CRIMINAL PROCEDURE SOURCEBOOK

Volume 2

CRIMINAL LAW AND URBAN PROBLEMS
Sourcebook Series
Number 6

CRIMINAL PROCEDURE SOURCEBOOK

Volume 2

Edited by

B. JAMES GEORGE, JR.
Associate Director
Practising Law Institute
and
Adjunct Professor of Law
New York University

and

JURIS CEDERBAUMS, ESQ.
New York Legal Aid Society

PRACTISING LAW INSTITUTE
New York City
with
ROSCOE POUND—AMERICAN TRIAL LAWYERS FOUNDATION

CONTENTS

Volume 1

CONTENTS

CONTENTS

CHAPTER 9

Trial Proceedings; Commencing Proof

A. Order of Procedures at Trial

LOUISIANA STATUTES ANNOTATED (WEST 1967),
CODE OF CRIMINAL PROCEDURE

Art. 761. Commencement of trial

A jury trial commences when the first prospective juror is called for examination. A trial by a judge alone commences when the first witness is sworn.

Art. 762. Place of sessions of court

Sessions of court shall be held at the parish courthouse but may be held at places within the parish other than the courthouse in the discretion of the court:

(1) To take the testimony of witnesses who are so incapacitated that they cannot attend the trial in the parish courthouse;

(2) To allow the jury or judge to view the place where the crime or any material part thereof is alleged to have occurred, or to view an object which is admissible in evidence but which is difficult to produce in court. At this view, the court shall not permit the taking of evidence except in connection with the place or object; or

(3) When the courthouse in which the sessions are usually held is unsuitable for use, or there is no courthouse.

Art. 763. Proceedings on holidays

Trials and hearings may commence or continue on a holiday or half-holiday in the discretion of the court.

Art. 764. Exclusion and conduct of witnesses

Upon its own motion the court may, and upon request of the state or the defendant the court shall, order that the witnesses be excluded from the courtroom or from where they can see or hear the proceedings and refrain from discussing the facts of the case or the testimony of any witness with anyone other than the district attorney or defense counsel. The court may modify its order in the interest of justice.

Art. 765.   Normal order of trial

The normal order of trial shall be as follows:

(1) The selection and swearing of the jury;

(2) The reading of the indictment;

(3) The reading of the defendant's plea on arraignment;

(4) The opening statements of the state and of the defendant;

(5) The presentation of the evidence of the state, and of the defendant, and of the state in rebuttal. The court in its discretion may permit the introduction of additional evidence prior to argument;

(6) The argument of the state, the defendant, and the state in rebuttal;

(7) The court's charge;

(8) The announcement of the verdict or mistrial in jury cases, or of the judgment in nonjury cases; and

(9) The discharge of the jury in jury cases.

When there is more than one defendant, the court shall determine the order of trial as between them.

A defendant may waive his opening statement.

Art. 766.   Opening statement by state; scope

The opening statement of the state shall explain the nature of the charge, and set forth, in general terms, the nature of the evidence by which the state expects to prove the charge.

Art. 767.   Same; prohibition against adverting to confessions

The state shall not, in the opening statement, advert in any way to a confession or inculpatory statement made by the defendant.

Art. 773.   Order of evidence

Neither the state nor the defendant can be controlled by the court as to the order in which evidence shall be adduced; but when the evidence requires a foundation for its admission, the foundation must be laid before the evidence is admissible.

*   *   *   *   *

New York Criminal Procedure Law (1971)

§ 260.30   Jury trial; in what order to proceed

The order of a jury trial, in general, is as follows:

1. The jury must be selected and sworn.

2. The court must deliver preliminary instructions to the jury.

3. The people must deliver an opening address to the jury.

4. The defendant may deliver an opening address to the jury.

5. The people must offer evidence in support of the indictment.

6. The defendant may offer evidence in his defense.

7. The people may offer evidence in rebuttal of the defense evidence, and the defendant may then offer evidence in rebuttal of the people's rebuttal evidence. The court may in its discretion permit the parties to offer further rebuttal or sur-rebuttal evidence in this pattern. In the interests of justice, the court may permit either party to offer evidence upon rebuttal which is not technically of a rebuttal nature but more properly a part of the offering party's original case.

8. At the conclusion of the evidence, the defendant may deliver a summation to the jury.

9. The people may then deliver a summation to the jury.

10. The court must then deliver a charge to the jury.

11. The jury must then retire to deliberate and, if possible, render a verdict.

§ 320.20 Non-jury trial; nature and conduct thereof

1. A non-jury trial of an indictment must be conducted by one judge of the superior court in which the indictment is pending.

2. The court, in addition to determining all questions of law, is the exclusive trier of all questions of fact and must render a verdict.

3. The order of the trial must be as follows:

(a) The court may in its discretion permit the parties to deliver opening addresses. If the court gives such permission to one party it must give it to the other also. If both parties deliver opening addresses, the people's address must be delivered first.

(b) The order in which evidence must or may be offered by the respective parties is the same as that applicable to a jury trial of an indictment as prescribed in subdivisions five, six and seven of section 260.30.

(c) The court may in its discretion permit the parties to deliver summations. If the court gives permission to one party, it must give it to the other also. If both parties deliver summations, the defendant's summation must be delivered first.

(d) The court must then consider the case and render a verdict.

4. The rules of evidence, motion practice and general procedure applicable to a jury trial are, wherever appropriate, equally applicable to a non-jury trial.

5. Before considering a multiple count indictment for the purpose of rendering a verdict thereon, and before the summations if there

be any, the court must designate and state upon the record the counts upon which it will render a verdict and the particular defendant or defendants, if there be more than one, with respect to whom it will render a verdict upon any particular count. In determining what counts, offenses and defendants must be considered by it and covered by its verdict, and the form of the verdict in general, the court must be governed, so far as appropriate and practicable, by the provisions of article three hundred governing the court's submission of counts and offenses to a jury upon a jury trial.

❂   ❂   ❂   ❂   ❂

B. Procedural Rights of the Defendant at Trial

1. Presence and Confrontation

CALIFORNIA v. GREEN, 399 U.S. 149 (1970)*

MR. JUSTICE WHITE delivered the opinion of the Court.

Section 1235 of the California Evidence Code, effective as of January 1, 1967, provides that "evidence of a statement made by a witness is not made inadmissible by the hearsay rule if the statement is inconsistent with his testimony at the hearing and is offered in compliance with § 770." In *People* v. *Johnson*, 68 Cal. 2d 646, 441 P.2d 111 (1968), cert. denied, 393 U.S. 1051 (1969), the California Supreme Court held that prior statements of a witness which were not subject to cross-examination when originally made, could not be introduced under this section to prove the charges against a defendant without violating the defendant's right of confrontation guaranteed by the Sixth Amendment and made applicable to the States by the Fourteenth Amendment. In the case now before us the California Supreme Court applied the same ban to a prior statement of a witness made at a preliminary hearing, under oath and subject to full cross-examination by an adequately counseled defendant. We cannot agree with the California court for two reasons, one of which involves rejection of the holding in *People* v. *Johnson*. . . .

. . . Porter's story at the preliminary hearing was subjected to extensive cross-examination by respondent's counsel—the same counsel who represented respondent at his subsequent trial. At the conclusion

* Footnotes, and concurring and dissenting opinions omitted.

of the hearing, respondent was charged with furnishing marihuana to a minor in violation of California law.

Respondent's trial took place some two months later before a court sitting without a jury. The State's chief witness was again young Porter. But this time Porter, in the words of the California Supreme Court, proved to be "markedly evasive and uncooperative on the stand." . . .

At various points during Porter's direct examination, the prosecutor read excerpts from Porter's preliminary hearing testimony. This evidence was admitted under § 1235 for the truth of the matter contained therein. With his memory "refreshed" by his preliminary hearing testimony, Porter "guessed" that he had indeed obtained the marihuana from the backyard of respondent's parents' home, and had given the money from its sale to respondent. On cross-examination, however, Porter indicated that it was his memory of the preliminary testimony which was "mostly" refreshed, rather than his memory of the events themselves, and he was still unsure of the actual episode. See App., 25. Later in the trial, Officer Wade testified, relating Porter's earlier statement that respondent had personally delivered the marihuana. This statement was also admitted as substantive evidence. Porter admitted making the statement, App., 59, and insisted that he had been telling the truth as he then believed it both to Officer Wade and at the preliminary hearing; but he insisted that he was also telling the truth now in claiming inability to remember the actual events.

Respondent was convicted. The District Court of Appeal reversed, holding that the use of Porter's prior statements for the truth of the matter asserted therein, denied respondent his right of confrontation under the California Supreme Court's recent decision in *People* v. *Johnson, supra.* The California Supreme Court affirmed, finding itself "impelled" by recent decisions of this Court to hold § 1235 unconstitutional insofar as it permitted the substantive use of prior inconsistent statements of a witness, even though the statements were cross-examined at a prior hearing. We granted the State's petition for certiorari. 396 U.S. 1001 (1970). . . .

Section 1235 of the California Evidence Code represents a considered choice by the California legislature between two opposing positions concerning the extent to which a witness' prior statements may be introduced at trial without violating hearsay rules of evidence. The orthodox view, adopted in most jurisdictions, has been that the out-of-court statements are inadmissible for the usual reasons that have led to the exclusion of hearsay statements: the statement may not have been made under oath; the declarant may not have been subjected to cross-examination when he made the statement; and the jury cannot observe the declarant's demeanor at the time he made the statement. Accordingly, under this view, the statement may not be offered to show the truth of the matters asserted therein, but can be introduced under appropriate limiting instructions to impeach the credibility of the witness who has changed his story at trial.

In contrast, the minority view adopted in some jurisdictions and supported by most legal commentators and by recent proposals to codify the law of evidence would permit the substantive use of prior inconsistent statements on the theory that the usual dangers of hearsay are largely nonexistent where the witness testifies at trial. "The whole purpose of the Hearsay rule has been already satisfied [because] the witness is present and subject to cross-examination [and] [t]here is ample opportunity to test him as to the basis for his former statement."

Our task in this case is not to decide which of these positions, purely as a matter of the law of evidence, is the sounder. The issue before us is the considerably narrower one of whether a defendant's constitutional right "to be confronted with the witnesses against him" is necessarily inconsistent with a State's decision to change its hearsay rules to reflect the minority view described above. While it may readily be conceded that hearsay rules and the Confrontation Clause are generally designed to protect similar values, it is quite a different thing to suggest that the overlap is complete and that the Confrontation Clause is nothing more nor less than a codification of the rules of hearsay and their exceptions as they existed historically at common law. Our decisions have never established such a congruence; indeed, we have more than once found a violation of confrontation values even though the statements in issue were admitted under an arguably recognized hearsay exception. See *Barber* v. *Page,* 390 U.S. 719 (1968); *Pointer* v. *Texas,* 380 U.S. 400 (1965). The converse is equally true: merely because evidence is admitted in violation of a long-established hearsay rule does not lead to the automatic conclusion that confrontation rights have been denied.

Given the similarity of the values protected, however, the modification of a State's hearsay rules to create new exceptions for the admission of evidence against a defendant, will often raise questions of compatibility with the defendant's constitutional right to confrontation. Such questions require attention to the reasons for, and the basic scope of, the protections offered by the Confrontation Clause.

The origin and development of the hearsay rules and of the Confrontation Clause have been traced by others and need not be recounted in detail here. It is sufficient to note that the particular vice which gave impetus to the confrontation claim was the practice of trying defendants on "evidence" which consisted solely of *ex parte* affidavits or depositions secured by the examining magistrates, thus denying the defendant the opportunity to challenge his accuser in a face-to-face encounter in front of the trier of fact. Prosecuting attorneys "would frequently allege matters which the prisoner denied and called upon them to prove. The proof was usually given by reading depositions, confessions of accomplices, letters, and the like; and this occasioned frequent demands by the prisoner to have his 'accusers,' *i.e.*, the witnesses against him, brought before him face to face. . . ."

But objections occasioned by this practice appear primarily to have been aimed at the failure to call the witness to confront personally the defendant at his trial. So far as appears, in claiming confrontation rights no objection was made against receiving a witness' out-of-court depositions or statements, so long as the witness was present at trial to repeat his story and to explain or repudiate any conflicting prior stories before the trier of fact.

Our own decisions seem to have recognized at an early date that it is this literal right to "confront" the witness at the time of trial which forms the core of the values furthered by the Confrontation Clause:

> "The primary object of the constitutional provision in question was to prevent depositions or *ex parte* affidavits, such as were sometimes admitted in civil cases, being used against the prisoner in lieu of a personal examination and cross-examination of the witness in which the accused has an opportunity, not only of testing the recollection and sifting the conscience of the witness, but of compelling him to stand face to face with the jury in order that they may look at him, and judge by his demeanor upon the stand and the manner in which he gives his testimony whether he is worthy of belief." *Mattox* v. *United States,* 156 U.S. 237, 242–243 (1895).

Viewed historically, then, there is good reason to conclude that the Confrontation Clause is not violated by admitting a declarant's out-of-court statements, as long as the declarant is testifying as a witness and subject to full and effective cross-examination. . . .

We have no occasion in the present case to map out a theory of the Confrontation Clause that would determine the validity of all such hearsay "exceptions" permitting the introduction of an absent declarant's statements. . . .

We find nothing, then, in either the history or the purposes of the Confrontation Clause, or in the prior decisions of this Court, that compels the conclusion reached by the California Supreme Court concerning the validity of California's § 1235. Contrary to the judgment of that court, the Confrontation Clause does not require excluding from evidence the prior statements of a witness who concedes making the statements, and who may be asked to defend or otherwise explain the inconsistency between his prior and his present version of the events in question, thus opening himself to full cross-examination at trial as to both stories.

We also think that Porter's preliminary hearing testimony was admissible as far as the Constitution is concerned wholly apart from the question of whether respondent had an effective opportunity for confrontation at the subsequent trial. For Porter's statement at the preliminary hearing had already been given under circumstances closely approximating those that surround the typical trial. Porter was under oath; respondent was represented by counsel—the same counsel in fact who later represented him at the trial; respondent had every opportunity to cross-examine Porter as to his statement; and the proceedings were conducted before a judicial tribunal, equipped to provide a judicial record of the hearings. Under these circumstances, Porter's statement would, we think, have been admissible at trial even in Porter's absence if Porter had been actually unavailable, despite good-faith efforts of the State to produce him. That being the case, we do not think a different result should follow where the witness is actually produced.

This Court long ago held that admitting the prior testimony of an unavailable witness does not violate the Confrontation Clause. *Mattox* v. *United States,* 156 U.S. 237 (1895). That case involved testimony given at the defendant's first trial by a witness who had died by the time of the second trial, but we do not find the instant preliminary hearing significantly different from an actual trial to warrant distinguishing the two cases for purposes of the Confrontation Clause. Indeed, we indicated as much in *Pointer* v. *Texas,* 380 U.S. 400, 407 (1965), where we noted that "the case before us would be quite a different one had Phillips' statement been taken at a full-fledged hearing at which petitioner had been represented by counsel who had been given a complete and adequate opportunity to cross examine." And in *Barber* v. *Page,* 390 U.S. 719, 725–726 (1968), although noting that the preliminary hearing is ordinarily a less searching exploration into the merits of a case than a trial, we recognized that "there may be some justification for holding that the opportunity for cross-examination of a witness at a preliminary hearing satisfies the demands of the Confrontation Clause where the witness is shown to be actually unavailable . . . ." In the present case respondent's counsel does not appear to have been significantly limited in any way in the scope or nature of his cross-examination of the witness Porter at the preliminary hearing. If Porter had died or was otherwise unavailable, the Confrontation Clause would not have been violated by admitting his testimony given at the preliminary hearing—the right of cross-examination then afforded provides substantial compliance with the purposes behind the confrontation requirement, as long as the declarant's inability to give live testimony is in no way the fault of the State. Compare *Barber* v. *Page, supra,* with *Motes* v. *United States,* 178 U.S. 458 (1900).

But nothing in *Barber* v. *Page* or in other cases in this Court indicates that a different result must follow where the State produces the declarant and swears him as a witness at the trial. It may be that the rules of evidence applicable in state or federal courts would restrict resort to prior sworn testimony where the declarant is present at the trial. But as a constitutional matter, it is untenable to construe the Confrontation Clause to permit the use of prior testimony to prove the State's case where the declarant never appears, but to bar that testimony where the declarant is present at the trial, exposed to the defendant and the trier of fact, and subject to cross-examination. As in the case where the witness is physically unproducible, the State here has made every effort to introduce its evidence through the live testimony of the witness; it produced Porter at trial, swore him as a witness, and tendered him for cross-examination. Whether Porter then testified in a manner consistent or inconsistent with his preliminary hearing testimony, claimed a loss of memory, claimed his privilege against compulsory self-incrimination, or simply refused to answer, nothing in the Confrontation Clause prohibited the State from also relying on his prior testimony to prove its case against Green. . . .

✣　✣　✣　✣　✣

EDITORS' NOTE

HEARSAY EVIDENCE UNDER THE CONFRONTATION CLAUSE

Admissibility of co-defendant confessions. Confessions are of course hearsay, and are admitted against their source only through an exception to the hearsay rule that presumes whatever a person says about himself is true. Therefore, one man's confession is not admissible against another other than in the rare instance in which the two are coconspirators and the statement is made in the course of and in furtherance of the conspiracy. The federal case law does not ordinarily view confessions by conspirators in police custody as within this rule [*e.g., Krulewitch v. United States,* 336 U.S. 440 (1949)].

What, however, if two or more of the co-criminals are tried jointly as co-defendants, and the statement of one of them is offered against him even though its contents implicate others than the maker? In the *Delli Paoli* case [*Delli Paoli v. United States,* 352 U.S. 232 (1957)], the Supreme Court held that there was no objection to this as long as the jury was given a precautionary instruction to consider the confession as evidence only against the defendant who made it.

In 1968, however, the Supreme Court overturned *Delli Paoli,* in *Bruton v. United States* [391 U.S. 123 (1968)]. The basic constitutional doctrine invoked is the right to confrontation, in that if the cautionary instructions are ignored, evidence against the second defendant is offered, in the form of the first defendant's confession, yet because of the privilege against self-incrimination the second defendant cannot call the first to the stand. The right of confrontation is violated if, for example, a hostile witness' claim of privilege disables the defendant from cross-examining him [*Douglas v. Alabama,* 380 U.S. 415 (1965)]. Therefore, unless the jury could be expected to abide by the precautionary instructions, receipt of one codefendant's confession impaired the right of confrontation and cross-examination on the part of others implicated in that confession.

The Court concluded that reliance on the ability of juries to understand and abide by precautionary instructions, on which *Delli Paoli* rested, was misplaced. For this proposition it relied in part on *Jackson v. Denno* [*see infra* at 581] and its unwillingness to assume that a jury could completely disregard a confession that it had found to have been obtained in violation of constitutional mandates; it also quoted at length Chief Justice Traynor's application of *Jackson* reasoning to the *Delli Paoli* situation in *Aranda* [*People v. Aranda,* 63 Cal. 2d 518, 407 P.2d 265, 47 Cal. Rptr. 353 (1965)]. As an additional source of support, the Court cited the 1966 amendment to Federal Rule 14, governing severance of trial, which provided that "in ruling on a motion by a defendant for severance the court may order the attorney for the government to deliver to the court for inspection *in camera* any statements or confessions made by the defendants which the government intends to introduce in evidence at the trial." Therefore, since curative instructions were a futile gesture, and prejudicial misuse of one defendant's confession against another by the jury a likelihood, the practice approved in *Delli Paoli* was held to violate the defendant's Sixth Amendment right of confrontation.

As Justice White indicates in his dissenting opinion, only three alternatives are available to the government or state. One is to proceed to trial against the joint defendants without using any confessions. The second is to excise all portions of the one defendant's confession that directly or indirectly implicate the other defendant or defendants. This might be possible in some instances, but in others might render the residue misleading and intrinsically unacceptable. The third would be to try the defendants separately. Though joint trials are permitted under the Federal Rules, *Bruton* may mean that in many instances this cannot be done. The consequences are summarized in Justice White's dissent:

> . . . Unquestionably, joint trials are more economical and minimize the burden on witnesses, prosecutors and courts. They also avoid delays in bringing those accused of crime to trial. This much the Court concedes. It is also worth saying that separate trials are apt to have varying consequences for legally indistinguishable defendants. The unfairness of this is confirmed by the common prosecutorial experience of seeing codefendants who are tried separately strenuously jockeying for position with regard to who should be the first to be tried. . . . [391 U.S. at 143]

> . . . I persist in believing that the reversal of *Delli Paoli* unnecessarily burdens the already difficult task of conducting criminal trials, and therefore I dissent in this case. [391 U.S. at 144]

Since the right of confrontation applied in *Bruton* is a part of Fourteenth Amendment due process, state courts will have to adjust their practices to conform.

Retroactivity. *Bruton* bears sufficiently on fundamental fairness of trial that it is retroactive [*Roberts v. Russell*, 392 U.S. 293 (1968)].

Impact on joint trials. *Bruton* does not apply if the co-defendant takes the stand later in the trial and thus becomes available for cross-examination [*Santoro v. United States*, 402 F.2d 920 (9th Cir. 1968); *In re Hill*, 80 Cal. Rptr. 537, 458 P.2d 449 (1969); *People v. Williams*, 105 Ill. App. 2d 25, 245 N.E.2d 17 (1969)]. Under these circumstances, the defendant confronts the source of the earlier confession and can cross-examine him about it.

Otherwise, there are few ways of admitting confessions without running afoul of the *Bruton* doctrine. Its requirements are sometimes complied with if the confession can be redacted so that there is no remaining reference to the non-confessing defendant. This, however, may be difficult to accomplish [*see United States ex rel. La Belle v.*

Mancusi, 404 F.2d 690 (2d Cir. 1968); *State v. Taylor,* 9 Ariz. App. 290, 648 P.2d 451 (1969); *People v. Jackson,* 22 N.Y.2d 446, 239 N.E.2d 869, 293 N.Y.S.2d 265 (1968)]. If redaction is impossible and the confession is to be used, there is no choice but to sever [*People v. Cefaro,* 23 N.Y.2d 283, 244 N.E.2d 42, 296 N.Y.S.2d 345 (1968)].

Bruton is violated if a police officer testifies to the codefendant's admissions [*United States v. Guajardo-Mendez,* 401 F.2d 35 (7th Cir. 1968)]. But the fact that some evidence implicates the co-defendant but not the defendant does not pose a *Bruton* problem [*Caton v. United States,* 407 F.2d 367 (8th Cir. 1969)].

Bruton also does not apply if the defendant calls an alibi witness to the stand, and the witness is then impeached by a confession [*State v. Cartagena,* 161 N.W.2d 392 (Wis. 1968)].

If none of these doctrines can be successfully invoked, the only remedy is to sever [*State v. Barnett,* 53 N.J. 559, 252 A.2d 33 (1969)]

Other forms of hearsay evidence. California v. Green does not purport to rule in general on the validity of exceptions to the hearsay rule, although it certainly lends little support to efforts to use the confrontation clause to attack traditional evidence law [*cf.* Note, *Confrontation, Cross-Examination, and the Right to Prepare a Defense,* 56 GEO. L.J. 939 (1968)]. However, the attack on certain exceptions cannot be ruled out on the basis of *Green,* and in any event a state can invoke the confrontation clause of its own constitution to rule out evidence on constitutional grounds even if the United States Supreme Court does not require it to do so. There is a gradually developing body of law which can be drawn upon in this regard.

For example, in one case a police officer was called to testify that the defendant had approached another prisoner with damaging admissions; the use of this hearsay on hearsay was held reversible error on constitutional grounds [*People v. Coleman,* —— Cal. ——, 459 P.2d 258, 80 Cal. Rptr. 920 (1969)]. So was testimony by a police officer as to what a third person told him about the defendant [*Rubey v. City of Fairbanks,* 456 P.2d 470 (Alaska 1969)]. Also erroneous was the admission in an embezzlement case of letters from hotel guests and their receipted bills without the guests having been called [*State v. Adrian,* 453 P.2d 221 (Hawaii 1969)].

Obviously all of these instances could have been taken care of on evidence law grounds alone. The invocation of constitutional grounds is important because the point can be raised in state and federal habeas corpus or other extraordinary writ proceedings long after normal appeal periods have elapsed [*see infra,* ch. 14].

❋   ❋   ❋   ❋   ❋

FEDERAL RULES OF CRIMINAL PROCEDURE, RULE 43

Presence of the Defendant

The defendant shall be present at the arraignment, at every stage of the trial including the impaneling of the jury and the return of the verdict, and at the imposition of sentence, except as otherwise provided by these rules. In prosecutions for offenses not punishable by death, the defendant's voluntary absence after the trial has been commenced in his presence shall not prevent continuing the trial to and including the return of the verdict. A corporation may appear by counsel for all purposes. In prosecutions for offenses punishable by fine or by imprisonment for not more than one year or both, the court, with the written consent of the defendant, may permit arraignment, plea, trial and imposition of sentence in the defendant's absence. The defendant's presence is not required at a reduction of sentence under Rule 35.

* * * * *

LOUISIANA STATUTES ANNOTATED (WEST 1967), CODE OF CRIMINAL PROCEDURE

Art. 832. Waiver by temporary voluntary absence

A defendant charged with a felony not punishable by death cannot object to his temporary voluntary absence at the proceedings listed in Article 831 if his counsel was present. However, the defendant may always object to his absence at the arraignment or plea to the merits, provided the objection is made before the commencement of trial.

Art. 833. Presence of defendant when prosecution is for misdemeanor

The court may permit a defendant charged with a misdemeanor to be arraigned, plead guilty, or be tried, in his absence, if he is represented by counsel who consents to proceed. Otherwise he must be present.

A plea of not guilty of a misdemeanor may always be entered through counsel and in the absence of the defendant.

Art. 834. When presence of defendant not necessary

The defendant has a right to be present, but his presence is not essential to the validity of any of the following proceedings in a criminal prosecution:

(1) The making, hearing of, or ruling on a preliminary motion or application addressed to the court;

(2) The making, hearing of, or ruling on a motion or application addressed to the court during the trial when the jury is not present; except as provided in Clause (4) of Article 831; and

(3) The making, hearing of, or ruling on a motion or application made after his conviction.

Art. 835. Presence of defendant at pronouncement of sentence

In felony cases the defendant shall always be present when sentence is pronounced. In misdemeanor cases the defendant shall be present when sentence is pronounced, unless excused by the court. If a sentence is improperly pronounced in the defendant's absence, he shall be resentenced when his presence is secured.

Art. 836. Presence of corporation or association

When a corporation, partnership, or other association is a defendant, the requirements of this Title are fulfilled if its counsel is present.

* * * * *

ILLINOIS v. ALLEN, 397 U.S. 337 (1970) *

MR. JUSTICE BLACK delivered the opinion of the Court.

The Confrontation Clause of the Sixth Amendment to the United States Constitution provides that "In all criminal prosecutions, the accused shall enjoy the right . . . to be confronted with the witnesses against him. . . ." We have held that the Fourteenth Amendment makes the guarantees of this clause obligatory upon the States. *Pointer* v. *Texas,* 380 U.S. 400 (1965). One of the most basic of the rights guaranteed by the Confrontation Clause is the accused's right to be present in the courtroom at every stage of his trial. *Lewis* v. *United States,* 146 U.S. 370 (1892). The question presented in this case is whether an accused can claim the benefit of this constitutional right to remain in the courtroom while at the same time he engages in speech and conduct which is so noisy, disorderly, and disruptive that it is exceedingly difficult or wholly impossible to carry on the trial.

The issue arose in the following way. The respondent, Allen, was convicted by an Illinois jury of armed robbery and was sentenced to serve 10 to 30 years in the Illinois State Penitentiary. The evidence against him showed that on August 12, 1956, he entered a tavern in Illinois and, after ordering a drink, took $200 from the bartender at gunpoint. The Supreme Court of Illinois affirmed his conviction. *People* v. *Allen,* 37 Ill. 2d 167, 226 N.E.2d 1 (1967), and this Court

---

* Footnotes, and concurring opinions omitted.

denied certiorari. 389 U.S. 907 (1967). Later Allen filed a petition for a writ of habeas corpus in federal court alleging that he had been wrongfully deprived by the Illinois trial judge of his constitutional right to remain present throughout his trial. Finding no constitutional violation, the District Court declined to issue the writ. The Court of Appeals reversed, 413 F.2d 232 (1969), Judge Hastings dissenting. The facts surrounding Allen's expulsion from the courtroom are set out in the Court of Appeals' opinion sustaining Allen's contention:

"After his indictment and during the pretrial stage, the petitioner [Allen] refused court-appointed counsel and indicated to the trial court on several occasions that he wished to conduct his own defense. After considerable argument by the petitioner, the trial judge told him, 'I'll let you be your own lawyer, but I'll ask Mr. Kelly [court-appointed counsel] [to] sit in and protect the record for you, insofar as possible.'

"The trial began on September 9, 1956. After the State's Attorney had accepted the first four jurors following their *voir dire* examination, the petitioner began examining the first juror and continued at great length. Finally, the trial judge interrupted the petitioner, requesting him to confine his questions solely to matters relating to the prospective juror's qualifications. At this point, the petitioner started to argue with the judge in a most abusive and disrespectful manner. At last, and seemingly in desperation, the judge asked appointed counsel to proceed with the examination of the jurors. The petitioner continued to talk, proclaiming that the appointed attorney was not going to act as his lawyer. He terminated his remarks by saying, 'When I go out for lunchtime, you're [the judge] going to be a corpse here.' At that point he tore the file which his attorney had and threw the papers on the floor. The trial judge thereupon stated to the petitioner, 'One more outbreak of that sort and I'll remove you from the courtroom.' This warning had no effect on the petitioner. He continued to talk back to the judge, saying, 'There's not going to be no trial, either. I'm going to sit here and you're going to talk and you can bring your shackles out and straight jacket and put them on me and tape my mouth, but it will do no good because there's not going to be no trial.' After more abusive remarks by the petitioner, the trial judge ordered the trial to proceed in the petitioner's absence. The petitioner was removed from the courtroom. The *voir dire* examination then continued and the jury was selected in the absence of the petitioner.

"After a noon recess and before the jury was brought into the courtroom, the petitioner, appearing before the judge, complained about the fairness of the trial and his appointed attorney. He also said he wanted to be present in the court during his trial. In reply, the judge said that the petitioner would be permitted to remain in the courtroom if he 'behaved [himself] and [did] not interfere with the introduction of the case.' The jury was brought in and seated. Counsel for the petitioner then moved to exclude the witnesses from the courtroom. The defendant protested this effort on the part of his attorney, saying: 'There is going to be no proceeding. I'm going to start talking and I'm going to keep on talking all through the trial. There's not going to be no trial like this. I want my sister and my friends here in court to testify for me.' The trial judge thereupon ordered the petitioner removed from the courtroom." 413 F.2d, at 233–234.

After this second removal, Allen remained out of the courtroom during the presentation of the State's case-in-chief, except that he was brought in on several occasions for purposes of identification. During one of these latter appearances, Allen responded to one of the judge's questions with vile and abusive language. After the prosecution's case had been presented, the trial judge reiterated his promise to Allen that he could return to the courtroom whenever he agreed to conduct himself properly. Allen gave some assurances of proper conduct and was permitted to be present through the remainder of the trial, principally his defense, which was conducted by his appointed counsel. . . .

The Court of Appeals felt that the defendant's Sixth Amendment right to be present at his own trial was so "absolute" that, no matter how unruly or disruptive the defendant's conduct might be, he could never be held to have lost that right so long as he continued to insist upon it, as Allen clearly did. Therefore the Court of Appeals concluded that a trial judge could never expel a defendant from his own trial and that the judge's ultimate remedy when faced with an obstreperous defendant like Allen who determines to make his trial impossible is to bind and gag him. We cannot agree that the Sixth Amendment, the cases upon which the Court of Appeals relied, or any other cases of this Court so handicap a trial judge in conducting a criminal trial. The broad dicta in *Hoyt* v. *Utah, supra,* and *Lewis* v. *United States,* 146 U.S. 370 (1892), that a trial can never continue in the defendant's absence has been expressly rejected. *Diaz* v. *United States,* 223 U.S. 442 (1912). We accept instead the statement of Mr. Justice Cardozo who, speaking for the Court in *Snyder* v. *Massachusetts,* 291 U.S. 97,

106 (1938), said: "No doubt the privilege [of personally confronting witnesses] may be lost by consent or at times even by misconduct." Although mindful that courts must indulge every reasonable presumption against the loss of constitutional rights, *Johnson* v. *Zerbst,* 304 U.S. 458, 464 (1938), we explicitly hold today that a defendant can lose his right to be present at trial if, after he has been warned by the judge that he will be removed if he continues his disruptive behavior, he nevertheless insists on conducting himself in a manner so disorderly, disruptive, and disrespectful of the court that his trial cannot be carried on with him in the courtroom. Once lost, the right to be present can, of course, be reclaimed as soon as the defendant is willing to conduct himself consistently with the decorum and respect inherent in the concept of courts and judicial proceedings.

It is essential to the proper administration of criminal justice that dignity, order, and decorum be the hallmarks of all court proceedings in our country. The flagrant disregard in the courtroom of elementary standards of proper conduct should not and cannot be tolerated. We believe trial judges confronted with disruptive, contumacious, stubbornly defiant defendants must be given sufficient discretion to meet the circumstances of each case. No one formula for maintaining the appropriate courtroom atmosphere will be best in all situations. We think there are at least three constitutionally permissible ways for a trial judge to handle an obstreperous defendant like Allen: (1) bind and gag him, thereby keeping him present; (2) cite him for contempt; (3) take him out of the courtroom until he promises to conduct himself properly.

I

Trying a defendant for a crime while he sits bound and gagged before the judge and jury would to an extent comply with that part of the Sixth Amendment's purposes that accords the defendant an opportunity to confront the witnesses at the trial. But even to contemplate such a technique, much less see it, arouses a feeling that no person should be tried while shackled and gagged except as a last resort. Not only is it possible that the sight of shackles and gags might have a significant effect on the jury's feelings about the defendant, but the use of this technique is itself something of an affront to the very dignity and decorum of judicial proceedings that the judge is seeking to uphold. Moreover, one of the defendant's primary advantages of being present at the trial, his ability to communicate with his counsel, is greatly reduced when the defendant is in a condition of total physical restraint. It is in part because of these inherent disadvantages and limitations in this method of dealing with disorderly defendants that we decline to hold with the Court of Appeals that a defendant cannot under any possible circumstances be deprived of his right to be present at trial. However, in some situations which we need not attempt to foresee, binding and gagging might possibly be the fairest and most reasonable way to handle a defendant who acts as Allen did here.

II

In a footnote the Court of Appeals suggested the possible availability of contempt of court as a remedy to make Allen behave in his robbery trial, and it is true that citing or threatening to cite a contumacious defendent for criminal contempt might in itself be sufficient to make a defendant stop interrupting a trial. If so, the problem would be solved easily, and the defendant could remain in the courtroom. Of course, if the defendant is determined to prevent *any* trial, then a court in attempting to try the defendant for contempt is still confronted with the identical dilemma that the Illinois court faced in this case. And criminal contempt has obvious limitations as a sanction when the defendant is charged with a crime so serious that a very severe sentence such as death or life imprisonment is likely to be imposed. In such a case the defendant might not be affected by a mere contempt sentence when he ultimately faces a far more serious sanction. Nevertheless, the contempt remedy should be borne in mind by a judge in the circumstances of this case.

Another aspect of the contempt remedy is the judge's power, when exercised consistently with state and federal law, to imprison an unruly defendant such as Allen for civil contempt and discontinue the trial until such time as the defendant promises to behave himself. This procedure is consistent with the defendant's right to be present at trial, and yet it avoids the serious shortcomings of the use of shackles and gags. It must be recognized, however, that a defendant might conceivably, as a matter of calculated strategy, elect to spend a prolonged period in confinement for contempt in the hope that adverse witnesses might be unavailable after a lapse of time. A court must guard against allowing a defendant to profit from his own wrong in this way.

III

The trial court in this case decided under the circumstances to remove the defendant from the courtroom and to continue his trial in his absence until and unless he promised to conduct himself in a manner befitting an American courtroom. As we said earlier, we find nothing unconstitutional about this procedure. Allen's behavior was clearly of such an extreme and aggravated nature as to justify either his removal from the courtroom or his total physical restraint. Prior to his removal he was repeatedly warned by the trial judge that he would be removed from the courtroom if he persisted in his unruly conduct, and, as Judge Hastings observed in his dissenting opinion, the record demonstrates that Allen would not have been at all dissuaded by the trial judge's use of his criminal contempt powers. Allen was constantly informed that he could return to the trial when he would agree to conduct himself in an orderly manner. Under these circumstances we hold that Allen lost his right guaranteed by the Sixth and Fourteenth Amendments to be present throughout his trial. . . .

❋   ❋   ❋   ❋   ❋

EDITORS' NOTE

If the defendant is absent "involuntarily" from the courtroom, any procedure conducted in his absence is without legal effect [e.g., Saul v. State, 6 Md. App. 540, 252 A.2d 282 (1969) (copy of statute sent at jury's request when the defendant was out of the courtroom)]. The close interrelationship between the rights of presence and of confrontation is illustrated in an Arizona case [State v. Cumbo, 9 Ariz. App. 253, 451 P.2d 333 (1969)]. Trial was conducted in Cumbo's absence in reliance on an Arizona court rule, under circumstances which brought about a federal district court ruling that his right of presence at trial had been violated. One result was to preclude subsequent use of testimony by the now deceased victim given at the first trial at which Cumbo was not present.

❋   ❋   ❋   ❋   ❋

2. Compulsory Process

WASHINGTON V. TEXAS, 388 U.S. 14 (1967) *

MR. CHIEF JUSTICE WARREN delivered the opinion of the Court.

We granted certiorari in this case to determine whether the right of a defendant in a criminal case under the Sixth Amendment to have compulsory process for obtaining witnesses in his favor is applicable to the States through the Fourteenth Amendment, and whether that

* Certain footnotes omitted.

right was violated by a state procedural statute providing that persons charged as principals, accomplices, or accessories in the same crime cannot be introduced as witnesses for each other.

Petitioner Jackie Washington was convicted in Dallas County, Texas, of murder with malice and was sentenced by a jury to 50 years in prison. The prosecution's evidence showed that petitioner, an 18-year-old youth, had dated a girl named Jean Carter until her mother had forbidden her to see him. The girl thereafter began dating another boy, the deceased. Evidently motivated by jealousy, petitioner with several other boys began driving around the City of Dallas on the night of August 29, 1964, looking for a gun. The search eventually led to one Charles Fuller, who joined the group with his shotgun. After obtaining some shells from another source, the group of boys proceeded to Jean Carter's home, where Jean, her family and the deceased were having supper. Some of the boys threw bricks at the house and then ran back to the car, leaving petitioner and Fuller alone in front of the house with the shotgun. At the sound of the bricks the deceased and Jean Carter's mother rushed out on the porch to investigate. The shotgun was fired by either petitioner or Fuller, and the deceased was fatally wounded. Shortly afterward petitioner and Fuller came running back to the car where the other boys waited, with Fuller carrying the shotgun.

Petitioner testified on his own behalf. He claimed that Fuller, who was intoxicated, had taken the gun from him, and that he had unsuccessfully tried to persuade Fuller to leave before the shooting. Fuller had insisted that he was going to shoot someone, and petitioner had run back to the automobile. He saw the girl's mother come out of the door as he began running, and he subsequently heard the shot. At the time, he had thought that Fuller had shot the woman. In support of his version of the facts, petitioner offered the testimony of Fuller. The record indicates that Fuller would have testified that petitioner pulled at him and tried to persuade him to leave, and that petitioner ran before Fuller fired the fatal shot.

It is undisputed that Fuller's testimony would have been relevant and material, and that it was vital to the defense. Fuller was the only person other than petitioner who knew exactly who had fired the shotgun and whether petitioner had at the last minute attempted to prevent the shooting. Fuller, however, had been previously convicted of the same murder and sentenced to 50 years in prison, and he was confined in the Dallas County jail. Two Texas statutes provided at the time of the trial in this case that persons charged or convicted as co-participants in the same crime could not testify for one another, although there was no bar to their testifying for the State. On the basis of these statutes the trial judge sustained the State's objection and refused to allow Fuller to testify. Petitioner's conviction followed, and it was upheld on appeal by the Texas Court of Criminal Appeals. 400 S.W.2d 756. We granted certiorari. 385 U.S. 812, 87 S.Ct. 123, 17 L.Ed.2d 54. We reverse.

I.

We have not previously been called upon to decide whether the right of an accused to have compulsory process for obtaining witnesses in his favor, guaranteed in federal trials by the Sixth Amendment, is so fundamental and essential to a fair trial that it is incorporated in the Due Process Clause of the Fourteenth Amendment. At one time, it was thought that the Sixth Amendment had no application to state criminal trials. That view no longer prevails, and in recent years we have increasingly looked to the specific guaranties of the Sixth Amendment to determine whether a state criminal trial was conducted with due process of law. We have held that due process requires that the accused have the assistance of counsel for his defense, that he be confronted with the witnesses against him, and that he have the right to a speedy and public trial.

The right of an accused to have compulsory process for obtaining witnesses in his favor stands on no lesser footing than the other Sixth Amendment rights that we have previously held applicable to the States. This Court had occasion in In re Oliver, 333 U.S. 257, 68 S.Ct. 499, 92 L.Ed. 682 (1948), to describe what it regarded as the most basic ingredients of due process of law. It observed that:

> "A person's right to reasonable notice of a charge against him, and an opportunity to be heard in his defense—a right to his day in court—are basic to our system of jurisprudence; and these rights include, as a minimum, a right to examine the witnesses against him, to offer testimony, and to be represented by counsel." 333 U.S., at 273, 68 S.Ct. at 507 (footnote omitted).

The right to offer the testimony of witnesses, and to compel their attendance, if necessary, is in plain terms the right to present a defense, the right to present the defendant's version of the facts as well as the prosecution's to the jury so it may decide where the truth lies. Just as an accused has the right to confront the prosecution's witnesses for the purpose of challenging their testimony, he has the right to present his own witnesses to establish a defense. This right is a fundamental element of due process of law.

II.

Since the right to compulsory process is applicable in this state proceeding, the question remains whether it was violated in the circumstances of this case. The testimony of Charles Fuller was denied to the defense not because the State refused to compel his attendance, but because a state statute made his testimony inadmissible whether he was present in the courtroom or not. We are thus called upon to decide whether the Sixth Amendment guarantees a defendant the right under any circumstances to put his witnesses on the stand, as well as the right to compel their attendance in court. The resolution of this question requires some discussion of the common-law context in which the Sixth Amendment was adopted. . . .

The federal courts followed the common-law restrictions for a time, despite the Sixth Amendment. In United States v. Reid, 12 How. 361, 13 L.Ed. 1023 (1852), the question was whether one of two defendants jointly indicted for murder on the high seas could call the other as a witness. Although this Court expressly recognized that the Sixth Amendment was designed to abolish some of the harsh rules of the common law, particularly including the refusal to allow the defendant in a serious criminal case to present witnesses in his defense, it held that the rules of evidence in the federal courts were those in force in the various States at the time of the passage of the Judiciary Act of 1789, including the disqualification of defendants indicted together. The holding in United States v. Reid was not satisfactory to later generations, however, and in 1918 this Court expressly overruled it, refusing to be bound by "the dead hand of the common law rule of 1789," and taking note of "the conviction of our time that the truth is more likely to be arrived at by hearing the testimony of all persons of competent understanding who may seem to have knowledge of the facts involved in a case, leaving the credit and weight of such testimony to be determined by the jury or by the court * * *." Rosen v. United States, 245 U.S. 467, 471, 38 S.Ct. 148, 150, 62 L.Ed. 406 (1918).

Although Rosen v. United States rested on nonconstitutional grounds, we believe that its reasoning was required by the Sixth Amendment. In light of the common-law history, and in view of the recognition in the *Reid* case that the Sixth Amendment was designed in part to make a defendant's witnesses admissible on his behalf in court, it could hardly be argued that a State would not violate the clause if it made all defense testimony inadmissible as a matter of procedural law. It is difficult to see how the Constitution is any less violated by arbitrary rules that prevent whole categories of defense witnesses from testifying on the basis of *a priori* categories that presume them unworthy of belief.

The rule disqualifying an alleged accomplice from testifying on behalf of the defendant cannot even be defended on the ground that it rationally sets apart a group of persons who are particularly likely to commit perjury. The absurdity of the rule is amply demonstrated by the exceptions that have been made to it. For example, the accused accomplice may be called by the prosecution to testify against the defendant. Common sense would suggest that he often has a greater interest in lying in favor of the prosecution rather than against it, especially if he is still awaiting his own trial or sentencing. To think that criminals will lie to save their fellows but not to obtain favors from the prosecution for themselves is indeed to clothe the criminal class with more nobility than one might expect to find in the public at large. Moreover, under the Texas statutes, the accused accomplice is no longer disqualified if he is acquitted at his own trial. Presumably, he would then be free to testify on behalf of his comrade, secure in the knowledge that he could incriminate himself as freely as he liked in his testimony, since he could not again be prosecuted for the same offense. The Texas law leaves him free to testify when he has a great incentive to perjury, and bars his testimony in situations when he has a lesser motive to lie.

We' hold that the petitioner in this case was denied his right to have compulsory process for obtaining witnesses in his favor because the State arbitrarily denied him the right to put on the stand a witness who was physically and mentally capable of testifying to events that he had personally observed, and whose testimony would have been relevant and material to the defense.[21] The Framers of the Constitution did not intend to commit the futile act of giving to a defendant the right to secure the attendance of witnesses whose testimony he

[21] Nothing in this opinion should be construed as disapproving testimonial privileges, such as the privilege against self-incrimination or the lawyer-client or husband-wife privileges, which are based on entirely different considerations from those underlying the common-law disqualifications for interest. Nor do we deal in this case with nonarbitrary state rules that disqualify as witnesses persons who, because of mental infirmity or infancy, are incapable of observing events or testifying about them.

had no right to use. The judgment of conviction must be reversed. It is so ordered.

Reversed.

* * * * *

NEW YORK CRIMINAL PROCEDURE LAW (1971)

§ 610.10   Securing attendance of witnesses by subpoena; in general

1. Under circumstances prescribed in this article, a person at liberty within the state may be required to attend a criminal court action or proceeding as a witness by the issuance and service upon him of a subpoena.

2. A "subpoena" is a process of a court directing the person to whom it is addressed to attend and appear as a witness in a designated action or proceeding in such court, on a designated date and any recessed or adjourned date of the action or proceeding. If he is given reasonable notice of such recess or adjournment, no further process is required to compel his attendance on the adjourned date.

3. As used in this article, "subpoena" includes a "subpoena duces tecum." A subpoena duces tecum is a subpoena requiring the witness to bring with him and produce specified physical evidence.

§ 610.20   Securing attendance of witnesses by subpoena; when and by whom subpoena may be issued

1. Any criminal court may issue a subpoena for the attendance of a witness in any criminal action or proceeding in such court.

2. A district attorney, or other prosecutor where appropriate, as an officer of a criminal court in which he is conducting the prosecution of a criminal action or proceeding, may issue a subpoena of such court, subscribed by himself, for the attendance in such court or a grand jury thereof of any witness whom the people are entitled to call in such action or proceeding.

3. An attorney for a defendant in a criminal action or proceeding, as an officer of a criminal court, may issue a subpoena of such court, subscribed by himself, for the attendance in such court of any witness whom the defendant is entitled to call in such action or proceeding. An attorney for a defendant may not issue a subpoena duces tecum of the court directed to any department, bureau or agency of the state or of a political subdivision thereof, or to any officer or representative thereof. Such a subpoena duces tecum may be issued in behalf

of a defendant upon order of a court pursuant to the rules applicable to civil cases as provided in section two thousand three hundred seven of the civil practice law and rules.

§ 610.30 Securing attendance of witnesses by subpoena; where subpoena may be served

1. A subpoena of any criminal court, issued pursuant to section 610.20, may be served anywhere in the county of issuance or anywhere in an adjoining county.

2. A subpoena of a superior court, issued pursuant to section 610.20, may be served anywhere in the state.

3. A subpoena of a district court or of the New York City criminal court, issued pursuant to section 610.20, may be served anywhere in the state; provided that, if such subpoena is issued by a prosecutor or by an attorney for a defendant, it may be served in a county other than the county of issuance or an adjoining county only if such court, upon application of such prosecutor or attorney, endorses upon such subpoena an order for the attendance of the witness.

4. A subpoena of a city court or a town court or a village court, issued pursuant to section 610.20, may be served in a county other than the one of issuance or an adjoining county if a judge of a superior court, upon application of the issuing court or the district attorney or an attorney for the defendant, endorses upon such subpoena an order for the attendance of the witness.

§ 610.40 Securing attendance of witnesses by subpoena; how and by whom subpoena may be served

A subpoena may be served by any person more than eighteen years old. Service must be made in the manner provided for by the civil practice law and rules for the service of subpoenas in civil cases.

❉　❉　❉　❉　❉

LOUISIANA STATUTES ANNOTATED (WEST 1967), CODE OF CRIMINAL PROCEDURE

Art. 732.　Subpoena duces tecum

A subpoena may order a person to produce at the trial or hearing, books, papers, documents, or any other tangible things in his possession or under his control, if a reasonably accurate description thereof is given; but the court shall vacate or modify the subpoena if it is unreasonable or oppressive.

Art. 733.   Form

A subpoena shall be issued under the seal of the court, shall state the name of the court and the title of the case, and shall command the attendance of a witness at a time and place specified.

Art. 737.   Contempt; attachment of witnesses failing to appear

Contumacious failure to comply with a subpoena, proof of service of which appears of record, constitutes a direct contempt of the court which issued the subpoena, and the court may order the witness attached and brought to court immediately.

If an order of attachment is issued, it may be executed in any parish by the sheriff of the parish from which the attachment was issued, or by the sheriff of the parish where the witness is found.

Art. 738.   Number of witnesses allowed

At a trial or hearing, each defendant in a misdemeanor case shall be allowed to summon six witnesses at the expense of the parish, and in a felony case twelve witnesses. A defendant shall have the right of compulsory process for additional witnesses at his own expense.

Comments

(a) This article is a combination of the source provisions. It continues the procedure of former R.S. 15:150 authorizing at the expense of the parish, six witnesses in a misdemeanor case and twelve witnesses in a felony case.

There is no reason for a defendant to summon more than six witnesses in a misdemeanor case and twelve witnesses in a felony case at the expense of the parish as was authorized by former R.S. 15:151, and that authorization is omitted. If the defendant is indigent, Art. 739 gives him the right to summon as many witnesses as are necessary at the expense of the parish. If the defendant is not indigent, he may summon as many additional witnesses as he deems necessary at his own expense, as was authorized by former R.S. 15:151.

(b) If a criminal charge involves more than one defendant, each defendant has the right to summon six witnesses in a misdemeanor case and twelve witnesses in a felony case at the expense of the parish. Cf. State v. Carter, 51 La.Ann. 442, 25 So. 385 (1899).

(c) The provisions of Art. 740 must be complied with in order to obtain out-of-parish witnesses, regardless of who pays the expenses under this article or under Art. 739.

(d) The above article, unlike former R.S. 15:150 and 15:151, does not apply to the state, because all expenses incurred in summoning the state's witnesses should be paid by the state, regardless of the number of witnesses called by the state.

Art. 739. Indigent defendant

If a defendant is indigent and unable to pay for witnesses desired by him in addition to those summoned at the expense of the parish, he shall make a sworn application to the court for the additional witnesses. The application must allege that the testimony is relevant and material and not cumulative and that the defendant cannot safely go to trial without it.

The court shall make a private inquiry into the facts, and if satisfied that the defendant is entitled to the privilege, it shall render an order permitting the defendant to subpoena additional witnesses at the expense of the parish. If the application is denied, the court shall state the reasons for the denial in writing, which shall become part of the record.

Art. 741. Method of obtaining a witness from another state

If a person in any state, which by its laws has made provision for commanding persons within its borders to attend and testify in criminal prosecutions or grand jury investigations commenced or about to commence in this state, is a material witness in a prosecution pending in a court of record in this state, or in a grand jury investigation which has commenced or is about to commence, a judge of such court may issue a certificate under the seal of the court stating these facts and specifying the number of days the witness shall be required. This certificate shall be presented to a judge of a court of record in the county (parish) in which the witness is found.

If the certificate recommends that the witness be taken into immediate custody and delivered to an officer of this state to assure his attendance in this state, the judge may direct that the witness be forthwith brought before him. The judge being satisfied of the desirability of custody and delivery, for which determination the certificate shall be prima facie proof, may order that the witness be forthwith taken into custody and delivered to an officer of this state. The order shall be sufficient authority for the officer to take the witness into custody and hold him unless and until he may be released by bail, recognizance, or order of the judge issuing the certificate.

If the witness is summoned to attend and testify in this state he shall be tendered the sum of ten cents a mile for each mile and five dollars for each day that he is required to travel and attend as a witness. A witness who has appeared in accordance with the provisions of the summons shall not be required to remain within the state a longer period of time than the period mentioned in the certificate, unless otherwise ordered by the court. If the witness fails without good cause to attend and testify as directed in the summons, he shall be punished in a manner provided for the punishment of any witness who disobeys a summons issued from the court of record of this state.

Art. 742.   Method of summoning a witness in this state
to testify in another state

If a judge of a court of record in any state which by its laws has made provision for commanding persons within that state to attend and testify in this state, certifies under seal of court that there is a criminal prosecution pending in that court, or that a grand jury investigation has commenced or is about to commence, that a person being within this state is a material witness in the prosecution or grand jury investigation, and that his presence will be required for a specified number of days, upon presentation of the certificate to any judge of a court of record in the parish (county) in which the person is, the judge shall fix a time and place for a hearing and shall make an order directing the witness to appear at a time and place certain for the hearing.

If at a hearing the judge determines that the witness is material and necessary, that it will not cause undue hardship to the witness to be compelled to attend and testify in the prosecution or grand jury investigation in the other state, and that the laws of the state in which the prosecution is pending, or grand jury investigation has commenced or is about to commence, will give to him protection from arrest and the service of civil and criminal process, he shall issue a summons, with a copy of the certificate attached, directing the witness to attend and testify in the court where the prosecution is pending, or where a grand jury investigation has commenced or is about to commence at a time and place specified in the summons. In any such hearing the certificate shall be prima facie evidence of all the facts stated therein.

If the certificate recommends that the witness be taken into immediate custody and delivered to an officer of the requesting state to assure his attendance in the requesting state, the judge may, in lieu of notification of the hearing, direct that the witness be forthwith brought before him for the hearing. The judge at the hearing being satisfied of the desirability of custody and delivery, for which determination the certificate shall be prima facie proof of desirability may, in lieu of issuing subpoena or summons, order that the witness be forthwith taken into custody and delivered to an officer of the requesting state.

If the witness, who is summoned as above provided, after being paid or tendered by some properly authorized person the sum of ten cents a mile for each mile and five dollars for each day, that he is required to travel and attend as a witness, fails without good cause to attend and testify as directed in the summons, he shall be punished in the manner provided by law for the punishment of any witness who disobeys a summons issued from a court of record in this state.

Art. 743. Exemption from arrest and service of process

If a person comes into this state in obedience to a summons directing him to attend and testify in this state, he shall not, while in this state pursuant to such summons or order, be subject to arrest or the service of process, civil or criminal, in connection with matters which arose before his entrance into this state under the summons.

If a person passes through this state while going to another state in obedience to a summons or order to attend and testify in that state or while returning therefrom, he shall not, while so passing through this state be subject to arrest, or the service of process, civil or criminal, in connection with matters which arose before his entrance into this state under the summons or order.

Art. 744. Witness; state; defined

"Witness" as used in Articles 741 through 743 shall include a person whose testimony is relevant and material and desired in any proceeding or investigation by a grand jury or in a criminal action, prosecution, or proceeding.

"State" shall include any territory of the United States and the District of Columbia.

Art. 745. Uniformity of interpretation

Articles 741 through 744 shall be so interpreted and construed as to effect their general purpose to make uniform the law of the states which enact similar provisions.

❋   ❋   ❋   ❋   ❋

3. Public Trial

[For an extensive treatment of the right to a public trial, *see* Note, *The Accused's Right to a Public Trial*, 42 NOTRE DAME LAWYER 499 (1967).]

4. Counsel

[See Chapter 7, *supra*, at 349]

5. Speedy Trial

[See Chapter 8, *supra*, at 519]

6. Privilege Against Self-Incrimination

Coverage of the Privilege

Traditionally, the Fifth Amendment privilege against self-incrimination applied only to federal proceedings. States were free to adopt it or not, although almost all did so in their own constitutions. However, in 1964 the Supreme Court brought the privilege clause within Fourteenth Amendment due process [*Murphy v. Waterfront Comm'n*, 378 U.S. 52 (1964); *Malloy v. Hogan*, 378 U.S. 1 (1964)].

Three Privileges

There is not one privilege, but in effect three—the witness privilege, the party privilege and the defendant privilege. Each had a different historical inception, and in detail each differs from the others.

Witness privilege. The witness privilege is historically the oldest, antedating as it does the time when parties could testify in their own causes. It applies to any kind of proceeding—criminal, civil, administrative and legislative. This privilege does not permit the witness to refuse to take an oath, but only to refuse to answer specific questions. [*See Morgan v. U.S.F. & G. Co.*, 222 So. 2d 820 (Miss. 1969) on procedures for handling a witness claim of privilege in a civil case.]

It is of course undesirable from the point of view of the party seeking the information to have the witness claim privilege, but there is nothing he can do about it. If the witness for the first time claims privilege on cross-examination, the remedy is to strike the direct testimony [*Smith v. State*, 225 Ga. 328, 168 S.E.2d 587 (1969)]; if curative instructions are not likely in fact to be curative because of the importance of the witness's testimony, the only effective remedy is probably a mistrial.

In a criminal case, it is not error *per se* for the prosecutor to call to the witness stand a criminal participant who is not a co-defendant, even though there is a possibility or even a probability that he may claim privilege [*Namet v. United States*, 373 U.S. 179 (1963); *State v. Chaffin*, 92 Idaho 629, 448 P.2d 243 (1968)]. However, if he persists in asking questions after the witness begins to claim privilege, this may lend "critical weight" to the prosecution case and require a reversal because of the unfairness of the tactic as far as the defendant is concerned [*Namet v. United States, supra; Price v. State*, 37 Wis. 2d 117, 154 N.W.2d 222 (1967)].

Party privilege. The Supreme Court in the waiver context has in effect approved a party privilege rule [*Brown v. United States*, 356 U.S. 148 (1958)]. If a party is called as a witness by the adverse party, the usual witness privilege applies, but if he takes the stand in the presentation of his own case, he cannot claim privilege against self-incrimination to defeat cross-examination about what he testified to on direct. The purpose is to avoid an unfair advantage over the opponent. However, there is no unfair advantage when one party is summoned by the other in pretrial discovery proceedings [*Steinbrecher v. Wapnick*, 24 N.Y.2d 354, 248 N.E.2d 419, 300 N.Y.S.2d 555 (1969)].

Permitting a party to claim privilege can have adverse impact on effectuation of the policy underlying the substantive rule on the basis of which the proceedings are brought. If a spouse and his paramour are permitted to assert privilege when the wife is seeking a divorce based on adultery [*Zonver v. Superior Court*, —— Cal. App. ——, 76 Cal. Rptr. 10 (1969); *Simkins v. Simkins*, 219 So. 2d 724 (Fla. App. 1969)], or an alleged putative father can claim privilege in a paternity suit [*Pouncy v. Carraway*, 5 Conn. Cir. 571, 258 A.2d 483 (1969)], this preserves the concept of privilege at the expense of the aims embodied in the divorce and paternity statutes. An immunity statute is the only way traditionally by which the privilege can be dispensed with, but it is unlikely that such legislation will be forthcoming outside the criminal law field. Similar policy problems underlie decisions permitting a judgment debtor to claim privilege when asked to testify in a civil action affecting real property, on the ground a fraudulent conveyance would make an income tax violation a possibility [*State ex rel. Howard v. Allison*, 431 S.W.2d 233 (Mo. App. 1968)].

Defendant privilege. The defendant privilege is the later of the old privileges to develop, in that until well into the nineteenth century no party to a proceeding was competent to give testimony. Thus, the defendant in a criminal case could not offer testimony on his own behalf, but neither could he be called to the stand by the prosecution.

When parties, including criminal defendants, became competent as witnesses, the federal and state constitutional provisions protecting against self-incrimination "in any criminal case" were invoked to protect criminal defendants against being called to the stand at the behest of the prosecution. This is so much a commonplace that it is difficult to find instances in which the prosecutor has tried to call the defendant as a witness, though an occasional one appears [*People v. Talle*, 111 Cal. App. 2d 650, 245 P.2d 633 (1952)]. The more likely instance is when one defendant tries to call a co-defendant to the stand. This of course violates the co-defendant's privilege [*e.g., Coleman v. United States*, 420 F.2d 616 (D.C. Cir. 1969); *United States v. Carella*, 411 F.2d 729 (2d Cir. 1969); *People v. Lilliock*, 265 Cal. App. 2d 419, 71 Cal. Rptr. 434 (1968); *People v. Owen*, 22 N.Y.2d 93, 238 N.E.2d 715, 291 N.Y.S.2d 313 (1968); *State v. Smith*, 74 Wash. 2d 744, 446 P.2d 571 (1968)].

A troublesome question has been when one acquires the status of defendant. Under the traditional view, there must be a formal charge laid before one is considered a defendant. A formal complaint, information or indictment clearly confers defendant status. But what if the grand jury has not yet formally indicted, yet calls a prime suspect before it? The traditional view is that only the witness privilege applies, so that the witness cannot resist the subpoena or oath [*e.g., United States v. Levinson*, 405 F.2d 971 (6th Cir. 1968); *United States v. Cipaldo*, 402 F.2d 821 (2d Cir. 1968); *People v. Robinson*, 306 Mich. 167, 10 N.W.2d 817 (1943) (so-called one-man grand jury); *Boikess v. Aspland*, 24 N.Y.2d 136, 247 N.E.2d 135, 299 N.Y.S.2d 163 (1969); the basic authority cited is usually *Hale v. Henkel*, 201 U.S. 43 (1906)]. However, some decisions apply the defendant privilege to prime suspects before the grand jury [*e.g., People v. Calhoun*, 50 Cal. 2d 137, 323 P.2d 427 (1958); *People v. De Feo*, 308 N.Y. 595, 127 N.E.2d 592 (1955); *People v. Smith*, 257 Mich. 319, 241 N.W. 186 (1932)] or corner's inquest [*People v. Keelin*, 136 Cal. App. 2d 860, 289 P.2d 520 (1955)]. Certainly the latter cases are closer in spirit to *Miranda*, which of course rests on the privilege concept [*see supra* at 145].

Even under the most extended view of when one becomes a defendant, the proceedings must be directed toward the ultimate defendant at least in a preliminary way. Thus, the defendant cannot object to the fact that he was called as a witness in another case several days before he was indicted and no warnings given him about the possible use of his statements against him [*Beckley v. State*, 443 P.2d 51 (Alaska 1968)].

Subject Matter of Privilege

The traditional view has been that the privilege in any of its forms extends only to (a) testimonial utterances, that is, statements the content of which is offered to prove a point in issue, and (b) anything ordered to be produced under subpoena duces tecum or similar process [*see, e.g., United States v. Cohen,* 338 F.2d 464 (9th Cir. 1967)]; an I.R.S. summons can be included in the second category [*Stuart v. United States,* 416 F.2d 459 (5th Cir. 1969)]. It does not, however, extend to demonstrative evidence obtained from the person, like blood-test evidence [*Schmerber v. California,* 384 U.S. 757 (1964)], lineup identification [*United States v. Wade,* 388 U.S. 219 (1967)], handwriting exemplars [*Gilbert v. California,* 388 U.S. 263 (1967)], or to the performance of acts in or out of court, like donning clothing in court [*Holt v. United States,* 218 U.S. 245 (1910). Rather, the control is exercised through search and seizure concepts [*cf. Davis v. Mississippi,* 394 U.S. 721 (1969), *supra* at 88].

Testing the Presence of Incrimination

It is necessary to determine when a statement or documents elicited from the defendant or witness can be considered incriminating. In the case of the defendant, anything whatever elicited from him at the instance of court, co-defendant's counsel or prosecutor is automatically considered incriminating.

In the case of the witness, however, greater precision is necessary. Historically, the question had to go directly to the material elements of a crime before an answer would be considered incriminating. However, in recent years the Supreme Court has adopted the position that before a witness's claim of privilege can be rejected, it must be "*perfectly* clear, from a careful consideration of all the circumstances in the case, that the witness is mistaken, and that the answer cannot possibly have such tendency 'to incriminate'" [*Hoffman v. United States,* 341 U.S. 479, 488 (1951)]. Anything that might "furnish a link in the chain of evidence needed to prosecute" is enough.

Nor is there much room for trial court inquiry into the matter. In *Malloy* [*Malloy v. Hogan,* 378 U.S. 1 (1964)], the Connecticut court had specifically ruled that the witness was not subject to prosecution under Connecticut law for anything he said. Nevertheless, the Supreme Court speculated that his answers might possibly have proven useful in some subsequent Connecticut proceeding, and so held that his privilege had been violated by forcing answers from him on threat of contempt penalties. One court has taken this to mean that the burden is on the prosecution to show the impossibility of incrimination [*Murphy v. Commonwealth,* 354 Mass. 81, 235 N.E.2d 552 (1968); *cf. State ex rel. Howard v. Allison,* 431 S.W.2d 233 (Mo. App. 1968)]. This being the procedural setting, there is nothing that can be absolutely ruled out as information potentially within the privilege [*e.g., People v.*

Lilliock, 265 Cal. App. 2d 419, 71 Cal. Rptr. 434 (1968) (age, when identification an issue)].

If the court should err in granting a claim of privilege, the party desiring the testimony can appeal [8 H. WIGMORE, EVIDENCE § 2270(2) (Rev. ed. 1961); *Poling v. State*, 6 Md. App. 45, 250 A.2d 126 (1969)].

The incrimination must be within the law of the United States or one of the states. It cannot rest in the law of another country [*In re Parker*, 411 F.2d 1067 (10th Cir. 1969) (Canadian law)].

Privilege Personal

The privilege cannot be invoked to protect anyone other than the defendant or witness himself [*Matter of Levy*, 255 N.Y. 223, 174 N.E. 461 (1931); *State v. Dilworth*, 159 N.W.2d 795 (S.D. 1968)]. An attorney, however, may call a witness's attention to the existence of the privilege [*Farmer v. State*, 5 Md. App. 546, 248 A.2d 809 (1968)], and there is authority that under certain circumstances the attorney may actually assert the privilege on behalf of the witness [*Poling v. State*, 6 Md. App. 45, 250 A.2d 126 (1969)]. Because the witness privilege belongs to the witness and not to the party against whom he is called, the latter cannot appeal if for any reason the witness decides not to invoke privilege [*Poling v. State, supra*].

This tradition has also been applied in the special *Miranda* setting of privilege, so that one defendant cannot assert a violation of a codefendant's rights [*United States v. Bruton*, 414 F.2d 905 (8th Cir. 1969)].

The privilege also protects only natural persons. A corporation, partnership, unincorporated association or labor union has no privilege, since it is not viewed as a "person" within the meaning of the Fifth Amendment [*United States v. Kordel*, 397 U.S. 1 (1970) (corporation); *Campbell Painting Corp. v. Reid*, 392 U.S. 287 (1968) (family corporation); *United States v. White*, 322 U.S. 594 (1944) (labor union); *Hale v. Henkel*, 201 U.S. 43 (1906) (corporation)]. Therefore, an official in such an organization cannot claim privilege unless he himself is incriminated as an individual by the documents he is called upon to produce or the testimony he is required to give [*United States v. Kordel, supra; Curcio v. United States*, 354 U.S. 118 (1957)]. The same approach is taken to officials of governmental units; they may claim privilege as to purely personal records, but not to public records [*In re Addonizio*, 53 N.J. 107, 248 A.2d 531 (1968)].

Waiver of Defendant Privilege

A defendant waives privilege by taking the stand to testify on his own behalf [authorities are gathered in 8 H. WIGMORE EVIDENCE § 2276

(Rev. ed. 1968)]. A lawyer conducting his own defense waives with reference to everything he says in court, including his own testimony [*United States v. Lacob*, 416 F.2d 756 (7th Cir. 1969)].

Traditionally there has been no obligation on the part of the court to warn a defendant of his privilege. Laymen unrepresented by counsel, therefore, were sometimes held to have waived a right of which they were ignorant. This hardly comports with the current test of waiver as the "intentional relinquishment or abandonment of a known right or privilege" [*Johnson v. Zerbst*, 304 U.S. 458, 464 (1938)]. As a practical matter, however, the sweeping extension of the right to counsel [*Coleman v. Alabama*, 399 U.S. 1, 38 U.S.L.W. 4535 (June 22, 1970); *Gideon v. Wainwright*, 372 U.S. 335 (1963)] should mean that relatively few defendants actually go to trial unrepresented and without being aware of the consequences of what they do.

If the defendant does validly waive by taking the stand, and testifies in his own behalf, he may be cross-examined as any other witness may be, and may be prosecuted for perjury if he lies under oath [*cf. People v. Tomasello*, 21 N.Y.2d 143, 234 N.E.2d 190, 287 N.Y.S.2d 1 (1967) (perjury committed during testimony under grant of immunity)].

At the particular stage of the proceeding, the extent of the waiver is determined by the scope of cross-examination under the prevailing evidence law [*People v. Eaton*, —— Cal. App. ——, 80 Cal. Rptr. 192 (1969)].

Waiver through testimony does not constitute waiver of the right to attack the underlying criminal statute on privilege grounds [*Leary v. United States*, 395 U.S. 6 (1969)].

An important aspect of waiver is the extent to which the statements made after a valid waiver are available for later use as party admissions.

The defendant will not be held to a concept of waiver of privilege if the alternative is waiver of some other constitutional right. In the *Simmons* case [*Simmons v. United States*, 390 U.S. 377 (1968)], the defendant had taken the stand to testify about his claim to the property he was seeking to suppress, a claim necessary to afford him standing [see *supra* at 470]. After the motion was denied and the defendant was put on trial, the United States attorney offered the defendant's testimony at the motion hearing as evidence of unlawful possession. The trial court permitted this on traditional waiver theory. The Supreme Court, however, reversed:

> It seems obvious that a defendant who knows that his testimony may be admissible against him at trial will sometimes be

deterred from presenting the testimonial proof of standing necessary to assert a Fourth Amendment claim. The likelihood of inhibition is greatest when the testimony is known to be admissible regardless of the outcome of the motion to suppress. But even in jurisdictions where the admissibility of the testimony depends upon the outcome of the motion, there will be a deterrent effect in those marginal cases in which it cannot be estimated with confidence whether the motion will succeed. Since search-and-seizure claims depend heavily upon their individual facts and since the law of search and seizure is in a state of flux, the incidence of such marginal cases cannot be said to be negligible. In such circumstances, a defendant with a substantial claim for the exclusion of evidence may conclude that the admission of the evidence, together with the Government's proof linking it to him, is preferable to risking the admission of his own testimony connecting himself with the seized evidence.

The rule adopted by the courts below does not merely impose upon a defendant a condition which may deter him from asserting a Fourth Amendment objection—it imposes a condition of a kind to which this Court has always been peculiarly sensitive. For a defendant who wishes to establish standing must do so at the risk that the words which he utters may later be used to incriminate him. Those courts which have allowed the admission of testimony given to establish standing have reasoned that there is no violation of the Fifth Amendment's Self-Incrimination Clause because the testimony was voluntary. As an abstract matter, this may well be true. A defendant is "compelled" to testify in support of a motion to suppress only in the sense that if he refrains from testifying he will have to forgo a benefit, and testimony is not always involuntary as a matter of law simply because it is given to obtain a benefit. However, the assumption which underlies this reasoning is that the defendant has a choice: he may refuse to testify and give up the benefit. When this assumption is applied to a situation in which the "benefit" to be gained is that afforded by another provision of the Bill of Rights, an undeniable tension is created. Thus, in this case Garrett was obliged either to give up what he believed, with advice of counsel, to be a valid Fourth Amendment claim or, in legal effect, to waive his Fifth Amendment privilege against self-incrimination. In these circumstances, we find it intolerable that one constitutional right should have to be surrendered in order to assert another. We therefore hold that when a defendant testifies in support of a motion to suppress evidence on Fourth Amendment grounds, his testimony may not thereafter be admitted against him at trial on the issue of guilt unless he makes no objection. [390 U.S. at 392–94 (footnotes omitted).]

In other applications of *Simmons,* in a bifurcated trial, testimony by the defendant at the guilt portion did not serve as a waiver at the penalty hearing in which recidivism was an issue [*Brumfield v. State,* 445 S.W.2d 732 (Tex. Crim. App. 1969)]. Testimony at a confession suppression hearing does not waive privilege, so that the prosecutor could not thereafter comment on the defendant's failure to testify to other matters [*Calloway v. Wainwright,* 409 F.2d 59 (5th Cir. 1969)]. However, in the confession hearing itself, it has been held that it is no violation of the defendant's privilege to cross-examine him about whether he believed he was guilty at the time he was interrogated [*State v. Miranda,* 104 Ariz. 174, 450 P.2d 364 (1969)].

One court rejected the defendant's contention that his privilege was impaired because he could not take the stand to testify on the issue of character, when the jury determines capital punishment, without undergoing cross-examination on the merits [*State v. Crampton,* 18 Ohio St. 2d 182, 248 N.E.2d 614 (1969)]. Despite the dilemma in which the defendant finds himself, it would appear unlikely that *Simmons* will be extended to protect the defendant as witness from the same cross-examination other witnesses receive. The practical solution probably lies in making clear procedural separation between hearings on admissibility of evidence and the principal trial, and between the main trial and hearings bearing on disposition, since if the procedural separation is clear, *Simmons* provides adequate protection to the defendant.

Waiver of Witness Privilege

A witness waives by answering individual questions. After answering, he must submit to cross-examination (or in the appropriate instance, further direct examination) on whatever has been opened up by his response [*McCarthy v. Arndstein,* 262 U.S. 355 (1923); *United States v. St. Pierre,* 132 F.2d 837 (2d Cir. 1942)]. The traditional position has been that the waiver extends throughout the particular phase of the proceeding, but not to later phases of the same proceeding or to separate proceedings [*see* authorities in C. McCormick, Evidence § 130 (1954)]. However, one court has held that if a witness with knowledge of the privilege waives by testifying before the grand jury, the waiver extends to the trial itself if it is promptly held [*Ellis v. United States,* 416 F.2d 791 (D.C. Cir. 1969)].

On the use of the statements themselves as evidence in later proceedings if the witness becomes unavailable, see *supra* at 528.

One who turns over documents to a governmental agency without claiming privilege is considered to have waived privilege with reference to them. There is authority that there cannot be a belated claim of privilege when a second agency obtains them from the first for use in a criminal investigation [*In re Clark*, 256 A.2d 278 (Del. Ch. 1969) (records turned over in bankruptcy proceeding available for attorney-general investigation of embezzlement)].

Extinction of Incrimination

It has already been indicated that the privilege against self-incrimination protects the witness or defendant against answering an inquiry in formal proceedings unless he waives his privilege. Only a pardon or the extinction of the state's right to prosecute because of the running of the statute of limitations or the repeal of the criminal statute without a saving clause, removes the possibility of incrimination, so that the witness may be forced to answer [*Brown v. Walker*, 161 U.S. 591 (1896); *Matter of Doyle*, 257 N.Y. 244, 177 N.E. 489 (1931)].

A related question is whether a plea of guilty or a conviction removes the privilege as far as the particular offense is concerned [*see* Annot., 9 A.L.R.3d 990 (1966)]. This problem could arise when the defendant is called to testify against a fellow criminal tried separately, to respond to questions about the plea of guilty itself, or to reply to questions at the time of sentencing. The federal-state relationship problem following *Murphy v. Waterfront Commission* may complicate the matter. In one recent case, when a federal judge questioned a defendant at the time of sentencing on a federal crime, but the statements were later offered in a state proceeding, the state court held that though the federal privilege with reference to the federal crime had been extinguished, incrimination was still possible as far as the state offense was concerned, so that the admissions made during sentencing on the federal crime were inadmissible in the state proceeding [*State v. Castonguay*, 240 A.2d 747 (Me. 1968)].

Immunity Legislation

If the possibility of incrimination is not removed through extinction of criminality or accepted through waiver of privilege, the only other way through which needed testimony can be obtained is by means of immunity legislation [*see* N.Y. CRIMINAL PROCEDURE LAW §§ 190.40–190.50 (1971) and Staff Comments, *supra* at 316]. The principal problems are the acts necessary to trigger the immunity provisions and the scope of immunity conferred.

It is a matter of legislative choice when immunity is conferred. It may be that a judicial order is required, based on an application by the official conducting the inquiry in question. In this event, the witness has no control over the process. It may also be that the witness must specifically claim immunity before he testifies, if immunity is to be conferred [e.g., *People v. Ianniello*, 21 N.Y.2d 418, 235 N.E.2d 439, 288 N.Y.S.2d 462, *cert. denied*, 393 U.S. 827 (1968) (under pre-1971 provisions)]. Under some forms of legislation, however, the statute is triggered by the very fact of testifying [e.g., *State v. Panagoulis*, 253 Md. 699, 253 A.2d 877 (1969); *see also* Wexler, *Automatic Witness Immunity Statutes and the Inadvertent Frustration of Criminal Prosecutions: A Call for Congressional Action*, 55 GEO. L.J. 656 (1969)]. A system that places control over the process in the prosecutor is probably preferable, but it should be stated again that this is a matter for legislative choice.

The same thing cannot be said, however, about the second problem, that of scope of immunity. As a matter of logic, it would seem to be enough that the compelled testimony and its direct fruits are rendered inadmissible in later proceedings. However, language in the first case in the field [*Counselman v. Hitchcock*, 142 U.S. 547 (1892)] indicated that to be valid an immunity statute would have to achieve what its title indicated—confer absolute immunity against prosecution for the crimes to which the inquiry related. For many years this was the controlling assumption on which state courts and legislatures proceeded.

Recently, however, there has been an indication of a shift back to the earliest assumption. In *Murphy v. Waterfront Commission*, the Court indicated that a state immunity statute had to be broad enough so that "the compelled testimony and its fruits cannot be used in any manner" [378 U.S. at 79]. Two courts have read this as an abandonment of the *Counselman* language, so that absolute immunity need not be conferred [*Zicarelli v. New Jersey State Comm'n of Investigation*, 55 N.J. 249, 269 A.2d 129 (1970); *People v. LaBello*, 24 N.Y.2d 598, 249 N.E.2d 412, 301 N.Y.S.2d 544 (1969)].

If the individual has obtained immunity under a valid statute it does not give him a license to commit perjury or contempt [*People v. Ianniello*, 21 N.Y.2d 418, 235 N.E.2d 439, 288 N.Y.S.2d 462 (1968); *People v. Tomasello*, 21 N.Y.2d 143, 234 N.E.2d 190, 287 N.Y.S.2d 1 (1967)]. Nor need it protect the individual against loss of official employment as a result of answers given [*Headley v. Baron*, 228 So. 2d 281 (Fla. 1969); *cf.* the counterpart problem of prohibited penalities, *infra* at 566].

Derivative Evidence Rule

As indicated above, the derivative evidence rule covers the compelled statements or materials, or anything derived from them, unless the prosecution carries the burden of showing an independent source for the disputed evidence [*Murphy v. Waterfront Comm'n*, 378 U.S. 52, 79 n.18 (1964)]. Material gotten under a federal immunity statute is unavailable in federal proceedings and in state proceedings as well as a matter of federal supremacy [*see State v. Castonguay*, 240 A.2d 747 (Me. 1968)]. To protect the operation of state immunity legislation, the Court also adopted a rule of exclusion for federal proceedings affecting testimony or documents gotten by state officials under a state immunity statute. The question is still open whether a sister state must also immunize against the use of material obtained under another state's immunity proceedings [*cf. People v. Den Uyl*, 318 Mich. 645, 29 N.W.2d 284 (1947), *with State v. Dilworth*, 159 N.W.2d 795 (S.D. 1968)].

Comment on Failure to Testify

It is an impairment of the defendant's privilege against self-incrimination for the prosecutor to comment on the defendant's failure to take the stand [*Griffin v. California*, 380 U.S. 609 (1965)], unless the court is able to say beyond a reasonable doubt that the error is harmless under the circumstances [*Chapman v. California*, 386 U.S. 18 (1967)]. The Court has not been willing to consider anything more than trifling comments harmless [*Fontaine v. California*, 390 U.S. 593 (1968); *Anderson v. Nelson*, 390 U.S. 523 (1968)].

There is no agreement whether the test is purely an objective one of whether the statement on the basis of its content amounts to a comment, or whether a subjective element is a part of it. The Illinois Supreme Court takes the latter position, holding that the test is whether the reference was intended or calculated to direct the jury's attention to the defendant's failure to testify [*People v. Mills*, 40 Ill. 2d 4, 237 N.E.2d 697 (1968)]. Most cases, however, appear to turn on what is said, *e.g.*, that "the defendant called no witnesses" [*People v. Mirenda*, 23 N.Y.2d 439, 245 N.E.2d 194, 297 N.Y.S.3d 532 (1969)] or that the prosecution evidence is "uncontradicted" [*e.g., Doty v. United States*, 416 F.2d 887 (10th Cir. 1969); Annot., 14 A.L.R.3d 723 (1967)]. A statement that the testimony of prosecution witnesses remains uncontradicted was not, however, considered a veiled comment on the defendant's failure to take the stand [*United States ex rel. Leak v. Follette*, 418 F.2d 1266 (2d Cir. 1969)].

The prohibition on comment also extends to the court. In one case the defendant tried on trousers allegedly worn by the criminal to show that they did not fit, but made no other statement. The judge then commented, as he was permitted to do as a matter of procedural law, that the defendant did not deny other evidence against him [*United States ex rel. Fioravanti v. Yeager*, 404 F.2d 675 (3d Cir. 1968)]. There is also much litigation over whether the court can instruct the jury to draw no inference from the defendant's failure to testify, because of the fact that the jurors may in fact be reminded to do this [*see People v. Brady*, —— Cal. App. ——, 80 Cal. Rptr. 418 (1969) and authorities cited therein; Annot., 18 A.L.R.3d 1335 (1968)].

The defense counsel may handle the trial in a way to bring out the fact of defendant's failure to testify. For example, defense counsel stated in final argument that it had been his choice that the defendant not take the stand, and that he would rely on his cross-examination of prosecution witnesses. The county attorney in rebuttal asked if there might not be some other reason for the defendant's refusal. The court held this to be an improper statement by the prosecutor, but one brought on by defense counsel so that there would be no reversal [*State v. Sage*, 162 N.W.2d 502 (Iowa 1968)].

It will be recalled that *Miranda* rests on the privilege clause, and that comment on the defendant's refusal to make a statement to police is an impairment of privilege [*see supra* at 184]. If the defendant takes the stand, however, thus waiving privilege, he can be asked on cross-examination why he did not offer the same explanation to police at the time of his arrest [*Sharp v. United States*, 410 F.2d 959 (5th Cir. 1969)]. A police officer of course should not testify that the defendant failed to respond to questioning. A casual reply to that effect might be ignored as harmless, but when the prosecutor returns to the answer in final arugment, the error becomes manifest enough that reversal can be ordered despite the fact that the point was raised for the first time on appeal [*United States v. Arnold*, 425 F.2d 204, 7 Cr.L. 2181 (10th Cir. 1970)].

If a substantive statute is held void on privilege grounds, the comment doctrine may come into play. As discussed below [*see infra* at 572], the Supreme Court has voided certain registration statutes as in violation of the privilege. Therefore, it is error to point out the fact that the defendant held a gambler's tax stamp issued under the void law [*Nolan v. United States*, 423 F.2d 1031 (10th Cir. 1969)].

The concept of comment extends to cross-examination of a defendant about whether he asserted a claim of privilege at the preliminary examination [*State ex rel. Riendeau v. Tahash*, 276 Minn. 26, 148 N.W.2d 557 (1967)] or in separate proceedings in which he was called as a witness [*Dean v. Commonwealth*, 209 Va. 666, 166 S.E.2d 228 (1969)].

If there are co-defendants, each is protected against comment by anyone, including counsel for other co-defendants. Thus the court can (and should) refuse to let one attorney comment on the fact that the other defendants did not testify [*Gurleski v. United States*, 405 F.2d 253 (5th Cir. 1969); *People v. Haldeen*, 267 Cal. App. 2d 478, 73 Cal. Rptr. 102 (1968); *State v. Smith*, 74 Wash. 2d 744, 446 P.2d 571 (1968)].

If the action is not criminal, the failure of the adverse party to present his position can be commented on [*Smith v. Lautenschlager*, 15 Ohio App. 2d 212, 240 N.E.2d 109 (1968) (bastardy action)]. However, the general rule is that no inference can be drawn by either party to an action if a witness claims privilege [*see* Annot., 24 A.L.R.2d 895 (1953)], although there is authority to the contrary [*e.g., Morgan v U.S.F. & G. Co.*, 222 So. 2d 820 (Miss. 1969)].

Prohibited Penalties

The traditional view has been that loss of employment is not a "penalty" within the coverage of the Fifth Amendment [*Ullman v. United States*, 350 U.S. 422 (1956)]. Consequently, a person could not claim privilege on the basis that he might lose his employment, and the material elicited from him could be used as a basis for suspension or revocation of licenses [*e.g., Matter of Randel*, 158 N.Y. 216, 52 N.E. 1106 (1899)]. This tradition has been substantially affected by several recent decisions of the Supreme Court, though whether the net result is simply a change in the formula of questions put to employees about their employment-related activities remains to be seen.

In *Spevack v. Klein* [385 U.S. 511 (1967)], the Court overruled *Cohen v. Hurley* [366 U.S. 117 (1961)], and held that an attorney named in disbarment proceedings could claim privilege against a subpoena ordering him to produce incriminating records, without being disbarred for his refusal to comply. Five of the Justices joined in holding that the claim of privilege was properly made under the circumstances. Four of them, speaking through Mr. Justice Douglas, held that disbarment is a penalty within the meaning of the Fifth Amendment, and that the protection of the privilege "should not be watered down by imposing the dishonor of disbarment and the deprivation of a livelihood as a price for asserting it" [385 U.S. at 514]. Having concluded this, the four did not find it necessary to consider whether the "required records" doctrine of the *Shapiro* case [*Shapiro v. United States*, 355 U.S. 1 (1948); *see infra* at 573] was still viable.

Justice Fortas concurred in the judgment. He felt that lawyers as private citizens could remain silent without fearing loss of employment, but made no commitment that the same could be said of public employees like the police officers in *Garrity* [*see infra* at 570]. He also left open the question, which he thought not to be presented on the facts, of whether lawyers could be required by statute or court rule to maintain and produce certain records in connection with their practice, and be disbarred for their refusal to comply. He did indicate, however, that he was "not prepared to indicate doubt as to the essential validity of *Shapiro*" [385 U.S. at 520].

The four dissenting Justices were gravely concerned about the impact the decision would have on safeguarding and upgrading the standards of the legal profession. And indeed it seems difficult to reconcile the traditions of the profession, including the status of its members as officers of the court, with the assumption on the part of the majority that the practice of law is purely private employment; as Justice Harlan observed, "this decision can hardly fail to encourage oncoming generations of lawyers to think of their calling as imposing on them no higher standards of behavior than might be acceptable in the general market-place" [385 U.S. at 521; *cf. State v. McIntyre*, 41 Wis. 2d 481, 164 N.W.2d 235 (1969) (*Spevack* destroys power of disciplinary authority to subpoena the lawyer's records)].

The *Spevack* decision thus seemed to raise particularly critical questions about the ability to maintain the standards of the legal profession. Unless the "required records" exception of *Shapiro* could be utilized, discipline or disbarment would be possible only if full testimony or complete records on the part of witnesses enabled the requisite findings to be made without resort to the respondent attorney's own files. These apprehensions, however, may have been allayed somewhat as the result of a related decision in the October 1967 Term.

In *Gardner v. Broderick* [392 U.S. 273 (1968)], the applicant sued for reinstatement and back pay after he had been dismissed because of his claim of privilege and his refusal to sign a waiver of immunity in connection with a grand jury investigation. Under the New York Constitution [Art. 1, § 6 (McKinney Supp. 1968)], this required his dismissal. Though *Spevack* and *Garrity v. New Jersey* [*see infra* at 570] were cited to it, the New York Court of Appeals thought they were to be distinguished because Gardner was a public official. As the Supreme Court summarized the New York court's position:

> . . . Unlike the lawyer, he is directly, immediately, and entirely responsible to the city or State which is his employer. He owes his entire loyalty to it. He has no other "client" or principal. He is a trustee of the public interest, bearing the burden of great and total responsibility to his public employer. Unlike the lawyer who is directly responsible to his client, the policeman is either responsible to the State or to no one. [392 U.S. at 277–78]

Therefore, the New York Court of Appeals sustained the dismissal.

The Supreme Court reversed, however. In its view, Gardner's dismissal impaired his Fifth Amendment privilege.

> . . . Here, petitioner was summoned to testify before a grand jury in an investigation of alleged criminal conduct. He was discharged from office not for failure to answer relevant questions about his official duties, but for refusal to waive a constitutional right. He was dismissed for failure to relinquish the protections of the privilege against self-incrimination. The Constitution of New York State and the City Charter both expressly provided that his failure to do so, as well as his failure to testify, would result in dismissal from his job. He was dismissed solely for his refusal to waive the immunity to which he is entitled if he is required to testify despite his constitutional privilege. . . .

> . . . New York City discharged him for refusal to execute a document purporting to waive his constitutional rights and to permit prosecution of himself on the basis of his compelled testimony. Petitioner could not have assumed—and certainly he was not required to assume—that he was being asked to do an idle act of no legal effect. In any event, the mandate of the great privilege against self-incrimination does not tolerate the attempt, regardless of its ultimate effectiveness, to coerce a waiver of the immunity it confers on penalty of loss of employment. It is clear that petitioner's testimony was demanded before the grand jury in part so that it might be used to prosecute him, and not solely for the purpose of securing an accounting of his performance of his public trust. If the latter had been the only purpose, there would have been no reason to seek to compel petitioner to waive his immunity. [392 U.S. at 279]

Therefore, the provision of the charter under which Gardner had been dismissed was held invalid.

In a companion case [*Uniformed Sanitation Men Ass'n, Inc. v. Comm'r of Sanitation,* 392 U.S. 281 (1968)], the Court applied *Gardner v. Broderick* to prevent the discharge of city trash collectors purely on the basis of their claim of privilege to directly incriminating material.

Whether, however, this means that public employees—and attorneys—are able both to retain their employment, and claim privilege against revealing incriminating matters arising out of their employment, turns on the implication to be drawn from other passages in two decisions. In *Gardner v. Broderick,* the Court acknowledged some relevancy in the description of the public employee's responsibility to the state [see *supra*]. It stated:

> We agree that these factors differentiate the situations. If appellant, a policeman, had refused to answer questions specifically, directly, and narrowly relating to the performance of his official duties, without being required to waive his immunity with respect to the use of his answers or the fruits thereof in a criminal prosecution of himself, . . . the privilege against self-incrimination would not have been a bar to his dismissal. [392 U.S. at 278]

This was elaborated upon in the *Sanitation Men* case. The Court noted:

> As we stated in *Gardner v. Broderick, supra,* if New York had demanded that petitioners answer questions specifically, directly, and narrowly relating to the performance of their official duties on pain of dismissal from public employment without requiring relinquishment of the benefits of the constitutional privilege, and if they had refused to do so, this case would be entirely different. In such a case, the employee's right to immunity as a result of his compelled testimony would not be at stake. But here the precise and plain impact of the proceedings against petitioners . . . was to present them with a choice between surrendering their constitutional rights or their jobs. Petitioners as public employees are entitled, like all other persons, to the benefit of the Constitution, including the privilege against self-incrimination. . . . At the same time, petitioners, being public employees, subject themselves to dismissal, after proper proceedings, if they refuse to account for their performance of their public trust which do not involve an attempt to coerce them to relinquish their constitutional rights. [392 U.S. at 284–85]

This caused Justice Harlan, one of the dissenters in *Spevack,* to concur in the two decisions. He stated:

. . . I do so with a good deal less reluctance than would otherwise have been the case because, despite the distinctions which are sought to be drawn between these two cases, on the one hand, and *Spevack* and *Garrity*, on the other, I find in these opinions a procedural formula whereby, for example, public officials may now be discharged and lawyers disciplined for refusing to divulge to appropriate authority information pertinent to the faithful performance of their offices. I add only that this is a welcome breakthrough in what *Spevack* and *Garrity* might otherwise have been thought to portend. [392 U.S. at 285]

What if instead of claiming immunity and being dismissed, the official incriminates himself? Can his statements be used to support a criminal prosecution against him? This is what is involved in *Garrity v. New Jersey*.

The decision in *Garrity v. New Jersey* [385 U.S. 493 (1967)] is in part an explanation of *Miranda* [see supra at 134] and in part an exposition of the privilege against self-incrimination as such. Garrity and his fellow defendants had been convicted of conspiracy to obstruct justice because of a "ticket-fixing" scheme in which they participated. The conviction was based in part on statements the defendants made to the state attorney-general during his investigation of the ticket-fixing operation. Under the New Jersey statute [N.J. REV. STAT. § 2A:81–17.1 (Supp. 1965); *cf.* N.Y. CONST. art. 1, § 6 (McKinney Supp. 1968)], a public official or employee who refuses to waive his immunity under the privilege may be removed from office and is thereafter ineligible to hold public office or employment in the state. Faced with this choice, Garrity and the others made statements of an incriminating nature.

The Supreme Court reversed the conviction. It felt that:

The choice given petitioners was either to forfeit their jobs or incriminate themselves. The option to lose their means of livelihood or to pay the penalty of self-incrimination is the antithesis of free choice to speak out or to remain silent. [385 U.S. at 497]

Therefore, "the statements were infected by the coercion inherent in this scheme of questioning and cannot be sustained as voluntary under our prior decisions" [385 U.S. at 497–98].

But it was also asserted that Garrity and his companions had in fact made their choice to speak, and therefore should be held to have waived the privilege. This did not impress the Court. "Where the choice is 'between the rock and the whirlpool,' duress is inherent in deciding to 'waive' one or the other" [385 U.S. at 498]. Nor did it matter that these men were police officers and not private citizens:

We now hold the protection of the individual under the Fourteenth Amendment against coerced statements prohibits use in subsequent criminal proceedings of statements obtained under threat of removal from office, and that it extends to all, whether they are policemen or other members of our body politic. [385 U.S. at 500]

The result of these several decisions seems to be, first, that no license or permit holder can have his license or permit revoked, and no public employee can be discharged because of his refusal to testify to directly incriminating questions. Second, if the individual chooses to incriminate himself rather than to lose his employment, the statement will not be usable against him in a criminal prosecution. Third, however, if specific statements are sought from him directly relating to public employment, and perhaps in fact to licensed employment like the practice of law, and he refuses to answer, this can be made the basis of dismissal or license revocation proceedings against him.

Thus, disciplinary proceedings cannot be stayed if a police disciplinary board is not permitted to discharge an officer simply for asserting privilege [*Luman v. Tanzler,* 411 F.2d 164 (5th Cir. 1969)]. If the officer refuses to answer questions put to him by a superior officer about his participation in a car theft ring, in an official inquiry during which no testimony was induced by a threat of discharge and no waiver of immunity required of him, the officer could be discharged [*Silverio v. Municipal Court,* 247 N.E.2d 379 (Mass.), *cert. denied,* 396 U.S. 878 (1969)].

There are also limits on how far the Court will press its self-incrimination doctrines to prevent the conduct of civil proceedings. It was asked to rule that the privilege clause ruled out the use of interrogatories under Federal Rule of Civil Procedure 33 in a civil forfeiture proceeding against a corporation until pending criminal proceedings were finally disposed of. The Court refused [*United States v. Kordel,* 397 U.S. 1 (1970)]. The corporation itself could not claim privilege, and could comply with the interrogatories through the testimony of an official who himself would not be incriminated by the responses. If the official were asked specifically incriminating questions, he remained free to claim privilege. Nor was the conduct of a civil action while a criminal prosecution was pending fundamentally unfair:

. . . The public interest in protecting consumers throughout the Nation from misbranded drugs requires prompt action by the agency charged with responsibility for administration of the federal food and drug laws. But a rational decision whether to proceed criminally against those responsible for the misbranding may have to wait consideration of a fuller record than that before the agency at the time of the civil seizure of the offending products. It would stultify enforcement of federal law to require a governmental agency such as the FDA invariably to choose either to forgo recommendation of a criminal prosecution once it seeks civil relief, or to defer civil proceedings pending the ultimate outcome of a criminal trial.

We do not deal here with a case where the Government has brought a civil action solely to obtain evidence for its criminal prosecution or has failed to advise the defendant in its civil proceeding that it contemplates his criminal prosecution; nor with a case where the defendant is without counsel or reasonably fears prejudice from adverse pretrial publicity or other unfair injury; nor with any other special circumstances that might suggest the unconstitutionality or even the impropriety of this criminal prosecution.

Overturning these convictions would be tantamount to the adoption of a rule that the Government's use of interrogatories directed against a corporate defendant in the ordinary course of a civil proceeding would always immunize the corporation's officers from subsequent criminal prosecution. . . . [O]n this record there was no . . . . departure from the proper administration of criminal justice. [397 U.S. at 11–13 (footnotes omitted)]

On the strength of *Kordel* it was held that a state does not have to defer disciplinary hearings against an attorney-judge until all possible criminal charges have been disposed of [*DeVita v. Sills,* 422 F.2d 1172 (3d Cir. 1970)].

Required Records

Modern government runs on taxation. To make these taxation schemes enforceable, taxpayers must be required to file returns and to maintain the records by which the sufficiency of those returns can be evaluated. When revenue law enforcement was attacked in part on the basis of self-incrimination inherent in filing a return, the Supreme Court denied the claim.

Thus, in the *Sullivan* case [*United States v. Sullivan,* 274 U.S. 259 (1927)], the taxpayer sought to defend against his failure to file an income tax return on the ground that it would have indicated revenue from bootlegging in violation of the National Prohibition Act. The Court held that to sustain this claim would amount to "an extreme if not an extravagant application" of the privilege [274 U.S. at 263], and so denied the claim that the entire return was within the privilege.

The *Shapiro* case [*Shapiro v. United States*, 335 U.S. 1 (1948)] involved wartime price control. Shapiro was ordered by Office of Price Administration attorneys to produce the records relating to fruit and produce sales that he had made, but claimed the privilege against self-incrimination concerning their contents. He later attacked his conviction for violating the price control act on the basis that it rested in part on the material exacted from him over his claim of privilege. The Court held that he could not make such a claim concerning records that he was required to keep under valid administrative regulations; the analogy used by the Court was a claim by a public officer that public records in his custody would incriminate him, a claim that is uniformly rejected. Since the price control records had "public aspects," the defendant as their custodian could not claim privilege with respect to them.

Whether encouraged by these decisions or not, Congress passed a number of reporting and registration statutes, for the most part in the guise of taxation measures. The most prominent of these were the federal wagering tax statutes which required gamblers to obtain special stamps and pay a ten per cent excise tax on gross amount of wagers, and the registration provisions of the National Firearms Act [26 U.S.C. §§ 5841, 5851]. When the federal wagering tax provisions were first attacked, the Court sustained the constitutionality of the registration and reporting requirements on the basis once more of the required records doctrine [*Kahriger v. United States*, 345 U.S. 22 (1953); *Lewis v. United States*, 348 U.S. 419 (1955)].

When, however, Congress began to extend reporting requirements to the political area, by requiring individual members of the Communist Party to register, the Court struck down the statute as violative of the privilege [*Albertson v. Subversive Activities Control Board*, 382 U.S. 70 (1965)]. Because Communist Party membership was itself a crime, the contents of the required report were patently and directly incriminating.

The *Albertson* decision brought about efforts to have the Court reconsider *Shapiro, Kahriger* and *Lewis*. As we have seen [*supra* at 567], the Court in *Spevack* refused to consider the question of the continued vitality of *Shapiro*. But in three decisions in the October 1967 Term the Court overturned *Kahriger* and *Lewis*.

The first of the three is the *Marchetti* case [*Marchetti v. United States*, 390 U.S. 39 (1968)]. Marchetti had been convicted of a willful failure to pay the wagering tax and to register before engaging in the business of accepting wagers. The government had relied on *Kahriger* as a ground for rejecting Marchetti's claim of privilege. The Supreme Court, however, found the basis on which *Kahriger* rested inadequate in light of the intervening privilege cases of *Murphy, Garrity* and *Spevack.* Gambling is widely prohibited by both federal and state laws. In particular, Connecticut, where Marchetti operated, had comprehensive laws against wagering. Information obtained by federal enforcement agencies was regularly turned over to state enforcement officials. Therefore, when the defendant was required to register as a gambler, he was being required to provide information that was directly incriminating.

The government also contended that if Marchetti complied with the act, he would be indicating only that future acts might take place, so that he was not at the moment incriminated. This argument, too, the Court rejected. The privilege could not rest on a "rigid chronological distinction," but rather turned on the question of whether "the claimant is confronted by substantial and 'real,' and not merely trifling or imaginary, hazards of incrimination." The hazards created by the wagering tax act registration requirement were, in the Court's view, quite real.

The Court was also asked by the government to create an immunity against state prosecution in order to validate the federal registration scheme. But the Court felt that immunity should come from legislation, and that the legislative intent of Congress was clearly to make the information obtained through administration of the federal system available to interested law enforcement authorities. Thus no immunity was intended. Moreover, to create immunity by judicial action would force state prosecutors to show that their evidence of gambling had an independent source [*see Murphy v. Waterfront Commission,* 378 U.S. 52, 79 n.18 (1964)], and this would be an undue burden to impose on them, one that would hamper law enforcement. Therefore, the registration requirement itself had to fall.

In the companion *Grosso* decision [*Grosso v. United States,* 390 U.S. 62 (1968)], the Court also struck down prosecutions for failure to pay the excise tax imposed by the act and for conspiracy to defraud the government through non-payment of the tax. The payment of the tax was in itself directly an indication of participation in illegal gambling activity, and in any event the government would not accept payment unless a return was filed, a return that itself required revelation of incriminating matter. The Court would not characterize the danger under these circumstances as "imaginary and unsubstantial." Since the failure to pay tax under these conditions could not be made a criminal act, it followed that there could be no crime of conspiracy not to pay that tax.

The third case, *Haynes* [*Haynes v. United States*, 390 U.S. 85 (1968)], voided the registration provisions of the National Firearms Act. Taking the statute as a whole, the Court concluded that possession of any of the firearms governed by the act would constitute a crime, and that in effect the registration requirement made the registrant report the fact of possession. Since the risk was "real and appreciable," the defendant could not be prosecuted for failure to register.

In all three cases the defendants sought also to have the Court overrule *Shapiro* and thus eliminate the required records doctrine completely. This, however, the Court refused to do. In each case the Court found *Shapiro* not to be applicable. In *Marchetti* the Court stated:

> We think that neither *Shapiro* nor the cases upon which it relied are applicable here . . . Moreover, we find it unnecessary for present purposes to pursue in detail the question, left unanswered in *Shapiro,* of what "limits . . . the Government cannot constitutionally exceed in requiring the keeping of records. . . ." It is enough that there are significant points of difference between the situations here and in *Shapiro* which in this instance preclude, under any formulation, an appropriate application of the "required records" doctrine. [390 U.S. at 56]

> Each of the three principal elements of the doctrine, as it is described in *Shapiro,* is absent from this situation. First, petitioner Marchetti was not, by the provisions now at issue, obliged to keep and preserve records "of a kind he has customarily kept"; he was required simply to provide information, unrelated to any records which he may have maintained, about his wagering activities. This requirement is not significantly different from a demand that he provide oral testimony . . . Second, whatever "public aspects" there were to the records at issue in *Shapiro*, there are none to the information demanded from Marchetti. The Government's anxiety to obtain information known to a private individual does not without more render that information public; if it did, no room would remain for the application of the constitutional privilege. Nor does it stamp information with a public character that the Government has formalized its demands in the attire of a statute; if this alone were sufficient, the constitutional privilege could be entirely abrogated by any Act of Congress. Third, the requirements at issue in Shapiro were imposed in "an essentially

noncriminal and regulatory area of inquiry" while those here are directed at a "selective group inherently suspect of criminal activities" . . . . The United States' principal interest is evidently the collection of revenue, and not the punishment of gamblers, . . . but the characteristics of the activities about which information is sought, and the composition of the groups to which inquiries are made, readily distinguish this situation from that in *Shapiro*. There is no need to explore further the elements and limitations of *Shapiro* and the cases involving public papers; these points of difference in combination preclude any appropriate application of these cases to the present one. [390 U.S. at 57]

In similar fashion, the statutory requirements in *Grosso* were viewed as "directed almost exclusively to individuals inherently suspect of criminal activities" [390 U.S. at 68]. The information sought also lacked any characteristic of a public document. Therefore, *Shapiro* was inapplicable. In *Haynes* as well, the Court noted that this was not among "regulatory programs of general application" sustained in *Sullivan* and *Shapiro*.

The Court further indicated the scope of its rulings in subsequent terms. It struck down the registration requirements of the Marihuana Tax Act [26 U.S.C. § 4744(a)(2)] as violative of self-incrimination because, granted the limited class of persons in possession of registered marijuana, compliance with the transfer tax provisions would identify the registrant unmistakably as a member of a "selective group inherently suspect of criminal activities" [*Leary v. United States*, 395 U.S. 6 (1969); *see also United States v. Covington*, 395 U.S. 57 (1969) (prosecution for failure to pay transfer tax barred)]. However, the Court sustained the validity of provisions penalizing sale of heroin and marijuana, in this instance to an undercover agent, because buyers would not comply with registration requirements under the statutes, so that any possibility of the illicit seller having to supply incriminating information is too remote to be acknowledged [*Minor v. United States*, 396 U.S. 87 (1969)].

The fact that the underlying registration provisions may be invalid does not mean that one who submits false data in feigned compliance with the statute receives immunity from a perjury prosecution [*United States v. Knox*, 396 U.S. 77 (1969) (false statements in wagering tax form under 26 U.S.C. § 4412); *Bryson v. United States*, 396 U.S. 64 (1969) (false anti-Communist affidavit filed with NLRB)].

The Court's privilege decisions have been used as a basis for attacking certain well-established reporting and examination requirements, with varying degrees of success. One is the requirement of reporting a vehicle accident. Though some courts have continued to hold that a requirement of reporting name and address, vehicle registration number and operator's permit number is not an impairment of privilege [*e.g. People v. Lucas*, 41 Ill. 2d 370, 243 N.E.2d 228 (1969); *State v. Lemme*, —— R.I. ——, 244 A.2d 585 (1968)], the California Supreme Court has held that *Marchetti et al.* apply to these statutes [*Byers v. Justice Court*, —— Cal. ——, 458 P.2d 465, 80 Cal. Rptr. 553 (1969)]. However, to save the statute the court created immunity to a charge of refusing to identify one's self.

Attacks have also been made on the statutory presumption of guilt of larceny based on possession of recently stolen goods, but thus far without success [*e.g., United States v. Prujansky*, 415 F.2d 1045 (6th Cir. 1969); *State v. Young*, 217 So. 2d 567 (Fla. 1968); *People v. Moro*, 23 N.Y.2d 496, 245 N.E.2d 226, 297 N.Y.S.2d 578 (1969)].

Statutes requiring defendants to submit to psychiatric examinations are also under close scrutiny [Note, *Requiring a Criminal Defendant to Submit to a Government Psychiatric Examination: An Invasion of the Privilege Against Self-Incrimination*, 83 HARV. L. REV. 648 (1970)]. The decisions are in a considerable state of confusion. One court has held that no examination can be held without notice to and presence of counsel, thus utilizing Sixth Amendment and not Fifth Amendment grounds [*Schantz v. Eyman*, 418 F.2d 11 (9th Cir. 1969)]. Other decisions hold that the order for a psychiatric examination is valid as long as the defendant can assert privilege against specific incriminating answers [*McGuire v. Superior Court*, —— Cal. App. ——, 79 Cal. Rptr. 155 (1969); *Commonwealth v. Brown*, —— Pa. ——, 265 A.2d 101 (1970)]. Whether or not the defendant specifically claims privilege, other decisions prohibit the prosecution psychiatrist from testifying to the defendant's statements about the crime as admissions [*Shepard v. Bowe*, 250 Ore. 288, 442 P.2d 238 (1968); *State v. Miner*, 258 A.2d 815 (Vt. 1969)], unless a defense psychiatrist has testified to the same kind of statements [*United States v. Baird*, 414 F.2d 700 (2d Cir. 1969)] or the defendant has otherwise put the issue into the case in a way making the psychiatrist's testimony about the interview necessary [*People v. Morse*, 70 Cal. 2d 711, 452 P.2d 607, 76 Cal. Rptr. 391 (1969) (precautionary instruction necessary)]. Other courts in effect take the position that the defendant waives any privilege protection by injecting the issue of his mental condition into the proceedings, whether in the form of incompetence to stand trial [*State v. Whitlow*, 45 N.J. 3, 210 A.2d 763 (1965)] or substantive insanity [*Alexander v. United States*, 380 F.2d 33 (8th Cir. 1967)]. The Supreme Court's recent decision on alibi notice and discovery for the prosecution [*Williams v. Florida*, 399 U.S. 78, 38 U.S.L.W. 4557 (June 22, 1970); *see supra* at 445] suggests that it might tend toward the *Baird* and *Morse* holding.

Privilege in Juvenile Proceedings

A striking application of the privilege clause is *In re Gault* [387 U.S. 1 (1967)], which for the first time laid down substantial constitutional regulations for the conduct of juvenile delinquency proceedings. Among the rights included is the privilege against self-incrimination, in both its judicial and its extra-judicial settings. The Court rejected the contention that the privilege has no application to juvenile delinquency proceedings that "may result in commitment to a state institution":

> It would indeed be surprising if the privilege against self-incrimination were available to hardened criminals but not to children. The language of the Fifth Amendment, applicable to the States by operation of the Fourteenth Amendment, is unequivocal and without exception. And the scope of the privilege is comprehensive. . . . [387 U.S. at 47]

The Court did not spell out the details of how the privilege applies in actual delinquency proceedings. One may assume that the analogy of the adult criminal proceeding is pertinent, and that it will be necessary to prove the delinquent acts other than by questioning the juvenile in court, as has so often been the case in traditional practice. This in turn will require a clearcut separation between the adjudicational hearing, at which the fact of delinquency is determined, and the dispositional hearing, which may be likened to the sentencing process in a regular criminal proceeding. Since the privilege has never been held applicable at the sentencing phase of the criminal case, there seems to be no reason why it should be available in the dispositional hearing in a delinquency proceeding, as long as there is no danger that the information offered by the juvenile can be used in support of the adjudication of delinquency itself.

It would seem to follow also that the fact of failure to testify in the adjudicational hearing cannot be used adversely to the respondent. Since, however, no jury is usually involved and the prudent judge would never state on the record that he has inferred guilt from silence, it is unlikely that the situation will arise in a form presentable to the appellate courts.

*   *   *   *   *

7. Double Jeopardy

[See Chapter 7, *supra* at 421–35; Chapter 12, *infra* at 745.]

C. *Jackson v. Denno* Hearings

NEW YORK CRIMINAL PROCEDURE LAW (1971)

§ 60.45 Rules of evidence; admissibility of statements of defendants

1. Evidence of a written or oral statement previously made by a defendant may not be received in evidence against him in a criminal proceeding if such statement was involuntarily made.

2. A confession, admission or other statement is "involuntarily made" by a defendant when it is obtained from him:

> (a) By any person by the use or threatened use of physical force upon the defendant or another person, or by means of any other improper conduct or undue pressure which impaired the defendant's physical or mental condition to the extent of undermining his ability to make a choice whether or not to make a statement; or
>
> (b) By a public servant engaged in law enforcement activity or by a person then acting under his direction or in cooperation with him:
>
>> (i) by means of any promise or statement of fact, which promise or statement creates a substantial risk that the defendant might falsely incriminate himself; or
>>
>> (ii) in violation of such rights as the defendant may derive from the constitution of this state or of the United States.

Staff Comments*

This section replaces that part of Criminal Code § 395 which declares:

> "A confession of a defendant, whether in the course of judicial proceedings or to a private person, can be given in evidence against him, unless made under the influence of fear produced by threats, or unless made upon a stipulation of the district attorney, that he shall not be prosecuted therefor. . . ."

* From 1967 Study Draft and Commission Report.

The quoted provision was enacted in the nineteenth century, largely to overcome an early rule that evidence of a confession made in a judicial proceeding (*e.g.*, before a magistrate) was not admissible upon a criminal trial of the confessor (People v. Mondon, 1886, 103 N.Y. 211, 220, 8 N.E. 496). In its modern setting, the Code section is anachronistic and grossly inadequate.

Speaking in something of a vacuum, the logical rule with respect to a confession or other inculpatory statement of a defendant would probably be that it is always admissible as an admission against interest but that its weight and truth may and should be reduced or discounted in the eyes of the triers of the facts by evidence that it was involuntarily made. In the case of statements made to law enforcement and other public officials, however, it has long been a public policy doctrine that proof of involuntariness precludes *admissibility* thereof. Although Code § 395 renders inadmissible an involuntary statement made to "a private person" as well as one made "in the course of judicial proceedings," the term "private person" is intended to embrace public officers (People v. Rogers, 1908, 192 N.Y. 331, 350, 85 N.E. 135); and, indeed, the only real importance of the *inadmissibility* rule lies in its application to statements made to public servants or to persons acting under their direction or in cooperation with them. The proposed section so limits its scope (subd. 1).

Subdivision 2 seeks to exclude from evidence every such statement obtained by any kind of pressure or under any circumstances which the courts and fair-minded people in general do or might consider coercive, unjust, improper or in any way conducive to possible false self-incrimination. Paragraph (ii) is chiefly designed to outlaw admissibility of any statement obtained in the absence of the kind of warnings declared by the Supreme Court of the United States to be essential to valid use thereof against the defendant pursuant to the federal Constitution (Miranda v. Arizona, 1966, 384 U.S. 436, 86 S.Ct. 1602).

It is to be noted that the proposed section is also much broader than Code § 395 in that it excludes any "statement"—not merely any "confession"—involuntarily obtained.

§ 60.50   Rules of evidence; statements of
defendants; corroboration

A person may not be convicted of any offense solely upon evidence of a confession or admission made by him without additional proof that the offense charged has been committed.

§ 710.20 Motion to suppress evidence; in general; grounds for

[The text of this section appears *supra* at 466].

✻ ✻ ✻ ✻ ✻

EDITORS' NOTE

PROCEDURE IN JACKSON V. DENNO HEARINGS

Constitutional Controls on Admission Process

Presence or absence of jury. Under the requirements of *Jackson v. Denno,* the trial court should usually make a determination of constitutional admissibility out of the presence of the jury. This has been somewhat further elucidated in the decision of *Sims v. Georgia* [385 U.S. 538 (1967)]. The trial court had found the testimony on the issue of voluntariness to be conflicting, refused to rule on the matter, and permitted the jury to make the final determination. The Georgia Supreme Court thought its procedures offered equivalent safeguards to those set out in *Jackson v. Denno.* The United States Supreme Court disagreed. It held:

> . . . A constitutional rule was laid down in [*Jackson v. Denno*] that a jury is not to hear a confession unless and until the trial judge has determined that it was freely and voluntarily given. The rule allows the jury, if it so chooses, to give absolutely no weight to the confession in determining the guilt or innocence of the defendant but it is not for the jury to make the primary determination of voluntariness. Although the judge need not make formal findings of fact or write an opinion, his conclusion that the confession is voluntary must appear on the record with unmistakable clarity. Here there has been absolutely no ruling on that issue and it is therefore impossible to know whether the judge thought the confession voluntary or if the jury considered it as such in its determination of guilt. [The *Jackson*] rule is, as we have said, a constitutional rule binding on the States and, under the Supremacy Clause of Article VI of the Constitution, it must be obeyed. [385 U.S. at 543–44]

Nevertheless, the question of whether the *Jackson v. Denno* hearing should be held in the presence or absence of the jury rests to a degree in the discretion of the trial court. In *Pinto v. Pierce* [389 U.S. 31 (1967)], it was not held error to hold the hearing in the jury's presence when the court ruled the confession admissible as evidence to be considered by the jury, and the defendant did not object to the procedure. The Court, however, did indicate that it is "prudent" to hold the hearing out of the jury's presence.

It is probably the fact that Pierce's confession was properly ruled admissible that accounts for the result in *Pinto v. Pierce*. It seems unlikely that the jury will erase their impressions of what they have heard if the trial court determines the statement inadmissible [*cf. Bruton v. United States*, 391 U.S. 123 (1968), discussed *supra* at 534]. Moreover, the fact that he has to make statements in the presence of the jury may very well inhibit the defendant in what he has to say [*cf. Turner v. United States*, 387 F.2d 333 (5th Cir. 1968)].

It is of course open to legislatures or state courts to require that the hearing always be held out of the presence of the jury. Congress in Section 3501(a) of the Crime Control Act of 1968 has now required this for federal trials, and some states also have held to this effect [*e.g., State v. Bishop*, 272 N.C. 283, 158 S.E.2d 511 (1968); *Andrews v. Langlois*, 252 A.2d 450 (R.I. 1969)]. In the long run, *Pinto v. Pierce* probably distills into nothing but a harmless error rule turning on its own fact situation.

Pretrial motions to suppress. Jackson v. Denno also does not purport to resolve the question of when the determination of admissibility is to be made, as long as the jury does not make the ruling on constitutional admissibility. Therefore, states may make provision for an objection to a confession to be made in a pretrial motion to suppress, a proceeding that makes more functional sense than an interruption of trial to raise the issue. Some of the new statutes and drafts provide for this [*e.g.*, Ill. Ann. Stat. ch. 38 § 114–11 (Smith-Hurd Supp. 1970), and şee *People v. Harper*, 36 Ill. 2d 398, 223 N.E.2d. 841 (1967); La. C. Crim. P. art. 703 (1967); N.Y. Crim. P. Law § 710.40 (1971)], and some state courts have taken this position without specific rules [*e.g., Freeman v. Commonwealth*, 425 S.W.2d 575 (Ky. App. 1968); *State v. Ferrara*, 92 N.J. Super. 549, 224 A.2d 159 (1966)].

If the matter is in fact handled in a pretrial motion, there is not thereafter a duty to stop trial for a second *Jackson v. Denno* hearing [*Bond v. United States*, 397 F.2d 162 (10th Cir. 1968)].

Procedural Aspects of Suppression Hearings

Requirement of a motion. The trial court is under no affirmative duty to inquire into the validity of a confession unless the defendant objects to its admissibility [*Lundberg v. Buckhoe*, 389 F.2d 154 (6th Cir. 1968); *Hammonds v. State*, 442 P.2d 39 (Alaska 1968); *State v. Davis*, 157 N.W.2d 907 (Iowa 1968); *State v. Steeves*, 279 Minn. 298,

157 N.W.2d 67 (1968); *State v. Gray*, 432 S.W.2d 593 (Mo. 1968); *State v. Oliva*, 183 Neb. 620, 163 N.W.2d 112 (1968)].

Standing is also an aspect of confession suppression hearings as it is of motions to suppress other forms of evidence. When the defendant offered an alibi witness whom the state impeached by proving a contrary confession, the defendant was held to have no standing to object to the way the confession was obtained [*State v. Cartagena*, 40 Wis. 2d 213, 161 N.W.2d 392 (1968)]. There is support for this approach in the way the Supreme Court handled the standing matter in its *Alderman* decision [*Alderman v. United States*, 394 U.S. 165, 171–72, 174–75 (1969)].

Discovery. The availability of discovery is often important to the success of confession suppression hearing [*cf.* FED. R. CR. P. 16]. If the statute or rule covers written but not oral confessions, it may be interpreted to include a video tape recording [*cf. State v. Hall*, 253 La. 425, 218 So. 2d 320 (1969)].

Hearings. Because the hearing is a part of the criminal proceeding as a whole, the right to public trial applies, so that spectators cannot be excluded [*United States ex rel. Bennett v. Rundle*, 419 F.2d 599 (3d Cir. 1969)]. The hearing is as much for the protection of the state as of the defendant, so that the court may properly disregard a defense motion to consider the matter on the basis of the preliminary examination transcript [*People v. Lauderdale*, 17 Mich. App. 191, 169 N.W.2d 171 (1969)].

For the most part, the usual rules of evidence apply. The prosecutor can cross-examine the defendant out of the hearing of the jury as to whether he believed himself innocent or guilty at the time of the interrogation [*State v. Miranda*, 104 Ariz. 174, 450 P.2d 364 (1969)]. In another instance, however, it was held that the defense attorney should not be permitted to ask the defendant to read from a book to demonstrate his lack of English language ability, because there was too much incentive for deception and the matter was not subject to effective cross-examination [*State v. Sandoval*, 92 Idaho 853, 452 P.2d 350 (1969)].

If the defendant testified only on the matter of the credibility of the confession, on the authority of *Simmons* [*Simmons v. United States*, 390 U.S. 377 (1968)] the waiver extends that far only, so that it is error for the prosecutor to comment to the jury that the defendant testified on that issue alone [*Calloway v. Wainwright*, 409 F.2d 59 (5th Cir. 1969) (on common-law credibility issue, but principle should be the same in *Jackson v. Denno* hearing context)].

Burden of producing evidence in support of motion. Is the only requirement imposed on defendant one of moving in good time, or must he produce some material showing that he confessed, and perhaps the circumstances surrounding the interrogation? If ordinary motion practice provided the pattern, then the defendant would have to do something more than move; there is authority to this effect [*e.g.*, *State v. Davis*, 157 N.W.2d 907 (Iowa 1968)].

The Pennsylvania Supreme Court, however, has taken a different view. The trial court had indicated that since the allegation had been made by the defendant, he ought to present some evidence on his own behalf. The supreme court reversed on the ground that this constituted an improper allocation of the burden of producing evidence, and that it should be the prosecution's responsibility to come forward with evidence showing the constitutional admissibility of the confession [*Commonwealth ex rel. Butler v. Rundle*, 429 Pa. 141, 239 A.2d 426 (1968)]. In effect, all that was required of the defendant was an unadorned pleading. Since, however, both sides had actually produced evidence, the error was harmless.

Burden of going forward: prosecution. If, depending on the procedural standard adopted by the particular court, the defendant has either pleaded without more or has offered some data to show that he has confessed, then the burden of producing or going forward with the evidence shifts to the prosecution; what is involved is actually the "risk of non-persuasion" [C. McCORMICK, EVIDENCE § 318 (1954)].

If the evidence offered in fact confirms that the officers acted improperly, this without more justifies an order of suppression [*e.g.*, *Sullins v. United States*, 389 F.2d 985 (10th Cir. 1968)]. What, however, if the hearing turns into a swearing contest in which it is the defendant's word against that of the police officer who has begun to lay foundation for admission of the confession?

The Washington Supreme Court recently faced this problem [*State v. Davis*, 73 Wash. 2d 271, 438 P.2d 185 (1968)]. The state had called only one of the two officers present at the interrogation, and did not produce the other even after a clear conflict developed between the first officer's testimony and that of the defendant. Under these circumstances, the court held, the failure of the state to produce the other officer justified the inference that his testimony would have supported the defendant's point of view and not the state's, under the so-called "missing witness" rule.

The prosecution had argued several points in opposition. It said first that the reason for the non-production of the second officer had been explained to defense counsel. This the appellate court refused to consider because it was not revealed in the record. It next asserted that the so-called "missing witness rule" on which the court relied was inapplicable because the officer was equally available to both parties, so that the defense could have called him if it had wanted. The court, however, thought that availability is more a matter of relationship to a party than it is of physical presence in the jurisdiction, and concluded that the officer was "peculiarly available" to the prosecution because of the close working relationship between the police department and the prosecutor's office. As a third ground, the state maintained that the witness' testimony would be merely cumulative; in a proper instance this may indeed excuse production of the other officer or officers [e.g., People v. Gross, 87 Ill. App. 2d 300, 232 N.E.2d 54 (1967)]. In this instance, however, the court did not believe the testimony would have been cumulative to a justification for admission already established. Finally, the prosecution urged that the withholding of the witness was not "willful," that is, a deliberate suppression. The court, though, refused to accept this interpretation of the requirement, and in effect equated withholding with non-production, whatever the reason. Therefore, the trial court should have invoked the missing witness rule at the pretrial hearing and in the form of a jury instruction when the defendant renewed his objection to the confession at trial on the issue of voluntariness.

While this is a rule of evidentiary law and not constitutional doctrine, the case suggests that in instances of sharply-conflicting testimony, all the officers participating in the interrogation had better be called or at least made available in the courtroom at the time of the motion if the defense attorney wishes to examine them. [See Sims v. Georgia, 389 U.S. 404 (1967), which seems to draw similar inferences from the failure to produce rebuttal testimony; Stevens v. State, 228 So. 2d 888 (Miss. 1969); Williams v. State, 220 So. 2d 325 (Miss. 1969) (state's burden cannot be sustained when it fails to call the other officer present at the interrogation)].

Burden of going forward: defense. Whatever the initial burden of presentation may be, it is also true that the defendant can be placed in the position of risking a finding of admissibility if all the testimony by the officers suggests compliance with constitutional requirements and the defendant has done nothing but allege involuntariness, nonwaiver or whatever. If this is the posture of the proof when viewed by an appellate court, the trial court's refusal to suppress the confession will be sustained [e.g., United States v. Hayes, 385 F.2d 375 (4th Cir. 1967); State v. Nolan, 423 S.W.2d 815 (Mo. 1968); State v. Bishop, 272 N.C. 283, 158 S.E.2d 511 (1968); State v. Morris, 248 Ore. 480, 435 P.2d 1018 (1967)].

Burden of persuasion. The *Miranda* opinion's only contribution to the matter of motions to suppress confessions was its statement that a "heavy burden" rests on the government or state to prove the validity of any claimed waiver of *Miranda* rights. This has caused courts to split on the question of exactly what the burden of persuasion is, a matter also evident in the field of traditional motions to suppress seized evidence. The question is complicated in both instances by the fact that the matter is tried initially before a judge in the absence of a jury, so that there is usually no occasion to formalize the matter of burden of persuasion in a formal instruction or statement of law.

As might be expected, the judicial holdings run the gamut. The statement may be simply that the court must be "satisfied" that the confession meets constitutional standards [*e.g., Keller v. State,* 2 Md. App. 623, 236 A.2d 313 (1967)]. To the Pennsylvania Supreme Court, the burden of "beyond a reasonable doubt" has no application to a determination of police misconduct alleged by the defendant; "a finding of voluntariness by a preponderance prevents the use of confessions obtained through improper police tactics, while guilt beyond a reasonable doubt is still required" [*Commonwealth ex rel. Butler v. Rundle,* 429 Pa. 141, 239 A.2d 426, 429 (1968)].

Other courts, however, have imposed the reasonable doubt standard in this context [*Pea v. United States,* 397 F.2d 627 (D.C. Cir. 1968)]. This may be done on the theory that such was the burden before *Jackson v. Denno* when the issue went to the jury, and that it should not be changed [*Fernandez v. Beto,* 281 F. Supp. 207 (N.D. Texas 1968)]. A more satisfactory theoretical basis, asserted by the Washington Supreme Court, is that the foreboding statements by the Supreme Court in *Miranda* concerning the heavy burden on the proponent of the confession can only be translated into the reasonable doubt standard traditional in criminal law [*Roney v. State,* 44 Wis. 2d 522, 171 N.W.2d 400 (1969); *State v. Davis,* 73 Wash. 2d 271, 438 P.2d 185 (1968)].

California, as indicated earlier, has adopted the "cat out of the bag" principle voiding a subsequent confession after an earlier unconstitutionally obtained one unless the confession is the product of an "independent act." A confrontation of the defendant with unlawfully obtained evidence is also a basis for excluding evidence under *Wong Sun* unless the relationship has become sufficiently "attenuated to remove the taint." In either instance, the burden is on the state to show the independent source or attenuation [*People v. Johnson,* 70 Cal. 541, 450 P.2d 865, 75 Cal. Rptr. 401 (1969)].

Trial court findings. Because of the likelihood of subsequent review, including later federal habeas corpus proceedings under *Townsend v. Sain* [372 U.S. 293 (1963)], a record should be kept and the trial court should enter specific findings [*State v. Bishop*, 272 N.C. 283, 158 S.E.2d 511 (1968)]. If after a preliminary denial of the defense motion additional facts are brought out suggesting that the confession should in fact be suppressed, an order to that effect should then be entered [*cf. People v. Hudson*, 38 Ill. 2d 616, 233 N.E.2d 403 (1968)].

Review of trial court findings. Whether the state can appeal from an order suppressing a confession depends both on when the motion itself is dealt with and whether there is an implementing statute. Under the double jeopardy rule in force in most states, if the confession determination is deferred until a *Jackson v. Denno* hearing in mid-trial, the defendant is already in jeopardy, so that if he is acquitted no appeal, other than perhaps an advisory appeal in the handful of states permitting that procedure, is possible. If the confession matter is handled in a pretrial motion, then the problem of appeal is no different than that for other varieties of pretrial interlocutory appeals.

If the ruling goes against the defendant, he can include this in his list of errors on appeal if he is convicted. Since there is a considerable element of trial court discretion involved, the appellate court looks principally for abuse of discretion in evaluating the evidence [*e.g., People v. Giovannini*, 260 Cal. App. 2d 597, 67 Cal. Rptr. 303 (1968); *People v. Hudson*, 38 Ill. 2d 616, 233 N.E.2d 403 (1968); *Commonwealth ex rel. Joyner v. Brierley*, 429 Pa. 156, 239 A.2d 434 (1968)]. The court looks to see if the "historical facts" in the record support the trial court conclusions on voluntariness [*Ball v. Gladden*, 250 Ore. 485, 443 P.2d 621 (1968)].

The "harmless error" rule is available as far as some collateral aspects of the confessions rules are concerned [*e.g., People v. Haston*, 69 Cal. App. 2d 233, 444 P.2d 91, 70 Cal. Rptr. 419 (1968) (failure to deny accusation as tacit admission); *State v. Galasso*, 217 So. 2d 326 (Fla. 1968) (error in form of warnings); *State v. Fleury*, 203 Kan. 888, 457 P.2d 44 (1969); *State v. Jefferson*, 101 N.J. Super. 519, 245 A.2d 30 (1968) (question to defendant on witness stand whether he had refused to confess)]. The Supreme Court ruling that the harmless error rule applies in *Bruton* situations [*Harrington v. California*, 395 U.S. 250 (1969); *see infra*] appears to support the basic premise of these decisions.

If the error is not harmless, the court must reverse for a new trial [*State v. Zackmeier*, 151 Mont. 256, 441 P.2d 737 (1968)]. Perhaps a new *Jackson v. Denno* hearing could be had if the state acquires different evidence on the matter, but this would not be so if the appellate court determines absolutely as a matter of law that the particular confession is constitutionally defective [*State v. Seal*, 160 N.W.2d 643 (S.D. 1968)].

Remedy on suppression. The primary remedy is suppression of the confession whether it bears on a direct or a collateral issue in the case [*United States v. Fox*, 403 F.2d 97 (2d Cir. 1968)]. If derivative evidence is affected by the ruling, an appropriate suppression order can no doubt be entered at the same time the confession itself is suppressed. If, however, defense counsel is aware that demonstrative evidence is derivative from a confession, he might be well-advised to submit a pretrial motion to suppress under the state equivalent to Federal Rule 41(e) rather than waiting until trial. If the state does not decide to submit the confession itself, there will be no *Jackson v. Denno* hearing, and there is some risk that if the defendant then objected to the demonstrative evidence on grounds of which he was aware before trial, the motion might be denied during trial as not timely.

As is the usual rule in the case of suppression of unlawfully seized evidence, the exclusion extends only to actions to which the state is a party. A confession allegedly obtained in violation of *Escobedo* and *Miranda* should not have been excluded when it was offered by the defendant in a civil action for malicious prosecution and slander [*Seelig v. Harvard Coop. Soc'y*, —— Mass. ——, 246 N.E.2d 642 (1969)].

Resubmission of the confession to the jury on credibility. Jackson v. Denno prohibited only an abdication of the judge's responsibility to determine initial admissibility of the confession by constitutional standards. If he rules against the admissibility of the confession, this ends the matter unless the defendant has not been placed in jeopardy yet and the state is authorized an interlocutory appeal. If, however, he rules that the confession meets constitutional standards, the possibility still remains of a second attack on the confession.

Under the orthodox rule, the jury considers only the question of credibility, although whether any limitation can be imposed on the data the jury hears as bearing on this issue is problematical [*see State v. Thundershield*, 160 N.W.2d 408 (S.D. 1968)]. Under the Massachusetts or "humane" rule, the jury is to reconsider directly the question of voluntariness [*see* PA. STAT. ANN. tit. 19, § 323 (Purdon Supp. 1970); *State v. Hancock*, 164 N.W.2d 330 (Iowa 1969); *Carlson v. State*, 445 P.2d 157 (Nev. 1968)].

The difference is probably in the instructions of law given to the jury. Under either rule, it is doubtful that the jury should hear about the *Miranda* rule as such. As the Washington Supreme Court noted [*State v. Aiken*, 72 Wash. 2d 306, 434 P.2d 10 (1967)]:

> . . . [T]he jury may redetermine the question of voluntariness as a matter of fact, as it relates to the weight and credibility to be given the confession. The jury may not, however, disregard a confession by measuring it against the foregoing legal tests of due process and reject the confession, as a judge would, if the tests are not fulfilled . . . [434 P.2d at 35]

Errors in instructing the jury will be evaluated by the usual test, to see if any omissions or inclusions would have misled the jurors under the circumstances [*e.g., State v. Morris*, 248 Ore. 480, 435 P.2d 1018 (1967)]. If there is any fact issue, it is error for the court to instruct the jury that the confession is voluntary; the jury must make the final determination of credibility [*Barkhart v. State*, 5 Md. App. 222, 246 A. 2d 280 (1968)].

If the defendant loses on a pretrial motion to suppress, an objection to the confession during trial and a request for an instruction on voluntariness have been held prerequisites for preserving the point on appeal [*People v. Cefaro*, 23 N.Y.2d 283, 244 N.E.2d 42, 296 N.Y.S.2d 345 (1968)].

❊ ❊ ❊ ❊ ❊

D. Screening Identification Evidence

NEW YORK CRIMINAL PROCEDURE LAW (1971)

§ 60.25 Rules of evidence; identification by means of previous recognition, in absence of present identification

1. In any criminal proceeding in which the defendant's commission of an offense is in issue, testimony as provided in subdivision two may be given by a witness when:

(a) Such witness testifies that:

(i) He observed the commission of such offense or an incident related thereto, and the presence or conduct thereat of the person claimed by the people to be the defendant; and

(ii) On an occasion subsequent thereto, but prior to the criminal proceeding, he physically observed, under circumstances consistent with such rights as an accused person may derive under the constitution of this state or of the United

States, a person whom he recognized as the same person whom he had observed on the first or incriminating occasion; and

(iii) He is unable at the proceeding to state, on the basis of present recollection, whether or not the defendant is the person in question; and

(b) It is established that the defendant is in fact the person whom the witness observed and recognized on the second occasion. Such fact may be established by testimony of another person or persons to whom the witness promptly declared his recognition on such occasion.

2. Under circumstances prescribed in subdivision one, such witness may testify at the criminal proceeding that he is certain that the person whom he observed and recognized on the second occasion is the same person whom he observed on the first or incriminating occasion. Such testimony, together with the evidence that the defendant is in fact the person whom the witness observed and recognized on the second occasion, constitutes evidence in chief.

Staff Comment *

This section is derived from, but materially changes, Criminal Code § 393–b, which declares:

"When identification of a person is in issue, a witness who has on a previous occasion identified such person may testify to such previous identification."

That section was enacted in 1927, assertedly to change an earlier case law doctrine that a witness making a trial identification of a defendant cannot bolster his testimony by the self-serving process of showing that he previously identified the defendant on an occasion some time after the crime but before trial (People v. Jung Hing, 1914, 212 N.Y. 393, 401, 106 N.E. 105). In a series of controversial decisions, § 393–b has been held to permit evidence of a previous identification made not only by a witness who identifies a defendant at trial but also by one who is unable to identify him in the courtroom. While the decisions construing this statute are not entirely clear, the following propositions emerge: that whether or not the witness is able to make a trial identification, he may ordinarily testify concerning his prior mak-

* From 1967 Study Bill and Commission Report.

ing of a pre-trial identification (although how this is to be done in the case of a witness who does not recognize the defendant at trial is not explained); that only the witness himself may testify to his previous identification, and not other persons who were present thereat; and that only proof of a previous identification made in person, and not of one made by photograph, is admissible (People v. Cioffi, 1955, 1 N.Y.2d 70, 73, 150 N.Y.S.2d 192; People v. Trowbridge, 1953, 305 N.Y. 471, 476–477, 113 N.E.2d 841; People v. Spinello, 1951, 303 N.Y. 193, 203, 101 N.E.2d 457; People v. Oliver, 1957, 4 App.Div.2d 28, 31, 163 N.Y.S.2d 235, aff'd 3 N.Y.2d 684, 171 N.Y.S.2d 811). Whether previous identification testimony constitutes evidence in chief or merely some kind of bolstering device is not really answered, although it is difficult to perceive anything to be "bolstered" in the case of a witness unable to make a trial identification (see People v. Spinello, supra).

Upon the premise that both § 393–b and the decisions construing it ignore the true purpose and value of "previous identification" testimony, the proposed section reformulates the principle along different lines.

The chief importance of identification by means of previous recognition lies in cases where the witness, owing to lapse of time or other factors, is unable to make a trial identification. A classic example is the factual situation in People v. Spinello, supra, a robbery case in which the trial did not occur until three years after the crime. The complainant, who had positively recognized and identified a man (in fact the defendant) in a police station a few hours after the robbery, was unable, on the basis of present recollection, to identify the defendant years later in the courtroom as the man who had held him up.

Under such circumstances, evidence concerning the prior recognition should be received; but not, as the present law declares, in the form of testimony by the witness that he *was* certain on such prior occasion that the man whom he then saw was the one who robbed him. To allow a conviction on the basis of the witness' earlier state of mind seems improper, especially since he conceivably could have changed his mind in the interim and concluded that he was wrong on the earlier occasion. In this setting, the only valid and salient testimony which he might give would be that he *is* certain *now*—as he sits on the witness stand—that the man whom he saw in the police station shortly after the holdup *is* the same man who robbed him. This, together with proof that the man whom he saw and recognized in the station house was in fact the defendant (proof which would necessarily have to be supplied by other witnesses) would establish a genuine, if indirect, *identification* and should constitute evidence in chief.

It is on the basis of this principle and consideration that the proposed section is formulated.

§ 60.30　Rules of evidence; identification by means of previous recognition, in addition to present identification

In any criminal proceeding in which the defendant's commission of an offense is in issue, a witness whose testimony demonstrates that (a) he observed the commission of such offense or an incident related thereto and the presence or conduct thereat of the person claimed by the people to be the defendant, and (b) he is certain, on the basis of present recollection, that the defendant is the person in question, and (c) on an occasion subsequent to such offense or incident but prior to the proceeding, he observed the defendant under circumstances consistent with such rights as an accused person may derive under the constitution of this state or of the United States and then also recognized him as the same person whom he had observed on the first or incriminating occasion, may, in addition to making an identification of the defendant at the criminal proceeding on the basis of present recollection as the person whom he observed on the first or incriminating occasion, also describe his previous recognition of the defendant and testify that he is certain that the person whom he observed on such second occasion is the same person whom he had observed on the first or incriminating occasion. Such testimony constitutes evidence in chief.

✿　✿　✿　✿　✿

EDITORS' NOTE

PROCEDURE IN SUPPRESSION HEARINGS

The Supreme Court in its lineup decisions indicated that the methods of enforcing its new lineup rule are two-fold. The most obvious one is to prohibit the witness from testifying in court that he had identified the defendant as the criminal in the course of the improper lineup. This would in effect be direct in-court use of the improperly-obtained identification [*see People v. Fowler,* 1 Cal. App. 3d 335, 461 P.2d 643, 82 Cal. Rptr. 363 (1969)]. The second, and most difficult to administer, is to prohibit the witness from testifying to identity at all if his in-court identification is in fact the product of the original lineup identification, and not "based upon observations of the suspect other than the lineup identification." This is the indirect "taint"-"fruit" test with which Justice Black took issue in his dissent.

The Court in laying down its derivative evidence rule gave little indication of the procedural setting in which this critical issue is to be determined by the trial court. In *Wade* and *Gilbert* the defense motion was to strike the witnesses' identification testimony after the circumstances of the lineup were developed to a degree. In each instance the Supreme Court found the record inadequate to determine whether the identification testimony, other than the direct testimony in *Gilbert* to the fact of identification in the lineup, was the product of the improper lineup, and so remanded the cases for a redetermination on that issue. This, however, goes to the adequacy of the records forwarded to the appellate court, and not to the procedure to be followed in the course of trial.

In fact, only four clues are found in the opinions. One, in *Gilbert*, is that "the admission of the in-court identifications without first determining that they were not tainted by the illegal lineup but were of independent origin was constitutional error" [388 U.S. at 272]. A second, in *Wade*, is that "derivative" identification testimony cannot be automatically excluded "without first giving the Government the opportunity to establish by clear and convincing evidence that the in-court identifications were based upon observations of the suspect other than the lineup identification" [388 U.S. at 240]. A third, again in *Gilbert*, is that as far as direct testimony concerning identification in the offending lineup is concerned, "the State is . . . not entitled to an opportunity to show that that testimony had an independent source," since "only a *per se* exlusionary rule as to such testimony can be an effective sanction to assure that law enforcement authorities will respect the accused's constitutional right to the presence of his counsel at the critical lineup" [388 U.S. at 273]. The fourth is that the "harmless error" rule of the *Chapman* case [*Chapman v. California*, 386 U.S. 18 (1967)] applies, so that if the trial court is able to declare the constitutional error "harmless beyond a reasonable doubt," there need be no reversal [*Gilbert*, 388 U.S. at 274]. Except for these points, however, the state and federal trial courts have had to develop on their own initiative the procedures for determining the admissibility of lineup-derived identification evidence.

One requirement consistent with traditional practice on motions to suppress is that the defendant must raise the issue, either by a specific motion [*e.g., Guam v. Cruz*, 415 F.2d 336 (9th Cir. 1969);

State v. Dessureault, 104 Ariz. 380, 453 P.2d 951 (1969)] or by a showing through cross-examination or otherwise that the witness in question participated in a lineup procedure [*Watts v. State,* 3 Md. App. 454, 240 A.2d 317 (1968)]. In the absence of some effort to raise the issue, the court is under no obligation to pursue the matter.

A related question is whether the matter must be raised before trial. There is a growing body of doctrine that either the hearing should be held [*e.g., Guam v. Cruz,* 415 F.2d 336 (9th Cir. 1969); *Solomon v. United States,* 408 F.2d 1306 (D.C. Cir. 1959); *Commonwealth v. Cooper,* —— Mass. ——, 248 N.E.2d 253 (Mass. 1969)] or may be held [*United States v. Hammond,* 419 F.2d 166 (4th Cir. 1969); *Smith v. State,* 6 Md. App. 59, 250 A.2d 285 (1969)] before trial commences. The same approach is also embodied in new provisions [*e.g.,* LA. C. CRIM. P. art. 703 (1967); NEW YORK CRIMINAL PROCEDURE LAW § 710.40 (1971)].

In many jurisdictions, however, the matter is apparently dealt with during trial. Prior to *Wade* and *Gilbert,* the issue of the original identification procedure would be a matter going to the credibility of the witness' testimony about identification, so that as a matter of course the jury would hear the evidence pro and con [*People v. Ford,* 89 Ill. App. 2d 69, 233 N.E.2d 51 (1967)]. However, once the jury hears the prejudicial matter, no amount of precautionary instructions from the judge will erase the matter from the jurors' minds, a matter that the Supreme Court now recognizes as a fact of judicial life [*Bruton v. United States,* 391 U.S. 123 (1968) (admission of codefendant's confession at joint trial)]. An illustration is the *Pedercine* case [*People v. Pedercine,* 256 Cal. App. 2d 328, 63 Cal. Rptr. 873 (1968)], in which the defense counsel was forced to bring out the prejudicial nature of a photograph identification procedure through cross-examination of a police officer. The court deplored the dilemma in which the defense attorney was placed in having either to let the identification go unchallenged or else putting "the inadmissible evidence before the jury to demonstrate its spurious nature" [63 Cal. Rptr. at 879]; only the overwhelming nature of the other proof caused the court to find the error harmless.

Therefore, the trend is to hold the witness taint hearings out of the presence of the jury [*Caples v. United States,* 391 F.2d 1018 (5th Cir. 1968); *State v. Woodward,* 102 N.J. Super. 419, 246 A.2d 130 (1968); *People v. Ballott,* 20 N.Y.2d 600, 233 N.E.2d 103, 286 N.Y.S.2d, (1967); *Thompson v. State,* 438 P.2d 287 (Okla. Crim. App. 1968); *Martinez v. State,* 437 S.W.2d 842, 4 Crim. L. Rptr. 2321 (Tex. Crim. 1969)]. Again the analogy is the *Jackson v. Denno* hearing in which the preferred practice [*Pinto v. Pierce,* 389 U.S. 31 (1967)] is to hold the hearing out of the presence of the jury. Only if the confession is properly held admissible would there be freedom from likelihood of prejudicial error, and the same approach would appear to be valid for lineup identification proceedings as well.

The matter of discovery also has arisen in the context of the lineup identification issue. In the *Simmons* case [*Simmons v. United States,* 390 U.S. 377 (1968)], defense counsel invoked the Jencks Act [18 U.S.C.A. § 3500], as the basis for a motion that photographs shown to witnesses before trial be turned over to him for use in cross-examination. The motion was made after direct examination of the first eyewitness, on the second trial day. The United States attorney replied that there were many pictures and that he was unsure whether he could learn which ones had been shown to the witness, but that he would furnish them if they could be found. The district judge held that Section 3500 was inapplicable and that he would not stop the trial to have the pictures made available. The Court affirmed:

> Although the pictures might have been of some assistance to the defendants, and although it doubtlessly would have been preferable for the Government to have labeled the pictures shown to each witness and kept them available for trial, we hold that in the circumstances the refusal of the District Court to order their production did not amount to an abuse of discretion, at least as to petitioner Simmons. The defense surely knew that photographs had played a role in the identification process. Yet there was no attempt to have the pictures produced prior to trial pursuant to Fed. Rules Crim. Proc. 16. When production of the pictures was sought at trial, the defense did not explain why they were needed, but simply argued that production was required under § 3500. Moreover, the strength of the eyewitness identifications of Simmons renders it highly unlikely that nonproduction of the photographs caused him any prejudice. [388 U.S. at 388–89]

Thus, discovery seems to be available, provided the procedural requirements set out in Federal Rule 16 are met.

One state court has also considered the question of discovery. It found that the request for police reports embodying information about possibly conflicting identifications, for impeachment use, was too broad and a "fishing expedition," but did not state that discovery was unavailable as a matter of law [*State v. Blevins,* 421 S.W.2d 263 (Mo. 1967)].

If transcripts of earlier proceedings in which the witness under attack testified are needed in support of the defense efforts to attack the identification as constitutionally unfair, it is a denial of equal protection to refuse to furnish them to an indigent free of charge [*People v. Ballott*, 20 N.Y.2d 600, 233 N.E.2d 103, 286 N.Y.S.2d 1 (1967)].

The ordinary rules of evidence apply. The defendant is under the burden of presenting some evidence showing that an illegal lineup may have occurred. At that point, the limited authority agrees that the burden shifts to the prosecution to show by clear and convincing proof that the lineup was in fact lawful [*State v. Dessureault*, 453 P.2d 951 (Ariz. 1969); *People v. Martin*, 78 Cal. Rptr. 552 (Ct. App. 1969); *Miller v. State*, 7 Md. App. 344, 255 A.2d 459 (1969); *cf. United States v. Broadhead*, 413 F.2d 1351 (7th Cir. 1969)]. The same basic procedural questions also arise when the issue is the admissibility of evidence about a photographic identification [*see Sutherland v. United States*, —— F.2d ——, 7 Cr. L. 2199 (5th Cir. 1970)].

Arizona appears to leave the issue to the jury [*State v. Dessureault, supra*]. Whether this is consistent with the Supreme Court doctrine in the analogous area of confessions hearings is questionable. This question aside, there is considerable discretion in the trial court in interpreting the evidence [*United States v. Hall*, 396 F.2d 841 (4th Cir. 1968); *People v. Bozigian*, —— Cal. App. ——, 75 Cal. Rptr. 876 (Ct. App. 1969)]. For example, the trial court did not have to accept the testimony of a psychologist offered on the psychology of witness recollection [*State v. Redmond*, 75 Wash. 2d 64, 448 P.2d 938 (1968)].

If the lineup is unlawful and the witness's testimony is found to be tainted, he cannot testify on the identification issue, although of course he can testify on other matters about the crime within his direct knowledge. The burden of non-disclosure to the jury is only on the prosecution, however. One court refused to give relief when the references to the unlawful lineup were elicited by defense counsel on cross-examination [*Sanders v. State*, 219 So. 2d 913 (Miss.), *cert. denied*, 396 U.S. 913 (1969)].

If the court rules against the validity of the lineup, then the jury would not be permitted to hear the witness testify to identity. If the ruling is in favor of the state, the question could arise whether the common-law doctrine permitting impeachment of credibility through an attack on pretrial identification procedures [*see People v. Ford*, 89 Ill. App. 2d 69, 233 N.E.2d 51 (1967)] can still be made. In the confessions area, if the constitutional problems are resolved adversely to the defendant, the common-law tests of credibility can still be submitted to the jury [*Smith v. State*, 6 Md. App. 59, 250 A.2d 285 (1969); *State v. Galloway*, —— Me. ——, 247 A.2d 104 (Me. 1968);

State v. Harris, 40 Wis. 2d 200, 161 N.W.2d 385 (1968)]. One case [*Graham v. State,* 422 S.W.2d 922 (Tex. Crim. App. 1968)] recently held that the trial court did not have to respond to a jury request, during deliberation, for information about police procedures used in a lineup, but this probably had to do more with the timing of the request than to the relevance of that information timely presented by counsel.

In the case of sketches or photographs, the primary materials themselves are inadmissible hearsay that cannot be shown to the jury [*People v. Turner,* 91 Ill. App. 2d 436, 235 N.E.2d 317 (Ill. App. 1968)]. However, if a witness testifies to identity, and the photographs are identified by him as part of his overall testimony, then of course they are admissible and available to the jury for inspection [*People v. Pedercine,* 256 Cal. App. 2d 328, 63 Cal. Rptr. 873 (1968)].

* * * * *

E. Competence to Stand Trial

PATE v. ROBINSON, 383 U.S. 375 (1966) *

I.

The State concedes that the conviction of an accused person while he is legally incompetent violates due process, Bishop v. United States, 350 U.S. 961, 76 S.Ct. 440, 100 L.Ed. 835 (1956), and that state procedures must be adequate to protect this right. It insists, however, that Robinson intelligently waived this issue by his failure to request a hearing on his competence at the trial; and further, that on the basis of the evidence before the trial judge no duty rested upon him to order a hearing *sua sponte.* A determination of these claims necessitates a detailed discussion of the conduct of the trial and the evidence touching upon the question of Robinson's competence at that time.

The uncontradicted testimony of four witnesses called by the defense revealed that Robinson had a long history of disturbed behavior. His mother testified that when he was between seven and eight years of age a brick dropped from a third floor hit Robinson on the head. "He blacked out and the blood run from his head like a faucet." Thereafter "he acted a little peculiar." The blow knocked him "cockeyed" and his mother took him to a specialist "to correct the crossness of his eyes." He also suffered headaches during his childhood, apparently stemming from the same event. His conduct became noticeably

---

* Some footnotes have been eliminated.

erratic about 1946 or 1947 when he was visiting his mother on a furlough from the Army. While Robinson was sitting and talking with a guest, "he jumped up and run to a bar and kicked a hole in the bar and he run up in the front." His mother asked "what on earth was wrong with him and he just stared at [her], and paced the floor with both hands in his pockets." On other occasions he appeared in a daze, with a "glare in his eyes," and would not speak or respond to questions. In 1951, a few years after his discharge from the service, he "lost his mind and was pacing the floor saying something was after him." This incident occurred at the home of his aunt, Helen Calhoun. Disturbed by Robinson's conduct, Mrs. Calhoun called his mother about six o'clock in the morning, and she "went to see about him." Robinson tried to prevent Mrs. Calhoun from opening the door, saying "that someone was going to shoot him or someone was going to come in after him." His mother testified that, after gaining admittance, "I went to him and hugged him to ask him what was wrong and he went to pushing me back, telling me to get back, somebody was going to shoot him, somebody was going to shoot him." Upon being questioned as to Robinson's facial expression at the time, the mother stated that he "had that starey look and seemed to be just a little foamy at the mouth." A policeman was finally called. He put Robinson, his mother and aunt in a cab which drove them to Hines Hospital. On the way Robinson tried to jump from the cab, and upon arrival at the hospital he was so violent that he had to be strapped in a wheel chair. He then was taken in an ambulance to the County Psychopathic Hospital, from which he was transferred to the Kankakee State Hospital. The medical records there recited:

> "The reason for admission: The patient was admitted to this hospital on the 5th day of June, 1952, from the Hines Hospital. Patient began presenting symptoms of mental illness about a year ago at which time he came to his mother's house. He requested money and when it was refused, he suddenly kicked a hole in her bar.

* * * * *

> "Was drinking and went to the Psychopathic Hospital. He imagined he heard voices, voices of men and women and he also saw things. He saw a little bit of everything. He saw animals, snakes and elephants and this lasted for about two days. He went to Hines. They sent him to the Psychopathic Hospital. The voices threatened him. He imagined someone was outside with a pistol aimed at him. He was very, very scared and he tried to call the police and his aunt then called the police. He thought he was

going to be harmed. And he says this all seems very foolish to him now. Patient is friendly and tries to cooperate.

*   *   *   *   *

"He went through an acute toxic episode from which he has some insight. He had been drinking heavily. I am wondering possibly he isn't schizophrenic. I think he has recovered from this condition. I have seen the wife and she is in a pathetic state. I have no objection to giving him a try."

After his release from the state hospital Robinson's irrational episodes became more serious. His grandfather testified that while Robinson was working with him as a painter's assistant, "all at once, he would come down [from the ladder] and walk on out and never say where he is going and whatnot and he would be out two or three hours, and at times he would be in a daze and when he comes out, he comes back just as fresh. He just says he didn't do anything. I noticed that he wasn't at all himself." The grandfather also related that one night when Robinson was staying at his house Robinson and his wife had a "ruckus," which caused his wife to flee to the grandfather's bedroom. Robinson first tried to kick down the door. He then grabbed all of his wife's clothes from their room and threw them out in the yard, intending to set them on fire. Robinson got so unruly that the grandfather called the police to lock him up.

In 1953 Robinson, then separated from his wife, brought their 18-month-old son to Mrs. Calhoun's home and asked permission to stay there for a couple of days. She observed that he was highly nervous, prancing about and staring wildly. While she was at work the next day Robinson shot and killed his son and attempted suicide by shooting himself in the head. It appeared that after Robinson shot his son, he went to a nearby park and tried to take his life again by jumping into a lagoon. By his mother's description, he "was wandering around" the park, and walked up to a policeman and "asked him for a cigarette." It was stipulated that he went to the South Park Station on March 10, 1953, and said that he wanted to confess to a crime. When he removed his hat the police saw that he had shot himself in the head. They took him to the hospital for treatment of his wound.

Robinson served almost four years in prison for killing his son, being released in September 1956. A few months thereafter he began to live with Flossie May Ward at her home. In the summer of 1957 or 1958 Robinson "jumped on" his mother's brother-in-law and "beat him up terrible." She went to the police station and swore out a warrant for his arrest. She described his abnormalities and told the officers that Robinson "seemed to have a disturbed mind." She asked the police "to pick him up so I can have him put away." Later she went back to see why they had not taken him into custody because of "the way he was fighting around in the streets, people were beating him up." She made another complaint a month or so before Robinson killed Flossie May Ward. However, no warrant was ever served on him.

The killing occurred about 10:30 p. m. at a small barbecue house where Flossie May Ward worked. At that time there were 10 customers in the restaurant, six of them sitting at the counter. It appears from the record that Robinson entered the restaurant with a gun in his hand. As he approached the counter, Flossie May said, "Don't start nothing tonight." After staring at her for about a minute, he walked to the rear of the room and, with the use of his hand, leaped over the counter. He then rushed back toward the front of the restaurant, past two other employees working behind the counter, and fired once or twice at Flossie May. She jumped over the counter and ran out the front door with Robinson in pursuit. She was found dead on the sidewalk. Robinson never spoke a word during the three to four minute episode.

Subsequently Robinson went to the apartment of a friend, Mr. Moore, who summoned the police. When three officers, two in uniform, arrived, Robinson was standing in the hall approximately half way between the elevator and the apartment. Unaware of his identity, the officers walked past him and went to the door of the apartment. Mrs. Moore answered the door and told them that Robinson had left a short time earlier. As the officers turned around they saw Robinson still standing where they had first observed him. Robinson made no attempt to avoid being arrested. When asked his address he gave several evasive answers. He also denied knowing anything about the killing.[4]

---

[4] According to the testimony of an arresting officer the following exchange took place:

"I asked him what his name was and he said, 'My name is Ted.' I said, 'What is your real name?' And he said, 'Theodore Robinson.' Then I asked him—I told him he was under arrest and he said, 'For what?' I said, 'Well, you are supposed to be wanted for killing two people on the south side.' I asked him did he know anything about it. He said, 'No, I don't know what you are talking about.' So then I asked him where he lived and he said, 'I don't live no place.'

"I said, 'What do you mean you don't live no place?' He said, 'That's what I said.'

"So then pretty soon asked him again and he said, 'Sometimes I stay with my mother.' And I said, 'Where does she live?' He said, 'Some address on East 44th Street.'

"So then we took him on to the 27th District and while we were making the arrest slip, asked him again his address and he said he lived at 7320 South Park-

Four defense witnesses expressed the opinion that Robinson was insane.[5] In rebuttal the State introduced only a stipulation that Dr. William H. Haines, Director of the Behavior Clinic of the Criminal Court of Cook County would, if present, testify that in his opinion Robinson "knew the nature of the charges against him and was able to cooperate with counsel" when he examined him two or three months before trial. However, since the stipulation did not include a finding of sanity the prosecutor advised the court that "we should have Dr. Haines' testimony as to his opinion whether this man is sane or insane. It is possible that the man might be insane and know the nature of the charge or be able to cooperate with his counsel. I think it should be in evidence, your Honor, that Dr. Haines' opinion is that this defendant was sane when he was examined." However, the court told the prosecutor, "You have enough in the record now. I don't think you need Dr. Haines." In his summation defense counsel emphasized "our defense is clear * * *. It is as to the sanity of the defendant at the time of the crime and also as to the present time." The court, after closing argument by the defense, found Robinson guilty and sentenced him to prison for his natural life.

II.

The State insists that Robinson deliberately waived the defense of his competence to stand trial by failing to demand a sanity hearing as provided by Illinois law. But it is contradictory to argue that a defendant may be incompetent, and yet knowingly or intelligently "waive" his right to have the court determine his capacity to stand trial. See Taylor v. United States, 282 F.2d 16, 23 (C.A. 8th Cir. 1960). In any event, the record shows that counsel throughout the proceedings insisted that Robinson's present sanity was very much in issue. He made a point to elicit Mrs. Robinson's opinion of Robinson's "present sanity." And in his argument to the judge, he asserted that Robinson "should be found not guilty and presently insane on the basis of the testimony that we have heard." Moreover, the prosecutor himself suggested at trial that "we should have Dr. Haines' testimony as to his opinion whether this man is sane or insane." With this record

---

way. That's about all he said. He didn't know anything about any killing or anything."

[5] His mother stated: "I think he is insane." Mrs. Calhoun testified as follows:

"Q. Do you have an opinion as to whether or not presently he is sane or insane?

"A. He is sick. He is insane.

"Q. First of all, do you have an opinion?

"A. Yes.

"Q. What is your opinion as to his present sanity?

"A. He is mentally sick."

we cannot say that Robinson waived the defense of incompetence to stand trial.[6]

We believe that the evidence introduced on Robinson's behalf entitled him to a hearing on this issue. The court's failure to make such inquiry thus deprived Robinson of his constitutional right to a fair trial.[7] See Thomas v. Cunningham, 313 F.2d 934 (C.A. 4th Cir. 1963). Illinois jealously guards this right. Where the evidence raises a *"bona fide* doubt" as to defendant's competence to stand trial, the judge on his own motion must impanel a jury and conduct a sanity hearing pursuant to Ill.Rev.Stat., c. 38, § 104–2 (1963). People v. Shrake, 25 Ill.2d 141, 182 N.E.2d 754 (1962). The Supreme Court of Illinois held that the evidence here was not sufficient to require a hearing in light of the mental alertness and understanding displayed in Robinson's "colloquies" with the trial judge. 22 Ill.2d, at 168, 174 N.E.2d, at 823. But this reasoning offers no justification for ignoring the uncontradicted testimony of Robinson's history of pronounced irrational behavior. While Robinson's demeanor at trial might be relevant to the ultimate decision as to his sanity, it cannot be relied upon to dispense with a hearing on that very issue. Cf. Bishop v. United States, 350 U.S. 961, 76 S.Ct. 440, 100 L.Ed. 835 (1956), reversing 96 U.S. App.D.C. 117, 223 F.2d 582, 585 (1955). Likewise, the stipulation of Dr. Haines' testimony was some evidence of Robinson's ability to assist in his defense. But, as the state prosecutor seemingly admitted, on the facts presented to the trial court it could not properly have been deemed dispositive on the issue of Robinson's competence. . . .

If the State elects to retry Robinson, it will of course be open to

---

[6] Although defense counsel phrased his questions and argument in terms of Robinson's present insanity, we interpret his language as necessarily placing in issue the question of Robinson's mental competence to stand trial. Counsel was simply borrowing the terminology of the relevant Illinois statutes and decisions. The state law in effect at the time of Robinson's trial differentiated between lack of criminal responsibility and competence to stand trial, but used "insanity" to describe both concepts. Ill.Rev.Stat., c. 38, §§ 592, 593 (1963). The judges likewise phrased their decisions only in terms of sanity and insanity. See, e. g., People v. Baker, 26 Ill.2d 484, 187 N.E.2d 227 (1962). The statutory provisions and terminology in this field have now been clarified by the enactment of an article dealing with the "competency of accused." Ill.Rev.Stat., c. 38, §§ 104–1 to 104–3 (1963), as amended by the Code of Criminal Procedure of 1963. Even if counsel may also have meant to refer to the statutory provisions dealing with commitment for present insanity, Ill.Rev.Stat., c. 38, § 592 (1963), this fact would not affect the determination that counsel's words raised a question as to competence that the trial judge should have considered.

[7] Moreover, as the Court of Appeals stressed, the trial judge did not give Robinson an opportunity to introduce expert testimony on the question of his sanity. The judge denied counsel's request for a continuance of several hours in order to secure the appearance of a psychiatrist from the Illniois Psychiatric Institute.

him to raise the question of his competence to stand trial at that time and to request a special hearing thereon. In the event a sufficient doubt exists as to his present competence such a hearing must be held. If found competent to stand trial, Robinson would have the usual defenses available to an accused.

The case is remanded to the District Court for action consistent with this opinion. It is so ordered.

* * * * *

WILSON V. UNITED STATES, 391 F.2d 460, 463–64 (D.C. Cir. 1968) *

Whether the accused suffers from a mental disorder as defined in the AMERICAN PSYCHIATRIC ASSOCIATION MANUAL is not decisive. Nor is it enough that the evidence of the defendant's guilt is substantial. He is entitled to a fair trial as well as a trial in which he is proven guilty. To have a fair trial the defendant must be competent to stand trial. The test of competency must be whether he has sufficient "present ability to consult with his lawyer with a reasonable degree of rational understanding—and whether he has a rational as well as factual understanding of the proceedings against him." Dusky v. United States, 362 U.S. 402, 80 S.Ct. 788, 4 L.Ed.2d 824 (1960). The accused must be able to perform the functions which "are essential to the fairness and accuracy of a criminal proceeding." Pouncey v. United States, 121 U.S.App.D.C. 264, 266, 349 F.2d 699, 701 (1965).

A prediction of the amnesic defendant's ability to perform these functions must, of course, be made before trial at the competency hearing. But where the case is allowed to go to trial, at its conclusion the trial judge should determine whether the defendant has in fact been able to perform these functions. He should, before imposing sentence, make detailed written findings, after taking any additional evidence deemed necessary, concerning the effect of the amnesia on the fairness of the trial. In making these findings the court should consider the following factors:

(1) The extent to which the amnesia affected the defendant's ability to consult with and assist his lawyer.

(2) The extent to which the amnesia affected the defendant's ability to testify in his own behalf.

(3) The extent to which the evidence in suit could be extrinsically reconstructed in view of the defendant's amnesia. Such

* Footnotes omitted.

evidence would include evidence relating to the crime itself as well as any reasonably possible alibi.

(4) The extent to which the Government assisted the defendant and his counsel in that reconstruction.

(5) The strength of the prosecution's case. Most important here will be whether the Government's case is such as to negate all reasonable hypotheses of innocence. If there is any substantial possibility that the accused could, but for his amnesia, establish an alibi or other defense, it should be presumed that he would have been able to do so.

(6) Any other facts and circumstances which would indicate whether or not the defendant had a fair trial.

After finding all the facts relevant to the fairness of the trial, considering the amnesia, the court will then make a judgment whether, under applicable principles of due process, the conviction should stand.

If the court determines that the conviction may not stand because of the unfairness of the trial caused by the defendant's amnesia, the court will vacate the conviction and give the Government an opportunity to retry the case. If on retrial the Government is unable to overcome the unfairness which would have thus voided the first conviction, the indictment will be dismissed.

So ordered.

❖   ❖   ❖   ❖   ❖

STATE V. HANCOCK, 247 Ore. 21, 27–30, 426 P.2d 872, 875–76 (1967)

Following the verdict and the entry of judgment thereon, defendant filed a motion for a new trial alleging "irregularity in the proceedings" by which "defendant was prevented from having a fair trial." Extensive testimony was taken by the court prior to its ruling. The motion was denied. The third assignment of error challenges that ruling. Referring to the trial, the motion asserts "that the defendant was under the influence of tranquilizers which impaired his mental functions and ability to confront his accusers." Both while in jail awaiting trial and during the trial itself, the defendant, pursuant to examination by and prescription of a duly licensed physician and qualified psychiatrist, was regularly receiving medication in the form of tranquilizers. The defendant concedes the tranquilizers were administered to him with his full knowledge and without any objection from him.

The state concedes and we recognize that:

"Every accused has a fundamental right to be present at his trial and to confront the witnesses against him, * * *." 83 A.L.R. 2d 1067, at 1069.

Obviously this means more than his physical presence at the trial. It includes the right to be present in such a physical and mental condition as to be able to comprehend the nature of the proceedings and to assist in his own defense.

Thus, if during his trial or any part thereof this defendant because of the narcotic effect of the tranquilizers being administered to him was deprived of his ability in the absence thereof to comprehend the nature of the proceedings and to assist in his own defense, then it follows that his conviction cannot stand.

The transcript of the evidence taken in connection with the motion for the new trial reveals that in January, 1966, the defendant by order of the court in connection with some six charges pending against him, including the instant charge, was sent for examination to the Oregon State Hospital to ascertain whether or not he could assist in his own defense. The diagnosis by the hospital disposition board made following extensive examinations was: "psychopathic personality disturbance, disassociation reaction." In addition it was determined that the defendant would upon occasion go into rages. When under emotional stress his blood pressure became "markedly elevated."

Because of these and other factors the drug, valium, a mild tranquilizer, was prescribed for and administered to him. The hospital disposition board concluded that he was able to assist in his own defense and he was returned to the Multnomah County Jail to await trial.

While there, as shown by the ledger record of medication maintained for prisoners at the jail, and from the testimony of the Multnomah County Health Department employee employed to administer and supervise all medication given at the jail where the defendant was confined, valium was administered to his as prescribed. The dosage prescribed was one ten-milligram tablet four times a day. The evidence shows the quantity and time of administration of every dose beginning with a week before and continuing to the conclusion of the trial. The medical testimony is uncontradicted that valium was administered to the defendant to assist him in handling his emotions; that as administered it did not affect his ability to communicate with other people; that it did not affect his memory in any way; and that from the dosage prescribed and administered there was no impairment of his mental function. The record further shows that the defendant actively participated in his trial. He testified at length himself.

He advised and cooperated with his own experienced counsel in arranging for and calling some five witnesses in his own behalf. He himself during the trial asked for a delay to communicate with his attorney and with witnesses, which was allowed by the court.

As a result of the careful and thorough inquiry conducted by the trial court it concluded that the drug, valium, as administered to the defendant before and during the trial "did not impair the defendant's mental function in any way during the trial" and that accordingly "there was no irregularity in the proceedings which prevented the defendant from having a fair trial." There was no abuse of discretion in so holding. This record reveals that the defendant was accorded an eminently fair and impartial trial.

The judgment is affirmed.

[Other cases from the use of narcotics or tranquilizers during the course of trial include *Hansford v. United States,* 365 F.2d 920 (D.C. Cir. 1966); *Kaufman v. United States,* 268 F. Supp. 484 (E.D. Mo. 1967); and *State v. Murphy,* 56 Wash. 2d 761, 355 P.2d 323, 83 A.L.R.2d 1061 (1960).—Eds.]

❖   ❖   ❖   ❖   ❖

F. Evidence

FEDERAL RULES OF CRIMINAL PROCEDURE

Rule 26.

EVIDENCE

In all trials the testimony of witnesses shall be taken orally in open court, unless otherwise provided by an act of Congress or by these rules. The admissibility of evidence and the competency and privileges of witnesses shall be governed, except when an act of Congress or these rules otherwise provide, by the principles of the common law as they may be interpreted by the courts of the United States in the light of reason and experience.

Rule 26.1.

DETERMINATION OF FOREIGN LAW

A party who intends to raise an issue concerning the law of a foreign country shall give reasonable written notice. The court, in determining foreign law, may consider any relevant material or source, including testimony, whether or not submitted by a party or admissible under Rule 26. The court's determination shall be treated as a ruling on a question of law.

Rule 27.

PROOF OF OFFICIAL RECORD

An official record or an entry therein or the lack of such a record or entry may be proved in the same manner as in civil actions.

✵ ✵ ✵ ✵ ✵

NEW YORK CRIMINAL PROCEDURE LAW (1971)

§ 60.10 Rules of evidence; in general

Unless otherwise provided by statute or by judicially established rules of evidence applicable to criminal cases, the rules of evidence applicable to civil cases are, where appropriate, also applicable to criminal proceedings.

§ 60.20 Rules of evidence; testimonial capacity; evidence given by children

1. Any person may be a witness in a criminal proceeding unless the court finds that, by reason of infancy or mental disease or defect, he does not possess sufficient intelligence or capacity to justify the reception of his evidence.

2. Every witness more than twelve years old may testify only under oath. A child less than twelve years old may not testify under oath unless the court is satisfied that he understands the nature of an oath. If the court is not so satisfied, such child may nevertheless be permitted to give unsworn evidence if the court is satisfied that he possesses sufficient intelligence and capacity to justify the reception thereof.

3. A defendant may not be convicted on an offense solely upon the unsworn evidence of a child less than twelve years old, given pursuant to subdivision two.

§ 60.35 Rules of evidence; impeachment of own witness by proof of prior contradictory statement

1. When, upon examination by the party who called him, a witness in a criminal proceeding gives testimony upon a material issue of the case which tends to disprove the position of such party, such party may introduce evidence that such witness has previously made

either a written statement signed by him or an oral statement under oath contradictory to such testimony.

2. Evidence concerning a prior contradictory statement introduced pursuant to subdivision one may be received only for the purpose of impeaching the credibility of the witness with respect to his testimony upon the subject, and does not constitute evidence in chief. Upon receiving such evidence at a jury trial, the court must so instruct the jury.

3. When a witness has made a prior signed or sworn statement contradictory to his testimony in a criminal proceeding upon a material issue of the case, but his testimony does not tend to disprove the position of the party who called him and elicited such testimony, evidence that the witness made such prior statement is not admissible, and such party may not use such prior statement for the purpose of refreshing the recollection of the witness in a manner that discloses its contents to the trier of the facts.

§ 60.22   Rules of evidence; corroboration of accomplice testimony

1. A defendant may not be convicted of any offense upon the testimony of an accomplice unsupported by corroborative evidence tending to connect the defendant with the commission of such offense.

2. An "accomplice" means a witness in a criminal action who, according to evidence adduced in such action, may reasonably be considered to have participated in:

(a) The offense charged; or
(b) An offense based upon the same or some of the same facts or conduct which constitute the offense charged.

3. A witness who is an accomplice as defined in subdivision two is no less such because a prosecution or conviction of himself would be barred or precluded by some defense or exemption, such as infancy, immunity or previous prosecution, amounting to a collateral impediment to such a prosecution or conviction, not affecting the conclusion that such witness engaged in the conduct constituting the offense with the mental state required for the commission thereof.

§ 60.40   Rules of evidence; proof of previous conviction;
when allowed

1. If in the course of a criminal proceeding, any witness, including a defendant, is properly asked whether he was previously convicted of a specified offense and answers in the negative or in an equivocal manner, the party adverse to the one who called him may indepen-

dently prove such conviction. If in response to proper inquiry whether he has ever been convicted of any offense the witness answers in the negative or in an equivocal manner, the adverse party may independently prove any previous conviction of the witness.

2. If a defendant in a criminal proceeding, through the testimony of a witness called by him, offers evidence of his good character, the people may independently prove any previous conviction of the defendant for an offense the commission of which would tend to negate any character trait or quality attributed to the defendant in such witness' testimony.

3. Subject to the limitations prescribed in section 200.60, the people may prove that a defendant has been previously convicted of an offense when the fact of such previous conviction constitutes an element of the offense charged, or proof thereof is otherwise essential to the establishment of a legally sufficient case.

❖ ❖ ❖ ❖ ❖

LOUISIANA STATUTES ANNOTATED (WEST 1967)
CRIMINAL CODE—ANCILLARIES

§ 275. Judge's control over examination of witnesses

In the discipline of his court, the trial judge is vested with a sound discretion to stop the prolonged, unnecessary and irrelevant examination of a witness, whether such examination be direct or cross, and even though no objection be urged by counsel.

§ 276. Self-incrimination of witness

No witness can be forced to criminate himself, but the judge is not bound by the witness' statement that the answer would criminate him, when from the nature of the question asked and the circumstances of the case such statement can not be true.

§ 277. Leading questions

A leading question is one which suggests to the witness the answer he is to deliver, and though framed in the alternative, is inadmissible when propounded to one's own witness, unless such witness be unwilling or hostile.

§ 278. Questions assuming facts or answers

Neither upon direct nor cross-examination is it permissible to propound a question which assumes as true that which the jury alone are charged with finding, or which assumes as proven facts which have not been proven, or which assumes that particular answers have been given that have not been given.

§ 279. Refreshing memory of witness

A witness may be allowed to refresh his memory by reference to his testimony given on the preliminary examination, or at a coroner's investigation, or on a previous trial, or, for the purpose of refreshing his present memory a witness may examine memoranda, and it is immaterial by whom or when the memoranda were made, provided that, after such inspection, the witness can testify to the fact.

§ 280. Scope of cross-examination

When a witness has been intentionally sworn and has testified to any single fact in his examination in chief, he may be cross-examined upon the whole case.

§ 281. Scope of redirect examination

The redirect examination must be confined to the subject matter of the cross-examination and to the explanation of statements elicited on cross-examination; but the application of this rule is within the discretion of the trial judge, provided that the opportunity be not denied to recross on the new matter brought out on the redirect.

§ 282. Right of prosecution to rebut defendant's evidence

The prosecution has the right to rebut the evidence adduced by the defendant, but the defendant is without right to rebut the prosecution's rebuttal.

✿   ✿   ✿   ✿   ✿

CHAPTER 10

Concluding Proof

A. Expert Evidence

FEDERAL RULES OF CRIMINAL PROCEDURE, RULE 28

EXPERT WITNESSES AND INTERPRETERS

(a) **Expert Witnesses.** The court may order the defendant or the government or both to show cause why expert witnesses should not be appointed, and may request the parties to submit nominations. The court may appoint any expert witnesses agreed upon by the parties, and may appoint witnesses of its own selection. An expert witness shall not be appointed by the court unless he consents to act. A witness so appointed shall be informed of his duties by the court in writing, a copy of which shall be filed with the clerk, or at a conference in which the parties shall have opportunity to participate. A witness so appointed shall advise the parties of his findings, if any, and may thereafter be called to testify by the court or by any party. He shall be subject to cross-examination by each party. The court may determine the reasonable compensation of such a witness and direct its payment out of such funds as may be provided by law. The parties also may call expert witnesses of their own selection.

(b) **Interpreters.** The court may appoint an interpreter of its own selection and may fix the reasonable compensation of such interpreter. Such compensation shall be paid out of funds provided by law or by the government, as the court may direct.

* * * * *

NEW YORK CRIMINAL PROCEDURE LAW (1971)

§ 60.55 **Rules of evidence; psychiatric testimony in certain cases**

When, in connection with a defense of mental disease or defect, a psychiatrist who has examined the defendant testifies concerning the defendant's mental condition at the time of the conduct charged to constitute a crime, he shall be permitted to make a statement as to the nature of the examination, the diagnosis of the mental condition of the defendant and his opinion as to the extent, if any, to which the capacity of the defendant to know or appreciate the nature and consequence of such conduct, or its wrongfulness, was impaired as a result of mental disease or defect at that time. The psychiatrist shall be permitted to make any explanation reasonably serving to clarify his diagnosis and opinion, and may be cross-examined as to any matter bearing on his competency or credibility or the validity of his diagnosis or opinion.

✿   ✿   ✿   ✿   ✿

AMERICAN LAW INSTITUTE MODEL CODE OF EVIDENCE
198–216 (1942) *

EXPERT AND OPINION EVIDENCE

Introductory Note: The entire body of the law dealing with opinion evidence of both lay and expert witnesses needs revision. The rules evolved in this country prohibiting a witness from stating in terms of inference relevant matters which he has perceived have been the sources of numerous trivial appeals and many undeserved reversals. They are uncertain in phrasing and capable of capricious application. There has appeared in the more recent decisions a tendency to disregard them or at least to refuse to interfere with their application by the trial courts.

Rule 401 deals with testimony given by witnesses, lay and expert, who are testifying to what they have perceived.

Rules 402–410 deal with testimony by experts. Precedents beginning in the fourteenth century show the judges availing themselves of the aid of experts without formally calling them as witnesses; from that time to this, expert testimony has been received in the common law courts. The necessity for it is everywhere conceded. The abuses which have developed since experts have come to be witnesses for litigants are everywhere deplored, not only by the bench and bar but also by members of the other learned professions. (See 2 Law and Contemporary Problems 401–527, Duke University, and other references collected in 2 Wigmore, Evidence (3d ed. 1940) § 563 Note 2.) Expert witnesses are all too frequently merely expert advocates. The most shocking exhibitions occur in criminal prosecutions and personal injury actions, but the evils are not thus confined. The National Conference of Commissioners on Uniform State Laws had this subject under consideration for three years, and in 1937 recommended a Uniform Act. In 1938 the Committee of the American Bar Association on Improvement of the Law of Evidence approved this Act. Rules 403–410 are substantially similar to the corresponding provisions of the Uniform Act.

Rule 401. Testimony in Terms of Opinion

(1) In testifying to what he has perceived a witness, whether or not an expert, may give his testimony in terms which include inferences and may state all relevant inferences, whether or not embracing ultimate issues to be decided by the trier of fact, unless the judge finds

(a) that to draw such inferences requires a special knowledge, skill, experience, or training which the witness does not possess, or

(b) that the witness can readily and with equal accuracy and adequacy communicate what he has perceived to the trier of fact without testifying in terms of inference or stating inferences, and his use of inferences in testifying will be likely to mislead the trier of fact to the prejudice of the objecting party.

(2) The judge may require that a witness, before testifying in terms of inference, be first examined concerning the data upon which the inference is founded.

Comment:

a. Changes in existing law. The American decisions concerning opinion evidence exhibit much confusion in statement and inconsistency in application. Most of them purport to reject all opinion, lay and expert, upon issues ultimately to be decided by the jury, but in many cases the fact that the opinion covers a jury issue is conveniently overlooked. Many exclude all lay opinion and most expert opinion concerning such qualities of human behavior as care, safety, propriety, reasonableness and their opposites, and, to a less degree, concerning qualities of things. There is much conflict as to the admissibility of opinion as to skill or competence. On the other hand, courts usually admit opinion evidence as to distance, time, speed, size, weight, direction, form, identity and similar matters, although their decisions show some conflict concerning the qualifications required of the witness. They receive also lay and expert opinion as to sanity, identity of handwriting and value of services or things.

This Rule applies to both lay and expert witnesses. It permits the lay witness to express himself in language ordinarily used in conversation and easily understood by the jury. It allows the expert to do likewise, but where the matter required special skill, Rules 402 to 409 are applicable.

b. Application. A witness under this rule may not only describe what he has experienced by using language which consists of or includes inferences; he may also state a relevant opinion after giving such a description.

A lay witness who is acquainted with the characteristics of X's handwriting may describe a document as being in X's handwriting. If he has had no first-hand knowledge of X's writing, he cannot describe the document in terms of X's writing, as a color-blind man cannot state the color of a given object. (See Rule 601). A witness who is well acquainted with X and has observed his conduct may give his opinion as to X's character. (See Rules 305, 306.) Reputation is composite hearsay opinion, and is a means of expressing in a compendious form what the community has observed concerning X's conduct. So W's opinion as to X's character is a summary statement of his perception of X's behavior.

c. Reasons for change. Where a witness is attempting to communicate the impressions made upon his senses by what he has perceived, any attempt to distinguish between so-called fact and opinion is likely to result in profitless quibbling. Analytically no such distinction is possible. The English common law does not attempt to prevent a witness from describing his experiences in terms including inferences. The witness whose statement is too general to suit the opponent may on cross-examination be required to expose its elements. If he hasn't the skill or experience required for drawing inferences, he will not be allowed to state them. His inferences, when received, may not be worth much, but they can do no harm. The court will not permit them to be given more weight than the basis upon which they are built will sustain, and that basis can be uncovered on cross-examination if the judge has not required that it be given in advance.

The Rule deals not with the weight of testimony but with its admissibility. Where the proffered evidence of opinion will be of slight weight and may tend to undue consumption of time or to confusion, it may be rejected under Rule 303. The judge at the trial is in so much better position than an appellate court to determine when a witness should be permitted to give opinion evidence that his rulings should be accepted save in the most exceptional circumstances.

Rule 402.   Expert Witness Defined

A witness is an expert witness and is qualified to give expert testimony if the judge finds that to perceive, know or understand the matter concerning which the witness is to testify requires special knowledge, skill, experience or training, and that the witness has the requisite special knowledge, skill, experience or training.

Comment:

This states the well settled law.

Rule 403.   Appointment of Experts

In an action in which the judge determines that expert evidence will be of substantial assistance, he may, of his own motion or at the request of a party, at any time during the pendency of the action

(a) order the parties

(i) to show cause why expert witnesses should not be appointed to give evidence in the action, and

(ii) to submit nominations for their appointment and objections to proposed appointments, and

(b) appoint one or more expert witnesses of his own selection to give evidence in the action except that, if the parties agree as to the experts to be appointed, he shall appoint only those designated in the agreement.

Comment:

a. Comparison with Uniform Act. This Rule embodies the substance of Sections 1, 2 and 4 of the Uniform Expert Testimony Act, which reads as follows:

"SECTION 1. (Court Empowered to Appoint Expert Witnesses.) Whenever, in a civil or criminal proceeding, issues arise upon which the court deems expert evidence is desirable, the court, on its own motion, or on the request of either the state or the defendant in a criminal proceeding, or of any party in a civil proceeding, may appoint one or more experts, not exceeding three on each issue, to testify at the trial.

"SECTION 2. (Notice When Called by Court.) The appointment of expert witnesses by the court shall be made only after reasonable notice to the parties to the proceeding of the names and addresses of the experts proposed for appointment."

"SECTION 4. (Agreement on Expert Witnesses by Parties.) Before appointing expert witnesses, the court may seek to bring the parties to an agreement as to the experts desired, and, if the parties agree, the experts so selected shall be appointed."

It will be noted that the Rule in providing for a hearing differs from the Act. It seems only fair to give the parties an opportunity to be heard on the question whether expert evidence is needed or desired as well as to present arguments for or against the selection of specified experts.

b. During pendency of the action. The motion and order may be made at any time during the pendency of the action, and the expert evidence may be received at any stage of the proceeding at which evidence may be offered. Ordinarily the evidence will be introduced at the trial upon the merits, but it may well be offered at a hearing either before or after such a trial.

c. Reasons. The chief reason for the distrust of expert evidence is that it comes from a biased source. All commentators agree that the control of the parties over the selection of experts must be limited. The distrust, it is true, cannot be eradicated by merely permitting the judge to appoint expert witnesses, so long as the parties may continue to call experts of their own selection; but the distrust can be greatly lessened; the jury will know that experts selected by the judge will ordinarily be impartial; and if these experts agree, the conflicting opinions of the partisan experts will be discounted. On the other hand, there may be some danger that the judge in the matter of appointment of expert witnesses will be subject to the temptation to which some judges have yielded in exercising the power of appointing receivers. Consequently, where the parties agree as to the experts to be appointed, the Rule requires the judge to appoint those so selected.

Rule 404. Testimony by Other Experts

Subject to Rule 105 (c), a party may call an expert witness who has not been appointed under Rule 403, if the judge finds that

(a) the party has given reasonable notice to each adverse party of the name and address of the witness to be called, or

(b) it is expedient, notwithstanding a failure to give such notice, to permit the witness to be called.

Comment:

This is in substance Section 3 of the Uniform Expert Testimony Act, which provides:

"SECTION 3. (Notice When Called by Parties.) Unless otherwise authorized by the court, no party shall call a witness, who has not been appointed by the court, to give expert testimony unless that party has given the court and the adverse party to the proceeding reasonable notice of the name and address of the expert to be called."

The notice will enable the adverse party not only to investigate the professional standing of the proposed expert but also to check his record as a witness in other litigation. The judge may find it expedient to allow an expert to testify even though no notice has been given in advance, as where an issue requiring expert testimony arises unexpectedly in the course of a trial or the subject matter of such testimony is comparatively simple and other experts are readily available.

Rule 405.   Examination and Report by Experts

(1) At any time after the appointment of an expert witness by the judge, or after notice of intention of a party to call an expert witness, the judge, on his own motion or that of a party, after reasonable notice to each party and hearing thereon, may make one or more of the following orders:

(a) that each party submit, for purposes of inspection and examination by each expert witness named in the order, his person and all persons, things and places under his control insofar as the judge deems necessary to enable the witness adequately to inform himself for the purpose of testifying;

(b) that at the time and place and under reasonable conditions set forth in the order each expert named therein make such inspection and examination of the person, thing, place or matter concerning which he is to give evidence as the judge deems necessary;

(c) that any expert witness prepare and file with the clerk of the court within a time fixed in the order a written report under oath of the inspection and examination made by him, including the inferences drawn by him therefrom;

(d) that two or more of the expert witnesses confer at or before a time fixed in the order and, if practicable, unite in a written report and file it with the clerk of the court.

(2) No inspection or examination ordered by the judge under this Rule shall be made unless each party has been given reasonable notice thereof and opportunity to be appropriately represented.

(3) On motion of a party or of a person having an interest in the subject matter of an inspection or examination ordered by the judge under this Rule, the judge shall determine the scope and manner of the inspection or examination or of any part thereof, as to which a dispute has arisen either before or during the inspection or examination.

Comment:

a. Application. At any time after it becomes apparent that expert evidence is to be offered in the action, the judge may take appropriate steps to require the experts to make adequate preparation for the effective performance of their functions and to compel the parties to afford them opportunity therefor. And in order to enable the parties to be in a position to scrutinize and meet the expert testimony, he may order the experts to file reports of their findings and opinions. Ordinarily he will take such action only upon motion of one of the parties, and in no case can he do so until after the parties have been given an opportunity to be heard. At the hearing, the time, place and condition of the inspection or examination of persons, places and things by the experts will usually be discussed and decided. The order under Clause (a) will, of course, exempt from compulsory disclosure all privileged material. If a dispute arises at the inspection or examination concerning its scope or propriety, the objecting party may secure a hearing and determination thereon by motion.

b. Comparison with Uniform Act. All of these provisions are found in Sections 5, 6 and 7 of the Uniform Expert Testimony Act, except that the Rule provides for the filing of reports by experts not appointed by the court. There seems to be no reason why they should be exempted. The sections of the Uniform Act read as follows:

"SECTION 5. (Inspection and Examination of Subject Matter by Experts.) Expert witnesses appointed by the court shall, at the request of the court or of any party, make such inspection and examination of the person or subject matter committed to them as they deem necessary for the full understanding thereof and such further reasonable inspection and examination as any party may request. Reasonable notice shall be given to each party of the proposed inspection and examination of persons, things, and places, and each party shall be permitted to be represented at such inspection and examination. Experts called by the court or by the parties in the proceeding shall be permitted access to the persons, things, or places under investigation for the purpose of inspection and examination.

"SECTION 6. (Report by Experts and Filing Thereof.) The court may require each expert it has appointed to prepare a written report under oath upon the subject he has inspected and examined. This report shall be placed on file with the clerk of the court at such time as may be fixed by the court and be open to inspection by any party. By order of the court, or on the request of any party, the report shall be read, subject to all lawful objections as to the admissibility of the report or any part thereof, by the witness at the trial.

"SECTION 7. (Conference and Joint Report by Expert Witnesses.) The court may permit or require a conference before the trial on the part of some or all of the expert witnesses, whether summoned by the court or the parties or both; and two or more of them may unite in a report which may be introduced at the trial by any party or by order of the court, subject to all lawful objections as to the admissibility of the report or any part thereof."

c. Reasons. If the experts are to testify adequately they must have opportunity to make all necessary inspections and examinations. Insofar as they agree, their evidence will have added value. If they are required to put down their conclusions and the data supporting them, and if those conclusions are subject to scrutiny by the adversary, the experts are likely to be more careful and thorough. Moreover, the adversary has protection against surprise. These provisions all harmonize with the purpose of modern rules and statutes governing discovery.

Rule 406. Reports Open to Inspection

Each report filed pursuant to Rule 405 shall be open to inspection by each party to the action immediately after filing. No expert witness who made or joined in making a report shall be called as a witness until a reasonable time after the filing of the report.

Comment:

The first sentence of this provision is contained in Section 6 of the Uniform Expert Testimony Act. See Rule 405, Comment *b.* The second sentence gives effect to the purpose intended to be served by the requirement as to filing and inspection.

Rule 407. Examination of Expert Appointed by Judge

An expert witness appointed by the judge may be called as a witness by the judge or by a party and may be examined by each party as if the witness had been called by an adverse party. The fact of the appointment by the judge shall be made known to the trier of fact.

Comment:

This Rule puts expert witnesses called by the judge in the same class for purposes of cross-examination as other witnesses called by him. (See Rule 105 (g), (h).) The fact that the witness has been appointed by the judge and has not been selected by a party must be disclosed to the trier of fact in order that his testimony may be properly valued. Section 8 of the Uniform Act contains similar provisions.

Rule 408.   Reading of Report by Expert

An expert witness may at the trial read in evidence any report which he made or joined in making except matter therein which would be inadmissible if offered as oral testimony by the witness.

Comment:

A somewhat similar provision is found in Section 6 of the Uniform Expert Testimony Act. See Rule 405, Comment *b*. This rule harmonizes with Rule 503 (b). The desirability of presenting such testimony to the jury in a connected narrative and the most lucid form is obvious; and this provision will tend to accomplish that object.

Rule 409.   Opinion without Previous Statement of Data

An expert witness may state his relevant inferences from matters perceived by him or from evidence introduced at the trial and seen or heard by him or from his special knowledge, skill, experience or training, whether or not any such inference embraces an ultimate issue to be decided by the trier of fact, and he may state his reasons for such inferences and need not, unless the judge so orders, first specify, as an hypothesis or otherwise, the data from which he draws them; but he may thereafter during his examination or cross-examination be required to specify those data.

Comment:

a. Comparison with Uniform Act. This Rule does away with the necessity of using the hypothetical question but does not forbid its use. Its substance is found in Section 9 of the Uniform Act, which reads:

"SECTION 9. (Examination of Experts.) (1) An expert witness may be asked to state his inferences, whether these inferences are

based on the witness' personal observation, or on evidence introduced at the trial and seen or heard by the witness, or on his
technical knowledge of the subject, without first specifying hypo-
thetically in the question the data on which these inferences are
based.

"(2) An expert witness may be required, on direct or cross-
examination, to specify the data on which his inferences are
based."

The Rule expressly provides that the expert may state the reasons
for his inferences, because some decisions forbid him to do so. It also
makes clear that either the judge or a party may require him to state
the data upon which his opinion rests.

b. *Reasons.* That the hypothetical question is theoretically an effective device for presenting expert opinion to the jury where the facts
are in dispute, no one will deny. But in practice it has been so grossly
abused as to be almost a scandal. It has been said to be "the most
horrific and grotesque wen upon the fair face of justice."

Mr. Wigmore has put the case against the existing practice and has
suggested a solution consonant with this Rule as follows (2 Wigmore,
Evidence (3 ed. 1940) sec. 686):

"Its abuses have become so obstructive and nauseous that no
remedy short of extirpation will suffice. It is a logical necessity,
but a practical incubus; and logic must here be sacrificed. After
all, Law (in Mr. Justice Holmes' phrase) is much more than
Logic. It is a strange irony that the hypothetical question, which
is one of the few truly scientific features of the rules of Evidence,
should have become that feature which does most to disgust men
of science with the law of Evidence.

"The hypothetical question, misused by the clumsy and abused
by the clever, has in practice led to intolerable obstruction of
truth. In the first place, it has artificially clamped the mouth of
the expert witness, so that his answer to a complex question may
not express his actual opinion on the actual case. This is because
the question may be so built up and contrived by counsel as to
represent only a partisan conclusion. In the second place, it has
tended to mislead the jury as to the purport of actual expert
opinion. This is due to the same reason. In the third place, it has
tended to confuse the jury, so that its employment becomes a
mere waste of time and a futile obstruction.

"No partial limitation of its use seems feasible, by specific rules.
Logically, there is no place to stop short; practically, any specific

limitations would be more or less arbitrary, and would thus tend to become mere quibbles.

"How can the extirpating operation be performed? By exempting the offering party from the *requirement* of using the hypothetical form; by according him the *option* of using it—both of these to be left to the trial Court's discretion; and by permitting the opposing party, *on cross-examination,* to call for a hypothetical specification of the data which the witness has used as the basis of the opinion. The last rule will give sufficient protection against a misunderstanding of the opinion, when any actual doubt exists.

"The foregoing proposals, be it understood, represent a mere practical rule of thumb. They do violence to theoretical logic. But in practice they would produce less actual misleading of the jury than the present complex preciosities. After all, the only theoretical object of the hypothetical question (*ante*, § 672) is to avoid misunderstanding; and 'if the salt have lost its savor, wherewith shall it be salted? It is thenceforth good for nothing but to be cast out and trodden under foot of men.' The present proposal does not tread under foot the hypothetical question, but merely transfers its function to the hands of the cross-examiner."

Rule 410. Compensation of Expert Witness

The compensation of each expert witness appointed by the judge shall be fixed at a reasonable amount. In a criminal action it shall be paid by [insert name of the proper public authority] under order of the judge. In a civil action it shall be paid as the judge shall order; he may order that it be paid by the parties in such proportions and at such times as he shall prescribe, or that the proportion of any party be paid by [insert name of the proper public authority], and that, after payment by the parties or [insert name of the public authority] or both, all or part or none of it be taxed as costs in the action. Any witness appointed by the judge who receives any compensation other than that fixed by the judge and any person who pays or offers or promises to pay such other compensation shall be guilty of contempt of court. The fee of an expert witness called by a party but not appointed by the judge shall be paid by the party calling him but shall not be taxed as costs in the action.

Comment:

a. Comparison with the Uniform Act. Section 10 of the Uniform Act reads:

"SECTION 10. (Compensation of Expert Witnesses.) The compensation of expert witnesses appointed by the court shall be fixed by the court at a reasonable amount. In criminal proceedings it shall be paid by the (county) under the order of the court, as a part of the costs of the action. In civil proceedings the compensation of experts appointed by the court shall, after it has been fixed by the court, be paid in equal parts by the opposing litigants to the clerk of the court at such time as the court shall prescribe, and thereafter assessed as costs of the suit. The fee of an expert witness called by a party but not appointed by the court shall be paid by the party by whom he was called and the amount of such fee shall be disclosed if requested upon cross-examination. The receipt by any witness appointed by the court of any compensation other than that fixed by the court, and the payment of, or the offer or promise by any person to pay such other compensation shall be unlawful."

b. Reasons. It is essential to the satisfactory operation of rules governing expert testimony that provision be made for the compensation of expert witnesses appointed by the judge. In criminal prosecutions it seems reasonably clear that the expense should be borne by the authority which is prosecuting. That authority will differ in different jurisdictions. Consequently, the rule provides merely for payment by the proper public authority. No satisfactory allocation of the expense for such experts can be made applicable to all civil cases. Consequently the rule puts the matter entirely in the discretion of the trial judge. No doubt in the usual case the judge will provide that the expense of the experts shall be taxed as costs and paid by the loser. He may require the parties to contribute proportionate shares of the fee in advance. He may think it wise to excuse an impecunious party from paying his proportionate share. Indeed, he may in unusual circumstances provide that the entire fee be paid by the State. His power to impose any obligations upon a public authority will of course depend upon statutes making provision for appropriate funds.

The Rule attempts to discourage the use of experts not appointed by the court by providing that sums paid for fees to them shall not be taxed as costs. In many jurisdictions the existing law is in accord. The Rule also seeks to insure impartiality of the expert's opinion by having the court rather than the parties determine both the amount and the source of his compensation. The provision of the Uniform Act requiring disclosure of the amount of the expert's fee if requested on cross-examination is omitted as unnecessary. The admissibility of such evidence is governed by Rule 303; no attempt should be made to control the trial judge's discretion.

* * * * *

B. Sequestration of Jurors and Witnesses

New York Criminal Procedure Law (1971)

§ 270.45   Trial jury; when separation permitted

During the period extending from the time the jurors are sworn to the time they retire to deliberate upon their verdict, the court may in its discretion either permit them to separate during recesses and adjournments or direct that they be continuously kept together during such periods under the supervision of an appropriate public servant or servants. In the latter case, such public servant or servants may not speak to or communicate with any juror concerning any subject connected with the trial nor permit any other person to do so, and must return the jury to the court room at the next designated trial session.

* * * * *

Louisiana Statutes Annotated (West 1967)
Code of Criminal Procedure

Art. 764.   Exclusion and conduct of witnesses

Upon its own motion the court may, and upon request of the state or the defendant the court shall, order that the witnesses be excluded from the courtroom or from where they can see or hear the proceedings and refrain from discussing the facts of the case or the testimony of any witness with anyone other than the district attorney or defense counsel. The court may modify its order in the interest of justice.

Art. 791.   Sequestration of jurors and jury

A jury is sequestered by being kept together in charge of an officer of the court so as to be secluded from outside communication.

In capital cases, after each juror is sworn he shall be sequestered.

In noncapital cases, the jury shall be sequestered after the court's charge, and may be sequestered at any time upon order of the court.

* * * * *

C. Fair Trial and Free Press

FEDERAL RULES OF CRIMINAL PROCEDURE, RULE 53

REGULATION OF CONDUCT IN THE COURT ROOM

The taking of photographs in the court room during the progress of judicial proceedings or radio broadcasting of judicial proceedings from the court room shall not be permitted by the court.

✼　✼　✼　✼　✼

AMERICAN BAR ASSOCIATION PROJECT ON STANDARDS FOR THE ADMINISTRATION OF CRIMINAL JUSTICE, STANDARDS RELATING TO FAIR TRIAL AND FREE PRESS (Approved Draft 1968)

PART I. RECOMMENDATIONS RELATING TO THE CONDUCT OF ATTORNEYS IN CRIMINAL CASES

1.1   Revision of the Canons of Professional Ethics

It is recommended that the Canons of Professional Ethics be revised to contain the following standards relating to public discussion of pending or imminent criminal litigation:

It is the duty of the lawyer not to release or authorize the release of information or opinion for dissemination by any means of public communication, in connection with pending or imminent criminal litigation with which he is associated, if there is a reasonable likelihood that such dissemination will interfere with a fair trial or otherwise prejudice the due administration of justice.

With respect to a grand jury or other pending investigation of any criminal matter, a lawyer participating in the investigation shall refrain from making any extrajudicial statement, for dissemination by any means of public communication, that goes beyond the public record or that is not necessary to inform the public that the investigation is underway, to describe the general scope of the investigation, to obtain assistance in the apprehension of a suspect, to warn the public of any dangers, or otherwise to aid in the investigation.

From the time of arrest, issuance of an arrest warrant, or the filing of a complaint, information, or indictment in any criminal matter until the commencement of trial or disposition without trial, a lawyer associated with the prosecution or defense shall not release or authorize the release of any extrajudicial statement, for dissemination by any means of public communication, relating to that matter and concerning:

(1) The prior criminal record (including arrests, indictments, or other charges of crime), or the character or reputation of the defendant, except that the lawyer may make a factual statement of the defendant's name, age, residence, occupation, and family status, and if the defendant has not been apprehended, may release any information necessary to aid in his apprehension or to warn the public of any dangers he may present;

(2) The existence or contents of any confession, admission, or statement given by the defendant, or the refusal or failure of the defendant to make any statement;

(3) The performance of any examinations or tests or the defendant's refusal or failure to submit to an examination or test;

(4) The identity, testimony, or credibility of prospective witnesses, except that the lawyer may announce the identity of the victim if the announcement is not otherwise prohibited by law;

(5) The possibility of a plea of guilty to the offense charged or a lesser offense;

(6) Any opinion as to the accused's guilt or innocence or as to the merits of the case or the evidence in the case.

The foregoing shall not be construed to preclude the lawyer during this period, in the proper discharge of his official or professional obligations, from announcing the fact and circumstances of arrest (including time and place of arrest, resistance, pursuit, and use of weapons), the identity of the investigating and arresting officer or agency, and the length of the investigation; from making an announcement, at the time of seizure of any physical evidence other than a confession, admission or statement, which is limited to a description of the evidence seized; from disclosing the nature, substance, or text of the charge, including a brief description of the offense charged; from quoting or referring without comment to public records of the court in the case; from announcing the scheduling or result of any stage in the judicial process; from requesting assistance in obtaining evidence; or from announcing without further comment that the accused denies the charges made against him.

During the trial of any criminal matter, including the period of selection of the jury, no lawyer associated with the prosecution or defense shall give or authorize any extrajudicial statement or interview, relating to the trial or the parties or issues in the trial, for dissemination by any means of public communication, except that the lawyer may quote from or refer without comment to public records of the court in the case.

After the completion of a trial or disposition without trial of any criminal matter, and prior to the imposition of sentence, a lawyer associated with the prosecution or defense shall refrain from making or authorizing any extrajudicial statement for dissemination by any means of public communication if there is a reasonable likelihood that such dissemination will affect the imposition of sentence.

Nothing in this Canon is intended to preclude the formulation or application of more restrictive rules relating to the release of information about juvenile or other offenders, to preclude the holding of hearings or the lawful issuance of reports by legislative, administrative, or investigative bodies, or to preclude any lawyer from replying to charges of misconduct that are publicly made against him.

PART II. RECOMMENDATIONS RELATING TO THE
CONDUCT OF LAW ENFORCEMENT OFFICERS AND
JUDICIAL EMPLOYEES IN CRIMINAL CASES

2.1 Rule of court relating to disclosures by law enforcement officers

It is recommended that the following rule be promulgated in each jurisdiction by the appropriate court:

Release of information by law enforcement officers.

From the time of arrest, issuance of an arrest warrant, or the filing of any complaint, information, or indictment in any criminal matter within the jurisdiction of this court, until the completion of trial or disposition without trial, no law enforcement officer subject to the jurisdiction of this court shall release or authorize the release of any extrajudicial statement, for dissemination by any means of public communication, relating to that matter and concerning:

(1) The prior criminal record (including arrests, indictments, or other charges of crime), or the character or reputation of the defendant, except that the officer may make a factual statement of the defendant's name, age, residence, occupation, and family status, and if the defendant has not been apprehended, may release any information necessary to aid in his apprehension or to warn the public of any dangers he may present;

(2) The existence or contents of any confession, admission, or statement given by the defendant, or the refusal or failure of the defendant to make any statement;

(3) The performance of any examinations or tests or the defendant's refusal or failure to submit to an examination or test;

(4) The identity, testimony, or credibility of prospective witnesses,

except that the officer may announce the identity of the victim if the announcement is not otherwise prohibited by law;

(5) The possibility of a plea of guilty to the offense charged or a lesser offense;

(6) The defendant's guilt or innocence, or other matters relating to the merits of the case or the evidence in the case, except that the officer may announce the circumstances of arrest, including the time and place of arrest, resistance, pursuit, and use of weapons; may announce the identity of the investigating and arresting officer or agency and the length of the investigation; may make an announcement, at the time of the seizure, describing any evidence seized; may disclose the nature, substance, or text of the charge, including a brief description of the offense charged; may quote from or refer without comment to public records of the court in the case; may announce the scheduling or result of any stage in the judicial process; and may request assistance in obtaining evidence.

The court may, in its discretion, initiate proceedings for contempt for violation of this rule, either on its own motion or on the petition of any person.

Nothing in this rule is intended to preclude any law enforcement officer from replying to charges of misconduct that are publicly made against him, to preclude any law enforcement authority from issuing rules not in conflict herewith on this or related subjects, to preclude any law enforcement officer from participating in any legislative, administrative, or investigative hearing, or to supersede any more restrictive rule governing the release of information concerning juvenile or other offenders.

For purposes of this rule, the term 'law enforcement officer' includes any person employed or retained by any governmental agency to assist in the investigation of crime or in the apprehension or prosecution of persons suspected of or charged with crime.

2.2 Departmental rules

It is recommended that law enforcement authorities in each jurisdiction promulgate an internal regulation (1) embodying the prohibitions of the preceding section and (2) directing that releases not prohibited by that section be withheld during the relevant period if the information would be highly prejudicial and if public disclosure would serve no significant law enforcement function. It is further recommended that such agencies adopt the following internal regulations:

(a) A regulation governing the release of information, relating to the commission of crimes and to their investigation, prior to the making of an arrest or the filing of formal charges. This regulation should establish appropriate procedures for the release of information. It should further provide that, when a crime is believed to have been committed, pertinent facts relating to the crime itself may be made available but the identity of a suspect prior to arrest and the details of investigative procedures shall not be disclosed except to the extent necessary to assist in the apprehension of the suspect, to warn the public of any dangers, or otherwise to aid in the investigation.

(b) A regulation prohibiting (i) the deliberate posing of a person in custody for photographing or televising by representatives of the news media and (ii) the interviewing by representatives of the news media of a person in custody unless he requests an interview in writing after being adequately informed of his right to consult with counsel.

(c) A regulation providing for the enforcement of the foregoing by the imposition of appropriate disciplinary sanctions.

2.3 Rule of court relating to disclosures by judicial employees

It is recommended that a rule of court be adopted in each jurisdiction prohibiting any judicial employee from disclosing, to any unauthorized person, information relating to a pending criminal case that is not part of the public records of the court and that may tend to interfere with the right of the people or of the defendant to a fair trial. Particular reference should be made in this rule to the nature and result of any argument or hearing held in chambers or otherwise outside the presence of the public and not yet available to the public under the standards in section 3.1 and section 3.5(d) of these recommendations. Appropriate discipline, including proceedings for contempt, should be provided for infractions of this rule.

PART III. REOMMENDATIONS RELATING TO THE CONDUCT OF JUDICIAL PROCEEDINGS IN CRIMINAL CASES

3.1 Pretrial hearings

It is recommended that the following rule be adopted in each jurisdiction by the appropriate court:

Motion to exclude public from all or part of pretrial hearing.

In any preliminary hearing, bail hearing, or other pretrial hearing in a criminal case, including a motion to suppress evidence, the defendant may move that all or part of the hearing be held in chambers or otherwise closed to the public on the ground that dissemination of evidence or argument adduced at the hearing may disclose matters that will be inadmissible in evidence at the trial and is therefore likely to interfere with his right to a fair trial by an impartial jury. The motion shall be granted unless the presiding officer determines that there is no substantial likelihood of such interference. With the consent of the defendant, the presiding officer may take such action on his own motion or at the suggestion of the prosecution. Whenever under this rule all or part of any pretrial hearing is held in chambers or otherwise closed to the public, a complete record of the proceedings shall be kept and shall be made available to the public following the completion of trial or disposition of the case without trial. Nothing in this rule is intended to interfere with the power of the presiding officer in any pretrial hearing to caution those present that dissemination of certain information by any means of public communications may jeopardize the right to a fair trial by an impartial jury.

3.2   Change of venue or continuance

It is recommended that the following standards be adopted in each jurisdiction to govern the consideration and disposition of a motion in a criminal case for change of venue or continuance based on a claim of threatened interference with the right to a fair trial.

(a) Who may request.

Except as a federal or state constitutional provisions otherwise require, a change of venue or continuance may be granted on motion of either the prosecution or the defense.

(b) Methods of proof.

In addition to the testimony or affidavits of individuals in the community, which shall not be required as a condition to the granting of a motion for change of venue or continuance, qualified public opinion surveys shall be admissible as well as other materials having probative value.

(c) Standards for granting motion.

A motion for change of venue or continuance shall be granted whenever it is determined that because of the dissemination of potentially prejudicial material, there is a reasonable likelihood that in the absence of such relief, a fair trial cannot be had. This determination may be based on such evidence as qualified public opinion surveys or opinion testimony offered by individuals, or on the court's own evaluation of the nature, frequency, and timing of the material involved. A showing of actual prejudice shall not be required.

(d) Same; time of disposition.

If a motion for change of venue or continuance is made prior to the impaneling of the jury, the motion shall be disposed of before impaneling. If such a motion is permitted to be made, or if reconsideration or review of a prior denial is sought, after the jury has been selected, the fact that a jury satisfying prevailing standards of acceptability has been selected shall not be controlling if the record shows that the criterion for the granting of relief set forth in subsection (c) has been met.

(e) Limitations; waiver.

It shall not be a ground for denial of a change of venue that one such change has already been granted. The claim that the venue should have been changed or a continuance granted shall not be considered to have been waived by the waiver of the right to trial by jury or by the failure to exercise all available peremptory challenges.

3.3 Waiver of jury

In those jurisdictions in which the defendant does not have an absolute right to waive a jury in a criminal case, it is recommended that the defendant be permitted to waive whenever it is determined that (1) the waiver has been knowingly and voluntarily made, and (2) there is reason to believe that, as a result of the dissemination of potentially prejudicial material, the waiver is required to increase the likelihood of a fair trial.

3.4 Selecting the jury

It is recommended that the following standards be adopted in each jurisdiction to govern the selection of a jury in those criminal cases in which questions of possible prejudice are raised.

(a) Method of examination.

Whenever there is believed to be a significant possibility that individual talesmen will be ineligible to serve because of exposure to potentially prejudicial material, the examination of each juror with respect to his exposure shall take place outside the presence of other chosen and prospective jurors. An accurate record of this examination shall be kept, by court reporter or tape recording whenever possible. The questioning shall be conducted for the purpose of determining what the prospective juror has read and heard about the case and how his exposure has affected his attitude towards the trial, not to convince him that he would be derelict in his duty if he could not cast aside any preconceptions he might have.

(b) Standard of acceptability.

Both the degree of exposure and the prospective juror's testimony as to his state of mind are relevant to the determination of acceptability. A prospective juror who states that he will be unable to overcome his preconceptions shall be subject to challenge for cause no matter how slight his exposure. If he has seen or heard and remembers information that will be developed in the course of trial, or that may be inadmissible but is not so prejudicial as to create a substantial risk that his judgment will be affected, his acceptability shall turn on whether his testimony as to impartiality is believed. If he admits to having formed an opinion, he shall be subject to challenge for cause unless the examination shows unequivocally that he can be impartial. A prospective juror who has been exposed to and remembers reports of highly significant information, such as the existence or contents of a confession, or other incriminating matters that may be inadmissible in evidence, or substantial amounts of inflammatory material, shall be subject to challenge for cause without regard to his testimony as to his state of mind.

(c) Source of the panel.

Whenever it is determined that potentially prejudicial news coverage of a given criminal matter has been intense and has been concentrated primarily in a given locality in a state (or federal district), the court shall have authority to draw jurors from other localities in that state (or district).

3.5   Conduct of the trial

It is recommended that the following standards be adopted in each jurisdiction to govern the conduct of a criminal trial when problems relating to the dissemination of potentially prejudicial material are raised.

(a) Use of the courtroom.

Whenever appropriate in view of the notoriety of the case or the number or conduct of news media representatives present at any judicial proceeding, the court shall ensure the preservation of decorum by instructing those representatives and others as to the permissible use of the courtroom, the assignment of seats, and other matters that may affect the conduct of the proceeding.

(b) Sequestration of jury.

Either party shall be permitted to move for sequestration of the jury at the beginning of trial or at any time during the course of the trial, and, in appropriate circumstances, the court shall order sequestration on its own motion. Sequestration shall be ordered if it is determined that the case is of such notoriety or the issues are of such a nature that, in the absence of sequestration, highly prejudicial matters are likely to come to the attention of the jurors. Whenever sequestration is ordered, the court in advising the jury of the decision shall not disclose which party requested sequestration.

(c) Cautioning parties and witnesses; insulating witnesses.

Whenever appropriate in light of the issues in the case or the notoriety of the case, the court shall instruct parties and witnesses not to make extrajudicial statements, relating to the case or the issues in the case, for dissemination by any means of public communication during the course of the trial. The court may also order sequestration of witnesses, prior to their appearance, when it appears likely that in the absence of sequestration they will be exposed to extra-judicial reports that may influence their testimony.

(d) Exclusion of the public from hearings or arguments outside the presence of the jury.

If the jury is not sequestered, the defendant shall be permitted to move that the public be excluded from any portion of the trial that takes place outside the presence of the jury on the ground that dissemination of evidence or argument adduced at the hearing is likely to interfere with the defendant's right to a fair trial by an impartial jury. The motion shall be granted unless it is determined that there is no substantial likelihood of such interference. With the consent of the defendant, the court may take such action on its own motion or at the suggestion of the prosecution. Whenever such action is taken, a complete record of the proceedings from which the public has been excluded shall be kept and shall be made available to the public following the completion of the trial. Nothing in this recommendation is intended to interfere with the power of the court, in connection with any hearing held outside the presence of the jury, to caution those present that dissemination of specified information by any means of public communication, prior to the rendering of the verdict, may jeopardize the right to a fair trial by an impartial jury.

(e) Cautioning jurors.

In any case that appears likely to be of significant public in-interest, an admonition in substantially the following form shall be given before the end of the first day if the jury is not sequestered.

> During the time you serve on this jury, there may appear in the newspapers or on radio or television reports concerning this case, and you may be tempted to read, listen to, or watch them. Please do *not* do so. Due process of law requires that the evidence to be considered by you in reaching your verdict meet certain standards—for example, a witness may testify about events he himself has seen or heard but not about matters of which he was told by others. Also, witnesses must be sworn to tell the truth and must be subject to cross-examination. News reports about the case are not subject to these standards, and if you read, listen to, or watch these reports, you may be exposed to misleading or inaccurate information which unduly favors one side and to which the other side is unable to respond. In fairness to both sides, therefore, it is essential that you comply with this instruction.

If the process of selecting a jury is a lengthy one, such an admonition shall also be given to each juror as he is selected. At the end of each subsequent day of the trial, and at other recess periods if the court deems necessary, an admonition in substantially the following form shall be given:

> For the reasons stated earlier in the trial, I must remind you not to read, listen to, or watch any news reports concerning this case while you are serving on this jury.

(f) Questioning jurors about exposure to potentially prejudicial material in the course of the trial; standard for excusing a juror.

If it is determined that material disseminated during the trial raises serious questions of possible prejudice, the court may on its own motion or shall on motion of either party question each juror, out of the presence of the others, about his exposure to that material. The method of examination shall be the same as that recommended in section 3.4(a), above. The standard for excusing a juror who is challenged on the basis of such exposure shall be the same as the standard of acceptability recommended in section 3.4(b), above, except that a juror who has seen or heard reports of potentially prejudicial material shall be excused if the material in question would furnish grounds for a mistrial if referred to in the trial itself.

3.6 Setting aside the verdict

It is recommended that, on motion of the defendant, a verdict of guilty in any criminal case be set aside and a new trial granted whenever, on the basis of competent evidence, the court finds a substantial likelihood that the vote of one or more jurors was influenced by exposure to an extrajudicial communication of any matter relating to the defendant or to the case itself that was not part of the trial record on which the case was submitted to the jury. Nothing in this recommendation is intended to affect the rule in any jurisdiction as to whether and in what circumstances a juror may impeach his own verdict or as to what other evidence is competent for that purpose.

PART IV. RECOMMENDATIONS RELATING TO THE
EXERCISE OF THE CONTEMPT POWER

4.1 Limited use of the contempt power

The use of the contempt power against persons who disseminate information by means of public communication, or who make statements for dissemination, can in certain circumstances raise grave constitutional questions. Apart from these questions, indiscriminate use of that power can cause unnecessary friction and stifle desirable discussion. On the other hand, it is essential that deliberate action constituting a serious threat to a fair trial not go unpunished and that valid court orders be obeyed. It is therefore recommended that the contempt power shall be used only with considerable caution but should be exercised in at least the following instances, in addition to those specified in sections 1.3, 2.1, and 2.3, above:

(a) Against a person who, knowing that a criminal trial by jury is in progress or that a jury is being selected for such a trial:

(i) disseminates by any means of public communication an extrajudicial statement relating to the defendant or to the issues in the case that goes beyond the public record of the court in the case, if the statement is reasonably calculated to affect the outcome of the trial and seriously threatens to have such an effect; or

(ii) makes such a statement with the expectation that it will be so disseminated.

(b) Against a person who knowingly violates a valid judicial order not to disseminate until completion of the trial or disposition without trial, specified information referred to in the course of a judicial hearing from which the public is excluded under sections 3.1 or 3.5(d) of these recommendations.

4.2 Reimbursement of defendant

In the event that a mistrial or change of venue is granted or a conviction set aside, as a result of an extrajudicial statement held to be in contempt of court, it is recommended that the court have the authority to require that all or part of the proceeds of any fine be used to reimburse the defendant for the additional legal fees and other expenses fairly attributable to the order that the case be tried in a different venue or tried again in the same venue.

❊   ❊   ❊   ❊   ❊

AMERICAN BAR ASSOCIATION PROJECT ON STANDARDS FOR THE ADMINISTRATION OF CRIMINAL JUSTICE, STANDARDS RELATING TO PROSECUTION AND DEFENSE FUNCTION (Tentative Draft 1970)

1.3 Public statements

(a) The lawyer representing an accused should avoid personal publicity connected with the case before trial, during trial and thereafter.

(b) The lawyer should comply with the ABA Standards on Fair Trial and Free Press.

Commentary

a. Personal publicity

A minority of lawyers have sometimes exploited newsworthy cases for their own personal aggrandizement. Often this operates to the detriment of the particular client, and it is always demeaning of the proper role of defense counsel. The opportunity for personal publicity may color the lawyer's professional judgment and lead him to take steps which are not in the best interests of his clients, the profession and, most importantly, the administration of justice.

b. Trial publicity

The tendency of a minority of lawyers, including both prosecutors and defense counsel, to indulge in "trial by press" is a disservice to the client and to the fair administration of justice.

A separate Committee of this ABA Project was given the responsibility of considering the problem of publicity as it affects criminal litigation, including the role of counsel in public discussion of criminal cases. A major portion of its report consists of detailed recommendations for controls on the conduct of attorneys in criminal cases. ABA STANDARDS, FAIR TRIAL AND FREE PRESS §§ 1.1–1.3 (Approved Draft, 1968). These recommendations have been approved by the House of Delegates of the American Bar Association and are covered in ABA CODE DR 7–107. This Committee endorses these standards and urges their prompt and vigorous implementation. They strike a careful balance between the needs of the public for information and the interest in preserving fairness of the trial procedure. Moreover, they are designed to preserve and uphold the role of counsel as the courtroom advocate who defends the case by evidence and argument rather than as one who appeals to the public outside the courtroom on the basis of emotion and prejudice. See State v. Kavanaugh, 52 N.J. 7, 243 A.2d 225, *cert. denied sub nom.*, Matzner v. New Jersey, 393 U.S. 924 (1968).

1.3 Public statements

(a) The prosecutor should not exploit his office by means of personal publicity connected with a case before trial, during trial and thereafter.

(b) The prosecutor should comply with the ABA Standards on Fair Trial and Free Press.

Commentary

The prosecutor's responsibility to the administration of justice requires that he do nothing which will impair the right of the accused to a fair and impartial treatment in every case. As the representative of the public interest, his only interest is to see that justice is done. He should not exploit the power and prestige of his office for his own personal aggrandizement. Circumspection in this regard is most acutely required in cases which excite public interest. The very nature of his function as an administrator of justice requires that the prosecutor unselfishly avoid personal publicity in connection with the cases he prosecutes.

The problem of publicity as it affects the administration of criminal justice has been the subject of a separate study in this ABA Project, ABA STANDARDS, FAIR TRIAL AND FREE PRESS (Approved Draft, 1968). The product of long and thoughtful consideration of the problem, it contains detailed standards governing the role of attorneys associated with the prosecution and defense in public discussion of criminal cases. See *id.* §§ 1.1–1.3. It is incumbent upon the prosecutor to know and comply with these standards. ABA CODE DR 7–107.

* * * * *

[The leading cases from the Supreme Court on this subject are *Estes v. Texas*, 381 U.S. 532 (1965), and *Sheppard v. Maxwell*, 384 U.S. 333 (1966).—Eds.]

CHAPTER 11

Summation, Instructions and Jury Verdict

A. Motions During and at the Close of Proof

FEDERAL RULES OF CRIMINAL PROCEDURE, RULE 29

MOTION FOR JUDGMENT OF ACQUITTAL

(a) **Motion Before Submission to Jury.** Motions for directed verdict are abolished and motions for judgment of acquittal shall be used in their place. The court on motion of a defendant or of its own motion shall order the entry of judgment of acquittal of one or more offenses charged in the indictment or information after the evidence on either side is closed if the evidence is insufficient to sustain a conviction of such offense or offenses. If a defendant's motion for judgment of acquittal at the close of the evidence offered by the government is not granted, the defendant may offer evidence without having reserved the right.

(b) **Reservation of Decision on Motion.** If a motion for judgment of acquittal is made at the close of all evidence, the court may reserve decision on the motion, submit the case to the jury and decide the motion either before the jury returns a verdict or after it returns a verdict of guilty or is discharged without having returned a verdict.

(c) **Motion After Discharge of Jury.** If the jury returns a verdict of guilty or is discharged without having returned a verdict, a motion for judgment of acquittal may be made or renewed within 7 days after the jury is discharged or within such further time as the court may fix during the 7-day period. If a verdict of guilty is returned the court may on such motion set aside the verdict and enter judgment of acquittal. If no verdict is returned the court may enter judgment of acquittal. It shall not be necessary to the making of such a motion

639

that a similar motion has been made prior to the submission of the case to the jury.

*   *   *   *   *

NEW YORK CRIMINAL PROCEDURE LAW (1971)

§ 280.10   Motion for mistrial

At any time during the trial, the court must declare a mistrial and order a new trial of the indictment under the following circumstances:

1. Upon motion of the defendant, when there occurs during the trial an error or legal defect in the proceedings, or conduct inside or outside the courtroom, which is prejudicial to the defendant and deprives him of a fair trial. When such an error, defect or conduct occurs during a joint trial of two or more defendants and a mistrial motion is made by one or more but not by all, the court must declare a mistrial only as to the defendant or defendants making or joining in the motion, and the trial of the other defendant or defendants must proceed;

2. Upon motion of the people, when there occurs during the trial, either inside or outside the courtroom, gross misconduct by the defendant or some person acting on his behalf, or by a juror, resulting in substantial and irreparable prejudice to the people's case. When such misconduct occurs during a joint trial of two or more defendants, and when the court is satisfied that it did not result in substantial prejudice to the people's case as against a particular defendant and that such defendant was in no way responsible for the misconduct, it may not declare a mistrial with respect to such defendant but must proceed with the trial as to him;

3. Upon motion of either party or upon the court's own motion, when it is physically impossible to proceed with the trial in conformity with law.

Staff Comment *

This motion is primarily applicable to discharge of a jury prior to its retirement for deliberation; . . .

The Criminal Code contains a smattering of unsatisfactory sections which, though not phrased in "mistrial" terminology, authorize the court to discharge a jury on various grounds before the case has been submitted to it (*e.g.*, §§ 402, 404, 416, 430). The most comprehensive of these is § 430, providing that, when a jury has been discharged (without dismissal of the indictment)

* From 1967 Study Bill and Commission Report.

"by reason of an accident or other cause," the case "may be again tried at the same or another term." As indicated by the structure of that statute, many of the problems arising in the so-called "mistrial" area are basically double jeopardy issues. In short, the real question presented upon the declaration of a mistrial is not whether the jury could properly be discharged but whether the defendant may be re-tried after termination of the first trial under the given circumstances. Code § 430, with its vague clause, "by reason of accident or other cause," provides little in the way of criteria for determining what kinds of facts or circumstances justify a court in terminating a trial without concomitantly precluding a re-trial, and one is necessarily relegated to case law upon this subject.

No constitutional issue with respect to re-trial, of course, is presented when a mistrial is declared upon motion of the defendant, and the problems of this area are relatively simple. While no precise standards are to be found, it may' be broadly stated that a mistrial order upon the defendant's motion is warranted by any prejudicial error or occurrence which so clearly deprives him of a fair trial that it would require a reversal on appeal of a prospective judgment of conviction (see People v. Byrne, 1966, 17 N.Y.2d 209, 270 N.Y.S.2d 193; People ex rel. Costello v. La Valle, 1961, 13 App.Div.2d 601, 212 N.Y.S.2d 216; People v. Montlake, 1918, 184 App. Div. 578, 172 N.Y.S. 102).

The delicate issues arise in connection with mistrial orders issued upon motion of the people or upon the court's own motion and without the defendant's consent. Only under exceptional circumstances, it is held, may a trial be so terminated without precluding a re-trial on double jeopardy grounds, and the reason for the termination "must be a necessitous one, actual and substantial" (Nolan v. Court of General Sessions, 1962, 11 N.Y.2d 114, 118–119, 227 N.Y.S.2d 1).

One kind of "exceptional" circumstance meeting this standard consists of some occurrence rendering it physically impossible to proceed with the trial, such as death or serious illness of the judge or other essential court personnel (People ex rel. Epting v. Devoe, 1955, 309 N.Y. 818, 130 N.E.2d 616; People ex rel. Brinkman v. Barr, 1928, 248 N.Y. 126, 130, 161 N.E. 444). Rarely, however, may a mistrial safely be declared solely because of prejudice or misfortune affecting the people's case. Nevertheless, it has been held that such action was warranted by the serious illness of a prosecution witness (People v. Kelly, 1961, 9 N.Y.2d

697, 212 N.Y.S.2d 755) and by flagrant tactical chicanery practiced by the defendant at a trial (People v. Strick, 1965, 15 N.Y.2d 692, 694, 256 N.Y.S.2d 137); nor can it be doubted that bribery or corruption of a juror would constitute sufficient basis (see Matter of McCabe, 1960, 24 Misc.2d 477, 480, 199 N.Y.S.2d 247).

The proposed section is formulated in accordance with the foregoing principles, and also with some assistance from the American Law Institute's Model Penal Code (§ 1.08[4b]). Thus, the relatively mild requirement for a mistrial order upon the defendant's motion is the occurrence of error or defect "which is prejudicial to the defendant and deprives him of a fair trial" (subd. 1). The much stricter requirement for a mistrial declaration upon the people's motion is "gross misconduct by the defendant or some person acting on his behalf, or by a juror, resulting in substantial and irreparable prejudice to the people's case" (subd. 2). And physical impossibility of proceeding with the trial is a ground for the order upon motion of either party or of the court itself (subd. 3).

It may further be observed that the proposed section contains certain safeguards in connection with multiple defendant trials which, in appropriate situations, require continuation of the trial with respect to a defendant who wishes to proceed after the declaration of a mistrial with respect to another defendant (subds. 1, 2).

§ 280.20   Motion for mistrial; status of indictment upon new trial

Upon a new trial resulting from an order declaring a mistrial, the indictment is deemed to contain all the counts which it contained at the time the previous trial was commenced, regardless of whether any count was thereafter dismissed by the court prior to the mistrial order.

§ 290.10   Trial order of dismissal

1. At the conclusion of the people's case or at the conclusion of all the evidence, the court may, except as provided in subdivision two, upon motion of the defendant, issue a "trial order of dismissal," dismissing any count of an indictment upon the ground that the trial evidence is not legally sufficient to establish the offense charged therein or any lesser included offense.

2. Despite the lack of legally sufficient trial evidence in support of a count of an indictment as described in subdivision one, issuance

of a trial order of dismissal is not authorized and constitutes error when the trial evidence would have been legally sufficient had the court not erroneously excluded admissible evidence offered by the people.

3. When the court excludes trial evidence offered by the people under such circumstances that the substance or content thereof does not appear in the record, the people may, in anticipation of a possible subsequent trial order of dismissal emanating from the allegedly improper exclusion and erroneously issued in violation of subdivision two, and in anticipation of a possible appeal therefrom pursuant to subdivision two of section 450.20, place upon the record, out of the presence of the jury, an "offer of proof" summarizing the substance or content of such excluded evidence. Upon the subsequent issuance of a trial order of dismissal and an appeal therefrom, such offer of proof constitutes a part of the record on appeal and has the effect and significance prescribed in subdivision two of section 450.40. In the absence of such an order and an appeal therefrom, such offer of proof is not deemed a part of the record and does not constitute such for purposes of an ensuing appeal by the defendant from a judgment of conviction.

4. Upon issuing a trial order of dismissal which dismisses the entire indictment, the court must immediately discharge the defendant from custody if he is in custody of the sheriff, or, if he is at liberty on bail, it must exonerate the bail.

* * * * *

Louisiana Statutes Annotated (West 1967)
Code of Criminal Procedure

Art. 770. Prejudicial remarks; basis of mistrial

Upon motion of a defendant, a mistrial shall be ordered when a remark or comment, made within the hearing of the jury by the judge, district attorney, or a court official, during the trial or in argument, refers directly or indirectly to:

(1) Race, religion, color or national origin, if the remark or comment is not material and relevant and might create prejudice against the defendant in the mind of the jury;

(2) Another crime committed or alleged to have been committed by the defendant to which evidence is not admissible;

(3) The failure of the defendant to testify in his own defense; or

(4) The refusal of the judge to direct a verdict.

An admonition to the jury to disregard the remark or comment shall not be sufficient to prevent a mistrial. If the defendant, however, requests that only an admonition be given, the court shall admonish the jury to disregard the remark or comment but shall not declare a mistrial.

Art. 771.   Admonition

In the following cases, upon the request of the defendant or the state, the court shall promptly admonish the jury to disregard a remark or comment made during the trial, or in argument within the hearing of the jury, when the remark is irrelevant or immaterial and of such a nature that it might create prejudice against the defendant, or the state, in the mind of the jury:

(1) When the remark or comment is made by the judge, the district attorney, or a court official, and the remark is not within the scope of Article 770; or

(2) When the remark or comment is made by a witness or person other than the judge, district attorney, or a court official, regardless of whether the remark or comment is within the scope of Article 770.

In such cases, on motion of the defendant, the court may grant a mistrial if it is satisfied that an admonition is not sufficient to assure the defendant a fair trial.

Art. 775.   Mistrial; grounds for

A mistrial may be ordered, and in a jury case the jury dismissed, when:

(1) The defendant consents thereto;

(2) The jury is unable to agree upon a verdict;

(3) There is a legal defect in the proceedings which would make any judgment entered upon a verdict reversible as a matter of law;

(4) The court finds that the defendant does not have the mental capacity to proceed;

(5) It is physically impossible to proceed with the trial in conformity with law; or

(6) False statements of a juror on voir dire prevent a fair trial.

Upon motion of a defendant, a mistrial shall be ordered, and in a jury case the jury dismissed, when prejudicial conduct in or outside the courtroom makes it impossible for the defendant to obtain a fair trial, or when authorized by Article 770 or 771.

A mistrial shall be ordered, and in a jury case the jury dismissed, when the state and the defendant jointly move for a mistrial.

❖   ❖   ❖   ❖   ❖

AMERICAN BAR ASSOCIATION PROJECT ON STANDARDS FOR THE
ADMINISTRATION OF CRIMINAL JUSTICE, STANDARDS RELATING
TO TRIAL BY JURY (Approved Draft 1968)

4.5 Motion for judgment of acquittal

(a) After the evidence on either side is closed, the court on motion
of a defendant or on its own motion shall order the entry of a judgment of acquittal of one or more offenses charged if the evidence is
insufficient to sustain a conviction of such offense or offenses. Such a
motion by the defendant, if not granted, shall not be deemed to withdraw the case from the jury or to bar the defendant from offering
evidence.

(b) If the defendant's motion is made at the close of the evidence
offered by the prosecution, the court may not reserve decision on the
motion. If the defendant's motion is made at the close of all the
evidence, the court may reserve decision on the motion, submit the
case to the jury and decide the motion either before the jury returns
a verdict or after it returns a verdict of guilty or is discharged without
having returned a verdict.

(c) If the jury returns a verdict of guilty or is discharged without
having returned a verdict, the defendant's motion may be made or
renewed within a certain time, set by statute or rule, after discharge
of the jury or within such further time as the court may fix. Such a
motion is not barred by defendant's failure to make a similar motion
prior to the submission of the case to the jury.

Commentary

Section 4.5 generally

This standard, for the most part, is patterned after FED. R. CRIM. P.
29, as amended in 1966. State procedures consistent with the standard
are commonly provided for by rule or statute, although, depending
upon the circumstances and the precise procedures used, they may be
known by a variety of names, such as motion for directed verdict,
motion to exclude the evidence, or motion for judgment notwithstanding the verdict. ORFIELD, CRIMINAL PROCEDURE FROM ARREST
TO APPEAL 434–38 (1947); 5 BUSCH, LAW AND TACTICS IN JURY TRIALS
§§ 618, 620, 626 (1963). The matter is dealt with in this section because it involves important notions of the allocation of responsibility
between judge and jury and because there are some jurisdictions in
which the judge is unduly limited in his ability to control the jury in
this fashion.

Section 4.5 (a)

This subsection deals with what is most commonly known as a motion for directed verdict. It is similar in form to FED. R. CRIM. P. 29(a) and UNIFORM RULES OF CRIMINAL PROCEDURE, rule 38(a), and is also consistent with ALI CODE OF CRIMINAL PROCEDURE § 321 (1930). For citations to some state statutes in accord, see *id.* at 961–62.

The first sentence recognizes the power of the trial judge, upon his own motion or the motion of the defendant, to take the case from the jury because the evidence is insufficient to sustain a conviction. Such a motion is appropriate after the conclusion of the prosecution's case or at the close of all the evidence. This is currently the rule in the overwhelming majority of jurisdictions. Winningham, *The Dilemma of the Directed Acquittal,* 15 VAND. L. REV. 699 (1962). However, a small group of states are not in accord; they deny the trial judge the power to take the case from the jury. In a few states this results from statutes to the effect that the judge may advise the jury to acquit but that the jury is not bound by the advice, *e.g.*, OKLA. STAT. ANN. tit. 22, § 850 (1958), although there is a growing tendency for appellate courts to ignore these statutes and rule that it is the duty of the trial judge to direct a verdict when he deems the evidence insufficient, Snow v. State, 325 P.2d 754 (Okla. 1958). Elsewhere it has been ruled that the jury is the exclusive judge of the facts and that therefore the judge may not direct a verdict. Dykes v. State, 201 Tenn. 65, 296 S.W.2d 861 (1956); State v. Haddad, 221 La. 337, 59 So.2d 411 (1951); Myers v. Commonwealth, 132 Va. 746, 111 S.E. 463 (1922).

The arguments which have been presented in favor of the minority rule are that directed verdicts make possible abuse by the courts and that they prejudice the prosecution by an unappealable acquittal. Winningham, *The Dilemma of the Directed Acquittal,* 15 VAND. L. REV. 699, 718 (1962). These arguments have been rejected by the Advisory Committee. This risk of abuse does not seem great, and what statistics are available show that directed verdicts are not granted in a large number of cases. *Id.* at 718–19; KALVEN & ZEISEL, THE AMERICAN JURY 508 (1966). Withholding relief until the case reaches the appellate level casts an unnecessary burden on the defendant and transfers the sufficiency-of-all-the-evidence question from the judge who heard the evidence to others who must determine the issue solely upon the basis of the record.

The last sentence of this subsection enumerates two consequences which are *not* to follow from the fact that the defendant has moved for a directed verdict. For one thing, if the motion is made at the conclusion of the prosecution's case and is denied, the defendant is not

thereby barred from presenting his evidence. Because of some doubt
on this score, it is not uncommon for judgment-of-acquittal provisions
to make this clear. FED. R. CRIM. P. 29(a); UNIFORM RULES OF
CRIMINAL PROCEDURE, rule 38(a). There is no good reason for requiring the defendant to make this sacrifice in order to move for acquittal
when the government's case is in. (Of course, if the motion is denied,
the defendant must decide whether to put in evidence and thus waive
the right to appeal from the denial of the motion, or whether instead
to introduce no evidence and preserve the right to appeal on this
point. The former course does not bar the defendant from again moving for acquittal at the close of all the evidence, but at this time the
court may properly consider evidence damaging to the defendant
which may have come out during presentation of the defendant's case.
Thus, an erroneous denial of the motion for acquittal made at the conclusion of the prosecutor's case may be cured by subsequent developments at the trial. Although it has been argued that this rule comes
perilously close to compelling the defendant to incriminate himself,
Note, 70 YALE L. J. 1151 [1961], the argument is not believed to be
persuasive, and no deviation from the majority rule is recommended
here.)

The second consequence which is not to follow from the fact that
defendant has moved for acquittal is removal of the case from the jury
even if the motion is denied. In those few jurisdictions where the
ancient practice of demurrer to the evidence still exists, the effect of
such a demurrer, if joined in by the state, is to withdraw the case from
the jury. 5 BUSCH, LAW AND TACTICS IN JURY TRIALS § 620 (1963).
There is no good reason for requiring the defendant to risk his right to
jury trial whenever he questions the sufficiency of the government's
case.

Section 4.5 (b)

The first sentence of this subsection rests upon the notion that if a
defendant moves for acquittal at the end of the government's case, he
should have the benefit of a ruling on that motion prior to his election
whether or not to present evidence on his own behalf. As the court said
in Jackson v. United States, 250 F.2d 897, 901 (5th Cir. 1958), in
holding that the federal rules did not permit the judge to reserve decision until both sides had rested, the motion "would be a futile thing
if the court could reserve its ruling and force the defendant to an
election between resting and being deprived of the benefit of the
motion." The commentators have expressed approval of the position
taken in *Jackson*. Note, 70 YALE L. J. 1151, 1163 (1961); Winningham,

The Dilemma of the Directed Acquittal, 15 VAND. L. REV. 699, 703–04 (1962).

The second sentence of this subsection permits the court to reserve decision on a motion made at the end of all the evidence. The objection stated above is not present in this situation, and it is well expressly to recognize the power of the judge to render a decision on the motion even after the jury has returned a guilty verdict or is discharged without having returned a verdict. This portion of the standard, based upon FED. R. CRIM. P. 29(b), expressly recognizes the propriety of what often is referred to as a judgment notwithstanding the verdict. This practice is currently recognized in some but not all jurisdictions. ORFIELD, CRIMINAL PROCEDURE FROM ARREST TO APPEAL 436 (1947). The arguments against the practice—that there is a possibility of abuse by the courts and that it is unfair to confront the prosecution with an unappealable acquittal after a jury conviction, *id.* at 437—are not thought to be persuasive. On the contrary, it is desirable that the court not lose its power to direct a verdict once the jury retires and that it not be thereafter confined to granting a new trial. *Id.* at 438.

Section 4.5 (c)

Illustrative of a provision conforming to this subsection is FED. R. CRIM. P. 29(c), which allows the motion within seven days after the jury is discharged or within such further time as the court may fix during that seven-day period. See also UNIFORM RULES OF CRIMINAL PROCEDURE, rule 38(b). For the reasons stated above, it is desirable that the judge have the power to so act within a limited time after the case has been heard.

The last sentence in this subsection may be contrary to the law in several jurisdictions; a motion by the defendant after the case has been sent to the jury was not permitted in federal practice until the most recent revision of rule 29(c). As the federal Advisory Committee on Criminal Rules noted as to this change: "No legitimate interest of the government is intended to be prejudiced by permitting the court to direct an acquittal on a post-verdict motion. The constitutional requirement of a jury trial in criminal cases is primarily a right accorded to the defendant." It is undoubtedly true that in practice such motions "are ordinarily made as a matter of course at the end of the government's case and the close of the evidence" and that it is unwise to defer such a motion until after the verdict "in view of the impact a guilty verdict is likely to have on the court's determination of the motion." Rezneck, *The New Federal Rules of Criminal Procedure*, 54

GEO. L. J. 1276, 1313 (1966). Yet, as the federal rules committee concluded, it does not seem desirable to bar the motion because it was not made earlier, prior to the submission of the case to the jury.

* * * * *

B. Closing Argument

LOUISIANA STATUTES ANNOTATED (WEST 1967)
CODE OF CRIMINAL PROCEDURE

Art. 774. Argument; scope
The argument shall be confined to evidence admitted, to the lack of evidence, to conclusions of fact that the state or defendant may draw therefrom, and to the law applicable to the case.

The argument shall not appeal to prejudice.

The state's rebuttal shall be confined to answering the argument of the defendant.

* * * * *

Schrempp, *Summation*, in HOW TO DEFEND A CRIMINAL CASE—
FROM ARREST TO VERDICT 389–97 (V. Lawyer & B. George ed. 1967)*

That portion of the trial devoted to summation probably presents the most well-known image of the attorney in the mind of the public. Even in law school, most of the students dream of the day when they may stand before the twelve "friends and neighbors" and, with the eloquence of a Demosthenes, sway their captive audience to the principles of truth and justice which, in the mind of the lawyer, represent his side of the controversy. To most of the lawyers that will be, the ultimate objective in their minds will be the day when they stand before the jury and speak in the traditional "tongue of men and of angels." The art of summation, like most facets of the trial of any lawsuit, either civil or criminal, is a constantly changing thing and must be recognized as such by the practitioner. The arguments of the great lawyers of old were excellent and appropriate for their times; but the complexion of the public and, ultimately, the jury, is, and always will be, a changing thing. It is obvious that juries today are much more sophisticated than the juries of yesterday; and the summations of lawyers must conform to the increased sophistication of their audience. The keynote is an approach of sincerity and logic, as opposed to an appeal based upon high emotion alone.

We must face the realization that the image of the criminal lawyer is not, and may never be, the type of image that we completely desire. The very term, "criminal lawyer," in some areas causes the general public to become defensive in their attitude toward him. While the image has brightened somewhat through the years, the factors of adverse newspaper publicity, literature concerning law enforcement drives, motion pictures and television, and even the general recent back-lash of the public toward the decisions of our Supreme Court, have not combined to help matters very much. Illustrative of this is the well-known story of the stranger who visited a small community and asked one of the local people, "Do you have a criminal lawyer in town?" After an appropriate deposit of tobacco juice in a spittoon, the local personage replied, "By golly, we think we have; but we just can't prove it yet!" The criminal lawyer must, therefore, be as above suspicion as Caesar's wife; and his approach to the jury, from the beginning of the trial to the end, must be designed to convince the jury of his own honesty and sincerity, as well as that of his client.

Thus, it is particularly true in summation that high-flung phrases, and obvious appeals to emotion only, place the criminal advocate in a position of confirming the jury's preconceived ideas. This is not to say that emotion has no part in the successful advance of a criminal case. A criminal case is a dramatic, moving and emotional experience for the jury, as well as the participants. The jury must be, and will be, from the voir dire to the final argument, convinced of the fact that they are not dealing with mere money or property, and that personal rights of the individual and the preservation of our system of criminal justice transcend all considerations that would be important in the trial of a civil case.

A summation should, by its nature, be one of the easiest and most spontaneous activities of a lawyer on either side of a case, be it civil or criminal. Throughout the trial, the advocate has been forced to repress his argumentative questions as being improper. He may not, during the trial, make the pointed comments and observations during the examination of a witness that television audiences are led to believe a lawyer has the right to do. But, at long last, when he speaks in summation, his arguments, thoughts and comments usually virtually gush forth. In this geyser of rhetoric lies one of the dangers of summation. A lawyer must be constantly alert to the possibility that what he thinks is a major point may be a triviality or technicality to a jury of his client's peers.

A lawyer must also be a psychologist who is under the obligation of anticipating at all times what catastrophes can happen in summation by the wrong phrase or the wrong situation. As illustrative of this, in one of the author's very early cases, the defendant was a man who, despite the charges of the prosecution and despite his possible deviation from the paths of righteousness throughout his life, had an honest and sincere appearance. He did not take the witness stand, for reasons well known in the trial of criminal cases. In attempting to make the most of the appearance of his client and combat the effect of his failure to appear on the witness stand, his lawyer whirled about during the summation, pointed to the client and asked the jury, "Can you see any evidence of guilt in the face of that man?" The client had not been forewarned of this maneuver. Under the stress of the moment, the surprise of the situation and the pointing finger of his counsel, his reaction was to twist his face into a maniacal, homicidal, Jack the Ripper-type attempted grin which was, to say the least, both hideous and revolting. This points up the lack of psychological preparation of the client, as well as a failure properly to diagnose in advance the reaction of a given person under a given set of facts. It also constituted the last use of that particular maneuver in summation by this particular advocate.

Semantics in a criminal case are not only on a par with, but are probably more important than, semantics in a civil case. Why give the attorney for the State, or the Government, or the People, or the Commonwealth, the advantage of clothing him in that title of respectability? Call him the prosecutor, because that is what he is. As a matter of semantics, some jurors may not like the word prosecutor. They may feel that it is somehow linguistically connected with the word persecutor. Avoid referring to your client as "the defendant," because that phrase is cold and impersonal, and juries are more prone to wreak their vengeance upon cold and impersonal objects than they are upon the warmth of a living fellow human. Refer to your client by his proper name, or even indulge in the friendliness of using his first name, if the rules of your local tribunal do not forbid it.

If your client is a family man, the jury should have a chance at least to see the other members of the family in the courtroom, avoiding at all times the pitfall of letting it appear that this is your only defense. A good approach in summation is to state to the jury that you feel you are representing not only one person, but several, because, in truth and fact, you are. A jury should be reminded that the impact of a guilty verdict on the accused may cause an even greater injury to the innocent members of his family who have done no wrong.

There is a great temptation to discard arguments that you have made, perhaps successfully, time and time again, merely because, to you, they have begun to sound trite and even "cornball." You have heard them many times, but always remember that the jury has not.

A technique which may often be used to good advantage is to stress in argument that there is no burden on the defense to produce any evidence, and to ask the jury to indulge in the hypothesis that your client had availed himself of this right. The thesis is then predicated upon your attack on the credibility of prosecution witnesses, and your plea to the jury is simply that, even if the defense had produced no evidence, your client would be entitled to an acquittal under the doctrines of reasonable doubt and presumption of innocence. Argue, then, that even though you could have rested without any evidence, your client insisted that he be allowed to tell his side of the story to the jury.

In arguing reasonable doubt, it is well to impress the jury with the idea that any doubt that has arisen in their minds must, of necessity, be a reasonable doubt, on the basis of the fact that the jury is presumed to be composed of reasonable people, and that if even one of the reasonable persons among the entire twelve has a doubt of any kind in his mind, your client has the right to be acquitted. Often times during an argument, when you are merely referring to "doubts," the prosecutor may object and ask you to use the qualifying phrase, "reasonable doubt," to which you can, of course, reply, "You may not agree with me, Mr. Prosecutor, but I, at least, assume these twelve folks are all reasonable people and that any doubt in the mind of any one of them is a reasonable doubt."

With respect to instructions of the court, it is obvious that defense counsel will refer to the standard instructions in a criminal case. Rather than merely saying, "Judge Smith will instruct you," why not particularize the instruction to the case in trial by saying, "I feel that, under the evidence in *this* case, Judge Smith will agree to instruct you as follows: . . ."

Under the doctrine of reasonable doubt, the failure of the prosecution to produce any witness that has figured in the evidence can be turned into a most telling argument. The jury should not be asked to go through life wondering what the missing witness would have said, had he been produced by the prosecution. It was the prosecution's duty to produce him, because the burden of proof never shifts to your client.

Demonstrative evidence and the use of court reporter transcripts of portions of the evidence are as invaluable in a criminal case as in a civil case. With respect to such objects, photographs, written-up excerpts and other items that may be either seen or read, it is particularly important in summation to have such material well organized, because there is nothing more distracting than having to hunt through a bundle of messed-up papers to find the one that illustrates the point you are trying to make. A fumbler for exhibits loses his audience while he fumbles, and the magic spell may be broken.

When during the trial, and usually on cross-examination, you have elicited some astounding admission from a prosecuting witness which just cannot be true, have that portion written up by the court reporter. It is often well to say, "I thought that Mr. Jones testified that he was making his claimed observations from a point one hundred yards away in a dark alley, and I couldn't believe my ears, so I went back and checked with the court reporter to make sure. When I found that that witness had actually made that incredible claim, I had the court reporter write it up. I have it here in my hand, and I will read it back to you again." After finishing the reading of the excerpt, it might be well to ask the jury, "Does that raise a doubt in your minds? Are you reasonable people?"

As is well known to practitioners who are on the plaintiffs' side of civil cases, there is a distinct advantage in having the last argument to the jury, which advantage is enjoyed by the prosecutor in most jurisdictions. What can be done to lessen the effect of the prosecutor's final argument?

First, you must anticipate the damning arguments that you know the prosecutor is holding back for rebuttal, and answer them in advance as best you can.

Second, it is sometimes well to group together as many unanswerable questions as will serve to depreciate the State's case, and fire those questions at the prosecutor at the very end of the defense argument, with an admonition to the jury of, "Make Mr. Prosecutor answer these questions to your satisfaction. Don't let him tell you that you have to perform the grisly task of convicting a fellow human being of a felony without doing his job of leaving no unanswered questions in your minds. Don't let Mr. Prosecutor tell you that he can force you to go through the rest of your lives with a still, small voice in the back of your mind saying, 'What would have been the testimony of that witness?' He has the final argument. Make him answer these questions."

Often, the prosecutor will fail to answer some of the questions that have been fired at him, and this may be well remembered by some jurors in their deliberation. On the other hand, if the prosecutor decides to try to answer all of your questions, he may not answer some to the jury's satisfaction, and his attempt to do so may well upset his beautifully preconceived plan of rebuttal argument.

Remember always that the trial judge, who has probably worked with the same jury panel before, is usually looked upon by the jury as the ultimate in sagacity and fair play. It is obvious that in any sharp exchanges between defense counsel and the bench, in front of the jury, the bench will prevail.

In summation, it is particularly important that the jury feel that you and the judge are cooperating to preserve the rights of your client and the principles of American jurisprudence. However, in the life of every lawyer, there falls some rain. Some day, somewhere, you will be trying a criminal case before a judge who probably gained his political prestige as a prosecuting attorney, and forgets from time to time that he is supposed to have changed his role. If and when you feel that the jury has perhaps resented the manner in which the judge has made things difficult throughout the trial for you and your client, it is perfectly proper and ethical, in summation, to remind the jury that in their hands lies the power of a general verdict. A possible approach, in summation, to the problem would be as follows: "I think you realize that from the standpoint of the defense, this has been a particularly hard case. I think you, ladies and gentlemen of the jury, now realize why it was that the founders of this country and the legislators of this State long ago took the power to acquit or convict out of the hands of judges and, in their wisdom, placed it exclusively in the hands of twelve jurors such as yourselves."

There is nothing contentious about such a statement, because it is a statement of fact; all you are doing is commenting favorably upon the system of justice under which the case is being tried.

Many jurors feel that even though they should make a mistake in convicting a defendant, the whole thing will be cured on appeal if they are wrong. Obviously this is not true, and a portion of a summation should be devoted to clarifying the fact that the jurors are the sole judges of the facts of the case and that their decision in that field is final and unalterable.

Referring again to matters of semantics, it is sometimes quite dangerous, under the rules in some jurisdictions, for a defense lawyer to state that the verdict in non-capital felony cases will send his client to the penitentiary, because as a matter of practice this sometimes "opens the door" for an otherwise objectionable prosecution argument that the jury "is not sending anyone to prison; only the judge can do that."

This is an adroit prosecution argument, in that it allows the jury to pass the buck to the court and console themselves by saying, "We didn't hurt anyone; only the judge can do that." If the judge is a kindly, whitehaired, fair-appearing old gentleman, the jury may well believe that he would not hurt anyone, even though their verdict was guilty, not knowing that at that moment his bailiff is in chambers, at the judge's instructions, looking up the maximum penalty for the offense charged. A manner of reminding the jury of the seriousness of their task, without suggesting that they will inflict the punishment, is to couch your references in terms of "convicting a fellow man of a felony" or "making a convicted felon" of the defendant.

As another portion of the summation, it may be well to remind the jury of how they answered, under oath, the questions asked them on the voir dire, recalling to their minds the sworn pledges that they would be fair and impartial and would follow the doctrines of presumption of innocence, burden of proof and reasonable doubt.

A fair-minded jury is presumed to be composed of twelve people who are neither brutal nor sadistic. It must be further assumed that normal human beings do not enjoy hurting other human beings, under ordinary circumstances. It is well to remind the jury that, before they can be asked to perform the cruel, grisly and unpleasant duty of convicting a fellow human being of a felony, the prosecutor must have fulfilled his sworn duty of producing evidence beyond a reasonable doubt. If he has failed in his duty in this regard, it is completely unfair on his part to ask the jury for a conviction under these circumstances, even though the jury might have some passing belief that the defendant is guilty as charged.

Obviously, the limitations of the charge should be the object of defense comment in summation. How many Sam Sheppards have been convicted of murder on evidence of adultery? A good approach to this problem is to tell the jury, in summation, that the prosecution may have proved that your client is a drunkard or a libertine or an essentially bad or foul-mouthed man, and to plead him guilty to all these things if they constitute offenses under the law, but that he would never plead guilty to the charge under which the indictment is framed because, as to that charge, he is innocent. It might be suggested that punishment for moral turpitude or other delinquencies not contained within the charge of the indictment is not the concern of the jury, and that if such punishment is called for, it may be administered by another tribunal in another world, not by this jury in this court room on this day.

The summations are over. The jury has been instructed and is deliberating. You are now in what is known as the third summation, the three being: (1) the argument you planned; (2) the argument you gave; and (3) the argument you thought of afterward.

❊ ❊ ❊ ❊ ❊

Raggio, *Opening and Closing Arguments,* in TRIAL PRACTICE IN CRIMINAL CASES 97–104 (National District Attorneys Association, ca. 1967)[*]

Closing Argument: General

This really is what might be termed for the prosecutor, the "time to put up or shut up." With the "final shot" at the jury, the prosecutor should definitely shift gears. At this stage, the prosecutor should have the feeling that he has adequately covered his presentation in the opening, and should convey to the jury his determination and competency to meet the points raised by the defendant.

Acknowledging Jury's Service

It is always appropriate at the outset to thank the jury for its participation. Undoubtedly the defense counsel has in some way alluded to his obligation to his client; it is proper reference for you to remind them of your obligation to the people of the state, to the society of which they are a part. This again rightfully identifies you with the jury and the jury with your cause. You are not there to seek victims; but their obligation, as deciders of fact, must be made clear to them.

Instructions

This is the time to emphasize those instructions which you feel have particular application to your case, and which, if followed, will support your theory of the case. When numbered, emphasize these by marking the numbers on the blackboard. Apply the evidence to these instructions, leaving with the jury the realization that there can be no other valid explanation.

Witnesses

This is a fine opportunity, before the real thrust of your argument, to pinpoint the reliability of witnesses, to compare the caliber of witnesses offered by each side, to point up any bias motive or feelings

[*] Reprinted by permission.

that witnesses may have, and to remind them of the points on which witnesses have been effectively impeached. In this regard, it is important that sufficient background information has been brought out during the examination of the witnesses.

Reference to Opening Statement

It is well to remind the jury of what you predicted in your opening statement, and if the defendant has also made one, to indicate what he has failed to prove. Show them you have kept your word and that the defendant has not. This is especially useful where your opponent's proof has fallen way short.

Reference to Jurors' Answers on Voir Dire; to Opening Statements

It is usually quite effective to refer, in argument, to the jurors' own answers during voir dire examination. You may adroitly remind them of their sworn statement to apply a principle of law, even though they might personally disagree that it should be the law, for example. You may also remind them that you are confident they will decide the case fairly and squarely upon the evidence presented, as they have already indicated they would do.

Where such inquiry is allowed by the trial court, reference may be made to voir dire examination concerning the prospective juror's feeling on applicable legal principles. It is well to inquire, too, if the juror will return his verdict without regard to sympathy, pity, passion or other emotions. If such questions have been asked of each juror, he may be reminded of his answer given under oath. This is particularly true where you have the duty to answer a purely emotional appeal. Remind the jury that they have sworn not to decide the case on that basis.

Meeting Defendant's Argument

There is one basic rule that must apply here. *An explanation must now be offered as to all issues* which seem to materially aid the defendant's cause. The prosecutor must meet head on those portions of the defense argument which have hurt the state most.

This is the time for criticizing and pulling apart all of the illogical parts of the defendant's argument. Stress the matters that he has failed to answer. Emphasize the questions which you have posed and show that these have been ignored, evaded or sloughed over.

Improper Argument: in General

Although most courts are liberal in the latitude permitted counsel in summing up the evidence, his argument must, by law, be confined to the evidence and reasonable inferences to be drawn therefrom. It is improper, of course, to argue matters not in evidence or to misstate the evidence; to refer to evidence which has been excluded; to criticize the court's rulings or misstate the law; or to comment upon the failure of the defendant to take the stand in his own defense.[1] The United States Supreme Court has now clearly established that it is reversible error to comment upon the failure of the defendant to take the stand.[2]

Improper Argument: Defendant's Bad Reputation

It has also been held error to comment on the defendant's bad reputation where it has not been put in issue.[3]

A reversal will often result when there has been abusive characterization of the defendant. This is especially true when such characterization is not warranted by the evidence.

Failure of Defense to Produce Evidence

It is legitimate argument to comment upon the failure of your adversary to produce relevant evidence which is within his power to obtain or which is clearly subject to his control.[4] The prosecutor must clearly avoid any inference, however, that he is referring to the failure of the defendant to testify.

It has been held error for a prosecutor to make remarks during argument indicating that opposing counsel was attempting to suppress evidence by his failure to produce a particular witness, or was attempting to suppress physical evidence. Generally, however, where an explanation could be offered by such evidence, and it would clearly be within the province of the defendant to produce same, such reference is not objectionable.[5]

Such comment can be held improper if the witnesses are more readily accessible to the state.[6]

[1] Am. Jur., Pros. Attys. § 21, p. 256.
[2] Griffin v. California, 380 U.S. 609, 85 S.Ct. 1229, 14 L.Ed.2d 106 (1965).
[3] Fletcher v. State, 49 Ind. 124, 19 Am. Rep. 673 (1874); State v. Upham, 38 Me. 261 (1854).
[4] See Busch, *Law & Tactics in Jury Trials*, s. 518.
[5] 29 A.L.R.2d 996.
[6] People v. Rubin, 366 Ill. 195, 7 N.E.2d 890 (1937); People v. DePaulo, 235 N.Y. 39, 138 N.E. 498 (1923); Cole v. State, 92 Tex. Crim. 368, 243 S.W. 1100 (1922).

Likewise, the prosecutor may not make adverse comment upon the failure of defendant's spouse to testify for or against the other spouse where, for example, the wife of defendant is made incompetent to testify by statute, or pursuant to a privilege granted, the witness-spouse or both spouses must consent.[7]

Improper Argument: Prosecutor's Opinion as to Guilt

The prosecuting attorney must be careful not to express his personal belief or opinion in the guilt of the defendant, when the opinion is not based on the evidence adduced upon the trial.[8] It has been stated:

> "The role of the prosecuting attorney is a difficult one in many respects, and his argument to the jury is a particularly difficult problem in discrimination. He must pursue his duty as a diligent prosecutor without transgressing his responsibility as an officer of the state, and, above all, he must refrain from unduly oppressing or burdening the accused with the vast resources or dominating position of the state government. In particular, he must at all times bear in mind that defendant is innocent until proved guilty, and, while it is his duty to forcefully present all material facts from which the judge or jury may conclude that defendant is guilty, he must, nevertheless, refrain from pre-condemning the accused on the authority of the government he represents."[9]

A great deal of latitude is, of course, allowed in argument to the jury.[10] A prosecutor may lead the jurors to his own judgment by pointing out to them, independently and impartially, the evidence which cannot fairly justify any other conclusion. Although some cases have held that such assertion or belief merely puts into words what the very act of prosecution implies, it is wise to avoid such a direct statement. The test generally seems to be whether or not the conclusion reached by the prosecution is based on the evidence. In the absence of any indication to the contrary, the prosecutor's expressed opinion or belief will ordinarily be construed as his conclusion from the evidence introduced upon the trial.[11] Error has been assigned to

---

[7] Graves v. United States, 150 U.S. 118, 14 S.Ct. 40 (1893); Zumwalt v. State, 16 Ariz. 82, 141 P. 710 (1914); Johnson v. State, 63 Miss. 313 (1885).

[8] 50 A.L.R.2d 766.

[9] State v. Gulbrandsen, 238 Minn. 508, 57 N.W.2d 419 (1953).

[10] State v. Buttry, 199 Wash. 228, 90 P.2d 1026 (1939).

[11] People v. Ross, 120 Cal. App.2d 882, 262 P.2d 343 (1953); State v. Pisano, 33 N.J. Super. 559, 111 A.2d 279 (1955).

a statement in argument that the prosecutor would not have prosecuted the case unless he believed the defendant to be guilty. A great deal depends on whether the statement may be justified in final argument as being incited or provoked by statements of the defense counsel.

Clearly, the prosecuting attorney may not express his personal opinion or belief as to the guilt of the accused in such a way as to permit the jury to think that his opinion is based on information not placed in evidence or of which the prosecutor has some independent knowledge.[12]

Reading Law or Arguing Law

Although some jurisdictions hold otherwise, it is generally considered proper for the prosecutor to read and argue the law as given by the court. It is improper to read or argue law which has not been given by the court unless the law quoted has clear application and is correct in its statement.[13]

Improper Argument: Attacks Upon Counsel

While each case will have to determine its own byplay between adversary counsel, and will depend upon their particular traits or personalities, it is wise for the prosecutor to avoid, at all costs, attacks on opposing counsel. Whether or not such remarks will constitute prejudicial error depends on the facts of the particular case. Such remarks can run the gamut from charges of dishonesty to lesser acts of impropriety, and the like. The test as to whether or not such remarks are prejudicial will generally be an inquiry as to whether they brought to the jury's attention matters which it should not have considered.

It is certainly the duty of the prosecutor to conform to the high ethical standards expected of him as a representative of the people. Even though it is common practice for the defense counsel to "try" the prosecutor, as well as all the other persons involved except the defendant, such tactics usually defeat themselves and should not be dignified by counter-tactics of this nature.[14]

Reference to Release upon Acquittal for Insanity

Where a prosecutor has commented during argument that the defendant would be released from an institution if he were acquitted

[12] 42 J. Cr. L., C. & P.S. 73 (1951).
[13] 67 A.L.R.2d 245.
[14] 99 A.L.R.2d 508.

for insanity, the cases have produced opposite results.[15] Although such reference is generally considered harmless if the trial court takes some prompt curative action, it would seem best to avoid such direct reference to release. In most states where this issue arises, the defendant is entitled to an instruction that, upon acquittal by reason of insanity, he is to be committed to a mental hospital or similar institution. Without benefit of comment, this places the state in a difficult position. Since the only issue properly before the jury is that of insanity, references to the nature of treatment and/or release are usually improper. This argument should be sufficient to instill in the minds of the jury the necessity for determining guilt and not taking the easy way out, or compromising merely for the purpose of placing the defendant in a mental institution. A strong argument on the issue of insanity is the most effective approach. Testimony of an alienist as to unlikelihood of defendant's response to treatment is helpful at this point.

Improper Argument: Appeals to Prejudice

The prosecutor should avoid appeals to racial, national or religious bias. Statements which are reasonably calculated to appeal to, or evoke, racial, national or religious prejudice are universally condemned.[16]

Although such comments have been characterized by courts as hitting below the belt,[17] there are occasions when such statements are made inadvertently or may be provoked by argument of defense counsel. Such action can be rendered "harmless" by careful action on the part of the prosecutor or the court, by apology, deletion, or proper instruction. The test generally is whether such remark was calculated to engender such prejudice, whether the remark was unjustified, and whether the defendant has been deprived of his right to a fair and impartial trial.

Improper Argument: Reference to Public Opinion

It is generally held that prejudicial error would be assigned upon a prosecuting attorney's argument to the effect that the people of the state, county or community "want" or "expect" a conviction in the case, on the basis that the remark is a fact not in evidence and therefore a departure from the record.[18] Some courts have overlooked this where guilt was clearly shown by the entire record, or where the

[15] 44 A.L.R.2d 979.
[16] People v. Simon, 80 Cal. App. 675, 252 P. 758 (1927); 45 A.L.R.2d 303.
[17] Ross v. United States, 180 F.2d 160 (6th Cir. 1950).
[18] 85 A.L.R.2d 1137.

remark falls short of indicating a public demand for conviction. A remark that the people of the state would expect the jury to perform its duty has been held as not objectionable, and a general reference to the fact that jury verdicts as a whole establish a standard of conduct for others in the community has been held proper. Again, a great deal may depend upon what has been said by the defense attorney regarding the jurors' obligations in the case, and as to any reference made to community feeling. Recognizing that some latitude is allowed in summation, some courts have viewed such statements as being the usual rhetoric appeal to the jury and have considered the same harmless.

Punishment

In most states the jury has no duty to fix punishment, and in most jurisdictions where this is the exclusive function of the court, it is improper to make reference to the punishment prescribed by law.

Where it is within the province of the jury to fix the punishment for the particular offense, it is wise to first discuss these alternatives during voir dire examination of the jurors. This is particularly true where one of the alternatives is the assessment of the death penalty.

The jury should be reminded that upon voir dire examination each indicated that he would return a true verdict based upon the evidence and the applicable law, without regard to pity or sympathy or extraneous feelings or matters.

I deem it inadvisable for the prosecutor, representing the state, to appear before the jury and "demand" any particular type of punishment. This can serve to detract from your position, and can often cause the jury to stiffen against your appeal. A better approach is to stress all the alternatives and to indicate that, although it is exclusively their choice, a capital verdict or other punishment would clearly be proper under the circumstances. This can be done in such a way that there can be no doubt about your suggestion, and without causing the jurors to take issue with your premise.

Argument Invited by Opposing Counsel

This does not mean that you have no recourse to defendant's argument where the door has been opened for comments by you. There is authority that where remarks have been provoked and invited by opposing counsel, an otherwise improper reply may be proper.[19] It is thus important to have the defense argument reported.

[19] State v. Lindsay, 192 Wash. 356, 73 P.2d 391 (1937); see 42 J. Crim. L., C. & P.S. 73.

The line that the prosecutor must draw between "hard blows" and "foul ones" is often fine, and it is easy for an earnest prosecutor to unintentionally make remarks of an improper nature. The "harmless error" rule has application in these cases, and if the court feels that the prosecutor's statements were error, but not so prejudicial that they adversely affected the verdict, the appellate court will grant no reversal.

CONCLUSION

Adequate preparation is essential for even the most articulate prosecutor in the making of an opening statement and the delivery of final summations. Familiarity with the case and knowledge of witnesses is vital to proper preparation. Use of a trial plan or outline is recommended. Develop a technique best suited to your own personality, bearing in mind the necessity of conveying sincerity to the jury. Explain everything that seems the least bit confusing, either as to the evidence or the law.

Anticipate a defense issue if it will soften the blow. And meet head on all issues of substance raised by the defendant.

While the opening argument should be complete and forceful, the real thrust of your summation should be reserved for final argument. You must be prepared to encounter the usual emotional appeal. But don't over-argue: many a case is lost or harmed by over-argument.

It is interesting to observe that most articles on this subject are geared to the defense lawyer in criminal cases,[20] brimful of artful ways in which to delude the prosecution and with suggestions as to how to detract from the issues. Yet any treatise suggesting similar tactics for the prosecutor would be undoubtedly condemned as lamentable and shocking. In view of the unilateral right of appeal, most decisions ignore the histrionics of the defense lawyer while concentrating on the comportment of the prosecutor. Although it remains an adversary proceeding, demeanor, in practice, becomes pretty much of a one-way street. The prosecutor is at all times expected to proceed with dignity and ward off the snipes and jabs of the defense with restraint.

The closing argument is, therefore, the most effective weapon of the prosecutor. Style and content must be convincing. This is your best pitch as advocate for the people. You have the last word. Use it wisely!

✻ ✻ ✻ ✻ ✻

[20] Goldstein, TRIAL TECHNIQUE (Callaghan & Co.); Cornelius, TRIAL TACTICS (M. Bender); Busch, LAW & TACTICS IN JURY TRIALS (Bobbs-Merrill); Cohn, CRIMINAL LAW SEMINAR (Central Book Co. 1st & 2d ed.).

C. Instructing the Jury

FEDERAL RULES OF CRIMINAL PROCEDURE, RULE 30

INSTRUCTIONS

At the close of the evidence or at such earlier time during the trial as the court reasonably directs, any party may file written requests that the court instruct the jury on the law as set forth in the requests. At the same time copies of such requests shall be furnished to adverse parties. The court shall inform counsel of its proposed action upon the requests prior to their arguments to the jury, but the court shall instruct the jury after the arguments are completed. No party may assign as error any portion of the charge or omission therefrom unless he objects thereto before the jury retires to consider its verdict, stating distinctly the matter to which he objects and the grounds of his objection. Opportunity shall be given to make the objection out of the hearing of the jury and, on request of any party, out of the presence of the jury.

✻   ✻   ✻   ✻   ✻

NEW YORK CRIMINAL PROCEDURE LAW (1971)

§ 300.10 Court's charge and instructions; in general

1. At the conclusion of the summations, the court must deliver a charge to the jury.

2. In its charge, the court must state the fundamental legal principles applicable to criminal cases in general. Such principles include, but are not limited to, the presumption of the defendant's innocence, the requirement that guilt be proved beyond a reasonable doubt and that the jury may not, in determining the issue of guilt or innocence, consider or speculate concerning matters relating to sentence or punishment. Upon request of a defendant who did not testify in his own behalf, but not otherwise, the court must state that such failure to testify is not in itself a factor from which any inference unfavorable to the defendant may be drawn. The court must also state the material legal principles applicable to the particular case, and, so far as practicable, explain the application of the law to the facts, but it need not marshal or refer to the evidence to any greater extent than is necessary for such explanation.

3. The court must specifically designate and submit, in accordance with the provisions of sections 300.30 and 300.40, those counts and

offenses contained and charged in the indictment which the jury are to consider, and it must define each offense so submitted. Except as otherwise expressly provided, it must instruct the jury to render a verdict separately and specifically upon each count submitted to it, and with respect to each defendant if there be more than one, and must require that the verdict upon each such count be one of the following:

(a) "Guilty" of the offense submitted, if there be but one; or

(b) Where appropriate, "guilty" of a specified one of two or more offenses submitted under the same count in the alternative pursuant to section 155.40; or

(c) "Not guilty"; or

(d) Where appropriate "Not guilty by reason of mental disease or defect,"

4. Both before and after the court's charge, the parties may submit requests to charge, either orally or in writing, and the court must rule upon each request. A failure to rule upon a request is deemed a denial thereof.

§ 300.30 Court's submission of indictment to jury; definitions of terms

The following definitions are applicable to this article:

1. "Submission of a count" of an indictment means submission of the offense charged therein, or of a lesser included offense, or submission in the alternative of both the offense charged and a lesser included offense or offenses. When the court "submits a count," it must, at the least, submit the offense charged therein if such is supported by legally sufficient trial evidence, or if it is not, the greatest lesser included offense which is supported by legally sufficient trial evidence.

2. "Consecutive counts" means two or more counts of an indictment upon which consecutive sentences may be imposed in case of conviction thereon.

3. "Concurrent counts" means two or more counts of an indictment upon which concurrent sentences only may be imposed in case of conviction thereon.

4. "Inclusory concurrent counts." Concurrent counts are "inclusory" when the offense charged in one is greater than any of those charged in the others and when the latter are all lesser offenses included within the greater. All other kinds of concurrent counts are "non-inclusory."

5. "Inconsistent counts." Two counts are "inconsistent" when guilt

of the offense charged in one necessarily negates guilt of the offense charged in the other. . . .

§ 300.50   Court's submission of lesser included offenses

1.   In submitting a count of an indictment to the jury, the court in its discretion may, in addition to submitting the highest offense which it is required to submit, submit in the alternative any lesser included offense if there is a reasonable view of the evidence which would support a finding that the defendant committed such lesser offense but did not commit the greater. If there is no reasonable view of the evidence which would support such a finding, the court may not submit such lesser offense. Any error respecting such submission, however, is waived by the defendant unless he objects thereto before the jury retires to deliberate.

2.   If the court is authorized by subdivision one to submit a lesser included offense and is requested by either party to do so, it must do so. In the absence of such a request, the court's failure to submit such offense does not constitute error.

3.   The principles prescribed in subdivisions one and two apply equally where the lesser included offense is specifically charged in another count of the indictment.

4.   Whenever the court submits two or more offenses in the alternative pursuant to this section, it must instruct the jury that it may render a verdict of guilty with respect to any one of such offenses, depending upon its findings of fact, but that it may not render a verdict of guilty with respect to more than one. A verdict of guilty of any such offense is not deemed an acquittal of any lesser offense submitted but is deemed an acquittal of every greater offense submitted.

*   *   *   *   *

AMERICAN BAR ASSOCIATION PROJECT ON STANDARDS FOR THE ADMINISTRATION OF CRIMINAL JUSTICE, STANDARDS RELATING TO TRIAL BY JURY (Approved Draft 1968)

4.6   Jury instructions

(a)   A collection of accurate, impartial, and understandable pattern jury instructions should be available for use in criminal cases in each jurisdiction. Counsel and the court should nonetheless remain responsible for ensuring that the jury is adequately instructed as dictated by the needs of the individual case, and to that end should modify and supplement the pattern instructions whenever necessary.

(b)   At the close of the evidence or at such earlier time as the court reasonably directs, the court should allow any party to tender written instructions and may direct counsel to prepare designated instructions in writing. Copies of tendered instructions and instructions prepared at the direction of the court should be furnished the other parties.

(c) At a conference on instructions, which should be held out of the hearing of the jury, and, on request of any party, out of the presence of the jury, counsel should be afforded an opportunity to object to any instruction tendered by another party or prepared at the direction of the court. The court should advise counsel what instructions will be given prior to their delivery and, in any event, before the arguments to the jury. No party should be permitted to raise on appeal the failure to give an instruction unless he shall have tendered it, and no party should be permitted to raise on appeal the giving of an instruction unless he objected thereto, stating distinctly the matter to which he objects and the grounds of his objection. However, if the interests of justice so require, substantial defects or omissions should not be deemed waived by failure to object to or tender an instruction.

(d) After the jury is sworn the court may give preliminary instructions deemed appropriate for their guidance in hearing the case. After the arguments are completed, the court should give the jury all necessary instructions.

(e) All instructions, whether given or refused, should become a part of the record. All objections made to instructions and the rulings thereon should be included in the record.

Commentary

Section 4.6 (a)

Instructions to jurors should be "clear, concise, accurate and impartial statements of the law written in understandable language and delivered in conversational tone which will be helpful guidance to the jurors." Devitt, *Ten Practical Suggestions About Federal Jury Instructions,* 38 F.R.D. 75 (1966). It is frequently difficult to realize these several objectives, often because they tend to come into conflict with one another. For example, an undue emphasis upon ensuring accuracy may result in an instruction which is not understandable to laymen. Thus, "the language of decisions and statutes may represent correct and unimpeachable statements of the law, but the phraseology may be far removed from the jurors' comprehension." Parnell, *Uniform Jury Instructions,* 32 WIS. B. BULL. 58 (Aug. 1959); see also Devitt, *supra,* at 76. The preparation of instructions which meet these objectives, then, calls for the highest skills of draftsmanship. Because this is so, it is believed that the quality of instructions will be improved if there is available in each jurisdiction a set of pattern or model instructions prepared after sustained efforts at research and drafting by leading members of the bench and bar.

Concern over the jury instruction problem is reflected in a growing trend toward the development of pattern jury instructions in several jurisdictions. Wormwood, *Instructing the Jury*, 15 DEFENSE L. J. 1, 9 (1966). At least nine states currently have pattern jury instructions in one form or another, and work on such instructions is progressing in several other states. Note, 40 N. DAK. L. REV. 164, 165 (1964). Typically, work on such instructions has commenced with attention to civil trials, particularly negligence cases, but in some states work has been completed on instructions for criminal cases. See, *e.g.*, WISCONSIN JURY INSTRUCTIONS—CRIMINAL (1962); CALIFORNIA JURY INSTRUCTIONS—CRIMINAL (rev. ed. 1958). In other states, *e.g.*, Illinois and New York, work is currently under way on jury instructions for criminal cases. Such instructions are used by the military; see *e.g.*, AIR FORCE MANUAL 110–5.

"The reasons given for adoption of pattern jury instructions vary from state to state, and in order of importance; but generally there are five: accuracy, time savings, impartiality, intelligibility, uniformity." Note, 40 N. DAK. L. REV. 164, 165 (1964). The chairman of the Illinois jury instructions committee has set forth the virtues of pattern instructions as follows:

1. The judge will no longer be merely a reading agent reciting the argument of one side and then the other. Instead, he will talk to the jury about the law involved. The pattern instructions will provide a conversation in which the court tells the jury about the law, emphasizing the jury's province in applying the law.

2. The jury should have understandable, unslanted and accurate statements of the law in language the layman can understand.

3. There will be eliminated innumerable instructions now being given.

4. The time of both court and counsel needed to prepare and discuss instructions will be greatly reduced.

5. Attorneys practicing in different circuits, or even before different judges within the same circuit, will find a uniformity of opinion as to whether an instruction contains the proper language.

6. Conflicting decisions and interpretations of our courts on instructions now given, will be largely overcome.

7. The number of new trials granted and the reversals on appeal will be greatly reduced.

Snyder, *Illinois Pattern Jury Instructions*, 49 ILL. B. J. 230, 240 (1960). Other commentators have made similar observations. See, *e.g.*, Wiehl, *Instructing a Jury in Washington*, 36 WASH. L. REV. 378 (1961); Hannah, *Jury Instructions: An Appraisal by a Trial Judge*, 1963 U. ILL. L. F. 627; Corboy, *Pattern Jury Instructions—Their Function and Effectiveness*, 32 INS. COUNSEL J. 57 (1965).

The use of pattern jury instructions has been criticized by others. For example, the objection is made that pattern instructions tend to be more abstract and general in that they were prepared for continued use without the facts of any particular case in mind. Note, 40 N. DAK. L. REV. 164, 168 (1964). This may be a particularly cogent criticism with regard to instructions in civil negligence cases, involving an infinite variety of fact situations, Winslow, *The Instruction Ritual*, 13 HASTINGS L. J. 456 (1962), but would appear to be somewhat less applicable to instructions in criminal cases where the fact situations may be categorized to some extent by the various definitions and distinctions found in the substantive criminal code. That is, the chances of a pattern instruction on the elements of a particular offense being usable without alteration in a good many cases in which that offense is charged would seem to be greater than is true of many negligence instructions. Yet, even the draftsmen of pattern instructions for criminal cases acknowledge that these instructions must sometimes be modified or supplemented to suit the needs of an individual case. WISCONSIN JURY INSTRUCTIONS—CRIMINAL v (1962); CALIFORNIA JURY INSTRUCTIONS—CRIMINAL 14–15 (rev. ed. 1958).

The heart of the objection, then, goes not to the pattern instructions themselves, but rather to the practice which may develop by virtue of their existence. Counsel may come to rely unduly upon the pattern instructions and thus fail to modify or supplement these instructions as necessary to fit the needs of the individual case. Winslow, *supra*. Or, it may become "more and more difficult to convince the trial judge to accept even the slightest modification of the instructions . . . as well as to convince them to give any instruction that is not included" in the collection of pattern instructions. Close, *Theory and Practice of Standardized Jury Instructions*, 31 INS. COUNSEL J. 490 (1964). Thus, the second sentence of section (a) of the standard emphasizes the responsibility of both counsel and court to be alert to the possible need to modify and supplement the pattern instructions. See Devitt, *Ten Practical Suggestions About Federal Jury Instructions*, 38 F.R.D. 75,

77 (1966). Modified and supplemental instructions, of course, should also be simple, brief, impartial, and free from argument. See ILL. SUP. CT. RULE 239.

The standard merely states that pattern instructions should be available for use; it expresses no position on the degree to which these instructions should receive official sanction. Compare the situation in Illinois (which as yet has no pattern instructions for criminal cases), where the Supreme Court has directed that each applicable pattern instruction be used "unless the court determines that it does not accurately state the law," ILL. SUP. CT. RULE 239, with the situation in California, where the forms are not promulgated by statute or rule of court but it is the stated policy of some courts to use the instructions as far as practicable and to refuse specially prepared instructions where the subject matter is fully covered in the published instructions, Yerkes, *Standardized Jury Instructions in California,* 5 ST. LOUIS L. J. 347, 348–49 (1959), and with the situation in Wisconsin, where the instructions have been approved by the Board of Criminal Court Judges without certification that the instructions are free from error.

Section 4.6 (b)

State statutes and practice differ on the question of whether requests for instructions must be submitted in writing. UNIFORM RULES OF CRIMINAL PROCEDURE, rule 39, comment. The standard adopts the position of FED. R. CRIM. P. 30 and UNIFORM RULES OF CRIMINAL PROCEDURE, rule 39, that such requests should be in writing. "This makes for a good record and safeguards an objection on appeal." Devitt, *Ten Practical Suggestions About Federal Jury Instructions,* 38 F.R.D. 75 (1966).

The provision in the standard to the effect that the court may direct the preparation of certain instructions is not typically found in existing rules or statutes. The occasion for such direction would appear more likely where pattern instructions are in use; see ILL. SUP. CT. RULE 239 for a similar provision. In any event, this provision is particularly appropriate in criminal cases because of the special responsibility of the trial judge to ensure that certain essential instructions are given whether or not they are requested. See discussion in Commentary to § 4.6(c), *infra.*

The provision in the standard with regard to furnishing copies of instructions to other parties is similar to that found in FED. R. CRIM. P. 30 and UNIFORM RULES OF CRIMINAL PROCEDURE, rule 39. This ensures that there will be adequate opportunity for examination of the instructions by the other parties so that they may object to or concur in the content. While both the federal rule and the uniform rule refer to furnishing copies to "adverse parties," which is the language generally used, ILL. REV. STAT. ch. 110, § 67 (1965) (applicable also to criminal cases, ILL. SUP. CT. RULE 451) says copies are to be furnished "other parties." Use of the latter language in the standard is intended to make it clear that in a case in which there are several defendants represented by different counsel, each defense counsel should receive copies of instructions prepared by other defense counsel.

Section 4.6 (c)

The first two sentences of this subsection of the standard deal with matters typically covered in statutes or rules on jury instructions. It is, of course, important that counsel have an opportunity to raise objections to tendered instructions and to do so without being overheard by the jury, and that he be informed before the arguments to the jury what instructions will be given. See FED. R. CRIM. P. 30 and UNIFORM RULES OF CRIMINAL PROCEDURE, rule 39. Where, as contemplated in subsection (b) of this standard, the court may direct the preparation of instructions on a certain subject, it is necessary to recognize the right of any party to object to the instructions prepared at the direction of the court. See ILL. SUP. CT. RULE 239.

UNIFORM RULES OF CRIMINAL PROCEDURE, rule 39, provides that objections take place "out of the hearing of the jury." This language also appears in FED. R. CRIM. P. 30, but by virtue of a recent amendment there has been added thereto: "and, on request of any party, out of the presence of the jury." A third approach is that in ILL. REV. STAT. ch. 110 § 67 (1965), which provides for settling instructions at a conference which "must be out of the presence of the jury." Section 4.6(c) conforms to the recent amendment of Federal Rule 30; the Advisory Committee is of the view that it provides adequate protection.

It is not unusual to include in statutes or rules on jury instructions some provision on waiver. Generally, the position is that a defendant may not complain on appeal about instructions unless his counsel took sufficient action at trial, either by the tender of instructions or objection to proposed instructions, to apprise the trial judge of his view as to what the instructions should be. Thus, FED. R. CRIM. P. 30 reads: "No party may assign as error any portion of the charge or omission therefrom unless he objects thereto before the jury retires to consider its verdict, stating distinctly the matter to which he objects and the grounds of his objection." But, notwithstanding the existence of this provision and similar language in other jurisdictions, it is not strictly correct to say that appeal as to a matter of instructions is absolutely barred by a failure to object or tender the proper instruction. This is because the federal courts and most state courts have taken the position that in a criminal case the trial judge has a responsibility to ensure that certain essential instructions are given. Certain basic instructions, essential to a fair determination of the case by the jury (e.g., burden of proof, elements of offense charged), must be given, and the concept of waiver will not be employed to bar reversal if a defendant has been convicted in the absence of these instructions. See 1 MATTHEWS, How TO TRY A FEDERAL CRIMINAL CASE 666ff (1960) (federal); CALIFORNIA JURY INSTRUCTIONS—CRIMINAL 8–13 (rev. ed. 1958) (California); Note, 1963 WASH. U. L. Q. 353 (1963) (Missouri); Note, 33 ROCKY MT. L. REV. 427 (1961) (Colorado); Comment, 57 Nw. U.L. REV. 62, 68–71 (1962) (generally, but with special reference to duty as to lesser included offenses). Thus, the third sentence in subsection (c) of the standard is qualified by the fourth sentence, which is based upon ILL. SUP. CT. RULE 451.

Section 4.6 (d)

The first sentence in subsection (d) provides that the court may give certain instructions immediately after the jury is sworn. This is currently the practice, at least as to certain cases, in some states. Wormwood, *Instructing the Jury*, 15 DEFENSE L. J. 1, 2–4 (1966). In a number of appellate cases in which criminal defendants objected to the giving of instructions at that time, it has been held that the giving of certain instructions at the outset of the trial is proper. See cases collected in Annot., 89 A.L.R.2d 197, 200 n.2 (1963). A number of commentators have recommended the practice. Wormwood, *supra*, at 2; Winslow, *The Instruction Ritual*, 13 HASTINGS L. J. 456, 470 (1962); Prettyman, *Jury Instructions—First or Last?*, 46 A.B.A.J. 1066 (1960). Judge Prettyman states:

> I submit it makes no sense to have a juror listen to days of testimony only then to be told that he and his confreres are the sole judges of the facts, that the accused is presumed to be innocent, that the government must prove guilt beyond a reasonable doubt, etc. What manner of mind can go back over a stream of conflicting statements of alleged facts, recall the intonations, the demeanor, or even the existence of the witnesses, and retrospectively fit all these recollections into a pattern of evaluation and judgment given him for the first time after the events? The *human* mind cannot do so. It is not a magnetized tape from which recorded speech can be repeated at chosen speed and volume. The fact of the mat-

ter is that this order of procedure makes much of the trial of a law-suit mere mumbo jumbo. It sound all right to the professional technicians who are the judge and the lawyers. It reads all right to the professional technicians who are the court of appeals. But to the laymen sitting in the box, restricted to listening, the whole thing is a fog.

Why should not the judge, when the jury is sworn, then and there tell them the rules of the game: (a) the function of the in-dictment, (b) the function of the jury as the sole judges of the facts, (c) the restriction of their consideration to the evidence, (d) the presumption of innocence of the accused, (e) the burden of reasonable doubt, (f) matters concerning credibility, (g) the functions of court and counsel, (h) the elements of the crimes charged, (i) a glossary of some of the terms to be used, (j) ad-monition as to outside conversation, newspaper accounts, etc., (k) explanation of the verdict and how it is reached—all the explana-tory data which will put jurymen in the best possible position to perform the responsible task assigned to them.

Thus, the judge would instruct only as to the facets of functions and procedure which are general in application. And, of course, before the taking of the proof, he would not discuss any of the facts in the particular controversy about to be tried. The court should also instruct the jury at the end of the trial just before they retire. At that time should come his discussion of the case at hand, and he should recall then such parts of his initial instructions as need repeating.

I know we now have printed handbooks for jurors given them in advance, but these are no substitutes for the live, face-to-face, instruction and explanation from the judge on the bench. Some judges do instruct at the beginning of a trial. I submit to my brethren of the Bench and Bar it is a sensible course to follow.

Prettyman, *supra*, at 1066.

Even if certain instructions are given after the jury is sworn, it will nonetheless be necessary for the jury to be instructed before they re-tire for deliberations. The instructions given at this time will include at least some of the instructions which were given when the trial opened. The second sentence of subsection (d) provides for these instructions to be given after the arguments are completed.

FED. R. CRIM. P. 30 provides for instruction after argument, and a substantial number of states are in accord. In some jurisdictions, how-ever, it is the practice to instruct the jury prior to argument. UNIFORM

RULES OF CRIMINAL PROCEDURE, rule 39, comment. The latter practice has been criticized on the ground "that by the time the jury has sat through the bias and possibly heated comments of opposing counsel, what little law the jury may have comprehended from the charge will have entirely escaped them. It is said that this procedure leaves little chance for the court's words to make any impression upon the jurors." Comment, 49 MARQ. L. REV. 137, 140 (1965). On the other hand, it is contended that this practice "gives counsel the opportunity to explain the instructions, argue their application to the facts and thereby give the jury the maximum assistance in determining the issues and arriving at a good verdict on the law and the evidence. As an ancillary benefit, this approach aids counsel by supplying him with a natural outline, that is, his arguments may be directed to the essential fact issues which the jury must decide." Raymond, *Merits and Demerits of the Missouri System of Instructing Juries*, 5 ST. LOUIS L. J. 317 (1959). Similarly, it has been pointed out that it is preferable if counsel in argument can argue the facts as they apply to the law as already given to the jury in instructions, rather than for counsel to advise the jury that certain instructions will be forthcoming on the law. Wormwood, *Instructing the Jury*, 15 DEFENSE L. J. 1, 5 (1966). See also Blatt, *Judge's Charge to Jury Should Precede Arguments of Counsel*, 33 J. AM. JUD. SOC'Y 56 (1949). The Advisory Committee has found the case made for instruction after argument slightly more persuasive.

The Advisory Committee takes no position on whether all instructions should be in writing, read by the court to the jury, and then taken to the jury room by the jury. The practice of having written instructions read to the jury has been criticized by some commentators, who have expressed a preference for extemporaneous instructions. It has been contended that the practice "under which the written instructions are read verbatim by the court and then handed to the jury" is "at the root of many of the evils of the instructing system." Wright, *Adequacy of Instructions to the Jury: I*, 53 MICH. L. REV. 505, 509 (1955). The basic complaint is that "the obscurity of instructions results in a large part from the requirement in many states that they be written and be read to the jury verbatim" and that instructions would be far more meaningful to jurors upon an "oral presentation, with the repetition and emphasis necessary to convey meaning." Comment, 49 MARQ. L. REV. 137, 139 (1965). See also Editorial Notes, 15 DEFENSE L. J. 15, 16 (1966).

On the other hand, it is argued that the practice of reading written instructions, together with the use of pattern jury instructions and written submissions by the parties, is more likely to result in instructions which are accurate and free from reversible error. The use of written instructions, it is said, "results in a charge which will be better considered and more clearly expressed than an oral charge would ordinarily be." Comment, *supra*, at 139. "Many judges have the happy faculty of reading, but not appearing to read, their instructions and thus achieve the accuracy which reading ensures and the effectiveness which oral instructions afford." Devitt, *Ten Practical Suggestions About Federal Jury Instructions*, 38 F.R.D. 75, 79 (1966).

As to the matter of jurors carrying the written instructions to the jury room, this is a common but not universal practice. In a fairly recent survey of the law of the several states regarding this matter in criminal cases, it was found that 20 states permitted the taking of instructions to the jury room, 11 states required that they be taken, and only one state prohibited the practice. CALIFORNIA LAW REVISION COMMISSION, RECOMMENDATION AND STUDY RELATING TO TAKING INSTRUCTIONS TO THE JURY ROOM 15–17 (1956). The federal statutes and the federal rules are silent on the question, but a number of cases have upheld the practice of sending written instructions to the jury room. *Id.* at 10. The case for giving a copy of the instructions to the jury has been summarized as follows:

> The instructions are intended to guide the jury's deliberations. Yet, even in a relatively simple case they are usually lengthy and complex. It is hardly reasonable to suppose that the jury, composed as it is of persons unfamiliar with either law or legal language and having heard the instructions but once as given orally by the court, will be able to remember them in detail as it ponders the matters committed to it for decision. Thus, it would seem to be altogether fitting, if not indeed essential, that the jury have a copy of the instructions at hand with which to refresh its recollection as to the issues in the case and the law applicable thereto if it wishes to do so.

Id. at 10–11. See also Cunningham, *Should Instructions Go Into the Jury Room?*, 33 CALIF. S.B.J. 278 (1958).

While the Advisory Committee believes that there is some merit to the arguments which have been made in favor of the court reading written instructions and then sending them to the jury room, this procedure has not been included in section 4.6 because it is recognized that it would be impractical in many jurisdictions. Many judges do not have secretaries or law clerks available, and those who do ordinarily do not keep these personnel on duty until the case is submitted to a jury. Instructions submitted by attorneys often must be modified, and if they are not retyped there is a risk that jurors will give undue emphasis to interlineations and other modifications. Also, if instructions are to be send to the jury, then the same practice should ordinarily be followed as to additional instructions requested by the jury after some deliberation. See Commentary to § 5.3, *infra.* If a jury deliberating in the evening asks for additional instructions, it is unlikely that there will be someone present who could promptly reduce the additional instructions to writing.

Section 4.6 (e)

This part of the standard deals with the need for an adequate record with regard to jury instructions. It provides that all instructions, whether given or refused, should become a part of the record and that the record should include objections to and ruling on instructions. Such a record is necessary if the appellate court is to be able to consider alleged errors in instructions, particularly when there is no substantial defect and the defendant must establish that he made a specific objection or tendered a proper instruction. The record should also show what party tendered each instruction given or refused.

4.7   Summary of and comment on evidence

(a) The court, at the time it instructs the jury, may summarize and comment on the evidence, provided the jury is clearly and unequivocally instructed that it is the exclusive judge of the facts, that it is to determine the weight of the evidence and the credibility of witnesses, and that it is not bound by the comments of the court.

(b) The summary and comment permitted in subsection (a) is governed by the following principles:

(i) The court may analyze the evidence, draw the attention of the jury to important portions of the evidence, and fairly and accurately summarize the contentions of both the prosecution and the defense.

(ii) The court may not suggest a verdict of guilty or not guilty, nor may the court directly express any opinion on the guilt or innocence of the defendant.

(iii) The court may not present any item of evidence as a proven or undisputed fact unless the matter has been affirmatively conceded or is the subject of judicial notice.

(iv) The court may state the law and comment on matters in evidence bearing on the credibility of any witness, but may not directly express an opinion that certain testimony is worthy or unworthy of belief.

Commentary

Section 4.7 (a)

The practice of judicial comment on the evidence existed at common law from the beginning of jury trial. HALE, HISTORY OF THE COMMON LAW OF ENGLAND (5th ed. 1820). As the Supreme Court has observed, "A jury trial in which the judge is deprived of the right to comment on the evidence and to express his opinion on the facts . . . is not the jury trial which we inherited." Patton v. United States, 281 U.S. 276, 288 (1930). But, while the federal courts have retained this power, in the overwhelming majority of states this function of the trial judge was taken from him by constitutional provision, statute, or judicial decision. 9 WIGMORE, EVIDENCE § 2551 (3d ed. 1940); ORFIELD, CRIMINAL PROCEDURE FROM ARREST TO APPEAL 457 (1947). The constitutionality of statutes forbidding comment has been upheld. People v. Kelly, 347 Ill. 221, 179 N.E. 898 (1932).

While it has been said that there has been a "strong movement" to return to the common law power in the states since 1910, ORFIELD, *supra*, at 458, a great majority of the states still do not permit the practices allowed in the above standard. About 20 states allow neither comment nor summary, a slightly smaller number are said to allow summary only, while the rest allow both summary and comment on the evidence. KALVEN & ZEISEL, THE AMERICAN JURY 420 (1966). In about half of the states included in the intermediate position, the trial judge has in fact been so limited that he has little if any authority to summarize the evidence. Wright, *The Invasion of Jury: Temperature of the War*, 27 TEMPLE L. Q. 137, 161 (1953).

But, while approximately three-quarters of the states do not allow comment, with very few exceptions the articles and reports on the subject urge a return to the common law view. See materials cited, *id.* at 139–41. In 1938 the American Bar Association adopted a recommendation that "the common-law concept of the function and authority of the trial judge be uniformly restored in the states which have departed therefrom" and that the trial judge "should have power to advise them [the jury] as to the facts by summarizing and analyzing the evidence and commenting upon the weight and credibility of the evidence or upon any part of it, always leaving the final decision on questions of fact to the jury." VANDERBILT, MINIMUM STANDARDS OF JUDICIAL ADMINISTRATION 221 (1949). The ABA Section of Judicial Administration has continued to press for these reforms over the years. See, *e.g.*, AMERICAN BAR ASSOCIATION, THE IMPROVEMENT OF THE ADMINISTRATION OF JUSTICE (4th ed. 1961). The American Law Institute has taken the same view, as has the National Conference of Commissioners on Uniform State Laws, Subsection (a) of the above standard is based upon and is similar to the ABA recommendation, ALI CODE OF CRIMINAL PROCEDURE § 325 (1930); ALI MODEL CODE OF EVIDENCE, rule 8 (1942); and the UNIFORM RULES OF CRIMINAL PROCEDURE, rule 39.

The case in support of the view taken in the above standard has been stated in the following terms by one federal judge:

> A mere series of abstract principles of law stated by the judge is not always well understood, or practically applied by a group of laymen, if the judge is shorn of the power to discuss the facts and the evidence which must be measured by these rules. It is sometimes customary to speak of the right of the judge to discuss the facts and comment on the evidence. It should be better called the authority or power of the judge. It is the jury that has the right to receive the advice and assistance of the judge. It is the jury that under the prevailing state system is deprived of the aid to which it was entitled at common law. Necessarily, in such instances the judge is transformed into not much more than a presiding officer or a moderator at the trial, while the jury tends to become sovereign. Extreme appeals of advocacy are more likely to sway or to have undue effect on the jury under these circumstances, because it lacks the guidance and the stabilizing influence of the judge. Such criticisms as have been directed against the jury system generally relate to trials in the state courts and are due largely to these circumstances.
>
> The judge's discussion of the evidence is intended to assist the jury and thereby to aid it in arriving at a just result. It tends to clarify the issues, to enable the jury to discard extraneous matters that are at times injected into a trial, and to concentrate and focus the attention of the jury on the crucial points of the case. The judge is in a position to place the various items of evidence in their proper setting and to restore them to their correct proportions, rather than to permit them to remain in the distorted shape that they assume as a result of partisan presentation of counsel. On occasion the judge's observations may assist the jury in resolving doubts or misgivings as to the weight to be accorded or the importance to be attached to some phase of the evidence.
>
> The test of desirability of the common law procedure is whether it is conducive to just verdicts and therefore aids in a proper administration of justice. This question answers itself. It is capable

only of an affirmative response. Counsel for the parties are permitted to summarize the evidence and to comment on the facts from their standpoint. Their presentation must of necessity be one-sided and argumentative. The judge is the only impartial lawyer participating in the trial and the only lawyer in a position to give unbiased advice to the jury. It seems a paradox, therefore, to permit counsel to discuss the facts, but to bar the judge from doing so.

Holtzoff, *Modern Trends in Trial by Jury*, 16 WASH. & LEE L. REV. 27, 32–33 (1959). Others have likewise stated a persuasive case for return to the common law rule; see, *e.g.*, ABA, *supra*, at 66–67; DEVLIN, TRIAL BY JURY 115–16 (1956); ORFIELD, *supra*, at 457; VANDERBILT, *supra*, at 221–30; WIGMORE, *supra*, at § 2551a.

Some years ago a large number of lawyers with experience before judges who do comment on the evidence and before judges who do not were questioned concerning the relative merit of comment and no-comment rules:

> Of fifteen hundred and sixty-five lawyers with the requisite trial experience, eleven hundred and eighty-one, or more than seventy-five per cent, believe that the historic rule brings quicker verdicts and fewer disagreements than the currently prevailing rule. Of fifteen hundred and thirty-five, seven hundred and seventy-one, or slightly over fifty per cent, think it tends to reduce the number of new trials granted or applied for on the ground that the verdict is against the weight of the evidence. Of fifteen hundred and thirty-one, only three hundred and forty-seven, or less than twenty-three per cent, are of the opinion that it makes or would tend to make attorneys less exacting in empanelling the jury. And of fourteen hundred and eighty-six, at least three hundred and eighteen, or about twenty-two per cent, have observed its tendency to make the trial judge pay closer attention to the evidence. Of sixteen hundred and seventy-six, nine hundred and seven, or slightly more than fifty-four per cent, express the view that the court's comment upon the weight and credibility of the testimony assists the jury in reaching correct conclusions, but only six hundred and sixty-three out of fifteen hundred and nine, or less than forty-four per cent, believe that it cures errors in rulings upon evidence or in misconduct of counsel.

> From these statements the conclusion seems justified that in actual practice the privilege of proper comment has the following beneficial effects: (1) It saves time and expense by bringing

quicker verdicts, reducing the number of disagreements, and diminishing the number of new trials and applications for new trials. (2) It has an appreciable effect upon a substantial percentage of attorneys in making them spend less time in examining prospective jurors . . . . (3) It operates to a considerable degree to induce the trial judge to pay close attention to the conduct of the trial.

Report of The Commonwealth Fund, quoted in ALI MODEL CODE OF EVIDENCE 83–85 (1942).

Those who oppose the comment rule object that the trial judge may abuse the privilege of comment and engage in "partisan advocacy." *The Right of a Judge to Comment on the Evidence in His Charge to the Jury,* 6 F.R.D. 317, 330 (1947). However, the authority to comment is restricted and is subject to review. As the Supreme Court noted in Quercia v. United States, 289 U.S. 466, 470 (1933):

> This privilege of the judge to comment on the facts has its inherent limitations. His discretion is not arbitrary and uncontrolled, but judicial, to be exercised in conformity with the standards governing judicial office. In commenting upon testimony he may not assume the role of a witness. He may analyze and dissect the evidence, but he may not either distort it or add to it. His privilege of comment in order to give appropriate assistance to the jury is too important to be left without safeguard against abuses.

It would appear that the comment privilege of federal judges is not abused. One study covering 12 years noted that of 5,781 federal criminal cases tried to juries and appealed in only 85 cases was any complaint made about the judge's comments. The comments were held to be reversible error in but 30 of these cases, and were criticized in but two others. WIGMORE, *supra,* at § 2551a.

Some of those who oppose the comment rule have suggested that the trial judge should merely be allowed to summarize the evidence. 6 F.R.D. at 326. Because the advocates of the comment rule acknowledge that the comment prerogative is not often used, Wright, *Instructions to the Jury: Summary Without Comment,* 1954 WASH. U. L. Q. 177, it has been noted that it might be argued that an appropriate "compromise" might be a rule which allowed summary without comment. *Ibid.* Such a compromise has been rejected here, for "the brute fact is that this compromise has been tried since 1796, and has always failed. The compromise systems inevitably shrink into the custom of merely stating the pleadings, issues or contentions, or they expand into something substantially indistinguishable from the minority system." *Ibid.* The former is most likely, as where judges have the power to summarize only, they are reluctant to use it for fear of transgressing the no-comment rule. ABA, *supra,* at 66. It should also be noted that the fact the comment power is not frequently used does not mean that the power is unnecessary. The mere existence of the power serves to deter abuse by counsel. VANDERBILT, *supra,* at 225.

Section 4.7 (b)

This standard should not be read as embracing all forms of summary and comment which at one time or another have been approved by federal courts or by courts in the few states permitting summary and comment. There has been general but not universal agreement on some of the more important principles governing this power, and they are set forth in section 4.7(b). However, there is a considerable divergence of opinion as to certain other practices, and section 4.7(b) generally takes a restrictive view of these.

Section 4.7(b)(i) provides that "the court may analyze the evidence" and "draw the attention of the jury to important portions of the evidence." This is substantially the language used by the Supreme Court in Quercia v. United States, 289 U.S. 466 (1933) in defining and circumscribing the power to summarize and comment. Section 4.7(b)(i) also emphasizes that it is the responsibility of the court, in summarizing and commenting on the evidence, to ensure that he does not merely state the evidence of the prosecution or that of the defense. See Boatright v. United States, 105 F.2d 737 (8th Cir., 1939). It is the responsibility of the trial judge to fairly and accurately set forth the relevant evidence, both that which is favorable and that which is unfavorable to the accused. Byford v. United States, 185 F.2d 171 (10th Cir. 1950). His statements must not be argumentative, but impartial and dispassionate. *Ibid.* The trial judge must exercise restraint and be careful to be impartial in appearance as well as in fact. Holmes v. United States, 271 F.2d 635 (4th Cir. 1959).

Section 4.7(b)(ii) provides that the court "may not suggest a verdict of guilty or not guilty, nor may the court directly express an opinion on the guilt or innocence of the defendant." This proscription, of course, relates to cases which go to the jury, and has no effect upon the power of the court to grant a judgment of acquittal. See § 4.5. Because the judge does not have the power to direct a conviction, it follows that he is not authorized to advocate a verdict of guilty in his instructions. Buchanan v. United States, 244 F.2d 916 (6th Cir. 1957).

Under current law, an expression of belief in the defendant's guilt is not absolutely barred. In Horning v. District of Columbia, 254 U.S. 135 (1920), the Court held that such an expression was not reversible error where all the facts were admitted, but in United States v. Murdock, 290 U.S. 389 (1933), the Court admonished that such an expression should be limited to "exceptional cases." Subsequent federal cases have been quite strict, holding that the judge should not express such an opinion even when the defendant introduces no evidence or when the defendant testifies to the most implausible story, but a handful of states "have ignored the policy of the *Murdock* decision and allowed comment on the guilt issue as long as such comment is 'fair and temperate.'" Comment, 9 VILL. L. REV. 440, 452 (1964). The Advisory Committee is of the view that the trial judge should not be authorized to "urge his own view of the guilt or innocence of the accused." Billeci v. United States, 184 F.2d 394 (D.C. Cir. 1950).

What section 4.7(b)(ii) prohibits is a direct expression of an opinion on guilt or innocence, such as "It is my belief that the defendant is guilty" or "If I had the power to direct you to find the defendant guilty I would." Such direct expressions are to be distinguished from comments on the evidence which may tend to show the strengths or weaknesses of the case presented by the prosecution or defense.

Section 4.7(b)(iii) provides that the trial judge should not "present any item of evidence as a proven or undisputed fact unless the matter has been affirmatively conceded or is the subject of judicial notice." This means that in the course of summarizing the evidence, the judge should not set forth the testimony on one side or another as if it consisted of established facts. See Hardy v. United States, 335 F.2d 288, 290 n.2 (D.C. Cir. 1964), and Blunt v. United States, 244 F.2d 355 (D.C. Cir. 1957), for illustrations of the kind of summary prohibited. The exception in the standard, it should be noted, is stated more narrowly than it has been expressed by some courts. Sometimes it is said that an instruction which assumes an admitted *or* uncontroverted fact is proper *e.g.*, United States v. Salliey, 360 F.2d 699 (4th Cir. 1966); Malone v. United States, 238 F.2d 851 (6th Cir. 1956). This position has been rejected by the Advisory Committee, as the failure of the defendant to present contradictory testimony or even to cross-examine on the fact testified to does not justify the conclusion that the defendant has accepted the government's contention or that the jury might not find a reasonable doubt to exist on this particular point. See United States v. Gollin, 166 F.2d 123 (3d Cir. 1948). It is likewise inappropriate to tell the jury that a portion of the government's evidence is "undisputed," as "all issues not affirmatively conceded are 'disputed' on a plea of not guilty," and "to tell the jury that something is undisputed may well suggest that it is conceded. If the court wishes to comment on the evidence, or to summarize the evidence, it should ordinarily do so in a manner that does not reflect on the defendant's failure to offer rebuttal." Flaherty v. United States, 355 F.2d 924 (1st Cir. 1966). See also Desmond v. United States, 345 F.2d 225 (1st Cir. 1965); Kitchell v. United States, 354 F.2d 715 (1st Cir. 1966).

Section 4.7(b)(iv) deals with comment regarding the credibility of a witness, which has proved to be a most troublesome area and one in which excessive comment is perhaps most frequent. The thrust of section 4.7(b)(iv) is that special caution must be exercised in making such comments. Illustrative of the kinds of comments not permitted are: that it may be assumed the witness is lying because of his mannerisms, Quercia v. United States, 289 U.S. 466 (1933); or that one witness was more worthy of belief because he was a stranger to the courts, United States v. Meltzer, 100 F.2d 739 (7th Cir. 1938). The standard permits the judge to put to the jury appropriate legal principles on credibility and to point out relevant matters in evidence, such as conflicts in testimony of a witness or between testimony of witnesses. But, the judge may not "intimate that certain testimony is worthy or unworthy of belief." United States v. Bookie, 229 F.2d 130 (7th Cir. 1956). As one court said of a trial judge's statement that in his opinion a witness was not to be believed, "however much justification there was for the inference drawn by the court and certified to the jury, the invasion by the court into the province of the jury in the determination of matters of credibility cannot be sanctional." Stevens v. United States, 306 F.2d 834 (5th Cir. 1962).

* * * * *

D. Jury Deliberation and Verdict

FEDERAL RULES OF CRIMINAL PROCEDURE, RULE 31

VERDICT

(a) **Return.** The verdict shall be unanimous. It shall be returned by the jury to the judge in open court.

(b) **Several Defendants.** If there are two or more defendants, the jury at any time during its deliberations may return a verdict or verdicts with respect to a defendant or defendants as to whom it has agreed; if the jury cannot agree with respect to all, the defendant or defendants as to whom it does not agree may be tried again.

(c) **Conviction of Less Offense.** The defendant may be found guilty of an offense necessarily included in the offense charged or of an attempt to commit either the offense charged or an offense necessarily included therein if the attempt is an offense.

(d) **Poll of Jury.** When a verdict is returned and before it is recorded the jury shall be polled at the request of any party or upon the court's own motion. If upon the poll there is not unanimous concurrence, the jury may be directed to retire for further deliberations or may be discharged.

*   *   *   *   *

NEW YORK CRIMINAL PROCEDURE LAW (1971)

§ 70.10   Standards of proof; definitions of terms

The following definitions are applicable to this chapter:

1. "Legally sufficient evidence" means evidence which, if accepted as true, would establish every element of an offense charged and the defendant's commission thereof; except that such evidence is not legally sufficient when corroboration required by law is absent.

2. "Reasonable cause to believe that a person has committed an offense" exists when evidence or information which appears reliable discloses facts or circumstances which are collectively of such weight and persuasiveness as to convince a person of ordinary intelligence, judgment and experience that it is reasonably likely that such offense was committed and that such person committed it. Except as otherwise provided in this chapter, such apparently reliable evidence may include or consist of hearsay.

§ 35.20   Standards of proof for conviction

No conviction of an offense by verdict is valid unless based upon trial evidence which is legally sufficient and which establishes beyond a reasonable doubt every element of such offense and the defendant's commission thereof.

§ 310.10   Jury deliberation; requirement of; where conducted

Following the court's charge, the jury must retire to deliberate upon its verdict in a place outside the courtroom. It must be provided with suitable accommodations therefor and must be continuously kept together under the supervision of an appropriate public servant or servants. Except when so authorized by the court or when performing administerial duties with respect to the jurors, such public servant or servants may not speak to or communicate with them or permit any other person to do so.

§ 310.20   Jury deliberation; use of exhibits and other material

Upon retiring to deliberate, the jurors may take with them:

1. Any exhibits received in evidence at the trial which the court, after according the parties an opportunity to be heard upon the matter, in its discretion permits them to take; and

2. A written list prepared by the court containing the offenses submitted to the jury by the court in its charge and the possible verdicts thereon.

§ 310.30   Jury deliberation; request for information

At any time during its deliberation, the jury may request the court for further instruction or information with respect to the law, with respect to the content or substance of any trial evidence, or with respect to any other matter pertinent to the jury's consideration of the case. Upon such a request, the court must direct that the jury be returned to the courtroom and, after notice to both the people and counsel for the defendant, and in the presence of the defendant, give such requested information or instruction as the court deems proper.

§ 310.40   Verdict; rendition thereof

1. The verdict must be rendered and announced by the foreman of the jury in the courtroom in the presence of both the court and the defendant. The prosecutor may as a matter of right be present but may waive such right.

2. Before rendering and announcing the verdict, the foreman of the jury must be asked whether the jury has agreed upon a verdict and must answer in the affirmative.

§ 310.50   Verdict; form; reconsideration of defective verdict

1. The form of the verdict must be in accordance with the court's instructions, as prescribed in article three hundred.

2. If the jury renders a verdict which in form is not in accordance with the court's instructions or which is otherwise legally defective, the court must explain the defect or error and must direct the jury to reconsider such verdict, to resume its deliberation for such purpose, and to render a proper verdict. If the jury persists in rendering a defective or improper verdict, the court may in its discretion either order

that the verdict in its entirety as to any defendant be recorded as an acquittal, or discharge the jury and authorize the people to retry the indictment or a specified count or counts thereof as to such defendant; provided that if it is clear that the jury intended to find in favor of a defendant upon any particular count, the court must order that the verdict be recorded as an acquittal of such defendant upon such count.

3. If the court accepts a verdict which is defective or incomplete solely by reason of the jury's failure to render a verdict upon every count upon which it was instructed to do so, such verdict is deemed to constitute an acquittal upon every such count improperly ignored in the verdict.

§ 310.60 Discharge of jury before rendition of verdict and effect thereof

1. A deliberating jury may be discharged by the court without having rendered a verdict only when:

    (a) The jury has deliberated for an extensive period of time without agreeing upon a verdict with respect to any of the charges submitted and the court is satisfied that any such agreement is unlikely within a reasonable time; or

    (b) The court, the defendant and the people all consent to such discharge; or

    (c) A mistrial is declared pursuant to section 280.10.

2. When the jury is so discharged, the defendant or defendants may be retried upon the indictment. Upon such retrial, the indictment is deemed to contain all the counts which it contained at the time the previous trial was commenced, regardless of whether any count was dismissed by the court in the course of such trial.

§ 310.70 Rendition of partial verdict and effect thereof

1. If a deliberating jury declares that it has reached a verdict with respect to one or more but not all of the charges submitted to it, or with respect to one or more but not all of the defendants, the court must proceed as follows:

    (a) If the possibility of ultimate agreement with respect to the other charges or defendants is so small and the circumstances are such that if they were the only matters under consideration the court would be authorized to discharge the jury pursuant to paragraph (a) of subdivision one of section 310.60, the court must terminate the deliberation and order the jury to render a partial verdict with respect to those counts and defendants upon which or with respect to whom it has reached a verdict, and judgment must eventually be imposed accordingly;

(b) If the court is satisfied that there is a reasonable possibility of ultimate agreement upon any of the unresolved charges with respect to any defendant, it may either:

(i) Order the jury to render its verdict with respect to those charges and defendants upon which or with respect to whom it has reached agreement and resume its deliberation upon the remainder; or

(ii) Refuse to accept a partial verdict at the time and order the jury to resume its deliberation upon the entire case.

2. Upon the rendition of a partial verdict pursuant to subdivision one, a defendant may be retried upon an unresolved count of an indictment when such unresolved count is consecutive, as that term is defined in subdivision two of section 300.30, as to every count upon which the jury did render a verdict, whether of guilty or not guilty.

§ 310.80 Recording and checking of verdict and polling of jury

After a verdict has been rendered, it must be recorded on the minutes and read to the jury, and the jurors must be collectively asked whether such is their verdict. Even though no juror makes any declaration in the negative, the jury must, upon application of either party, be polled and each juror separately asked whether the verdict announced by the foreman is in all respects his verdict. If upon either the collective or the separate inquiry any juror answers in the negative, the court must refuse to accept the verdict and must direct the jury to resume its deliberation. If no disagreement is expressed, the jury must be discharged from the case, except as otherwise provided in sections 125.30 and 125.35 of the penal law.

* * * * *

In re Winship, 397 U.S. 358 (1970)

. . . . The requirement that guilt of a criminal charge be established by proof beyond a reasonable doubt dates at least from our early years as a Nation. The "demand for a higher degree of persuasion in criminal cases was recurrently expressed from ancient times, [though] its crystallization into the formula 'beyond a reasonable doubt' seems to have occurred as late as 1798. It is now accepted in common law jurisdictions as the measure of persuasion by which the prosecution must convince the trier of all the essential elements of guilt." McCormick, Evidence, § 321, at 681–682 (1954); see also 9 Wigmore, Evidence, § 2497 (3d ed. 1940). Although virtually unanimous adherence to the reasonable-doubt standard in common-law jurisdictions may not conclusively establish it as a requirement of due process, such adherence does "reflect a profound judgment about the way in which law should be enforced and justice administered." *Duncan* v. *Louisiana*, 391 U.S. 145, 155 (1968). . . .

The reasonable-doubt standard plays a vital role in the American scheme of criminal procedure. It is a prime instrument for reducing the risk of convictions resting on factual error. The standard provides concrete substance for the presumption of innocence—that bed-rock "axiomatic and elementary" principle whose "enforcement lies at the foundation of the administration of our criminal law." *Coffin* v. *United States, supra*, at 453. As the dissenters in the New York Court of Appeals observed, and we agree, "a person accused of crime . . . would be at a severe disadvantage, a disadvantage amounting to a lack of fundamental fairness, if he could be adjudged guilty and imprisoned for years on the strength of the same evidence as would suffice in a civil case." 24 N.Y.2d, at 205, 247 N.E.2d, at 259.

The requirement of proof beyond a reasonable doubt has this vital role in our criminal procedure for cogent reasons. The accused during a criminal prosecution has at stake interests of immense importance, both because of the possibility that he may lose his liberty upon conviction and because of the certainty that he would be stigmatized by the conviction. Accordingly, a society that values the good name and freedom of every individual should not condemn a man for commission of a crime when there is reasonable doubt about his guilt. As we said in *Speiser* v. *Randall, supra*, at 525–526: "There is always in litigation a margin of error, representing error in factfinding, which both parties must take into account. Where one party has at stake an interest of transcending value—as a criminal defendant his liberty—this margin of error is reduced as to him by the process of placing on the other party the burden of . . . persuading the factfinder at the conclusion of the trial of his guilt beyond a reasonable doubt. Due process commands that no man shall lose his liberty unless the Government has borne the burden of . . . convincing the factfinder of his guilt." To this end, the reasonable-doubt standard is indispensable, for it "impresses on the trier of fact the necessity of reaching a subjective state of certitude on the facts in issue." Dorsen & Rezneck. *In re Gault* and the Future of Juvenile Law, 1 Family Law Quarterly, No. 4, at 26 (1967).

Moreover, use of the reasonable-doubt standard is indispensable to command the respect and confidence of the community in applications of the criminal law. It is critical that the moral force of the criminal law not be diluted by a standard of proof which leaves people in doubt whether innocent men are being condemned. It is also important in our free society that every individual going about his ordinary affairs have confidence that his government cannot adjudge him guilty of a criminal offense without convincing a proper factfinder of his guilt with utmost certainty.

Lest there remain any doubt about the constitutional stature of the reasonable-doubt standard, we explicitly hold that the Due Process Clause protects the accused against conviction except upon proof beyond a reasonable doubt of every fact necessary to constitute the crime with which he is charged.

*   *   *   *   *

AMERICAN BAR ASSOCIATION PROJECT ON STANDARDS FOR THE ADMINISTRATION OF CRIMINAL JUSTICE, STANDARDS RELATING TO TRIAL BY JURY (Approved Draft 1968)

4.2   Note taking by jurors

Jurors may take notes regarding the evidence presented to them and keep these notes with them when they retire for their deliberations. Such notes should be treated as confidential between the juror making them and his fellow jurors.

Commentary

The great majority of the states which have ruled on the question permit the trial judge, in his discretion, to allow jurors to take notes regarding the evidence presented to them during the trial. Only two states view note taking as an illegal practice, while in one other state it has been held that note taking is a matter of right with the jury. Petroff, *The Practice of Jury Note Taking—Misconduct, Right, or Privilege?*, 18 OKLA. L. REV. 125 (1965). See also Annot., 14 A.L.R.3d 831 (1967). The federal courts "have held uniformly that the trial judge may, in his discretion, permit the practice." *The Jury System in the Federal Courts*, 26 F.R.D. 409, 457–58 (1961). Nine states (Cal., Idaho, Iowa, Minn., Mont., Nev., N.Y., N. Dak., Utah have enacted statutes which provide that jurors may take their notes with them upon retiring for deliberation. For statutory citations, see United States v. Campbell, 138 F. Supp. 344, 349 (N.D. Iowa 1956). These statutes are generally viewed as giving jurors the right to take notes, and it is the general practice of jurors in these jurisdictions to take notes. Buzard, *Jury Note-Taking in Criminal Trials*, 42 J. Crim. L. & Crim. 490, 491 (1951).

4.3 Substitution of judge

If by reason of death, sickness or other disability the judge before whom a jury trial has commenced is unable to proceed with the trial, another judge, upon certifying that he has familiarized himself with the record of the trial, may proceed with and finish the trial.

Commentary

This standard is patterned after Fed. R. Crim. P. 25(a), which permits substitution under these circumstances of "any other judge regularly sitting in or assigned to the court." (Any jurisdiction following the above standard would likewise want to identify in some way what judges are eligible for substitution.) Similar provisions are found in a few states. See Alaska R. Crim. P. 25; Cal. Pen. Code § 1053 (1956). In contrast to some state provisions on substitution during trial, the standard follows the federal approach of permitting substitution only in cases of jury trial. Where the judge is also the trier of the facts, the same judge should hear all the witnesses, unless the parties consent to substitution.

5.1 Materials to jury room

(a) The court in its discretion may permit the jury, upon retiring for deliberation, to take to the jury room a copy of the charges against the defendant and exhibits and writings which have been received in evidence, except depositions.

(b) Among the considerations which are appropriate in the exercise of this discretion are:

(i) whether the material will aid the jury in a proper consideration of the case;

(ii) whether any party will be unduly prejudiced by submission of the material; and

(iii) whether the material may be subjected to improper use by the jury.

5.2 Jury request to review evidence

(a) If the jury, after retiring for deliberation requests a review of certain testimony or other evidence, they shall be conducted to the courtroom. Whenever the jury's request is reasonable, the court, after notice to the prosecutor and counsel for the defense, shall have the requested parts of the testimony read to the jury and shall permit the jury to reexamine the requested materials admitted into evidence.

(b) The court need not submit evidence to the jury for review beyond that specifically requested by the jury, but in its discretion the court may also have the jury review other evidence relating to the same factual issue so as not to give undue prominence to the evidence requested.

5.3 Additional instructions

(a) If the jury, after retiring for deliberation, desires to be informed on any point of law, they shall be conducted to the courtroom. The court shall give appropriate additional instructions in response to the jury's request unless: (i) the jury may be adequately informed by directing their attention to some portion of the original instructions; (ii) the request concerns matters not in evidence or questions which do not pertain to the law of the case; or (iii) the request would call upon the judge to express an opinion upon factual matters that the jury should determine.

(b) The court need not give additional instructions beyond those specifically requested by the jury, but in its discretion the court may also give or repeat other instructions to avoid giving undue prominence to the requested instructions.

(c) The court may recall the jury after they have retired and give them additional instructions in order: (i) to correct or withdraw an erroneous instruction; (ii) to clarify an ambiguous instruction; or (iii) to inform the jury on a point of law which should have been covered in the original instructions.

(d) The provisions of section 4.6 (c) and (e) also apply to the giving of all additional instructions, except that the court in its discretion shall decide whether additional argument will be permitted.

5.4 Length of deliberations; deadlocked jury

(a) Before the jury retires for deliberation, the court may give an instruction which informs the jury:

> (i) that in order to return a verdict, each juror must agree thereto;
>
> (ii) that jurors have a duty to consult with one another and to deliberate with a view to reaching an agreement, if it can be done without violence to individual judgment;

(iii) that each juror must decide the case for himself, but only after an impartial consideration of the evidence with his fellow jurors;

(iv) that in the course of deliberations, a juror should not hesitate to reexamine his own views and change his opinion if convinced it is erroneous; and

(v) that no juror should surrender his honest conviction as to the weight or effect of the evidence solely because of the opinion of his fellow jurors, or for the mere purpose of returning a verdict.

(b) If it appears to the court that the jury has been unable to agree, the court may require the jury to continue their deliberations and may give or repeat an instruction as provided in subsection (a). The court shall not require or threaten to require the jury to deliberate for an unreasonable length of time or for unreasonable intervals.

(c) The jury may be discharged without having agreed upon a verdict if it appears that there is no reasonable probability of agreement.

5.5 Polling the jury

When a verdict has been returned and before the jury has dispersed, the jury shall be polled at the request of any party or upon the court's own motion. The poll shall be conducted by the court or clerk of court asking each juror individually whether the verdict announced is his verdict. If upon the poll there is not unanimous concurrence, the jury may be directed to retire for further deliberations or may be discharged.

5.6 Judicial comment on verdict

While it is appropriate for the court to thank jurors at the conclusion of a trial for their public service, such comments should not include praise or criticism of their verdict.

5.7 Impeachment of the verdict

(a) Upon an inquiry into the validity of a verdict, no evidence shall be received to show the effect of any statement, conduct, event or condition upon the mind of a juror or concerning the mental processes by which the verdict was determined.

(b) The limitations in subsection (a) shall not bar evidence concerning whether the verdict was reached by lot.

(c) Subject to the limitations in subsection (a), a juror's testimony or affidavit shall be received when it concerns:

(i) whether matters not in evidence came to the attention of one or more jurors, under circumstances which would violate the defendant's constitutional right to be confronted with the witnesses against him; or

(ii) any other misconduct for which the jurisdiction permits jurors to impeach their verdict.

✻   ✻   ✻   ✻   ✻

PEOPLE V. CRIMMINS, 26 N.Y.2d 319, 258 N.E.2d 708, 310 N.Y.S.2d 300 (1970)

BURKE, J. Defendant was indicted for, and convicted of, killing her daughter. At the trial the People established that the child died of strangulation within two or three hours of her last meal. The body was found at about 2:00 P.M., on July 14, 1965, and an autopsy determined that death occurred approximately 8 to 24 hours prior to discovery. Two of the People's witnesses, Sophie Earomirski and Joseph Rorech, presented substantially all of the evidence which connected defendant to the crime. The former testified that at about 2:00 A.M., on July 14, 1965, she saw defendant carrying a bundle and holding the hand of a little boy; she was accompanied by a man. Defendant's companion took the bundle and threw it into an automobile, and Mrs. Earomirski, from her third floor window across the street, heard defendant say, "My God, don't do that to *her*." Mr. Rorech testified that at a subsequent time defendant admitted to him, "Joseph, please forgive me, I killed her."

Although defendant raised several alleged errors in the Appellate Division, reversal was predicated on only one—an unauthorized visit by three jurors to the neighborhood which was the subject of Mrs. Earomirski's testimony—and was based on our decision in *People* v. *De Lucia* (20 N.Y.2d 275). Leave to appeal to this court was granted on the People's application. They argue that reversal is mandated only when prejudice to the defendant is shown and that, as found by the Trial Justice, such prejudice is absent herein. They also argue that the evidence is legally sufficient to establish defendant's guilt beyond a reasonable doubt.

After the trial but before the imposition of sentence, defendant moved, on the basis of a juror's affidavit, to set aside the verdict because members of the jury had made an unauthorized visit to the street on which Sophie Earomirski lived. A hearing was held, and the juror, Samuel Ehrlich, testified that, after Mrs. Earomirski had testified, he wanted to see that area. He went there between 1:00 and 2:00 A.M. Ehrlich further testified that his visit did not influence his opinion.

Another visit was made by Ehrlich and two other jurors, Harry Tunis and Irving Furst, at about 5:30 P.M.

During the jury's deliberations the lighting in the area was discussed in "small talk" and, according to Ehrlich, someone mentioned that the area was well-lit. Another juror, Philip Seidman, testified that the subject was discussed.

During the length of the trial, the jurors were never admonished not to visit any place which had been the subject of testimony. Ironically, after Mrs. Earomirski had testified, defense counsel requested that the court arrange a controlled visit to the area. The court denied the visit as unnecessary.

In *People* v. *De Lucia*, this court held: "In this type of case, proof of the fact of the unauthorized visit is sufficient to warrant a new trial without proof of how such visit may have influenced individual jurors in their juryroom deliberations. *Such a visit, in and of itself, constitutes inherent prejudice to the defendants.*" (20 N.Y.2d 275, 280 [emphasis supplied].) Appellant's attempt to distinguish *De Lucia* fails to comprehend the nature of the decision in that case. Although the affidavit averred that the jurors had re-enacted the crime, we did not predicate our decision on actual prejudice. That discussion merely demonstrates one of the manifest evils of an unauthorized visit. Since *De Lucia* was in the court on mere allegations, a hearing was ordered, and the afore-quoted statement indicates the quantum of proof which would mandate a new trial. The defendants were not required to establish prejudice.

Moreover, our decision in *People* v. *Sher* (24 N.Y.2d 454) should not be construed as modifying *De Lucia* (*supra*). There, unlawful communications made to jurors were disclosed to the court during the trial and prior to deliberation. After examining the jurors, the trial court was satisfied that the impropriety would not affect their verdict. We held that the pre-deliberation examination was sufficient to "sterilize" the jury. The jury visit herein was not disclosed until after verdict. Without the benefit of a judicial admonition, the jurors, although not *consciously* affected by the visit, would not make the specific effort to disregard it. Thus, no court instruction was made to counteract or "sterilize" any possible *subconscious* effect.

The attempt to distinguish the view made herein from one of the scene of a crime is also without merit. Mrs. Earomirski's ability to see and hear the events to which she testified depended very much on the lighting in the area and the distances involved. And the credibility of her testimony is essential to the prosecution's case. The Legislature perceived the evil in such a view and directed court supervision of views of the place where the crime is alleged to have been committed or where "any material fact occurred" (Code Crim. Pro., § 411). The statutory inclusion is sound, and we ought not to make a tenuous distinction.

Finally, appellant argues that the error is harmless. Assuming that such a determination is not precluded by our holding in *De Lucia*, the question is nevertheless moot. Although, as the People argue, the evidence is legally sufficient to sustain the verdict of guilt, it was not so overwhelming that we can say, as a matter of law, that the error could not have influenced the verdict (*Harrington* v. *California*, 395 U.S. 250; *Chapman* v. *California*, 386 U.S. 18). Only two witnesses gave evidence which connected defendant directly with the crime. Rorech, of course, testified that defendant confessed to the slaying, and that testimony, together with that of the coroner, is sufficient to establish a prima facie case. (Code Crim. Pro., § 395.) But that testimony was seriously challenged, and the witness was subjected to searching cross-examination. Mrs. Earomirski was the other witness who implicated defendant, and it is the value of her testimony which may have been affected by the impropriety. Given such limited evidence, we cannot find the error harmless beyond a reasonable doubt.

Accordingly the order of the Appellate Division should be affirmed.

CHAPTER 12

Sentencing

A. Presentence Investigation Reports

FEDERAL RULES OF CRIMINAL PROCEDURE, RULE 32(c)

(c) Presentence Investigation

(1) When Made. The probation service of the court shall make a presentence investigation and report to the court before the imposition of sentence or the granting of probation unless the court otherwise directs. The report shall not be submitted to the court or its contents disclosed to anyone unless the defendant has pleaded guilty or has been found guilty.

(2) Report. The report of the presentence investigation shall contain any prior criminal record of the defendant and such information about his characteristics, his financial condition and the circumstances affecting his behavior as may be helpful in imposing sentence or in granting probation or in the correctional treatment of the defendant, and such other information as may be required by the court. The court before imposing sentence may disclose to the defendant or his counsel all or part of the material contained in the report of the presentence investigation and afford an opportunity to the defendant or his counsel to comment thereon. Any material disclosed to the defendant or his counsel shall also be disclosed to the attorney for the government.

❋ ❋ ❋ ❋ ❋

UNITED STATES CODE, Title 18, Section 4208 (b) (Supp. 1968)

(b) If the court desires more detailed information as a basis for determining the sentence to be imposed, the court may commit the defendant to the custody of the Attorney General, which commitment shall be deemed to be for the maximum sentence of imprisonment prescribed by law, for a study as described in subsection (c) hereof. The results of such study, together with any recommendations which the Director of the Bureau of Prisons believes would be helpful in determining the disposition of the case, shall be furnished to the court within three months unless the court grants time, not to exceed an additional three months, for further study. After receiving such reports and recommendations, the court may in its discretion: (1) Place the prisoner on probation as authorized by section 3651 of this title, or (2) affirm the sentence of imprisonment originally imposed, or reduce the sentence of imprisonment, and commit the offender under any applicable provision of law. The term of the sentence shall run from date of original commitment under this section.

✿   ✿   ✿   ✿   ✿

NEW YORK CRIMINAL PROCEDURE LAW (1971)

§ 390.10   Requirement of fingerprint report

In any case where the defendant is convicted of an offense specified in subdivision one of section 160.10, the court may not pronounce sentence until it has received a fingerprint report from the New York state identification and intelligence system. For such purpose, the court may use the original fingerprint report obtained after the arrest or arraignment of the defendant, or it may direct that a new fingerprint report be prepared and transmitted to it.

§ 390.20   Requirement of pre-sentence report

1. Requirement for felonies. In any case where a person is convicted of a felony, the court must order a pre-sentence investigation of the defendant and the court must not pronounce sentence until it has received a written report of such investigation.

2. Requirement for misdemeanors. Where a person is convicted of a misdemeanor a pre-sentence report shall not be required, but the court shall not pronounce any of the following sentences unless it has ordered a pre-sentence investigation of the defendant and has received a written report thereof:

(a) A sentence of probation;

(b) A reformatory or an alternative local reformatory sentence of imprisonment;

(c) A sentence of imprisonment for a term in excess of ninety days;

(d) Consecutive sentences of imprisonment for terms aggregating more than ninety days.

3. **Permissible in any case.** The court may, in its discretion, order a pre-sentence investigation and report in any case where it is pronouncing sentence, irrespective of whether such investigation and report is required by subdivision one or two of this section.

§ 390.30   Scope of pre-sentence investigation and report

1. **The investigation.** The pre-sentence investigation shall consist of the gathering of information with respect to the circumstances attending the commission of the offense, the defendant's history of delinquency or criminality, and the defendant's social history, employment history, family situation, economic status, education, and personal habits. Such investigation may also include any other matter the agency conducting the investigation deems relevant to the question of sentence, and shall include any matter the court directs to be included.

2. **Physical and mental examinations.** Whenever information is available with respect to the defendant's physical and mental condition the pre-sentence investigation shall include the gathering of such information. In the case of a felony or of a class A misdemeanor, or in any case where a person under the age of twenty-one is convicted of a crime, the court may order that the defendant undergo a thorough physical or mental examination in a designated facility and may further order that the defendant remain in such facility for such purpose for a period not exceeding thirty days.

3. **The report.** The report of the pre-sentence investigation shall contain an analysis of such of the information gathered in the investigation as the agency that conducted the investigation deems relevant to the question of sentence. The report shall also include any other information that the court directs to be included.

§ 390.40   Defendant's pre-sentence memorandum

The defendant may, at any time prior to the pronouncement of sentence, file with the court a written memorandum setting forth any information he may deem pertinent to the question of sentence. Such memorandum may include information with respect to any of the matters described in section 390.30 and the defendant may annex written statements by others in support of facts alleged in the memorandum.

§ 390.50   Confidentiality of pre-sentence reports and memoranda

1. **In general.** Any pre-sentence report or memorandum submitted to the court pursuant to this article and any medical, psychiatric or

social agency report or other information gathered for the court by a probation department, or submitted directly to the court, in connection with the question of sentence shall be confidential and shall not be made available to any person or public or private agency except where specifically required or permitted by statute or upon specific authorization of the court.

2. **Public agencies within this state.** A probation department shall make available a copy of its pre-sentence report and any medical, psychiatric or social agency report submitted to it in connection with its pre-sentence investigation or its supervision of a defendant to any court, or to the probation department of any court, within this state that subsequently has jurisdiction over such defendant for the purpose of pronouncing or reviewing sentence and to any state agency to which the defendant is subsequently committed or certified or under whose care and custody or jurisdiction the defendant subsequently is placed upon the official request of such court or agency therefor. In any such case, the court or agency receiving such material shall retain same under the same conditions of confidentiality as the probation department that made it available.

3. **Public agencies outside this state.** Upon official request of any probation, parole or public institutional agency outside this state, a probation department may make any information in its files available to such agency.

4. **New York state identification and intelligence system.** Nothing in this section shall be construed to prevent the voluntary submission by a probation department of data in its files to the New York state identification and intelligence system.

§ 390.60 Copy of reports to accompany defendant sentenced to imprisonment

1. **Cases where copy of report is required.** Whenever a person is sentenced to a term of imprisonment in excess of ninety days or to consecutive sentences of imprisonment aggregating more than ninety days or to a reformatory or any alternative local reformatory sentence of imprisonment or to an indeterminate sentence of imprisonment, a copy of the pre-sentence report, a copy of any pre-sentence memorandum filed by the defendant and a copy of any medical, psychiatric or social agency report submitted to the court or to the probation department in connection with the question of sentence shall be delivered to the person in charge of the correctional facility to which the defendant is committed at the time the defendant is delivered thereto.

2. **Effect of failure to deliver required report.** A commitment shall

not be deemed void in the case of failure to comply with the provisions of subdivision one of this section but the person in charge of the correctional facility to which the defendant has been delivered in execution of the sentence is authorized to refuse to accept custody of such person until the required report is delivered.

*　*　*　*　*

AMERICAN BAR ASSOCIATION PROJECT ON STANDARDS FOR THE
ADMINISTRATION OF CRIMINAL JUSTICE, STANDARDS RELATING
TO PROBATION (Approved Draft 1970)

PROBATION REPORTS

2.1　Availability and use

(a) All courts trying criminal cases should be supplied with the resources and supporting staff to permit a presentence investigation and a written report of its results in every case.

(b) The court should explicitly be authorized by statute to call for such an investigation and report in every case. The statute should also provide that such an investigation and report should be made in every case where incarceration for one year or more is a possible disposition, where the defendant is less than [21] years old, or where the defendant is a first offender, unless the court specifically orders to the contrary in a particular case.

2.2　Purpose of report

The primary purpose of the presentence report is to provide the sentencing court with succinct and precise information upon which to base a rational sentencing decision. Potential use of the report by other agencies in the correctional process should be recognized as a factor in determining the content and length of the report, but should be subordinated to its primary purpose. Where the presentence investigation discloses information useful to other correctional agencies, methods should be developed to assure that this data is made available for their use.

2.3　Content, scope and length of report

Presentence reports should be flexible in format, reflecting differences in the background of different offenders and making the best use of available resources and probation department capabilities. Each probation department should develop gradations of reports between:

(i) a short-form report for primary use in screening offenders in order to assist in a determination of when additional and more complete information is desirable. Short-form reports could also be useful in courts which do not have adequate probation services;

(ii) a full report, which normally should contain the following items:

(A) a complete description of the offense and the circumstances surrounding it, not limited to aspects developed for the record as part of the determination of guilt;

(B) a full description of any prior criminal record of the offender;

(C) a description of the educational background of the offender;

(D) a description of the employment background of the offender, including any military record and including his present employment status and capabilities;

(E) the social history of the offender, including family relationships, marital status, interests and activities, residence history, and religious affiliations;

(F) the offender's medical history and, if desirable, a psychological or psychiatric report;

(G) information about environments to which the offender might return or to which he could be sent should probation be granted;

(H) supplementary reports from clinics, institutions and other social agencies with which the offender has been involved;

(I) information about special resources which might be available to assist the offender, such as treatment centers, residential facilities, vocational training services, special educational facilities, rehabilitative programs of various institutions to which the offender might be committed, special programs in the probation department, and other similar programs which are particularly relevant to the offender's situation;

(J) a summary of the most significant aspects of the report, including specific recommendations as to the sentence if the sentencing court has so requested.

A special effort should be made in the preparation of presentence reports not to burden the court with irrelevant and unconnected details.

2.4 When prepared

(a) Except as authorized in subsection (b), the presentence investigation should not be initiated until there has been an adjudication of guilt.

(b) It is appropriate to commence the presentence investigation prior to an adjudication of guilt only if:

(i) the defendant, with the advice of counsel if he so desires, has consented to such action; and

(ii) adequate precautions are taken to assure that nothing disclosed by the presentence investigation comes to the attention of the prosecution, the court, or the jury prior tò an adjudication of guilt. The court should be authorized, however, to examine the report prior to the entry of a plea on request of the defense and prosecution.

2.5 Availability of report; challenge of its contents

Standards dealing with the disclosure of the presentence report and the resolution of controversy as to its accuracy are developed in the separate report of this Advisory Committee on Sentencing Alternatives and Procedures.

4.1 Presentence report; general principles

(a) The legislature should supply all courts trying criminal cases with the resources and supporting staff to permit a presentence investigation and a written report of its results in every case.

(b) The court should explicitly be authorized by statute to call for such an investigation and report in every case. The statute should also provide that such an investigation and report should be made in every case where incarceration for one year or more is a possible disposition, where the defendant is less than [21] years old, or where the defendant is a first offender, unless the court specifically orders to the contrary in a particular case.

(c) Standards relating to the preparation and contents of the presentence report will be developed in a separate report on probation.

Commentary

a. Background

One of the most fundamental issues involved in the resolution of how any part of the criminal process ought to function is that of determining the method by which the relevant and necessary information should be provided to the agency which is to make a decision. It is basic to any intelligent decision that it be sufficiently informed by fact. . . .

The prevailing pattern of the statutes on the subject is also widely variant. Four general types seem to be in use:

(1) The first makes the presentence report mandatory for certain classes of offenses. In California, for example, such a report is required for every felony, see CAL. PENAL CODE § 1203 (1966 Supp.), as is the case in Vermont. VT. STAT. ANN. tit. 28, §1008 (1965 Supp.). In Colorado, any person who has been convicted of either a misdemeanor or a felony (with certain limited exceptions) may make an application to the court to be released on probation. Once such an application is made, the court must defer sentence until a presentence report is compiled. See COLO. REV. STAT. ANN. § 39–16–3 (1964). For examples of other states where the presentence report is mandatory, see CONN. GEN. STAT. ANN. § 54–109 (1960) (mandatory for all first offenses punishable for more than one year; also mandatory for repeat offenders punishable for more than one year if the record discloses a conviction prior to three years from the present conviction); DEL. CODE ANN. tit. 11, § 4331(a) (1966 Supp.) (mandatory if sentence can exceed six months' imprisonment); IND. ANN. STAT. § 9–2252 (1966 Supp.) (mandatory for felonies); MICH. STAT. ANN. § 28.1144 (1954) (mandatory for felonies); N.J. CRIM. PRAC. RULES, Superior and County Courts, Rule 3:7–10(b) (1967) (mandatory in all cases before such courts); R.I. GEN. LAWS §12–19–6 (1966 Supp.) (mandatory for all crimes for which a sentence of more than one year may be imposed). Typically in such states, the trial judge has the explicit discretion to call for a presentence report for most other types of offenses. See, e.g., the California, Connecticut, Michigan and Vermont statutes cited, supra.

(2) The second type of statute makes use of the presentence report discretionary with the trial court. In Minnesota, for example, the original draft of the 1963 revision of the Criminal Code required a presentence report for all felonies, but the legislature substituted "may" for "shall" to make such reports discretionary. See MINN. STAT. ANN. § 609–115(1) (1964). For other statutes which permit but do not require the use of a presentence report, see FLA. STAT. ANN. § 948.01 (1966 Supp.); GA. CODE ANN. § 27–2709 (1966 Supp.); IOWA CODE ANN. § 247.20 (1966 Supp.); MONT. REV. CODE ANN. § 94-7831 (1967 Supp.); N.M. STAT. ANN. § 41–17–23 (1964); N.Y. CODE CRIM. PROC. §§ 482, 931(1) (1967 Supp.); N.C. GEN. STATS. § 15–198 (1965); Okla. Laws c. 276, § 1 (1967); ORE. REV. STAT. 137.530 (1965); WASH. REV. CODE ANN. § 9.95.200 (1960). This is also the approach in the federal courts. See FED. R. CRIM. P. 32(c)(1).

(3) The third type of statute is a hybrid of the first two. The statute typically makes use of the presentence report discretionary with the trial court, but at the same time precludes certain types of dispositions, usually probation, if a report is not prepared. Thus, under such a statute the report is mandatory if the judge is thinking of probation as a possible disposition. The following statutes exemplify this approach: ALA. CODE tit. 42, § 21 (1959); OHIO REV. CODE ANN. § 2951.03 (1965 Supp.); S.C. CODE ANN. § 55–592 (1962); W.VA. CODE ANN. § 62–12–7 (1966); WYO. STAT. ANN. §7–319 (1965 Supp.).

(4) The final type of statute expresses a wholly different attitude towards the use of the presentence report. Such statutes provide a method by which evidence considered on the sentence can come to the attention of the court which would appear to exclude the use of presentence reports entirely. The statutes in Utah, which appears to be the only remaining state in this category, provide that the court may hear evidence on the sentencing issue presented by either party, but that except for witnesses who are physically unable to be present, all such evidence must be presented in open court. See UTAH CODE ANN. §§ 77–35–12, –13 (1953). Until this year, the Oklahoma statutes contained almost identical provisions. See OKLA. STAT. ANN. c. 22 § 973 (1958); Okla. Laws 1967, c. 276, § 1. Compare ALI MODEL CODE CRIM. PROC. § 397 (1931).

There are in addition many states in which the statutes do not fit any of the above patterns. In several, for example, presentence reports appear to be in use without any statutory authorization. See Note, *Employment of Social Investigation Reports in Criminal and Juvenile Proceedings*, 58 COLUM. L. REV. 702, 703 (1958). In Virginia, where sentences are assessed by the trier of fact in contested cases, the statutes do not authorize presentence reports in those cases where the jury fixes the sentence. In cases where the court is the trier of fact, or where the defendant has pleaded guilty, the court "may, or on the motion of the defendant shall," order a presentence report in felony cases where a sentence of death or confinement for more than ten years is available. See VA. CODE ANN. § 53–278.1 (1967).

b. Availability

The President's Crime Commission recently recommended that "all courts should require presentence reports for all offenders, whether those reports result from full field investigations by probation officers or, in the case of minor offenders, from the use of short forms." PRESIDENT'S COMM'N, THE CHALLENGE OF CRIME 144. Such an objective is not extravagant.

Consider the uses to which such information can be put. The most obvious, of course, are with respect to the sentencing decision itself. If probation is a realistic possibility, it would be the rare case where more information than was learned at the trial would not be essential to a proper disposition of the defendant. The information would be particularly scanty if the defendant pleaded guilty without trial. On the other hand, in cases where probation or some other sanction short of total incarceration is not a possibility, there is an even more urgent need for the court to inform itself about the defendant. There may, for example, be grounds which were not disclosed at trial which indicate that the defendant is likely to present a serious risk of future crimes of a violent nature, in which case a reasonably long prison term would be indicated. Or the facts may indicate that the defendant would be more likely to respond to a special type of commitment which may be available than he would to a normal maximum security institution. The point, in any event, is that serious consequences turn on the correct resolution of the sentencing decision, and it is sheer folly to attempt such a decision without more information than is typically provided by the guilt determining process.

But the value of the presentence report continues beyond the sentencing decision. If the defendant is indeed placed on probation, the supervising officer can be saved the need to engage in independent investigation to develop much of the information on which to base his initial relationship with the offender. The same, of course, holds true for the institutional officials in the event of a commitment. Both the initial classification and treatment of the defendant, as well as subsequent decisions such as parole, can be immeasurably aided—by narrowing the need for independent investigation—by a properly prepared presentence report. See REPORT OF THE PRESIDENT'S COMMISSION ON CRIME IN THE DISTRICT OF COLUMBIA, Appendix, p. 690 (1966); Wallace, *Aids in Sentencing*, 40 F.R.D. 433, 434 (1965). See also NEWMAN, CONVICTION: THE DETERMINATION OF GUILT OR INNOCENCE WITHOUT TRIAL 14–18 (1966).

It should not be assumed that the above comments are applicable only to serious offenses. Indeed, a strong case can be made for giving high priority to juvenile proceedings and certain types of misdemeanor offenders because of the opportunity they present for a creative disposition that will prevent a criminal career. *Cf. Report of the Conference on Legal Manpower Needs of Criminal Law*, 41 F.R.D. 389, 398, 401 (1966). Careful attention to cases which may signal the beginning of a course of crime will more than justify the cost of the system.

Subsection (a) accordingly suggests that the major legislative effort in this regard ought to be aimed at the provision of sufficient resources and supporting staff to permit the compilation of a presentence report in every case. While the Advisory Committee will deal with the preparation and contents of the presentence report in a separate report on probation, it should perhaps be noted here that this does not mean that a lengthy investigation and a full report should be prepared in every case. A properly developed preliminary screening program designed to determine who among numerous minor offenders ought to be investigated in more detail can reduce much of the financial burden, as well as increase the efficiency of the probation service. *Cf.* SUBIN, CRIMINAL JUSTICE IN A METROPOLITAN COURT 102–05, 153 (1966). See also PRESIDENT'S COMM'N, THE COURTS 18–19.

c. Presumption

The first sentence of subsection (b) implements the principle developed above by suggesting that the legislature ought specifically to authorize the employment of a presentence report in every case. It is expressly stated as a standard so as to avoid any ambiguity in the matter, as well as to indicate the propriety of legislative encouragement of the use of such reports.

The legislature must also face the question of whether it is sound to require the use of the report in any particular class of cases. The Model Penal Code, for example, has suggested that presentence reports be *authorized* in every case, and *required* in all felony cases, in all cases where the defendant is less than twenty-two years old, and before an extended term can be imposed. See MODEL PENAL CODE § 7.07(1), Appendix B, *infra*. The commentary adds that:

> The ideal course would be to require a presentence investigation in every case that comes before the court. We recognize, however, that facilities and personnel do not now make this possible. The problem at the present time is rather to assure that our limited resources in this area are used where they are needed most; the problem of the future is to expand those resources to the point where they are reasonably adequate for the discharge of this important task.
>
> Viewing the matter in these terms, this section undertakes to specify the cases where the inquiry is most essential. We think a system reasonably satisfactory that provides pre-sentence study when conviction is of felony, when the defendant is under 21 [subsequently changed to 22 to conform to the Code definition of a young offender], when the defendant will be placed on pro-

bation [subsequently stated as an alternative "to take account of the possibility that the requirement of an investigation prior to sentence of probation, rather than in the course of supervision, may be impractical in many jurisdictions and may thus have the undesired effect of discouraging probationary disposition"] or when he will be sentenced to imprisonment for an extended term. If this is unattainable, we would sacrifice the inquiry in all felony cases in favor of all first convictions of a felony, retaining the investigation in the other categories. Where even this is unattainable, we think there is an absolute inadequacy in the resources employed for the assistance of the court in sentencing. Accordingly, the section makes the investigation a legal requirement in the cases specified. This goes further than prevailing legislation, though less far than much prevailing practice.

MODEL PENAL CODE § 7.07, comment, pp. 53–54 (Tent. Draft No. 2, 1954). See also NCCD, STANDARD PROBATION AND PAROLE ACT § 11 (1964); MODEL SENTENCING ACT § 2, Appendix C, infra.

The Advisory Committee is basically in accord with these observations. Such matters must at bottom turn on an allocation of priorities within the realm of the possible. But on the assumption that it is not feasible at this time to require a presentence report in every case, the Committee would approach the matter in a slightly different fashion. There will be some cases within the categories developed by the Code where a required presentence report would duplicate information already disclosed, or where a certain disposition, such as probation with minimal supervision, is immediately apparent from the known facts of the case. The Committee would accordingly view it as a better allocation of resources to authorize the report in every case, and to suggest strongly—by means of a statutory presumption—that it at least be used in certain obvious classes of cases. But as subsection (b) indicates, the Committee would leave it open to the court not to obtain a report if there are affirmative reasons which make it unnecessary. The sentencing court's decision in this respect should of course be subject to review. See ABA STANDARDS, APPELLATE REVIEW OF SENTENCES § 3.2(ii) (Tent. Draft, April 1967).

One advantage of such an approach is that it should permit the legislative provision of a larger class of cases in which the report should normally be obtained. The Advisory Committee would agree that the three situations outlined by the Penal Code should be included, but would add a fourth, namely where the defendant is a first offender. All recidivists were at some point convicted of a first offense; some need not have committed a second. *Cf.* SUBIN, CRIMINAL JUSTICE IN A METROPOLITAN COURT 153 (1966).

Finally, a word should be added in explanation of why the Advisory Committee has rejected the formulation in use in at least five states which precludes the use of probation unless a presentence report is obtained, but which permits any other disposition without such a report. The philosophy of such a provision would seem to be that informational inadequacy which leads to unnecessary incarceration can be tolerated, while on the other hand society at least deserves the protection of an informed probation decision so that the wrong people will not be roaming the streets. While the Advisory Committee would not disagree with the latter conclusion, it must not be lost sight of that there are other interests which should be recognized. The defendant too is in need of the protection of an informed decision, and more so as the severity of the sanction increases. Nor is society served by an unnecessary jail sentence. If the judgment in a particular jurisdiction is that a presentence report is necessary as a prerequisite for imposing probation, the Advisory Committee would add its judgment that the same requirement should be made for most more serious sanctions. Compare the commentary to the Model Penal Code, quoted *supra,* which adds the point that the probation decision might be unduly encumbered by a requirement that probation cannot be used unless a presentence report has been obtained.

d. Separate report

Subsection (c) notes that the Advisory Committee intends to develop standards in a separate report on probation dealing with the preparation and contents of the presentence report.

4.2 Presentence report; when prepared

(a) Except as authorized in subsection (b), the presentence investigation should not be initiated until there has been an adjudication of guilt.

(b) It is appropriate to commence the presentence investigation prior to an adjudication of guilt only if:

(i) the defendant, with the advice of counsel if he so desires, has consented to such action; and

(ii) adequate precautions are taken to assure that nothing disclosed by the presentence investigation comes to the attention of the prosecution, the court, or the jury prior to an adjudication of guilt. The court should be authorized, however, to examine the report prior to the entry of a plea on request of the defense and the prosecution.

Commentary

a. General principle

There are at least four reasons why the presentence investigation should not be undertaken until after the adjudication of guilt. The most fundamental is that the investigation will undoubtedly represent an unwarranted invasion of the defendant's privacy if he is later acquitted. The defendant's friends, employers and relatives must be questioned, and embarrassing questions asked. The second reason relates to the use of the defendant as a source of information. Most reports depend in large part on information acquired from the accused, and later verified by independent investigation. The defendant can be placed in an awkward position if he is expected to talk to a probation officer before he goes to trial. The third reason stems from the fact that much of what is contained in the presentence report is not admissible at the trial on the question of guilt. There is a chance that it may come to the attention of the court before guilt is determined. See, *e.g.*, Calland v. United States, 371 F.2d 295 (7th Cir. 1966). The possibilities of prejudice are obvious. And finally, there is a convincing economic argument against the compilation of a report which may never be used. There are few probation offices which can afford the luxury of such a practice.

b. Exception

On the other hand, if the defendant intends to plead guilty and is willing to cooperate, there are gains to be had by permitting an early start. For example, where a trial court sits in terms, it is to be expected that a great many guilty pleas will await the first day of each session. For the probation office to be able to conduct some investigations prior to the first day of the term should serve to spread its work load and mitigate the innundation of the office after the receipt of numerous pleas. See generally Sims, *Pre-Arraignment Investigations: A Partial Solution to the Time Problem*, Fed. Prob., March 1964, p. 24. There are similar advantages to be gained in counties or districts where the judge still rides circuit.

Subsection (b) thus recognizes the possibility of early commencement of the investigation in those cases where the defendant consents and where adequate precautions are taken to avoid prejudice on the issue of guilt. As is the practice in some federal courts, it is also required by the subsection that the defendant be given an opportunity to consult with counsel before he agrees to such a procedure. See Evjen, *Some Guidelines in Preparing Presentence Reports,* 37 F.R.D. 177, 178 (1965).

In addition Subsection (b)(ii) recognizes that there may be occasions when it is appropriate for the court to examine the report prior to the entry of the guilty plea. It may be to the defendant's advantage, for example, to seek a one-appearance disposition of his case, as where he is anxious to reduce the time he will serve in a local facility. See 30 F.R.D. 442 (1962). The reason for the requirement of consent by the prosecutor is in order to prevent the use of such a procedure as a device to get favorable but inadmissible information before the court prior to an adjudication of guilt.

4.3 Presentence report: disclosure; general principles

The presentence report should not be a public record. It should be available only to the following persons or agencies under the conditions stated:

(i) The report should be available to the sentencing court for the purpose of assisting it in determining the sentence. The report should also be available to all judges who are to participate in a sentencing council discussion of the defendant (section 7.1);

(ii) The report should be available to persons or agencies having a legitimate professional interest in the information likely to be contained therein. Examples of such persons or agencies would be a physician or psychiatrist appointed to assist the court in sentencing, an examining facility, a correctional institution, or a probation or parole department;

(iii) The report should be available to reviewing courts where relevant to an issue on which an appeal has been taken;

(iv) The report should be available to the parties under the conditions stated in section 4.4.

Commentary

a. Confidentiality

In several states, the presentence report is in effect a public record. In California, for example, the full report "must be made available to the Court and the prosecuting and defense attorneys at least two days prior to the time fixed by the court for the hearing and determination of such report and must be filed with the clerk of the court as a record in the case at the time of said hearing." CAL. PENAL CODE § 1203 (1966 Supp.). And in Virginia, the probation officer shall present his report in open court in the presence of the accused who shall be advised of the contents of the same and be given the right to cross-examine the investigating officer as to any matter contained therein and to present any additional facts bearing upon the matter which he may desire to present. The report of the investigating Officer shall be filed as a part of the record in the case.

VA. CODE ANN. § 53–278.1 (1967).

On the other hand, in most states the report is confidential, at best available only on a limited basis. For example, the provision in Ohio is that the report "shall be confidential and need not be furnished to the defendant or his counsel or the prosecuting attorney unless the court, in its discretion, so orders." OHIO REV. CODE ANN. § 2951.03 (1965 Supp.). Compare N.C. GEN. STAT. § 15–207 (1965); N.J. CRIM. PRAC. RULES, Superior and County Courts, Rule 3:7–10(b) (1967); FED. R. CRIM. P. 32(c)(2).

This section begins with the assertion that the presentence report should not be a public record. No affirmative purpose is seen for making the document public, whereas there are discernible detriments. The defendant, for example, is not served by a public disclosure of the intimate—and possibly irrelevant or unverified—details of his background. Those who are concerned that sources of information might be affected by disclosure might also be heard to object. But whereas competing considerations may overcome such an argument in other contexts, no such reasons are observable here.

The conclusion is thus expressed that the report should not be spread upon the record, and that it should only be available as circumstances warrant. What those circumstances are likely to be is developed in subsections (i) through (iv).

b. Sentencing court

The basic purpose of the report is to assist the court in the sentencing decision, and it must of course be available to that end. By the same token, the report should not be used by the court for other purposes, particularly on such questions as guilt in the case before it or in other cases against the same defendant. It is also provided in subsection (i) that the report should be available to the sentencing council described in section 7.1, *infra*.

c. Professional agencies

It is quite common for presentence report statutes to provide that in the event of the defendant's commitment the report should be transmitted to the corrections authorities. See, *e.g.,* ALA. CODE tit. 42, § 21 (1959); CAL. PENAL CODE § 1203 (1966 Supp.); CONN. GEN. STAT. ANN. § 54–109 (1960); IND. STATS. ANN. § 9–2252 (1966 Supp.); MICH. STAT. ANN. § 28.1144 (1954); MINN. STAT. ANN. § 609.115 (5) (1964); MONT. REV. CODE ANN. § 94–7831 (1967 Supp.); N.J. CRIM. PRAC. RULES, Superior and County Courts, Rule 3:7–10(b) (1967); N.M. STAT. ANN. § 41–17–23 (1964); N.Y. CODE CRIM. PROC. § 931(1) (1966 Supp.); OHIO REV. CODE ANN. § 2951.03 (1965 Supp.). See also NCCD, STANDARD PROBATION AND PAROLE ACT § 11 (1964); MODEL SENTENC-ING ACT § 4, Appendix C, *infra:* MODEL PENAL CODE § 7.07(7), Appendix B, *infra.* Although the statutes are normally silent on the point, it is also common for the report to be available to the officer who is to supervise the defendant's probation, whether or not the officer has himself prepared the report. The reasons for such provisions are sound: both the corrections authorities and the probation officer can better perform their tasks with the information contained in a good presentence report.

There are likewise good reasons for making the report available to other persons and agencies with a legitimate professional interest in the information it is likely to contain. A diagnostic facility, such as is contemplated by section 4.6, *infra,* will be provided with a good start on its inquiry if it can begin with a carefully prepared presentence report. There would likewise seem no reason why a private treatment institution should not have access to the report if its interest is legitimate. See generally Sharp, *The Confidential Nature of Presentence Reports,* 5 CATHOLIC U.L. REV. 127, 129 (1955).

d. Reviewing courts

Disclosure of the report to appellate courts follows from the Advisory Committee's position on appellate review of sentences. See ABA STANDARDS, APPELLATE REVIEW OF SENTENCES (Tent. Draft, April 1967). However, even if sentences are not to be reviewed, disclosure of the report to reviewing courts would be necessary in order to permit review of matters relating to sentencing procedure, such as the duty to obtain a complete and accurate report. *Cf.* State v. Laird, 85 N.J. Super. 170, 204 A.2d 220 (1964).

e. Parties

The question of disclosure of the presentence report to parties presents issues which are difficult of resolution and highly controversial. Because of the complexity of the problem, it is dealt with in the separate section which follows.

4.4 Presentence report: disclosure; parties

(a) Fundamental fairness to the defendant requires that the substance of all derogatory information which adversely affects his interests and which has not otherwise been disclosed in open court should be called to the attention of the defendant, his attorney, and others who are acting on his behalf.

(b) This principle should be implemented by requiring that the sentencing court permit the defendant's attorney, or the defendant himself if he has no attorney, to inspect the report. The prosecution should also be shown the report if it is shown to the defense. In extraordinary cases, the court should be permitted to except from disclosure parts of the report which are not relevant to a proper sentence, diagnostic opinion which might seriously disrupt a program of rehabilitation, or sources of information which has been obtained on a promise of confidentiality. In all cases where parts of the report are not disclosed under such authority, the court should be required to state for the record the reasons for its action and to inform the defendant and his attorney that information has not been disclosed. The action of the court in excepting information from disclosure should be subject to appellate review.

(c) The resolution of any controversy as to the accuracy of the presentence report should be governed by the principles stated in sections 4.5(b), 5.3(d), 5.3(f), and 5.4(a).

Commentary

a. Background

The question of disclosure of the presentence report to parties has produced much heated debate in the literature. See, *e.g.*, Lorensen, *The Disclosure to Defense of Presentence Reports in West Virginia*, 69 W.Va. L. Rev. 159 (1967); Guzman, *Defendant's Access to Presentence Reports in Federal Criminal Courts*, 52 Iowa L. Rev. 161 (1966); Roche, *The Position for Confidentiality of the Presentence Investigation Report*, 29 Albany L. Rev. 206 (1965); Higgins, *In Response to Roche*, 29 Albany L. Rev. 225 (1965); Higgins, *Confidentiality of Presentence Reports*, 28 Albany L. Rev. 12 (1964); Parsons, *The Presentence Investigative Report Must be Preserved as a Confidential Document*, Fed. Prob., March 1964, p. 3; Thomsen, *Confidentiality of the Presentence Report: A Middle Position*, Fed. Prob., March 1964, p. 8; *Symposium of Discovery in Federal Criminal Cases*, 33 F.R.D. 47, 122–28 (1963); Sharp, *The Confidential Nature of Presentence Reports*, 5 Catholic U.L. Rev. 127 (1955); Rubin, *What*

Privacy for Presentence Reports, Fed. Prob., Dec. 1952, p. 8; Note, *Right of Criminal Offenders to Challenge Reports Used in Determining Sentence,* 49 COLUM. L. REV. 567 (1949); Hincks, *In Opposition to Rule 34(c)(2), Proposed Federal Rules of Criminal Procedure,* Fed. Prob., Oct.–Dec. 1944, p. 3. Other articles are collected in Committee on Rules of Practice and Procedure, Second Preliminary Draft of Proposed Amendments to Rules of Criminal Procedure for the United States District Courts, p. 41 (March 1964) (Advisory Committee's note). See also Proposed Amendments to Rules of Criminal Procedure for the United States District Courts, 39 F.R.D. 168, 193–94 (1966).

There is also a division among statutes on the point, although none has been found which flatly forbids disclosure to the defendant. Most maintain a position of silence which is usually interpreted as placing disclosure within the discretion of the sentencing court. This, for example, was the position of the Federal Rules of Criminal Procedure prior to the 1966 revision. There are a few statutes, however, which specifically require disclosure, or which in terms leave the issue to the court. In addition to the statutes cited in comment *a* to section 4.3, *supra,* see MINN. STAT. ANN. § 609.115(4) (1964): "Any report made pursuant to subdivision 1 of this section shall be open to inspection by the prosecuting attorney and the defendant's attorney prior to sentence . . . ."

Finally, it should be noted that there have been numerous proposals which have attempted to draw an intermediate line between complete disclosure and complete secrecy. The President's Crime Commission recommended, for example, that "in the absence of compelling reasons for nondisclosure of special information, the defendant and his counsel should be permitted to examine the entire presentence report." PRESI-DENT'S COMM'N, THE CHALLENGE OF CRIME 145. See also PRESIDENT'S COMM'N, THE COURTS 20. Other proposals have often proceeded from the view that what the defendant needs is not the whole report, but merely the facts on which it is based. Sources of information, together with opinions of the probation officer, properly can remain a privileged communication between officer and judge. See, *e.g.,* Higgins, *Confidentiality of Presentence Reports,* 28 ALBANY L. REV. 12 (1964). The Model Penal Code, on the other hand, has varied slightly from this conclusion by suggesting that the Court should advise the defendant or his attorney "of the factual contents and conclusions" of any presentence or psychiatric reports. Again, "the sources of information need not . . . be disclosed." MODEL PENAL CODE § 7.07(5). Appendix B, *infra.* Still a fourth view was expressed by an amendment once proposed to the Federal Rules of Criminal Procedure. By this view, the disclosure requirements would be different depending on whether the defendant was represented by counsel; if he is represented, "the court before imposing sentence shall permit counsel for the defendant to read the report of the presentence investigation (from which the sources of confidential information may be excluded)"; if the defendant is unrepresented, "the court shall communicate, or have communicated, to the defendant the essential facts in the report of the presentence investigation (from which communication the sources of confidential information may be excluded)." Committee on Rules of Practice and Procedure, Second Preliminary Draft of Proposed Amendments to Rules of Criminal Procedure for the United States District Courts, p. 39 (March 1964). A previously suggested revision was to the effect that the courts be required to disclose "a summary" of the material contained in the report. See Higgins, *Confidentiality of Presentence Reports*, 28 ALBANY L. REV. 12, 13 (1964).

b. Considerations

There have been three basic arguments made against disclosure of the presentence report to the defendant. First, it is suggested that disclosure would dry up sources of information. "To get information, especially of an intimate sort, the social investigator must be able to give firm assurances of confidentiality; if people generally learn that supplying information will get them into court or plunge them into a neighborhood feud, they will no longer share their knowledge and impressions . . . ." Paulsen, *Kent v. United States: The Constitutional Context of Juvenile Cases*, 1966 SUP. CT. REV. 167, 180. Compare United States v. Fischer, 381 F.2d 509 (2d Cir. 1967). In addition, the files of social agencies, open only on a confidential basis, would have to be closed to probation officers if the information were required to be disclosed to the defendant. In other cases, the lives of informants may be endangered if their identity were disclosed.

The second reason commonly advanced for not disclosing the presentence report is that disclosure would interminably delay the proceedings: "To require the court to permit examination and controversy over each part of a probation report would, in large part, defeat the very purpose of the report by extending the process to the point at which it is no longer a practical tool for the court's guidance in the exercise of its discretion." People v. Peace, 18 N.Y.2d 230, 237, 219 N.E.2d 419, 423 (1966), *cert. denied*, 385 U.S. 1032 (1967). The fear is thus that the defendant will challenge everything in the report, and thereby transform the sentencing process into a much more lengthy affair than it has to be. In turn, it is predicted, this could lead to dispensing with the report altogether in order to avoid the delay.

Thirdly, there is the argument that disclosure of parts of some presentence reports would be affirmatively harmful to the rehabilitative efforts of the defendant; a psychiatrist hardly reveals his complete diagnosis to his patient at the beginning of their relationship. Similarly, and particularly if the defendant is to be supervised on probation by the same officer who compiled the report, it can impede the defendant's progress from the beginning if complete disclosure is made.

Finally, each of these arguments is buttressed by the contention that it is not unfair to the defendant to proceed against him in this manner. "After conviction a case ceases to be an action at law and becomes a social problem." Hincks, *In Opposition to Rule 34(c)(2), Proposed Federal Rules of Criminal Procedure*, Fed. Prob., Oct.–Dec. 1944, p. 7. Viewed in this light, there is not the scrupulous need for trial-type hearings with full disclosure and confrontation that properly governs the determination of guilt. The probation officers can be as trusted as can the defense attorney to ensure the accuracy of the report; and ensuring accuracy is the only interest which the defendant would protect if he were afforded full disclosure. . . .

The view which is reflected in subsection (b) is based upon both an assessment of the values which are served by non-disclosure and a balance of these values against basic fairness to the defendant. Specifically, the argument that sources of information will dry up if the defendant's attorney is permitted to examine the report falters on two grounds.

The first is based on the experience of those members of the Committee who have lived under a system in which disclosure is routine, and is supplemented by the Committee's examination of sample reports produced under such a system. The conclusion is that there is little factual basis for the fear that information will become unavailable if the report is disclosed. The quality and value of a presentence report will turn to an infinitely greater extent on the skill of the probation service and the availability of adequate supporting facilities than it will on whether its contents remain a secreet. This view is further supported by the experience of the Legal Aid Agency in the District of Columbia. In order to meet the informational needs of defense counsel who were denied access to the presentence report, the Agency instituted a program to supply the attorney with a separately prepared report for the defense. It was reported to the Advisory Committee that only rarely was difficulty encountered by reason of the fact that such reports were expressly prepared for the defendant. For a description of the project, see Keys, *Extra-Legal Help for Defendants*, Legal Aid Brief Case, Oct. 1965, p. 15.

The second reason is more fundamental. One of the basic values underlying the manner in which the guilt phase of a criminal case proceeds is that the defendant is entitled to know the details of the charge against him and is entitled to an opportunity to respond. It is believed that this value is subverted by a system which does not require disclosure of the information contained in the presentence report.

The irony is clear. The Committee majority believes that the need to protect sources of information should be given no more weight on the disclosure issue at the sentencing stage than it would be at the guilt stage or at a hearing on recidivist or sex offender proceedings. It can see no relevant distinction. Long since exploded is the theory that a defendant who has been convicted of crime no longer has any rights, or that any sentence less than the maximum is the result of an act of grace. See, *e.g.*, Kadish, *Legal Norm and Discretion in the Police and Sentencing Processes*, 75 HARV. L. REV. 904, 919–25 (1962). In terms of impact on the defendant, it would not seem to be maintainable that he is hurt more by the deprivation of notice on the guilt issue than he would be on the sentencing issue. Coupled with the belief that the system can function in just as informed a manner with disclosure as without it, this conclusion leads the majority to the view that with respect to the occurrence of historical events the presentence report should not be a sacrosanct document. As the Supreme Court recently observed in a different, but still strikingly similar context, "perhaps the point of it is that while non-disclosure may contribute to the comfort of the staff, disclosure does not cause heaven to fall." Kent v. United States, 383 U.S. 541, 564 n.32 (1966).

Nor can the majority of the Advisory Committee accept the argument that non-disclosure should follow because the proceedings will be delayed by disclosure. In the first place, such an argument is a difficult one to make in the face of a conclusion that basic fairness requires disclosure; it completely avoids the fundamental relevance of justice to the defendant as a factor in determining procedural requirements. In the second place, the majority believes that this too is a straw man which both is not likely to find support in the facts of many cases and which in most can be avoided by the presentence conference proposed by section 4.5, *infra*.

Most importantly, however, it is the conviction of the majority that a properly conducted sentencing proceeding could, and perhaps should, be *more* protracted rather than less because of non-disclosure of the report. As expressed in support of section 5.3(f)(iii), *infra,* one of the functions of the defense attorney is to assure that the sentence is based on adequate and accurate information. The only way he can meet this duty if not allowed access to the report is by painstaking investigation, followed by the detailed presentation of evidence which may already be contained in the report. An attorney who is to assure himself that an item of information—which may have been furnished to the probation officer by the defendant in the first place— will be before the sentencing court must delay the proceedings to determine whether it has already come to the attention of the judge.

Finally, the majority cannot accept the proposition that historical facts should be withheld because the disclosure of a diagnosis might harm the defendant's chances for rehabilitation. The majority would be quite prepared to accept the legitimacy of the thesis underlying this argument, as expressed in subsection (b), but at the same time cannot accept it as a reason for denying disclosure of information not relevant to the point. . . .

Finally, it should be noted that there may be constitutional grounds on which disclosure of the presentence report should be required. Already noted is the possibility of an argument proceeding from the need for the effective assistance of counsel. Cases such as Townsend v. Burke, 334 U.S. 736 (1948), and United States v. Myers, 374 F.2d 707 (3d Cir. 1967), strongly support the position that the purpose of counsel at the sentencing proceeding is to assure the accuracy of information to be used in framing the sentence, a function which he cannot perform without access to the presentence report. The constitutional requirement of notice prior to the taking of adverse action—heretofore operative in civil contexts as well as criminal—may also operate in this context. But whatever the result of the constitutional cases of the future, two points must be made. First, the Supreme Court has never explicitly held that disclosure is not required. Neither Williams v. New York, 337 U.S. 241 (1949), nor Specht v. Patterson, 386 U.S. 605 (1967), deals specifically with this issue. The second point is that the disclosure decision is not in any event a decision which should exclusively be controlled by constitutional considerations. The Committee majority is persuaded as a matter of policy that disclosure of the report ought to be required because such a practice will increase the fairness of the system, because it will increase the appearance of fairness, and because it will assure a greater degree of accuracy in the sentencing determination.

c. Subsection (b)

It remains to deal with several of the specifics of subsection (b). It is appropriate in the ordinary case that it be the attorney rather than the defendant who is to examine the report because of the need for an expert evaluation of its strengths and weaknesses and because it will be the attorney who is to prepare the presentations to be made at the sentencing proceeding. Of course, if the defendant is to represent himself at the sentencing proceeding, then it is he who must have access to the report. The court in such a case should advise him of his rights in this respect.

In addition, subsection (b) provides that there should be full disclosure to the prosecuting attorney. On this point, the majority follows the suggestion of the revision of Federal Rule 32(c)(2). Compare MINN. STAT. ANN. § 609.115(4) (1964), quoted in comment *a, supra*. The major reason for such a provision is that the prosecutor too should be concerned with the accuracy of the facts on which the sentence is based, and that his interests will thus be served by being able to compare the report against information at his disposal. See § 5.3(d) (i), *infra*. He also needs to be in a position to challenge or concede any inaccuracies asserted by the defendant.

Subsection (b) also provides that in extraordinary cases the court may withhold three types of information for stated reasons. There would be no purpose advanced if the defendant were shown scurrilous information which was clearly irrelevant to the sentencing decision. Of course such information should not be in the report in the first place, and in most instances will not be. But if it is there, the principle which generally supports disclosure need not be pushed to extremes if there is a chance that the information may do some positive harm. There are likewise good reasons for withholding from the defendant personally information of a diagnostic nature which may do positive harm to any effective program of rehabilitation. Similarly the sources of information actually obtained in exchange for assurances of confidentiality could in some cases be properly withheld. To the extent that disclosure of the information is tantamount to disclosure of its source, on the other hand, the balance would seem clearly in favor of the defendant's need to know.

The difficulty with exceptions such as these is that they may be abused, and result as a practical matter in little improvement in the disclosure patterns which presently exist. In an attempt to confront this danger directly, the majority would require that the court explicitly state for the record the reasons for the non-disclosure of any item of information, and that it inform the defendant that a deletion has occurred so that he may have the matter, along with all of the other issues in the case, reviewed on appeal. By endorsing a general policy in favor of disclosure, by making non-disclosure of specific items a burdensome task to be justified as an exception, and by providing for review to determine whether non-disclosure was justified, the majority believes that the danger will be minimized, but that an outlet will be available to accommodate justifiable fears in particular cases. In a very few cases, this position will result in disclosure of information which the advocates of secrecy would prefer not to disclose. Such is the price of a system which derives value from the fairness with which it operates.

4.5 Presentence report: time of disclosure; presentence conference

(a) The information made available to the parties under section 4.4 should be disclosed sufficiently prior to the imposition of sentence as to afford a reasonable opportunity for verification.

(b) In cases where the presentence report has been open to inspection, each party should be required prior to the sentencing proceeding to notify the opposing party and the court of any part of the report which he intends to controvert by the production of evidence. It may then be advisable for the court and the parties to discuss the possibility of avoiding the reception of evidence by a stipulation as to the disputed part of the report. A record of the resolution of any issue at such a conference should be preserved for inclusion in the record of the sentencing proceeding (section 5.7[a][iii]).

Commentary

. . . .

b. Presentence conference

One of the major arguments against disclosure of the presentence report to the defendant has been that interminable delays will result from the natural tendency of the defense to quibble with every minute detail of the report. Subsection (b) is designed to combat this tendency and to accommodate the legitimate interest expressed by this view.

The only statute known to the Advisory Committee which addresses itself to this point is the recently enacted provision in Minnesota. The provision there is that on the request of either prosecution or defense (the entire report is available to both) "a summary hearing in chambers shall be held on any matter brought in issue." MINN. STAT. ANN. § 609.115 (1964). Within the experience of one member of the Advisory Committee, this requirement almost always avoids the need for the formal reception of evidence in open court.

The recommendation here is slightly different from the Minnesota provision in theory, but undoubtedly rather close in practice. The suggestion is that the parties be required to notify each other and the court of any errors prior to the sentencing proceeding, at which point the court should have the authority to initiate a presentence conference for the purpose of ascertaining the nature of the dispute. Many courses are open at such a conference: it can be stipulated that the dispute is one which is of such minor importance to the sentencing decision that the challenged portion of the report can be ignored; it can be stipulated that the challenged part of the report is in error, and it can be corrected by stipulation; or if there is serious disagreement and the issue is important to the sentencing decision, an informal evidentiary hearing can be held—as indeed it should be if the issue is important to a proper sentence. In most cases, however, it is to be expected that the reception of evidence could be avoided by further investigation, by concession of the parties, or by other informal devices.

It is important, of course, that if changes in the report are made as a result of such a conference a record is made so that others who later use the report, such as corrections authorities or a probation officer, will be brought up to date. Subsection (b) accordingly provides that a record of the resolution of any disputes at a presentence conference should become part of the record of the sentencing proceeding. See § 5.7(a)(iii), *infra*. It would seem best if any such record were actually attached to the presentence report in order to avoid subsequent errors.

Finally, it may be appropriate for procedures to be adopted formalizing the presentence conference, the timing of the disclosure of the presentence report, or other related matters. It may also be appropriate for sanctions to be attached to the failure to abide by such procedures, although they should of course be flexible enough so as to prevent injustice. In the view of the Advisory Committee, however, such matters should be left for resolution on a local basis.

4.6 Additional services

(a) The sentencing decision is of such complexity that each sentencing court must have available to it a broad range of services and facilities from which it can obtain more complete information about the defendant's mental, emotional and physical condition than can be afforded in the presentence report. The court should be able to employ such services in any case in which more detailed information of this type is desired as the basis for a sentence.

(b) The need for such additional services can and should be met by a combination of local services or facilities, such as by authority to employ local physicians or clinics on a case-by-case basis, and of regional, statewide or nationwide services or facilities, such as a central reception and diagnostic center.

(c) There is an urgent need for the various disciplines which are in a position to provide such services to develop professional standards by which high quality can be assured.

(d) Reports which result from the use of such services or facilities should be subject to the same disclosure and verification provisions as those which govern presentence reports (sections 4.3–4.5, 5.4).

Commentary

a. Additional services

In every jurisdiction in this country the court is empowered to employ various types of sentences as an alternative to incarceration in a maximum security institution. In most, and under the sentencing structure proposed by this report, the court has additional determinations to make about such matters as the appropriate length of incarceration and parole eligibility.

Reliance on the trial court for such significant correctional decisions suggests the imperative need for informational services beyond the normal presentence report. There will inevitably be instances in which the presentence report together with other information acquired during the trial will either leave the court short of desired information or will have raised additional questions which can only be answered by an examination of the defendant's physical, emotional or mental condition. The lack of access to facilities which can supply such information will force the court to an uninformed guess as to the proper disposition.

Too much is at stake to place the court in such a position. On occasion the simple correction of a physical defect has altered the course of a seemingly incorrigible offender. The use of prison in such a context could reinforce the offender's anti-social tendencies. Similarly, the pattern of psychiatric study followed by appropriate treatment offers significant advantages over the simple detention which characterizes so many of our prisons. The system needs the ability to discover the cases where unusual factors may indicate the desirability of an unusual disposition. The availability of facilities such as are contemplated by this section is one step in providing that capability.

The federal government and many of the states have recognized this. The federal statutes, for example, authorize a diagnostic commitment to a facility maintained by the Bureau of Prisons for study prior to the final imposition of sentence. See 18 U.S.C. § 4208(b) (1964); PRESIDENT'S COMM'N, THE COURTS 21. See also CAL. PENAL CODE § 1203.03 (1966 Supp.); N.J. STAT. ANN. §§ 30:4A–1 to –17 (1964); MODEL SENTENCING ACT § 6, Appendix C, *infra;* MODEL PENAL CODE § 7.08(1), Appendix B, *infra.* For general discussions, see Guttmacher, *Adult Psychiatric Court Clinics,* in SLOVENKO, CRIME, LAW AND CORRECTIONS 470 (1966); Heller, *Mental Health and Criminal Behavior,* 40 F.R.D. 399 (1966); Smith, *Psychiatric Examinations in Federal Mental Competency Proceedings,* 37 F.R.D. 171 (1965); O'Connell, *Court Clinics—The American Experience,* Medicine, Science and the Law, Oct. 1964, p. 266; Smith, *Observation and Study of Defendants Prior to Sentence,* Fed. Prob., June 1962, p. 6; Brancale, *Diagnostic Techniques in Aid of Sentencing,* 23 LAW & CONTEMP. PROB. 442 (1958). A description of many existing facilities is provided in tabular form in the Guttmacher article cited above, at 488–93.

It is of course not feasible to establish for every court a separate court services department capable of providing such elaborate information. Rural courts do not have the volume to justify the expense.

But there are many alternatives. The court could be given the authority and the funds to employ local psychiatrists or psychologists on a case-by-case basis, or could be permitted to work out an arrangement with an existing clinic which is nearby. At the other extreme a reception and diagnostic center could be established to provide statewide service, much as the Bureau of Prisons operates from a single facility for the federal system. The same type of facility could be established for certain rural regions of the state, leaving to the high-crime city areas the development of separate facilities. Several states could combine in the construction of a single facility for service to all courts within the area. The Advisory Committee also believes that significant improvement in correctional treatment of offenders can be achieved if states which had doubts as to their capacity to support superior facilities of the type described immediately undertook to explore with neighboring states the feasibility of jointly sponsored institutions or even the compensated use of another state's facilities.

The possibilities are endless. The ultimate goal, however, should be to provide the court with sufficient information services to permit highly sophisticated studies in cases which present special problems. The "easy" solution of maximum security incarceration is merely a temporizing device. Employment of the tools of non-legal disciplines offers the far more substantial possibility—and in most cases at less cost to the taxpayer—of more permanent solutions.

At the same time, however, it should be emphasized that employment of the tools of other disciplines depends on the development within those disciplines of the capacity to render the needed assistance. Existing services tend to be of very uneven quality, for reasons ranging from under-funding to the failure to seek properly trained personnel. See Guttmacher, *Adult Psychiatric Court Clinics*, in SLOVENKO, CRIME, LAW AND CORRECTIONS 479 (1966). Subsection (c) invites attention to this problem and suggests the need for development of standards by which the high quality of such services can be assured.

b. Availability of report

Subsection (d) states that reports which result from the use of such services should be treated in very much the same way as the presentence report. Their purpose is to provide additional information to the court for its assistance in sentencing, and like the presentence report they should be prepared by one who is not in an adversary setting.

But the fact that the report is not prepared by an adversary, as in the case of the presentence report, is not a valid reason to withhold it from the parties. The Advisory Committee believes that the same reasons which support disclosure of the presentence report, developed in detail in the commentary to section 4.4, *supra*, are applicable in the context under discussion here. Several existing statutes specifically provide for this result. See, *e.g.*, D.C. CODE ANN. § 22–3506(b) (1961); MASS. GEN. LAWS ANN. c. 123A, § 7 (1966 Supp.); OHIO REV. CODE ANN. § 2947.25 (1965 Supp); *cf.* MICH. STAT. ANN. § 28.967(7) (1954); 28 U.S.C. § 2902(b), P.L. No. 89–793, 89th Cong., 2d Sess. § 101 (November 22, 1966). See also GUTTMACHER, THE MIND OF THE MURDERER 139 (1962); Whitty v. State, 149 N.W.2d 557 (Wis. 1967).

✸　✸　✸　✸　✸

B. Sentencing Procedure

McConnell v. Rhay, 393 U.S.2 (1968)

PER CURIAM.

The sole issue presented by these cases is whether our decision in *Mempa* v. *Rhay*, 389 U.S. 128 (1967), should be applied retroactively.

The facts in both cases are quite similar to those in *Mempa*. Petitioner Jack D. McConnell pleaded guilty to two counts of grand larceny by check. At a hearing on December 23, 1965, he was placed on probation for five years upon condition that he serve one year in the county jail. He was released from jail the following April, but five months later the prosecuting attorney moved that the December 23 order be revoked, alleging that McConnell had violated the terms of his probation. Two hearings on the motion followed—one on September 29, 1966, and the other on November 23, 1966. As a result of these hearings, McConnell was sentenced to two concurrent 15-year terms. At neither hearing was he represented by counsel or advised of his right to have counsel appointed. . . .

In habeas corpus proceedings, the Washington Supreme Court properly found that both petitioners' Sixth Amendment rights were violated at their deferred sentence hearings. That question was settled by our decision in *Mempa*. But the court denied relief in both cases, holding that *Mempa* should not be applied to cases in which probation and deferral or suspension of sentences had been revoked before November 13, 1967, the date upon which *Mempa* was decided. This was error.

This Court's decisions on a criminal defendant's right to counsel at trial, *Gideon* v. *Wainwright*, 372 U.S. 335 (1963); at certain arraignments, *Hamilton* v. *Alabama*, 368 U.S. 52 (1961); and on appeal, *Douglas* v. *California*, 372 U.S. 353 (1963), have been applied retroactively. The right to counsel at sentencing is no different. As in these other cases, the right being asserted related to "the very integrity of the fact-finding process." *Linkletter* v. *Walker*, 381 U.S. 618, 639 (1965); cf. *Roberts* v. *Russell*, 392 U.S. 293 (1968). As we said in *Mempa*, "the necessity for the aid of counsel in marshaling the facts, introducing evidence of mitigating circumstances and in general aiding and assisting the defendant to present his case as to sentence is apparent." 389 U.S., at 135. The right to counsel at sentencing must, therefore, be treated like the right to counsel at other stages of adjudication.

✻ ✻ ✻ ✻ ✻

SPECHT V. PATTERSON, 386 U.S. 605 (1967) ✻

MR. JUSTICE DOUGLAS delivered the opinion of the Court.

We held in *Williams* v. *New York*, 337 U.S. 241, that the Due Process Clause of the Fourteenth Amendment did not require a judge to have hearings and to give a convicted person an opportunity to participate

✻ Footnotes omitted.

in those hearings when he came to determine the sentence to be imposed. We said:

"Under the practice of individualizing punishments, investigational techniques have been given an important role. Probation workers making reports of their investigations have not been trained to prosecute but to aid offenders. Their reports have been given a high value by conscientious judges who want to sentence persons on the best available information rather than on guesswork and inadequate information. To deprive sentencing judges of this kind of information would undermine modern penological procedural policies that have been cautiously adopted throughout the nation after careful consideration and experimentation. We must recognize that most of the information now relied upon by judges to guide them in the intelligent imposition of sentences would be unavailable if information were restricted to that given in open court by witnesses subject to cross-examination. And the modern probation report draws on information concerning every aspect of a defendant's life. The type and extent of this information make totally impractical if not impossible open court testimony with cross-examination. Such a procedure could endlessly delay criminal administration in a retrial of collateral issues." *Id.*, 249–250.

That was a case where at the end of the trial and in the same proceeding the fixing of the penalty for first degree murder was involved —whether life imprisonment or death.

The question is whether the rule of the *Williams* case applies to this Colorado case where petitioner, having been convicted for indecent liberties under one Colorado statute that carries a maximum sentence of 10 years (Colo. Rev. Stat. Ann. § 40–2–32 (1963) but not sentenced under it, may be sentenced under the Sex Offenders Act, Colo. Rev. Stat. Ann. §§ 39–19–1 to 10 (1963), for an indeterminate term of from one day to life without notice and full hearing. The Colorado Supreme Court approved the procedure, when it was challenged by habeas corpus (153 Colo. 235, 385 P.2d 423) and on motion to set aside the judgment. 156 Colo. 12, 396 P.2d 838. This federal habeas corpus proceeding resulted, the Court of Appeals affirming dismissal of the writ, 357 F.2d 325. The case is here on a petition for certiorari, 385 U.S. 968.

The Sex Offenders Act may be brought into play if the trial court "is of the opinion that any . . . person [convicted of specified sex offenses], if at large, constitutes a threat of bodily harm to members of the public, or is an habitual offender and mentally ill." § 1. He then becomes punishable for an indeterminate term of from one day to life on the following conditions as specified in § 2:

> "(2) A complete psychiatric examination shall have been made of him by the psychiatrists of the Colorado psychopathic hospital or by psychiatrists designated by the district court; and
>
> "(3) A complete written report thereof submitted to the district court. Such report shall contain all facts and findings, together with recommendations as to whether or not the person is treatable under the provisions of this article; whether or not the person should be committed to the Colorado state hospital or to the state home and training schools as mentally ill or mentally deficient. Such report shall also contain the psychiatrist's opinion as to whether or not the person could be adequately supervised on probation."

This procedure was followed in petitioner's case; he was examined as required and a psychiatric report prepared and given to the trial judge prior to the sentencing. But there was no hearing in the normal sense, no right of confrontation and so on.

Petitioner insists that this procedure does not satisfy due process because it allows the critical finding to be made under § 1 of the Sex Offenders Act (1) without a hearing at which the person so convicted may confront and cross-examine adverse witnesses and present evidence of his own by use of compulsory process, if necessary; and (2) on the basis of hearsay evidence to which the person involved is not allowed access.

We adhere to *Williams* v. *New York, supra;* but we decline the invitation to extend it to this radically different situation. These commitment proceedings whether denominated civil or criminal are subject both to the Equal Protection Clause of the Fourteenth Amendment as we held in *Baxstrom* v. *Herold,* 383 U.S. 107, and to the Due Process Clause. We hold that the requirements of due process were not satisfied here.

The Sex Offenders Act does not make the commission of a specified crime the basis for sentencing. It makes one conviction the basis for commencing another proceeding under another Act to determine whether a person constitutes a threat of bodily harm to the public, or is an habitual offender and mentally ill. That is a new finding of fact (*Vanderhoof* v. *People,* 152 Colo. 147, 149, 380 P.2d 903, 904) that was not an ingredient of the offense charged. The punishment under the second Act is criminal punishment even though it is designed not so much as retribution as it is to keep individuals from inflicting future harm. *United States* v. *Brown,* 381 U.S. 437, 458.

The Court of Appeals for the Third Circuit in speaking of a comparable Pennsylvania statute said:

> "It is a separate criminal proceeding which may be invoked after conviction of one of the specified crimes. Petitioner therefore was entitled to a full judicial hearing before the magnified sentence was imposed. At such a hearing the requirements of due process cannot be satisfied by partial or niggardly procedural protections. A defendant in such a proceeding is entitled to the full panoply of the relevant protections which due process guarantees in state criminal proceedings. He must be afforded all those safeguards which are fundamental rights and essential to a fair trial, including the right to confront and cross-examine the witnesses against him." *Gerchman* v. *Maroney,* 355 F.2d 302, 312.

We agree with that view. Under Colorado's criminal procedure, here challenged, the invocation of the Sex Offenders Act means the making of a new charge leading to criminal punishment. The case is not unlike those under recidivist statutes where an habitual criminal issue is "a distinct issue" (*Graham* v. *West Virginia,* 224 U.S. 616, 625) on which a defendant "must receive reasonable notice and an opportunity to be heard." *Oyler* v. *Boles,* 368 U.S. 448, 452; *Chandler* v. *Fretag,* 348 U.S. 3, 8. Due process, in other words, requires that he be present with counsel, have an opportunity to be heard, be confronted with witnesses against him, have the right to cross-examine, and to offer evidence of his own. And there must be findings adequate to make meaningful any appeal that is allowed. The case is therefore quite unlike the Minnesota statute we considered in *Minnesota* v. *Probate Court,* 309 U.S. 270, where in a proceeding to have a person adjudged a "psychopathic personality" there was a hearing where he was represented by counsel and could compel the production of witnesses on his behalf. *Id.,* at 275. None of these procedural safeguards we have mentioned is present under Colorado's Sex Offenders Act. We therefore hold that it is deficient in due process as measured by the requirements of the Fourteenth Amendment, *Pointer* v. *Texas,* 380 U.S. 400.

Reversed.

❖   ❖   ❖   ❖   ❖

FEDERAL RULES ON CRIMINAL PROCEDURE, RULE 32 (a)–(b), (e)

(a) **Sentence**

(1) **Imposition of Sentence.** Sentence shall be imposed without unreasonable delay. Pending sentence the court may commit the defendant or continue or alter the bail. Before imposing sentence the court shall afford counsel an opportunity to speak on behalf of the defendant and shall address the defendant personally and ask him if he wishes to make a statement in his own behalf and to present any information in mitigation of punishment.

(2) **Notification of Right to Appeal.** After imposing sentence in a case which has gone to trial on a plea of not guilty, the court shall advise the defendant of his right to appeal and of the right of a person who is unable to pay the cost of an appeal to apply for leave to appeal in forma pauperis. If the defendant so requests, the clerk of the court shall prepare and file forthwith a notice of appeal on behalf of the defendant.

(b) **Judgment.** A judgment of conviction shall set forth the plea, the verdict or findings, and the adjudication and sentence. If the defendant is found not guilty or for any other reason is entitled to be discharged, judgment shall be entered accordingly. The judgment shall be signed by the judge and entered by the clerk. . . .

. . . .

(e) **Probation.** After conviction of an offense not punishable by death or by life imprisonment, the defendant may be placed on probation as provided by law.

✿   ✿   ✿   ✿   ✿

NEW YORK CRIMINAL PROCEDURE LAW (1971)

§ 380.10   **Applicability**

1. **In general.** The procedure prescribed by this title shall apply to sentencing for every offense, whether defined within or outside of the penal law.

2. **Exception.** Whenever a different or inconsistent procedure is provided by any other law in relation to sentencing for a non-criminal offense defined therein, such different or inconsistent procedure shall apply thereto.

§ 380.20   **Sentence required**

The court must pronounce sentence in every case where a conviction is entered. If an accusatory instrument contains multiple counts and a conviction is entered on more than one count the court must pronounce sentence on each count.

§ 380.30 Time for pronouncing sentence

1. **In general.** Sentence must be pronounced without unreasonable delay.

2. **Court to fix time.** Upon entering a conviction the court must:

(a) Fix a date for pronouncing sentence; or

(b) Fix a date for one of the pre-sentence proceedings specified in article four hundred; or

(c) Pronounce sentence on the date the conviction is entered in accordance with the provisions of subdivision three.

3. **Sentence on date of conviction.** The court may sentence the defendant at the time the conviction is entered if:

(a) A pre-sentence report or a fingerprint report is not required; or

(b) Where any such report is required, the report has been received.

Provided, however, that the court must not pronounce sentence at such time without inquiring as to whether an adjournment is desired by the defendant. Where an adjournment is requested, the defendant must state the purpose thereof and the court may, in its discretion, allow a reasonable time.

4. **Time for pre-sentence proceedings.** The court may conduct one or more of the pre-sentence proceedings specified in article two hundred five at any time before sentence is pronounced. Notice of any such proceeding issued after the date for pronouncing sentence has been fixed automatically adjourns the date for pronouncing sentence. In such case the court must fix a date for pronouncing sentence at the conclusion of such proceeding.

§ 380.40 Defendant's presence at sentencing

1. **In general.** The defendant must be personally present at the time sentence is pronounced.

2. **Exception.** Where sentence is to be pronounced for a misdemeanor or for a petty offense, the court may, on motion of the defendant, dispense with the requirement that the defendant be personally present. Any such motion shall be accompanied by a waiver, signed and acknowledged by the defendant, reciting the maximum sentence that may be imposed for the offense and stating that the defendant

waives the right to be personally present at the time sentence is pronounced.

3. **Corporations.** Sentence may be pronounced against a corporation in the absence of counsel if counsel fails to appear on the date of sentence after reasonable notice thereof.

§ 380.50   Statements at time of sentence

At the time of pronouncing sentence, the court must accord the prosecutor an opportunity to make a statement with respect to any matter relevant to the question of sentence. The court must then accord counsel for the defendant an opportunity to speak on behalf of the defendant. The defendant also has the right to make a statement personally in his own behalf, and before pronouncing sentence the court must ask him whether he wishes to make such a statement.

The court may, either before or after receiving such statements, summarize the factors it considers relevant for the purpose of sentence and afford an opportunity to the defendant or his counsel to comment thereon.

§ 380.60   Authority for the execution of a sentence

Except where a sentence of death is pronounced, a certificate of conviction showing the sentence pronounced by the court, or a certified copy thereof, shall constitute the authority for execution of the sentence and shall serve as the order of commitment, and no other warrant, order of commitment or authority is necessary to justify or to require execution of the sentence.

§ 380.70   Minutes of sentence

In any case where a person receives an indeterminate sentence of imprisonment or a reformatory or an alternative local reformatory sentence of imprisonment, a certified copy of the stenographic minutes of the sentencing proceeding must be delivered to the person in charge of the institution to which the defendant has been delivered within thirty days from the date such sentence was imposed, provided, however, that a sentence or commitment shall not be deemed defective in the case of failure to comply with the provisions of this section.

§ 400.10   Pre-sentence conference

1. **Authorization and purpose.** Before pronouncing sentence the court, in its discretion, may hold one or more pre-sentence conferences in open court or in chambers (a) to resolve any discrepancies between the pre-sentence report, or other information the court has

received, and the defendant's pre-sentence memorandum submitted pursuant to section 390.40, or (b) to assist the court in its consideration of any matter relevant to the sentence to be pronounced.

2. **Attendance.** Such conference may be held with defense counsel in the absence of the defendant or the court may direct that the defendant attend. The court may also direct that any person who has furnished or who can furnish information to the court concerning sentence attend. Reasonable notice of the conference shall be given to the prosecutor who shall be afforded an opportunity to participate therein.

3. **Procedure at conference.** The court may advise the persons present at the conference of the factual contents of any report or memorandum it has received and afford any of the participants an opportunity to controvert or to comment upon any fact. The court may also conduct a summary hearing at the conference on any matter relevant to sentence and for such purpose take testimony under oath. In the discretion of the court, all or any part of the proceedings at the conference may be recorded by a court stenographer and the transcript made part of the pre-sentence report.

§ 400.20 Procedure for determining whether defendant should be sentenced as a persistent felony offender

1. **Applicability.** The provisions of this section govern the procedure that must be followed in order to impose the persistent felony offender sentence authorized by subdivision two of section 70.10 of the penal law. Such sentence may not be imposed unless, based upon evidence in the record of a hearing held pursuant to this section, the court (a) has found that the defendant is a persistant felony offender as defined in subdivision one of section 70.10 of the penal law, and (b) is of the opinion that the history and character of the defendant and the nature and circumstances of his criminal conduct are such that extended incarceration and lifetime supervision of the defendant are warranted to best serve the public interest.

2. **Authorization for hearing.** When information available to the court prior to sentencing indicates that the defendant is a persistent felony offender, and when, in the opinion of the court, the available information shows that a persistent felony offender sentence may be warranted, the court may order a hearing to determine (a) whether the defendant is in fact a persistent felony offender, and (b) if so, whether a persistent felony offender sentence should be imposed.

3. **Order directing a hearing.** An order directing a hearing to determine whether the defendant should be sentenced as a persistent

felony offender must be filed with the clerk of the court and must specify a date for the hearing not less than twenty days from the date the order is filed. The court must annex to and file with the order a statement setting forth the following:

(a) The dates and places of the previous convictions which render the defendant a persistent felony offender as defined in subdivision one of section 70.10 of the penal law; and

(b) The factors in the defendant's background and prior criminal conduct which the court deems relevant for the purpose of sentencing the defendant as a persistent felony offender.

4. Notice of hearing. Upon receipt of the order and statement of the court, the clerk of the court must send a notice of hearing to the defendant, his counsel and the district attorney. Such notice must specify the time and place of the hearing and the fact that the purpose of the hearing is to determine whether or not the defendant should be sentenced as a persistent felony offender. Each notice required to be sent hereunder must be accompanied by a copy of the statement of the court.

5. Burden and standard of proof; evidence. Upon any hearing held pursuant to this section the burden of proof is upon the people. A finding that the defendant is a persistent felony offender, as defined in subdivision one of section 70.10 of the penal law, must be based upon proof beyond a reasonable doubt by evidence admissible under the rules applicable to the trial of the issue of guilt. Matters pertaining to the defendant's history and character and the nature and circumstances of his criminal conduct may be established by any relevant evidence, not legally privileged, regardless of admissibility under the exclusionary rules of evidence, and the standard of proof with respect to such matters shall be a preponderance of the evidence.

6. Constitutionality of prior convictions. A previous conviction in this or any other jurisdiction which was obtained in violation of the rights of the defendant under the applicable provisions of the Constitution of the United States may not be counted in determining whether the defendant is a persistent felony offender. The defendant may, at any time during the course of the hearing hereunder controvert an allegation with respect to such conviction in the statement of the court on the grounds that the conviction was unconstitutionally obtained. Failure to challenge the previous conviction in the manner provided herein constitutes a waiver on the part of the defendant of any allegation of unconstitutionality unless good cause be shown for such failure to make timely challenge.

7. Preliminary examination. When the defendant appears for the hearing the court must ask him whether he wishes to controvert any allegation made in the statement prepared by the court, and whether he wishes to present evidence on the issue of whether he is a persistent felony offender or on the question of his background and criminal conduct. If the defendant wishes to controvert any allegation in the statement of the court, he must specify the particular allegation or allegations he wishes to controvert. If he wishes to present evidence in his own behalf, he must specify the nature of such evidence. Uncontroverted allegations in the statement of the court are deemed evidence in the record.

8. Cases where further hearing is not required. Where the uncontroverted allegations in the statement of the court are sufficient to support a finding that the defendant is a persistent felony offender and the court is satisfied that (a) the uncontroverted allegations with respect to the defendant's background and the nature of his prior criminal conduct warrant sentencing the defendant as a persistent felony offender, and (b) the defendant either has no relevant evidence to present or the facts which could be established through the evidence offered by the defendant would not affect the court's decision, the court may enter a finding that the defendant is a persistent felony offender and sentence him in accordance with the provisions of subdivision two of section 70.10 of the penal law.

9. Cases where further hearing is required. Where the defendant controverts an allegation in the statement of the court and the uncontroverted allegations in such statement are not sufficient to support a finding that the defendant is a persistent felony offender as defined in subdivision one of section 70.10 of the penal law, or where the uncontroverted allegations with respect to the defendant's history and the nature of his prior criminal conduct do not warrant sentencing him as a persistent felony offender, or where the defendant has offered to present evidence to establish facts that would affect the court's decision on the question of whether a persistent felony offender sentence is warranted, the court may fix a date for a further hearing. Such hearing shall be before the court without a jury and either party may introduce evidence with respect to the controverted allegations or any other matter relevant to the issue of whether or not the defendant should be sentenced as a persistent felony offender. At the conclusion of the hearing the court must make a finding as to whether or not the defendant is a persistent felony offender and, upon a finding that he is such, must then make such findings of fact as it deems relevant to the question of whether a persistent felony offender sentence

is warranted. If the court both finds that the defendant is a persistent felony offender and is of the opinion that a persistent felony offender sentence is warranted, it may sentence the defendant in accordance with the provisions of subdivision two of section 70.10 of the penal law.

10. Termination of hearing. At any time during the pendency of a hearing pursuant to this section, the court may, in its discretion, terminate the hearing without making any finding. In such case, unless the court recommences the proceedings and makes the necessary findings, the defendant may not be sentenced as a persistent felony offender.

§ 400.22 Evidence of imprisonment

The certificate of the commissioner of correction or of the warden or other chief officer of any prison, or of the superintendent or other chief officer of any penitentiary under the seal of his office containing name of person, a statement of the court in which conviction was had, the date and term of sentence, length of time imprisoned, and date of discharge from prison or penitentiary, shall be prima facie evidence of the imprisonment and discharge of any person under the conviction stated and set forth in such certificate for the purposes of any proceeding under section 400.20.

§ 400.30 Procedure for determining the amount of a fine based upon the defendant's gain from the offense

1. Order directing a hearing. In any case where the court is of the opinion that the sentence should consist of or include a fine and that the amount of the fine should be based upon the defendant's gain from the commission of the offense, the court may order a hearing to determine the amount of such gain. The order shall be filed with the clerk of the court and shall specify the date for the hearing, which shall be not less than ten days from the date of the filing.

2. Notice of hearing. Upon receipt of the order, the clerk of the court shall send a notice of hearing to the defendant, his counsel and the district attorney. Such notice shall specify the time and place of the hearing and the fact that the purpose of the hearing is to determine the amount of the defendant's gain from the commission of the offense so that an appropriate fine can be imposed.

3. Hearing. When the defendant appears for the hearing the court shall ask him whether he wishes to make any statement with respect to the amount of his gain from commission of the offense. If the defendant does make a statement, the court may accept such state-

ment and base its finding thereon. Where the defendant does not make a statement, or where the court does not accept the defendant's statement, the court shall proceed with the hearing.

4. **Burden and standard of proof; evidence.** At any hearing held pursuant to this section the burden of proof shall be upon the people. A finding as to the amount of the defendant's gain from the commission of the offense must be based upon a preponderance of the credible evidence. Any relevant evidence, not legally privileged, may be received regardless of its admissibility under the exclusionary rules of evidence.

5. **Termination of hearing.** At any time during the pendency of a hearing pursuant to this section the court may, in its absolute discretion, terminate the hearing without making any finding.

§ 400.40   Procedure for determining prior convictions for the purpose of sentence in certain cases

1. **Applicability.** Where a conviction is entered for an unclassified misdemeanor or for a traffic infraction and the authorized sentence depends upon whether the defendant has previously been convicted of an offense, or where a conviction is entered for a violation defined outside the penal law and the amount of the fine authorized by the law defining such violation depends upon whether the defendant has previously been convicted of an offense, the question of whether the defendant has previously been so convicted shall be determined as provided in this section.

2. **Statement to be filed.** If it shall appear that the defendant has previously been so convicted and if the court is required, or in its discretion desires, to impose a sentence that would not be authorized in the absence of such previous conviction, a statement shall be filed after conviction and before sentence setting forth the date and place of the previous conviction or convictions and the court shall conduct a hearing to determine whether the defendant is the same person mentioned in the record of such conviction or convictions. In cases where an increased sentence is mandatory, the statement may be filed by the court or by the prosecutor. In cases where an increased sentence is discretionary, the statement may be filed only by the court.

3. **Preliminary examination.** The defendant shall be given a copy of such statement and the court shall ask him whether he admits or denies such prior conviction or convictions. If the defendant denies such prior conviction or convictions, or remains silent, the court may proceed with the hearing and, where the increased sentence is mandatory, it must impose such.

4. **Time for hearing.** In any case where a copy of the statement was not received by the defendant at least two days prior to the preliminary examination, the court must upon request of the defendant grant an adjournment of at least two days before proceeding with the hearing.

5. **Manner of conducting hearing.** A hearing pursuant to this section shall be before the court without a jury. The burden of proof shall be upon the people and a finding that the defendant has been convicted of any offense alleged in the statement must be based upon proof beyond a reasonable doubt by evidence admissible under the rules applicable to trial of the issue of guilt.

✻ ✻ ✻ ✻ ✻

AMERICAN BAR ASSOCIATION PROJECT ON STANDARDS FOR THE ADMINISTRATION OF CRIMINAL JUSTICE, STANDARDS RELATING TO SENTENCING ALTERNATIVES AND PROCEDURES (Approved Draft 1968)

5.1 Sentencing judge

(a) If guilt was determined after a trial, the judge who presided at the trial should impose the sentence unless there are compelling reasons in a specific case to provide otherwise. To accommodate cases where it becomes necessary for another judge to impose the sentence, a system should be established to acquaint the new judge with what occurred at the trial.

(b) If guilt was determined by plea, it is still desirable that the same judge who accepted the plea impose the sentence. It is recognized, however, that the rotation practices of many courts make it impossible in many instances for the same judge to sit in both capacities. In any event, the judge who imposes sentence should ascertain the facts concerning the plea and the offense.

(c) Management of the docket should be controlled by the court and should not be subject to manipulation by either party. Where possible, it is desirable that the same judge sentence all defendants who were involved in the same offense.

5.2 Multiple offenses: consolidation for sentencing; pleading to prior offenses

(a) To the extent possible, all outstanding convictions should be consolidated for sentencing at one time. All outstanding charges should be disposed of promptly and should likewise be consolidated for sentencing at one time. Charges filed after sentencing should be promptly prosecuted. Any sentence imposed on an offender already under sentence for another offense should be integrated with the prior sentence.

(b) After conviction and before sentence, the defendant should be permitted to plead guilty to other offenses he has committed which are within the jurisdiction of the sentencing court or any other court of coordinate or inferior jurisdiction in the same state. The plea should not be accepted without the written consent of the official responsible for prosecuting the charge. Submission of such a plea should constitute a waiver of any objections which the defendant otherwise might have to venue or, where no charge has yet been filed, to formal charge. If such a plea is tendered and accepted, the court should sentence the defendant for all of the offenses in one proceeding, subject to the limitations on consecutive sentences stated in section 3.4.

5.3 Duties of counsel

(a) The duties of the prosecution and defense attorneys do not cease upon conviction. While it should be recognized that sentencing is the function of the court, the attorneys nevertheless have a duty of assisting the court in as helpful a manner as possible.

(b) The prosecutor should recognize that the severity of the sentence is not necessarily an indication of the effectiveness or the efficiency of his office. In addition, the prosecutor, no less than the judge, has the duty to resist clamor or improper outside pressure of any sort.

(c) Although there will be occasions when sentencing recommendations by the prosecutor are appropriate, the prosecutor ordinarily should not make any specific recommendations as to the appropriate sentence.

(d) The duties of the prosecutor with respect to each specific sentence should include the following steps:

(i) The prosecutor should satisfy himself that the factual basis for the sentence will be both adequate and accurate, and that the record of the sentencing proceeding will accurately reflect relevant circumstances of the offense and characteristics of the defendant which were not disclosed during the guilt phase of the case:

(A) If the prosecutor has access to the presentence report, he should measure it against information at his disposal and prepare himself to amplify parts which do not sufficiently reveal matters which are relevant to a proper sentence. The prosecutor should also take proper steps to controvert any inaccuracies in the report. The first such step should normally involve an attempt to avoid the formal production of evidence in open court by reaching an informal agreement with the defense attorney;

(B) If the prosecutor does not have access to the presentence report, he should present at the sentencing proceeding those facts at his disposal which are not known by him to be before the court and which are relevant to a proper sentence;

(ii) The prosecutor should disclose to the defense and to the court at or prior to the sentencing proceeding all information in his files which is favorable to the defendant on the sentencing issue;

(iii) If a plea was the result of plea discussions or an agreement which included a position on the sentence, the prosecutor should disclose its terms to the court;

(iv) The prosecutor should determine whether there are grounds for the imposition of a special term based on particular characteristics of the defendant (sections 2.5[b], 3.1[c], 3.3). If he finds such grounds, he should cause the notice contemplated by section 5.5(b)(i) to be served on the defendant and his attorney. He may then prepare a factual case for presentation at the sentencing proceeding.

(e) The defense attorney should recognize that the sentencing stage is the time at which for many defendants the most important service of the entire proceeding can be performed.

(f) The duties of the defense attorney with respect to each specific sentence should include the following steps:

(i) The attorney should familiarize himself with all of the sentencing alternatives that are available for the offence of which his client has been convicted and with community and other facilities which may be of assistance in a plan for meeting the needs of the defendant. Such preparation should also include familiarization with the practical consequences of different sentences, and with the normal pattern of sentences for the offense involved;

(ii) The attorney should explain the consequences of the likely sentences to the defendant and assure himself that the defendant understands the nature of the sentencing proceeding. The attorney should ascertain the views of his client once such information has been conveyed;

(iii) The attorney should satisfy himself that the factual basis for the sentence will be both adequate and accurate, and that the record of the sentencing proceedings will accurately reflect relevant circumstances of the offense and characteristics of the defendant which were not disclosed during the guilt phase of the case:

(A) If the attorney has access to the presentence report, this duty should at a minimum involve verification of the essential bases of the report and amplification at the sentencing proceeding of parts which seem to be inadequate. The attorney should also take proper steps to controvert any inaccuracies in the report. The first such step should normally involve an attempt to avoid the formal production of evidence in open court by reaching an informal agreement with the prosecutor;

(B) If the attorney does not have access to the presentence report, this duty should at a minimum involve an attempt to the best of the means at his disposal to ascertain the relevant facts. The attorney should also have the obligation to present at the sentencing proceeding all facts which are not known by him to be before the court and which in the interest of his client ought to be considered in reaching a sentence;

(iv) If a plea was the result of plea discussions or an agreement which included a position of the prosecutor on the sentence, the attorney should disclose its terms to the court;

(v) In appropriate cases, the attorney should make special efforts to investigate the desirability of a disposition which would particularly meet the needs of the defendant, such as probation accompanied by employment of community facilities or commitment to an institution for special treatment. If such a disposition is available and seems appropriate, the attorney, with the consent of the defendant, should make a recommendation at the sentencing proceeding that it be utilized.

(g) It is inappropriate for either prosecution or defense counsel to re-try an individual sentence in the media of public communication.

5.4 Sentencing proceeding

(a) As soon as practicable after the determination of guilt and the examination of any presentence reports (sections 4.1–4.6), a proceeding should be held at which the sentencing court should:

(i) entertain submissions by the parties which are relevant to the sentence;

(ii) afford to the defendant his right of allocution; and

(iii) in cases where guilt was determined by plea, inform itself, if not previously informed, of the existence of plea discussions or agreements and the extent to which they involve recommendations as to the appropriate sentence.

(b) Where the need for further evidence has not been eliminated by a presentence conference (section 4.5[b]), evidence offered by the parties on the sentencing issue should be presented in open court with full rights of confrontation, cross-examination and representation by counsel.

5.5 Special requirements

(a) The sentencing court should be required to obtain and consider a presentence report (sections 4.1–4.5) supplemented by a report of the defendant's mental, emotional and physical condition (section 4.6) prior to the imposition of a minimum term of imprisonment (section 3.2), a consecutive sentence (section 3.4), a sentence as an habitual offender (section 3.3), or a special term based on exceptional characteristics of the defendant (sections 2.5[b], 3.1[c]).

(b) The sentencing court should not be authorized to impose a sentence as an habitual offender (section 3.3) or a sentence based on exceptional characteristics of the defendant (sections 2.5[b], 3.1[c]) without taking the following additional steps:

(i) Written notice should be served on the defendant and his attorney of the proposed ground on which such a sentence could be based a sufficient time prior to the imposition of sentence so as to allow the preparation of a submission on behalf of the defendant; and

(ii) With the exception of the presentence report and any supplemental reports on the defendant's mental, emotional and physical condition, all of the evidence presented to sustain the proposed grounds on which such a sentence could be based should be presented in open court with full rights of confrontation, cross-examination and representation by counsel. The defendant should be afforded an opportunity to offer opposition to the proposed action; and

(iii) The presentence report and any supplemental reports on the defendant's mental, emotional and physical condition should be disclosed to the prosecution and the defense at least to the extent required by sections 4.4 and 4.5; and

(iv) Each of the findings required as the basis for such a sentence should be found to exist by a preponderance of the evidence, and should be appealable to the extent normally applicable to similar findings; and

(v) If the conviction was by plea, it should affirmatively appear on the record that the plea was entered with knowledge that such a sentence was a possibility. If it does not so appear on the record, the defendant should not be subject to such a sentence unless he is first given an opportunity to withdraw his plea without prejudice.

(c) The procedure for revocation of a sentence not involving confinement and for revocation of a sentence involving partial confinement should conform as nearly as possible to the procedure outlined in subsections (b)(i) through (b)(iv) of this section. Standards dealing with the procedure for changes in the conditions under which such sentences will continue in effect will be set forth in a separate report dealing with probation.

5.6 Imposition of sentence

In addition to reaching the conclusions required as a prerequisite to imposition of the sentence selected, when sentence is imposed the court:

(i) should make specific findings on all controverted issues of fact which are deemed relevant to the sentencing decision;

(ii) normally should state for the record in the presence of the defendant the reasons for selecting the particular sentence to be imposed. In the exceptional cases where the court deems it in the best interests of the defendant not to state fully in his presence the reasons for the sentence, the court should prepare such a statement for inclusion in the record;

(iii) should assure that the record accurately reflects time already spent in custody for which credit will be given under the provisions of section 3.6; and

(iv) should state with care the precise terms of the sentence which is imposed.

5.7 Record

(a) As in the case of all other proceedings in open court, a record of the sentencing proceeding should be made and preserved in such a manner that it can be transcribed as needed. The following items should be available for inclusion in a transcription:

(i) a verbatim account of the entire sentencing proceeding, including a record of any statements in aggravation or mitigation made by the defendant, the defense attorney and the prosecuting attorney, together with any testimony received of witnesses on matters relevant to the sentence and any statements by the court explaining the sentence;

(ii) a verbatim account of such parts of the trial on the issue of guilt, or the proceedings leading to the acceptance of a plea, as are relevant to the sentencing decision;

(iii) copies of the presentence report and any other reports or documents available to the sentencing court as an aid in passing sentence. The part of the record containing such reports or documents should be subject to examination by the parties to the extent provided in sections 4.3 and 4.4. The record should reveal what parts of such reports or documents have been disclosed to the parties and by what method such disclosure was made. It should also contain any record of a presentence conference held in accordance with section 4.5(b).

(b) Adequate resources should be provided to the court so as to permit the transmission of relevant sentencing information to the prison authorities in the event of a commitment. If the defendant is sentenced to imprisonment for a maximum term in excess of one year, the court should be required to forward to the prison authorities a copy of the items described in section 5.7(a)(iii) and a verbatim transcript of the proceeding described in section 5.6. The court should also be authorized and encouraged to forward any other part of the record which is deemed relevant to the defendant's classification and treatment.

5.8 Procedure for awarding credit

The credit required by section 3.6 should be awarded in the following manner:

(i) It is good practice for the parties to communicate to the court at the time of sentencing the facts upon which credit for time served prior to sentencing will be based;

(ii) It is good practice for the court to inform the defendant at the time of sentencing of his status on the issue of credit for time previously served;

(iii) The court should assure that the record accurately reflects the facts upon which credit for time served prior to sentencing will be computed;

(iv) The custodian should communicate to the prison authorities at the time the defendant is delivered for commitment the amount of time spent in custody since the imposition of sentence;

(v) The credit to be awarded against the sentence should be computed by the prison authorities as soon as practicable and automatically awarded;

(vi) The prison authorities should inform the defendant of his status as soon as practicable;

(vii) The defendant should be afforded an avenue of post-conviction review for the prompt disposition of questions which may arise as to the amount of credit which should have been awarded.

❋ ❋ ❋ ❋ ❋

C. Judicial Control Over Sentence and Judgment

1. Legally erroneous sentence or judgment

FEDERAL RULES OF CRIMINAL PROCEDURE

RULE 32(d)

(d) **Withdrawal of Plea of Guilty.** A motion to withdraw a plea of guilty or of *nolo contendere* may be made only before sentence is imposed or imposition of sentence is suspended; but to correct manifest injustice the court after sentence may set aside the judgment of conviction and permit the defendant to withdraw his plea.

Rule 35

CORRECTION OR REDUCTION OF SENTENCE

The court may correct an illegal sentence at any time and may correct a sentence imposed in an illegal manner within the time provided herein for the reduction of sentence. The court may reduce a sentence within 120 days after the sentence is imposed, or within 120 days after receipt by the court of a mandate issued upon affirmance of the judgment or dismissal of the appeal, or within 120 days after entry of any order or judgment of the Supreme Court denying review of, or having the effect of upholding, a judgment of conviction. The court may also reduce a sentence upon revocation of probation as provided by law.

Rule 36

CLERICAL MISTAKES

Clerical mistakes in judgments, orders or other parts of the record and errors in the record arising from oversight or omission may be corrected by the court at any time and after such notice, if any, as the court orders.

✻ ✻ ✻ ✻ ✻

NORTH CAROLINA v. PEARCE, 395 U.S. 711 (1969) *

MR. JUSTICE STEWART delivered the opinion of the Court.

When at the behest of the defendant a criminal conviction has been set aside and a new trial ordered, to what extent does the Constitution limit the imposition of a harsher sentence after conviction upon retrial? That is the question presented by these two cases.

In No. 413 the respondent Pearce was convicted in a North Carolina court upon a charge of assault with intent to commit rape. The trial judge sentenced him to prison for a term of 12 to 15 years. Several years later he initiated a state post-conviction proceeding which culminated in the reversal of his conviction by the Supreme Court of North Carolina, upon the ground that an involuntary confession had unconstitutionally been admitted in evidence against him, 266 N.C. 234, 145 S.E.2d 918. He was retried, convicted and sentenced by the trial judge to an eight-year prison term, which, when added to the time Pearce had already spent in prison, the parties agree amounted to a longer total sentence than that originally imposed. The conviction and sentence was affirmed on appeal. 268 N.C. 707, 151 S.E.2d 571. Pearce then began this habeas corpus proceeding in the United States District Court for the Eastern District of North Carolina. That court held, upon the authority of a then very recent Fourth Circuit decision, *Patton* v. *North Carolina*, 381 F.2d 636, cert denied, 390 U.S. 905, that the longer sentence imposed upon retrial was "unconstitutional and void." Upon the failure of the state court to resentence Pearce within 60 days, the federal court ordered his release. This order was affirmed by the United States Court of Appeals for the Fourth Circuit, 397 F.2d 253, in a brief *per curiam* judgment citing its *Patton* decision, and we granted certiorari. 393 U.S. 922.

In No. 418 the respondent Rice pleaded guilty in an Alabama trial

* Footnotes omitted.

court to four separate charges of second degree burglary. He was sentenced to prison terms aggregating 10 years. Two and one-half years later the judgments were set aside in a state *coram nobis* proceeding, upon the ground that Rice had not been accorded his constitutional right to counsel. See *Gideon* v. *Wainwright*, 372 U.S. 335. He was retried upon three of the charges, convicted, and sentenced to prison terms aggregating 25 years. No credit was given for the time he had spent in prison on the original judgments. He then brought this habeas corpus proceeding in the United States District Court for the Middle District of Alabama, alleging that the state trial court had acted unconstitutionally in failing to give him credit for the time he had already served in prison, and in imposing grossly harsher sentences upon retrial. United States District Judge Frank M. Johnson, Jr., agreed with both contentions. While stating that he did "not believe that it is constitutionally impermissible to impose a harsher sentence upon retrial if there is recorded in the court record some legal justification for it," Judge Johnson found that Rice had been denied due process of law, because "[u]nder the evidence in this case, the conclusion is inescapable that the State of Alabama is punishing petitioner Rice for his having exercised his post-conviction right of review and for having the original sentences declared unconstitutional." 274 F. Supp. 116, 121, 122. The judgment of the District Court was affirmed by the United States Court of Appeals for the Fifth Circuit, "on the basis of Judge Johnson's opinion," 396 F.2d 499, 500, and we granted certiorari. 393 U.S. 932.

The problem before us involves two related but analytically separate issues. One concerns the constitutional limitations upon the imposition of a more severe punishment after conviction for the same offense upon retrial. The other is the more limited question whether, in computing the new sentence, the Constitution requires that credit must be given for that part of the original sentence already served. The second question is not presented in *Pearce*, for in North Carolina it appears to be the law that a defendant must be given full credit for all time served under the previous sentence. *State* v. *Stafford*, 274 N.C. 519, 164 S.E.2d 371; *State* v. *Paige*, 272 N.C. 417, 158 S.E.2d 522; *State* v. *Weaver*, 264 N.C. 681, 142 S.E.2d 633. In any event, Pearce was given such credit. Alabama law, however, seems to reflect a different view. *Aaron* v. *State*, 43 Ala. App. 450, 192 So. 2d 456; *Ex parte Merkes*, 43 Ala. App. 640, 198 So. 2d 789. And respondent Rice, upon being resentenced, was given no credit at all for the two and one-half years he had already spent in prison.

We turn first to the more limited aspect of the question before us—

whether the Constitution requires that, in computing the sentence imposed after conviction upon retrial, credit must be given for time served under the original sentence. We then consider the broader question of what constitutional limitations there may be upon the imposition of a more severe sentence after reconviction.

I.

The Court has held today, in *Benton v. Maryland, post,* p. 784, that the Fifth Amendment guarantee against double jeopardy is enforceable against the States through the Fourteenth Amendment. That guarantee has been said to consist of three separate constitutional protections. It protects against a second prosecution for the same offense after acquittal. It protects against a second prosecution for the same offense after conviction. And it protects against multiple punishments for the same offense. This last protection is what is necessarily implicated in any consideration of the question whether, in the imposition of sentence for the same offense after retrial, the Constitution requires that credit must be given for punishment already endured. The Court stated the controlling constitutional principle almost 100 years ago, in the landmark case of *Ex parte Lange,* 18 Wall. 163, 168:

> "If there is anything settled in the jurisprudence of England and America, it is that no man can be twice lawfully punished for the same offence. And . . . there has never been any doubt of [this rule's] entire and complete protection of the party when a second punishment is proposed in the same court, on the same facts, for the same statutory offence.

> ❋ ❋ ❋ ❋ ❋

> "[T]he Constitution was designed as much to prevent the criminal from being twice punished for the same offence as from being twice tried for it." *Id.,* at 173.

We think it is clear that this basic constitutional guarantee is violated when punishment already exacted for an offense is not fully "credited" in imposing sentence upon a new conviction for the same offense. The constitutional violation is flagrantly apparent in a case involving the imposition of a maximum sentence after reconviction. Suppose, for example, in a jurisdiction where the maximum allowable sentence for larceny is 10 years imprisonment, a man succeeds in getting his larceny conviction set aside after serving three years in prison. If, upon conviction, he is given a 10-year sentence, then, quite clearly, he will have received multiple punishments for the same offense. For he will have been compelled to serve separate prison terms of three years and 10 years, although the maximum single punishment for the offense is 10 years imprisonment. Though not so dramatically evident, the same principle obviously holds true whenever punishment already endured is not fully subtracted from any new sentence imposed.

We hold that the constitutional guarantee against multiple punishments for the same offense absolutely requires that punishment already exacted must be fully "credited" in imposing sentence upon a new conviction for the same offense. If, upon a new trial, the defendant is acquitted, there is no way the years he spent in prison can be returned to him. But if he is reconvicted, those years can and must be returned—by subtracting them from whatever new sentence is imposed.

II.

To hold that the second sentence must be reduced by the time served under the first is, however, to give but a partial answer to the question before us. We turn, therefore, to consideration of the broader problem of what constitutional limitations there may be upon the general power of a judge to impose upon reconviction a longer prison sentence than the defendant originally received.

A.

Long-established constitutional doctrine makes clear that, beyond the requirement already discussed, the guarantee against double jeopardy imposes no restrictions upon the length of a sentence imposed upon reconviction. At least since 1896, when *United States* v. *Ball,* 163 U.S. 662, was decided, it has been settled that this constitutional guarantee imposes no limitations whatever upon the power to *retry* a defendant who has succeeded in getting his first conviction set aside. "The principle that this provision does not preclude the Government's retrying a defendant whose conviction is set aside because of an error in the proceedings leading to conviction is a well-established part of our constitutional jurisprudence." *United States* v. *Tateo,* 377 U.S. 463, 465. And at least since 1919, when *Stroud* v. *United States,* 251 U.S. 15, was decided, it has been settled that a corollary of the power to retry a defendant is the power, upon the defendant's reconviction, to impose whatever sentence may be legally authorized, whether or not it is greater than the sentence imposed after the first conviction. "That a defendant's conviction is overturned on collateral rather than direct attack is irrelevant for these purposes, see *Robinson* v. *United States,* 144 F.2d 392, 396, 397, aff'd on another ground, 324 U.S. 282." *United States* v. *Tateo, supra,* at 466.

Although the rationale for this "well-established part of our constitutional jurisprudence" has been variously verbalized, it rests ultimately upon the premise that the original conviction has, at the defendant's behest, been wholly nullified and the slate wiped clean. As to whatever punishment has actually been suffered under the first conviction, that premise is, of course, an unmitigated fiction, as we have recognized in Part I of this opinion. But, so far as the conviction itself goes, and that part of the sentence that has not yet been served, it is no more than a simple statement of fact to say that the slate *has* been wiped clean. The conviction *has* been set aside, and the unexpired portion of the original sentence will never be served. A new trial may result in an acquittal. But if it does result in a conviction, we cannot say that the constitutional guarantee against double jeopardy of its own weight restricts the imposition of an otherwise lawful single punishment for the offense in question. To hold to the contrary would be to cast doubt upon the whole validity of the basic principle enunciated in *United States* v. *Ball, supra,* and upon the unbroken line of decisions that have followed that principle for almost 75 years. We think those decisions are entirely sound, and we decline to depart from the concept they reflect.

B.

The other argument advanced in support of the proposition that the Constitution absolutely forbids the imposition of a more severe sentence upon retrial is grounded upon the Equal Protection Clause of the Fourteenth Amendment. The theory advanced is that, since convicts who do not seek new trials cannot have their sentences increased, it creates an invidious classification to impose that risk only upon those who succeed in getting their original convictions set aside. The argument, while not lacking in ingenuity, cannot withstand close examination. In the first place, we deal here not with increases in existing sentences, but with the imposition of wholly new sentences after wholly new trials. Putting that conceptual nicety to one side, however, the problem before us simply cannot be rationally dealt with in terms of "classifications." A man who is retried after his first conviction has been set aside may be acquitted. If convicted, he may receive a shorter sentence, he may receive the same sentence, or he may receive a longer sentence than the one originally imposed. The result may depend upon a particular combination of infinite variables peculiar to each individual trial. It simply cannot be said that a State has invidiously "classified" those who successfully seek new trials, any more than that the State has invidiously "classified" those prisoners whose convictions are *not* set aside by denying the members of that group the opportunity to be acquitted. To fit the problem of this case into an equal protection framework is a task too Procrustean to be rationally accomplished.

C.

We hold, therefore, that neither the double jeopardy provision nor the Equal Protection Clause imposes an absolute bar to a more severe sentence upon reconviction. A trial judge is not constitutionally precluded, in other words, from imposing a new sentence, whether greater or less than the original sentence, in the light of events subsequent to the first trial that may have thrown new light upon the defendant's "life, health, habits, conduct, and mental and moral propensities." *Williams* v. *New York*, 337 U.S. 241, 245. Such information may come to the judge's attention from evidence adduced at the second trial itself, from a new presentence investigation, from the defendant's prison record, or possibly from other sources. The freedom of a sentencing judge to consider the defendant's conduct subsequent to the first conviction in imposing a new sentence is no more than consonant with the principle, fully approved in *Williams* v. *New York, supra,* that a State may adopt the "prevalent modern philosophy of penology that the punishment should fit the offender and not merely the crime." *Id.,* at 247.

To say that there exists no absolute constitutional bar to the imposition of a more severe sentence upon retrial is not, however, to end the inquiry. There remains for consideration the impact of the Due Process Clause of the Fourteenth Amendment.

It can hardly be doubted that it would be a flagrant violation of the Fourteenth Amendment for a state trial court to follow an announced practice of imposing a heavier sentence upon every reconvicted defendant for the explicit purpose of punishing the defendant for his having succeeded in getting his original conviction set aside. Where, as in each of the cases before us, the original conviction has been set aside because of a constitutional error, the imposition of such a punishment, "penalizing those who choose to exercise" constitutional rights, "would be patently unconstitutional." *United States* v. *Jackson,* 390 U.S. 570, 571. And the very threat inherent in the existence of such a punitive policy would, with respect to those still in prison, serve to "chill the exercise of basic constitutional rights." *Id.,* at 582. See also

Griffin v. *California,* 380 U.S. 609; cf. *Johnson* v. *Avery,* 393 U.S. 483. But even if the first conviction has been set aside for nonconstitutional error, the imposition of a penalty upon the defendant for having successfully pursued a statutory right of appeal or collateral remedy would be no less a violation of due process of law. "A new sentence, with enhanced punishment, based upon such a reason, would be a flagrant violation of the rights of the defendant." *Nichols* v. *United States,* 106 F.672, 679. A court is "without right to . . . put a price on an appeal. A defendant's exercise of a right of appeal must be free and unfettered. . . . [I]t is unfair to use the great power given to the court to determine sentence to place a defendant in the dilemma of making an unfree choice." *Worcester* v. *Commissioner,* 370 F.2d 713, 718. See *Short* v. *United States,* 344 F.2d 550, 552. "This Court has never held that the States are required to establish avenues of appellate review, but it is now fundamental that, once established, these avenues must be kept free of unreasoned distinctions that can only impede open and equal access to the courts. *Griffin* v. *Illinois,* 351 U.S. 12; *Douglas* v. *California,* 372 U.S. 353; *Lane* v. *Brown,* 372 U.S. 477; *Draper* v. *Washington,* 372 U.S. 487." *Rinaldi* v. *Yeager,* 384 U.S. 305, 310–311.

Due process of law, then, requires that vindictiveness against a defendant for having successfully attacked his first conviction must play no part in the sentence he receives after a new trial. And since the fear of such vindictiveness may unconstitutionally deter a defendant's exercise of the right to appeal or collaterally attack his first conviction, due process also requires that a defendant be freed of apprehension of such a retaliatory motivation on the part of the sentencing judge.

In order to assure the absence of such a motivation, we have concluded that whenever a judge imposes a more severe sentence upon a defendant after a new trial, the reasons for his doing so must affirmatively appear. Those reasons must be based upon objective information concerning identifiable conduct on the part of the defendant occurring after the time of the original sentencing proceeding. And the factual data upon which the increased sentence is based must be made part of the record, so that the constitutional legitimacy of the increased sentence may be fully reviewed on appeal.

We dispose of the two cases before us in the light of these conclusions. In No. 418 Judge Johnson noted that "the State of Alabama offers no evidence attempting to justify the increase in Rice's original sentences . . . ." 274 F. Supp., at 121. He found it "shocking that the State of Alabama has not attempted to explain or justify the increase in Rice's punishment—in these three cases, over threefold." *Id.*, at 121–122. And he found that "the conclusion is inescapable that the State of Alabama is punishing petitioner Rice for his having exercised his post-conviction right of review . . . ." *Id.*, at 122. In No. 413 the situation is not so dramatically clear. Nonetheless, the fact remains that neither at the time the increased sentence was imposed upon Pearce, nor at any stage in this habeas corpus proceeding, has the State offered any reason or justification for that sentence beyond the naked power to impose it. We conclude that in each of the cases before us, the judgment should be affirmed.

It is so ordered.

❖ ❖ ❖ ❖ ❖

Moon v. Maryland, 398 U.S. 319 (1970)

Per Curiam.

. . . In the present case the petitioner was found guilty of armed robbery by a Maryland jury and sentenced by the trial judge to 12 years' imprisonment. The conviction was set aside on appeal by the Maryland Court of Appeals. At a second trial for the same offense in 1966 the petitioner was again convicted, and this time the trial judge imposed a sentence of 20 years' imprisonment, less full credit for time served under the original sentence. This second conviction was affirmed on appeal. 250 Md. 468, 243 A.2d 564. We granted certiorari, requesting counsel to brief and argue the question of the retroactivity of *North Carolina* v. *Pearce, supra,* 395 U.S. 975.

The facts that have emerged since the grant of certiorari impel us to dismiss the writ as improvidently granted. As an appendix to its brief, the respondent has filed an affidavit of the judge who presided at the second trial, setting out in detail the reasons he imposed the 20-year prison sentence. Those reasons clearly include "objective information concerning identifiable conduct on the part of the defendant occurring after the time of the original sentencing proceeding." But the dispositive development is that counsel for the petitioner has now made clear that there is no claim in this case that the due process standard of *Pearce* was violated. As counsel forthrightly stated in the course of oral argument, "I have never contended that Judge Pugh was vindictive."

Accordingly, the writ is dismissed as improvidently granted.

❖ ❖ ❖ ❖ ❖

Price v. Georgia, 398 U.S. 323 (1970) *

We granted the writ to consider the power of a State to retry an accused for murder after an earlier guilty verdict on the lesser included offense of voluntary manslaughter had been set aside because of a trial error.

Petitioner was charged with the killing of Johnnie Mae Dupree in an indictment for the offense of murder filed in the Superior Court of Effingham County, Georgia. He entered a plea of not guilty and was tried on October 17, 1962; the jury returned a verdict of guilty to the lesser included crime of voluntary manslaughter and fixed the sentence at 10 to 15 years in the state penitentiary. The jury's verdict made no reference to the charge of murder.

The Court of Appeals of Georgia reversed the conviction because of an erroneous jury instruction and ordered a new trial. *Price* v. *State*, 108 Ga. App. 581, 133 S.E.2d 916 (1963).

On October 20, 1967, petitioner was again placed on trial for murder under the original indictment. Before the commencement of the second trial petitioner entered a plea of *autrefois acquit*, claiming that to place him again on trial for the offense of murder would expose him to double jeopardy in view of the verdict of voluntary manslaughter at the initial trial. The trial judge rejected the plea and, at the close of the trial, included instructions on the offense of murder in his charge to the jury so that the jury could have rendered a verdict of guilty on that offense. The jury, like the first, found petitioner guilty of voluntary manslaughter, and then fixed the penalty at 10 years' imprisonment. . . .

In *United States* v. *Ball*, 163 U.S. 662, 669 (1896), this Court observed: "The Constitution of the United States, in the Fifth Amendment, declares, 'nor shall any person be subject [for the same offense] to be twice put in jeopardy of life or limb.' The prohibition is not against being twice punished, but against being twice *put* in jeopardy . . . ." (Emphasis added.) The "twice put in jeopardy" language of the Constitution thus relates to a potential, *i. e.*, the risk that an accused for a second time will be convicted of the "same offense" for which he was initially tried.

The circumstances that give rise to such a forbidden potential have been the subject of much discussion in this Court. In the *Ball* case, for example, the Court expressly rejected the view that the double jeopardy provision prevented a second trial when a conviction had been set aside. In so doing, it effectively formulated a concept of

* Footnotes omitted.

continuing jeopardy that has application where criminal proceedings against an accused have not run their full course. See *Green* v. *United States,* 355 U.S. 184, 189 (1957).

The continuing jeopardy principle necessarily is applicable to this case. Petitioner sought and obtained the reversal of his initial conviction for voluntary manslaughter by taking an appeal. Accordingly, no aspect of the bar on double jeopardy prevented his retrial for that crime. However, the first verdict, limited as it was to the lesser included offense, required that the retrial be limited to that lesser offense. Such a result flows inescapably from the Constitution's emphasis on a risk of conviction and the Constitution's explication in prior decisions of this Court. . . .

Similar double jeopardy issues did not fully claim the Court's attention until the Court heard argument in *Green* v. *United States,* 355 U.S. 184 (1957). There the petitioner had been tried and convicted of first-degree murder after an earlier guilty verdict on the lesser included offense of second-degree murder had been set aside on appeal. A majority of the Court rejected the argument that by appealing the conviction of second-degree murder the petitioner had "waived" his plea of former jeopardy with regard to the charge of first-degree murder.

The Court in the *Green* case reversed the first degree murder conviction obtained at the retrial, holding that the petitioner's jeopardy for first-degree murder came to an end when the jury was discharged at the end of his first trial. This conclusion rested on two premises. First, the Court considered the first jury's verdict of guilty on the second degree murder charge to be an "implicit acquittal" on the charge of first-degree murder. Second, and more broadly, the Court reasoned that petitioner's jeopardy on the greater charge had ended when the first jury "was given a full opportunity to return a verdict" on that charge and instead reached a verdict on the lesser charge. 355 U.S., at 191. Under either of these premises, the holding in the *Kepner* case—that there could be no appeal from an acquittal because such a verdict ended an accused's jeopardy—was applicable.

The rationale of the *Green* holding applies here. The concept of continuing jeopardy implicit in the *Ball* case would allow petitioner's retrial for voluntary manslaughter after his first conviction for that offense had been reversed. But as the *Kepner* and *Green* cases illustrate, this Court has consistently refused to rule that jeopardy for an offense continues after an acquittal, whether that acquittal is express or implied by a conviction on a lesser included offense when the jury was given a full opportunity to return a verdict on the greater charge.

There is no relevant factual distinction between this case and *Green* v. *United States*. Although the petitioner was not convicted of the greater charge on retrial, whereas Green was, the risk of conviction on the greater charge was the same in both cases, and the Double Jeopardy Clause of the Fifth Amendment is written in terms of potential or risk of conviction, not punishment. . . .

One further consideration remains. Because the petitioner was convicted of the same crime at both the first and second trials, and because he suffered no greater punishment on the subsequent conviction, Georgia submits that the second jeopardy was harmless error when judged by the criteria of *Chapman* v. *California*, 386 U.S. 18 (1967), and *Harrington* v. *California*, 395 U.S. 250 (1969).

We must reject this contention. The Double Jeopardy Clause, as we have noted, is cast in terms of the risk or hazard of conviction, not of the ultimate legal consequences of the verdict. To be charged and to be subjected to a second trial for first-degree murder is an ordeal not to be viewed lightly. Further, and perhaps of more importance, we cannot determine whether or not the murder charge against petitioner induced the jury to find him guilty of the less serious offense of voluntary manslaughter rather than to continue to debate his innocence. . . .

* * * * *

2. Imprisonment

NEW YORK CRIMINAL PROCEDURE LAW (1971)

§ 430.10 Sentence of imprisonment not to be changed after commencement

Except as otherwise specifically authorized by law, when the court has imposed a sentence of imprisonment and such sentence is in accordance with law such sentence cannot be changed, suspended or interrupted once the term or period of the sentence has commenced.

§ 430.20 Commitment of the defendant

1. **In general.** When a sentence of imprisonment is pronounced, or when the sentence consists of a fine and the court has directed that the defendant be imprisoned until it is satisfied, the defendant must forthwith be committed to the custody of the proper agency or officer and detained until the sentence is complied with.

2. **Indeterminate sentence.** In the case of an indeterminate sentence of imprisonment commitment shall be to the custody of the state de-

partment of correction as provided in subdivision one of penal law section 70.20 and the order of commitment shall specify the institution, designated by the commissioner of correction in accordance with correction law section eight hundred one, to which the defendant shall be delivered.

3. **Reformatory sentence.** In the case of a reformatory sentence of imprisonment commitment shall be to the custody of the state department of correction as provided in penal law section 75.05 and the order of commitment shall specify, in accordance with correction law section eight hundred one, as follows:

(a) If the defendant is a male, the order shall specify that he be delivered to the reception center at Elmira;

(b) If the defendant is a female, the order shall specify that she be delivered to an institution designated by the state commissioner of correction.

4. **Definite sentence.** In the case of a definite sentence of imprisonment, commitment shall be as follows:

(a) In counties contained within the city of New York, or in any county that has a county department of correction, commitment shall be to the custody of the department of correction of such city or county;

(b) In any other case, commitment shall be to the county jail, workhouse or penitentiary, or to a penitentiary outside the county and the order of commitment shall specify the institution to which the defendant shall be delivered.

5. **Alternative local reformatory sentence.** In the case of an alternative local reformatory sentence of imprisonment, commitment must be to and the sentence must be served in the local reformatory as provided in subdivision three of penal law section 75.20.

6. **Mentally defective defendants.** In any case where the defendant may be committed upon a certificate of mental defect, as provided in sections four hundred thirty-eight and four hundred fifty-one of the correction law, the court may, notwithstanding any other provision of this section, commit the defendant to the custody of the state department of correction and in such case the order of commitment shall specify, in accordance with correction law section eight hundred one that the defendant be delivered as follows:

(a) If the defendant is a male, to the Beacon state institution; and

(b) If the defendant is a female, to the Albion state training school.

7. Commitment for failure to pay fine. Where the sentence consists of a fine and the court has directed that the defendant be imprisoned until it is satisfied, commitment shall be as follows:

(a) If the sentence also includes a term of imprisonment, commitment shall be to the same institution as is designated for service of the term of imprisonment, and the period of commitment shall commence at such time as the term of imprisonment is satisfied or at such time as the defendant becomes eligible for parole or conditional release whichever occurs first, provided, however, that if the court so directs the period of imprisonment for the fine shall run concurrently with the term of imprisonment; and

(b) In any other case commitment shall be to the agency or institution that would be designated in the case of a definite sentence.

§ 430.30   Duty to deliver defendant

In counties contained within New York City and in counties that have a commissioner of correction who is responsible for detention of defendants in criminal actions, it is the duty of the commissioner of correction of such city or county to deliver the defendant forthwith to the proper institution in accordance with the commitment. In all other counties it is the duty of the sheriff to deliver the defendant forthwith to the proper institution in accordance with the commitment.

* * * * *

AMERICAN BAR ASSOCIATION PROJECT ON STANDARDS FOR THE ADMINISTRATION OF CRIMINAL JUSTICE, STANDARDS RELATING TO SENTENCING ALTERNATIVES AND PROCEDURES (Approved Draft 1968)

6.1 Authority to reduce: general

(a) It may be appropriate to authorize the sentencing court to reduce or modify a sentence within a specified time after its imposition or the final resolution of an appeal if new factors bearing on the sentence are made known. It is inappropriate for defense counsel or others on the defendant's behalf to make an ex parte approach to the judge except, it is likewise inappropriate for a judge to reduce or modify a sentence by any proceeding which does not occur in open court.

(b) Under no circumstances should the sentencing court be authorized to increase a term of imprisonment once it has been imposed.

Commentary

a. **Authority to reduce**

At common law, a sentencing court had the authority to change an imposed term of imprisonment so long as it acted within the same term of court. See, *e.g.*, United States v. Benz, 282 U.S. 304 (1931); District Attorney v. Superior Court, 342 Mass. 119, 172 N.E.2d 245 (1961). This authority has been specifically carried over in many jurisdictions by the provision of authority to reduce a sentence, normally limited by a specific period of time rather than by the sitting or term of court. See, *e.g.*, FLA. STAT. ANN. § 921.25 (1966 Supp.) (within the longer of the same term of court, or sixty days from imposition or the resolution of an appeal); KAN. GEN. STAT. ANN. § 62–2239 (1965 Supp.) (within 120 days of imposition); DEL. SUP. CT. (Crim.) R. 35(b) (1966 Supp.) (recently lengthened to within four months of imposition or the resolution of an appeal; formerly sixty days); FED. R. CRIM. P. 35 (recently lengthened to within 120 days; formerly sixty days); MD. RULES 764(b)(1) (1966 Supp.) (within ninety days of imposition or resolution of an appeal); N.J. CRIM. PRAC. RULES 3:7–13(a) (1967) (within sixty days of judgment of conviction, or twenty days from the resolution of an appeal).

The Massachusetts Supreme Judicial Court has stated the argument in favor of such a provision:

> Occasions inevitably will occur where a conscientious judge, after reflection or upon receipt of new probation reports or other information, will feel that he has been too harsh or has failed to give weight to mitigating factors which properly he should have taken into account. In such cases the interests of justice and sound judicial administration will be served by permitting the trial judge to reduce the sentence within a reasonable time.

District Attorney v. Superior Court, 342 Mass. 119, 128, 172 N.E.2d 245, 250–51 (1961). The counter-argument, of course, is that the sentencing process must at some point come to an end. Particularly where there are other ameliorative devices such as appellate review of sentences, see ABA STANDARDS, APPELLATE REVIEW OF SENTENCES (Tent. Draft, April 1967), authority to reduce a minimum term to time served, see section 6.2, *Infra*, and authority to parole when it appears warranted, see section 3.2, *supra*, it can be argued that this additional power is unnecessary and possibly provocative of delay.

The Advisory Committee takes no position in subsection (a) on whether provisions which directly authorize the sentencing court to reduce a sentence are necessary or desirable in a particular jurisdiction. In all likelihood, it would be better within a given jurisdiction to continue the present pattern in this respect, while attempting to effect reforms along the lines mentioned above. It is far more likely that an unjust sentence will be corrected by another agency, or at least by the initiation of another agency, than it is that the judge who imposed it will have second thoughts. On the other hand, no reason is seen to suggest change in jurisdictions in which the device has been successfully employed.

The Advisory Committee would suggest, however, that it is inappropriate for the sentencing court to make a change in the imposed sentence unless new factors have been made known. Particularly is it undesirable for a statute of this type to be used to impose a newspaper sentence on one day and a quiet reduction several days later. For this reason, the Advisory Committee would require that all modifications should occur in open court. The statement that it is inappropriate to approach the judge except by motion or in open court is designed to prevent unwarranted intrusions on the judge at other times.

b. Increase

The Advisory Committee is clear, however, that the court should not be authorized to increase a sentence once it has been imposed. It is specifically so provided in at least one statute on the subject, whereas most others carry the clear implication that such is their intent. See, e.g., MD. RULES 764(b)(1) (1966 Supp.) ("The court may, pursuant to this section, modify or reduce, but shall not increase the length of a sentence."); FED. R. CRIM. P. 35 ("The court may reduce a sentence within 120 days . . . ."). The Committee would thus disapprove of a provision based on section 7.08 of the Model Penal Code to the extent that it seems to authorize the court to increase a sentence within a year of its imposition upon the petition of corrections authorities. See § 2.5, comment g, supra.

The reasons for this view closely parallel many of the reasons offered by the Advisory Committee on this point in related contexts. See § 3.8, supra; ABA STANDARDS, POST-CONVICTION REMEDIES § 6.3 (a) (Tent. Draft, Jan. 1967); ABA STANDARDS, APPELLATE REVIEW OF SENTENCES § 3.4 (Tent. Draft, April 1967).

6.2 Authority to reduce: minimum term

The sentencing court should be authorized to reduce an imposed minimum term (section 3.2) to time served upon motion of the corrections or releasing authorities made at any time.

Commentary

This section states the view that the decision to impose a minimum term should never be irrevocable. Little would seem to be served by freezing a decision that later turns out to have been erroneous. Provision that the sentencing court can undo what hindsight has demonstrated to have been a mistake seems the least that is due the victim.

Several states now authorize such a device, though the frequency with which it appears to be used is unfortunately another matter. See, e.g., D.C. CODE ANN. § 24–201c (1961); KAN. GEN. STAT. ANN. § 62–2239 (1965). Compare DEL. CODE ANN. tit. 11, § 4346(b) (1965 Supp.). The same principle is reflected in the provision in Washington which allows the administrative board that fixes the minimum sentence later to reconsider its decision. See WASH. REV. CODE ANN. § 9.95.050 (1961). A slightly different device is in use in Alabama, where a minimum sentence (which is normally the lesser of one-third of the definite sentence imposed or ten years) can be overridden by the unanimous decision of the parole authorities. See ALA. CODE tit. 42, § 8 (1959).

Finally, it should be noted that the Model Penal Code has adopted an approach which in some contexts can serve this function, but which falls considerably short of the provision recommended here. Section 7.08(2) of the Code provides that every sentence to imprisonment is to be deemed tentative for one year. During that time, section 7.08(3) authorizes the institutional authorities to approach the court and request re-sentencing if it appears that the sentence was based on a misapprehension as to the history, character or physical or mental condition of the offender. Section 7.08(5) then explicitly authorizes, after a hearing, the imposition of any sentence (apparently including an increase over the original sentence) that could originally have been imposed. In some contexts this provision can be used for the purpose envisaged by the position taken here. If it is discovered during the first year of a sentence that the minimum period is too high, then reduction can be sought. The Code authorizes minima to extend beyond a year, however, and thus an error which is discovered later cannot be corrected. The Advisory Committee would reject two aspects of the Code position: that which seems to authorize an increase in the sentence on motion of the institutional authorities (see § 6.1[b], *supra*), and that which limits the period of time during which an error in the imposition of a minimum term can be corrected.

6.3 Authority to terminate: use of special facilities

In the event that commitment to a special type of facility is authorized for a period beyond the maximum sentence normally applicable to the offense (section 2.6[b]), the sentencing court should be authorized to terminate the commitment or any supervision at any time. The custodial or supervisory authorities should be required annually to review the progress of the defendant and to make a showing to the court to the effect that contemplated treatment is actually being administered to the defendant and outlining the progress which the defendant has made.

❖ ❖ ❖ ❖ ❖

3. Probation

FEDERAL RULES OF CRIMINAL PROCEDURE, RULE 32(f)

(f) **Revocation of Probation.** The court shall not revoke probation except after a hearing at which the defendant shall be present and apprised of the grounds on which such action is proposed. The defendant may be admitted to bail pending such hearing.

❖ ❖ ❖ ❖ ❖

UNITED STATES CODE, Title 18 (1969)

§ 3651 Suspension of sentence and probation

Upon entering a judgment of conviction of any offense not punishable by death or life imprisonment, any court having jurisdiction to try offenses against the United States when satisfied that the ends of justice and the best interest of the public as well as the defendant will be served thereby, may suspend the imposition or execution of sentence and place the defendant on probation for such period and upon such terms and conditions as the court deems best.

Upon entering a judgment of conviction of any offense not punishable by death or life imprisonment, if the maximum punishment provided for such offense is more than six months, any court having jurisdiction to try offenses against the United States, when satisfied that the ends of justice and the best interest of the public as well as the defendant will be served thereby, may impose a sentence in excess of six months and provide that the defendant be confined in a jail-type institution or a treatment institution for a period not exceeding six months and that the execution of the remainder of the sentence be suspended and the defendant placed on probation for such period and upon such terms and conditions as the court deems best.

Probation may be granted whether the offense is punishable by fine or imprisonment or both. If an offense is punishable by both fine and imprisonment, the court may impose a fine and place the defendant on probation as to imprisonment. Probation may be limited to one or more counts or indictments, but, in the absence of express limitation, shall extend to the entire sentence and judgment.

The court may revoke or modify any condition of probation, or may change the period of probation.

The period of probation, together with any extension thereof, shall not exceed five years.

While on probation and among the conditions thereof, the defendant—

May be required to pay a fine in one or several sums; and

May be required to make restitution or reparation to aggrieved parties for actual damages or loss caused by the offense for which conviction was had; and

May be required to provide for the support of any persons, for whose support he is legally responsible.

The defendant's liability for any fine or other punishment imposed as to which probation is granted, shall be fully discharged by the fulfillment of the terms and conditions of probation.

§ 3653   Report of probation officer and arrest of probationer

When directed by the court, the probation officer shall report to the court, with a statement of the conduct of the probationer while on probation. The court may thereupon discharge the probationer from further supervision and may terminate the proceedings against him, or may extend the probation, as shall seem advisable.

Whenever during the period of his probation, a probationer heretofore or hereafter placed on probation, goes from the district in which he is being supervised to another district, jurisdiction over him may be transferred, in the discretion of the court, from the court for the district from which he goes to the court for the other district, with the concurrence of the latter court. Thereupon the court for the district to which jurisdiction is transferred shall have all power with respect to the probationer that was previously possessed by the court for the district from which the transfer is made, except that the period of probation shall not be changed without the consent of the sentencing court. This process under the same conditions may be repeated whenever during the period of his probation the probationer goes from the district in which he is being supervised to another district.

At any time within the probation period, the probation officer may for cause arrest the probationer wherever found, without a warrant. At any time within the probation period, or within the maximum probation period permitted by section 3651 of this title, the court for the district in which the probationer is being supervised or if he is no longer under supervision, the court for the district in which he was last under supervision, may issue a warrant for his arrest for violation of probation occurring during the probation period. Such warrant may be executed in any district by the probation officer or the United States marshal of the district in which the warrant was issued or of any district in which the probationer is found. If the probationer shall be arrested in any district other than that in which he was last supervised, he shall be returned to the district in which the warrant was issued, unless jurisdiction over him is transferred as above provided to the district in which he is found, and in that case he shall be detained pending further proceedings in such district.

As speedily as possible after arrest the probationer shall be taken before the court for the district having jurisdiction over him. Thereupon the court may revoke the probation and require him to serve the sentence imposed, or any lesser sentence, and, if imposition of sentence was suspended, may impose any sentence which might originally have been imposed.

❖ ❖ ❖ ❖ ❖

NEW YORK CRIMINAL PROCEDURE LAW (1971)

§ 410.10 Specification of conditions of the sentence

When the court pronounces a sentence of probation or of conditional discharge it must specify as part of the sentence the conditions to be complied with. Where the sentence is one of probation, the defendant must be given a written copy of the conditions at the time sentence is imposed. In any case where the defendant is given a written copy of the conditions, a copy shall be filed with and shall become part of the record of the case and it shall not be necessary to specify the conditions orally.

Commission of an additional offense, other than a traffic infraction, after imposition of a sentence of probation or of conditional discharge shall be grounds for revocation of such sentence irrespective of whether such fact is specified as a condition of the sentence.

§ 410.20 Modification or enlargement of conditions

The court may modify or enlarge the conditions of a sentence of probation or of conditional discharge at any time prior to the expiration or termination of the period of the sentence. Such action shall not, however, be taken unless the defendant is personally present. In any such case the modification or enlargement shall be specified in the same manner as the conditions originally imposed and shall become part of the sentence.

The procedure set forth in this section shall apply to the imposition of an additional period of conditional discharge as authorized by subdivision three of penal law section 65.05.

§ 410.40 Notice to appear, warrants

1. **Notice to appear.** The court may at any time order that a person who is under a sentence of probation or of conditional discharge appear before it. Such direction may be in the form of a notice, specifying the time and place of appearance, which shall be mailed to or served personally upon the defendant as the court may direct. Failure to appear as ordered without reasonable cause therefor shall be deemed a violation of the conditions of the sentence irrespective of whether such requirement is specified as a condition thereof.

2. **Warrants.** If at any time during the period of a sentence of probation or of conditional discharge the court has reasonable grounds to believe the defendant has violated a condition of the sentence the court may issue a warrant to an appropriate peace officer directing him to take the defendant into custody and bring him before the court.

§ 410.50 Custody and supervision of probationers

1. **Custody.** A person who is under a sentence of probation is in the legal custody of the court that imposed it pending expiration or termination of the period of the sentence.

2. **Supervision.** The probation department serving the court that imposed a sentence of probation has the duty of supervising the defendant during the period of such legal custody.

3. **Search order.** If at any time during the period of probation the court has reasonable cause to believe that the defendant has violated a condition of the sentence, it may issue a search order. Such order must be directed to a probation officer and may authorize such officer to search the person of the defendant and/or any premises in which he resides or any real or personal property which he owns or which is in his possession.

4. **Taking custody without warrant.** When a probation officer has reasonable cause to believe that a person under his supervision pur-

suant to a sentence of probation has violated a condition of the sentence, such officer may, without a warrant, take the probationer into custody and search his person.

5. **Assistance by police officer.** In executing a search order, or in taking a person into custody, pursuant to this section, a probation officer may be assisted by a police officer.

§ 410.60 Appearance before court

A person who has been taken into custody pursuant to section 410.40 or section 410.50 for violation of a condition of a sentence of probation or a sentence of conditional discharge must forthwith be brought before the court that imposed the sentence. If the court has reasonable cause to believe that such person has violated a condition of the sentence, it may commit him to the custody of the sheriff or fix bail or release such person on his own recognizance for future appearance at a hearing to be held in accordance with section 410.70. If the court does not have reasonable cause to believe that such person has violated a condition of the sentence, it must direct that he be released.

5. **Commitment.** Whenever the court has reasonable grounds to believe that a person appearing before the court has violated or is or was about to violate the conditions of a sentence of probation or of conditional discharge the court may commit such person with or without bail.

§ 410.30 Declaration of delinquency

If at any time during the period of a sentence of probation or of conditional discharge the court has reasonable grounds to believe that the defendant has violated a condition of the sentence, the court may declare the defendant delinquent and file such declaration of delinquency with the clerk. Upon filing a declaration of delinquency, the court shall promptly take reasonable and appropriate steps to cause the defendant to appear before it and to make a final determination as to the delinquency.

§ 410.70 Hearing on violation

1. **In general.** The court shall not revoke a sentence of probation or a sentence of conditional discharge unless (a) the court has found that the defendant has violated a condition of the sentence and (b) the defendant has had an opportunity to be heard. The defendant shall be entitled to a hearing in accordance with this section promptly after the court has filed a declaration of delinquency or has committed him pursuant to this article.

2. Statement; preliminary examination. The court shall file or cause to be filed with the clerk of the court a statement setting forth the condition or conditions of the sentence violated and a reasonable description of the time, place and manner in which the violation occurred. The defendant must appear before the court and the court must apprise him of the contents of the statement and furnish him with a copy thereof. At the time of such appearance the court shall ask the defendant whether he wishes to make any statement with respect to the violation. If the defendant does make a statement, the court may accept such statement and base its decision thereon. Where the defendant does not make a statement, or where the court does not accept the defendant's statement, the court shall proceed with the hearing. Provided, however, that upon request of the defendant, the court shall grant a reasonable adjournment to the defendant to enable him to prepare for the hearing.

3. Manner of conducting hearing. The hearing shall be a summary one by the court without a jury and the court may receive any relevant evidence not legally privileged. The defendant shall have the right of confrontation and cross examination and shall have the right to present evidence on his own behalf. A finding that the defendant has violated the conditions of his sentence must be based upon a preponderance of the credible evidence.

4. Counsel. The defendant shall be entitled to counsel at all stages of any proceeding under this section and the court must advise him of his right to counsel at the outset of the proceeding.

5. Revocation; modification; continuation. At the conclusion of the hearing the court may revoke, continue or modify the sentence of probation or conditional discharge. Where the court revokes the sentence, it must impose sentence as specified in subdivision two of penal law section 60.10.

§ 410.50   Custody and supervision of probationers

1. Custody. A person who is under a sentence of probation shall be in the legal custody of the court that imposed the sentence pending expiration or termination of the period of the sentence.

2. Supervision. The probation department serving the court that imposed a sentence of probation shall have the duty of supervising the defendant during the period of such legal custody.

§ 410.80   Transfer of supervision of probationers

1. Authority to transfer supervision. In any case where a sentence of probation is pronounced, if the defendant resides or desires to reside in a place other than one within the jurisdiction of the probation department that serves the sentencing court, such court may designate any other probation department within the state to perform the duties of probation supervision and may transfer supervision of the defendant thereto. Any such designation must be in accordance with rules adopted by the director of the state division of probation.

2. **Transfer of powers.** Where supervision of a probationer is transferred pursuant to subdivision one, the probation department and probation officers to which the duties of probation supervision have been transferred have the same powers and duties as otherwise would have been possessed by those serving the sentencing court. The court served by the probation department to which supervision is transferred has the powers specified in sections 410.30, 410.40, subdivision three of section 410.50, and section 410.60. If it appears that the defendant has violated a condition of his sentence, such court also has the power to:

(a) Commit the defendant to the custody of the sheriff, and direct such official to bring the defendant promptly before the court that imposed the sentence; or

(b) Conduct a hearing on the violation pursuant to subdivisions one through four of section 410.70 and make findings of fact. In such case, the court may then either (i) continue or modify the sentence, or (ii) commit the defendant as provided in paragraph (a) and send a certified copy of the transcript of the hearings and its findings to the court that imposed the sentence.

3. **Procedure upon return of the defendant.** When a defendant is returned to the court that imposed the sentence the transfer is terminated and such court must proceed in accordance with the provisions of sections 410.60 and 410.70. In any case where a hearing was conducted pursuant to paragraph (b) of subdivision two, the hearing and findings have the same effect as a hearing conducted by and findings made by the sentencing court. No person who has been returned to such court may be transferred back to supervision in the county that returned him without consent of the court that returned him.

4. **Costs of returning a probationer.** The costs incurred by a county in returning a probationer transferred thereto, including any costs necessary for a hearing conducted in such county, are charges upon the county in which the sentencing court is located.

5. **Interstate compact.** Nothing contained in this section affects or limits the provisions of section two hundred twenty-four of the correction law relating to out-of-state probation supervision.

*   *   *   *   *

AMERICAN BAR ASSOCIATION PROJECT ON STANDARDS FOR THE
ADMINISTRATION OF CRIMINAL JUSTICE, STANDARDS RELATING
TO PROBATION (Approved Draft 1970)

3.2 Nature and determination of conditions

(a) It should be a condition of every sentence to probation that
the probationer lead a law-abiding life during the period of his probation. No other conditions should be required by statute; but the
sentencing court should be authorized to prescribe additional conditions to fit the circumstances of each case. Development of standard
conditions as a guide to sentencing courts is appropriate so long as
such conditions are not routinely imposed.

(b) Conditions imposed by the court should be designed to assist
the probationer in leading a law-abiding life. They should be reasonably related to his rehabilitation and not unduly restrictive of his liberty or incompatible with his freedom of religion. They should not be
so vague or ambiguous as to give no real guidance.

(c) Conditions may appropriately deal with matters such as the
following:

(i) cooperating with a program of supervision;

(ii) meeting family responsibilities;

(iii) maintaining steady employment or engaging or refraining from engaging in a specific employment or occupation;

(iv) pursuing prescribed educational or vocational training;

(v) undergoing available medical or psychiatric treatment;

(vi) maintaining residence in a prescribed area or in a special
facility established or available to persons on probation;

(vii) refraining from consorting with certain types of people or
frequenting certain types of places;

(viii) making restitution of the fruits of the crime or reparation for loss or damage caused thereby.

(d) Conditions requiring payment of fines, restitution, reparation,
or family support should not go beyond the probationer's ability to pay.

(e) The performance bond now authorized in some jurisdictions
should not be employed as a condition of probation.

(f) Probationers should not be required to pay the costs of probation.

Commentary

Section 3.2(a)

It is very common, of course, for the statutes to confer discretion on
the sentencing courts to determine the content of the conditions of

probation. *See e.g.*, 18 U.S.C. § 3651 (1964); FLA. STAT. ANN. § 948.03 (1944); MASS. GEN. LAWS ANN. ch. 279, § 1 (1959); MINN. STAT. ANN. § 609.135 (1964); NEB. REV. STAT. § 29–2219 (1964); ORE. REV. STAT. § 137.540 (1968); PA. STAT. ANN. tit. 19, § 1051 (1964); WASH. REV. CODE ANN. § 9.95.210 (1961). *See also* MODEL PENAL CODE § 301.1 (P.O.D. 1962); NCCD, STANDARD PROBATION AND PAROLE ACT § 14 (1964); NCCD, MODEL SENTENCING ACT § 9 (1963). Subsection (a) continues this sound practice.

Subsection (a) also continues the practice of most jurisdictions in recommending that it is unsound for the enabling legislation itself to prescribe mandatory conditions for use in every probation case. The Advisory Committee does not believe that the legislature can anticipate all of the circumstances that may arise in cases to come before the courts, for reasons which parallel those offered in another context against mandatory sentences. *See* SENTENCING ALTERNATIVES § 2.1(c) & comment *e* at 55–56, § 2.3(a) & comment *b* at 66–67, § 3.2(a) & comment *b* at 144–53, § 3.3(b) & comment *d* at 165–67. As observed by the Attorney General's study.

> Probation conditions prove themselves to be of the greatest utility when they are designed to meet the particular needs of individual cases. The theory of an individualization of justice is one of the underlying tenets of the probation system. For this reason a policy of fixing by legislative act terms to meet all cases which may conceivably arise will prove to be impractical, inadequate, and often injurious. Most of the states in fact have left the determination of conditions largely to the discretion of their courts. This is as it should be since the court, aided by the probation officer, is closer to the circumstances of the individual offender than the legislature can ever be.
>
> Whether the courts have assumed their duty to fix special conditions to meet the requirements of each case is doubtful. . . . If probation statutes left the matter of conditions to the court's discretion, but in addition imposed an affirmative duty on the court to prescribe conditions of some individuality and applicability to the peculiar circumstances of each case, an improvement in this aspect of probation work might result.

2 ATTORNEY GENERAL'S SURVEY OF RELEASE PROCEDURES: PROBATION 257 (1939). For a somewhat contrary view, *see* Best & Birzon, *Conditions of Probation: An Analysis*, 51 GEO. L.J. 809, 834 (1963).

This subsection also deals with two other related points. The first is that the development of standard conditions, whether by all of the courts of a jurisdiction or by a single court, is undoubtedly a healthy practice which should be continued, so long, however, as the standards do not assume the rigidity that is the vice of legislated conditions. Guidance can, of course, be achieved by standards which perform a checklist function, but routine imposition of standard conditions can quickly cost the system the benefits of individualization.

Subsection (a) also states an exception to the proscription against mandatory conditions by suggesting that it should be a condition of every probationary sentence that the offender will lead a law-abiding life during the period of his probation. Many jurisdictions have held that a new offense would be a violation irrespective of whether lawful conduct was an explicit condition. Whitehead v. United States, 155 F.2d 460, 462 (6th Cir.), cert. denied, 329 U.S. 747 (1946). The Advisory Committee would provide this as an explicit condition in every case for two reasons. First, it needs to be emphasized that this is the essential aim of probation and that other conditions should be related to this goal. Second, there is value in making all conditions explicit, primarily as an aid to the offender in increasing his understanding of what is expected of him.

Section 3.2(b)

Subsection (b) reinforces the principle mentioned above, that the basic purpose of conditions is to aid the probationer in the development of a law-abiding life. As one court has observed:

> Probation conditions are a means to an end, not an end in themselves. We are on the path to greater success in our treatment of probationers when we are able to interpret to them the specific restrictions imposed on them, not as blueprints of the perfect man, but rather as guides to probationers' growth in their responsibility from day to day.

State v. Moretti, 50 N.J. Super. 223, 244, 141 A.2d 810, 823 (Super. Ct. 1958). See also DiCerbo, When Should Probation Be Revoked?, 30 FED. PROB., June 1966, at 12; Hendrick, Basic Concepts of Conditions and Violations, 2 N.P.P.A.J. 1 (1956).

The second sentence of subsection (b) is closely related to the proposition that probation conditions should be reasonably related to the offender's rehabilitation in the sense of helping him learn to conform to law. The principle is that conditions should not be unduly restrictive of liberty nor incompatible with freedom of religion. It is derived from the similar provision in MODEL PENAL CODE § 301.1(2) (1) (P.O.D. 1962). Freedom of religion was deemed to express more accurately the purpose of the Code's reference to freedom of conscience. The point, in any event, is that the conditions must achieve a balance between oppression and necessity, between interference and utility. For a sample of judicial opinion on this subject, see State v. Oyler, 92 Idaho 43, 436 P.2d 709 (1968); Sobota v. Williard, 247 Ore. 151, 427 P.2d 758 (1967); Sweeney v. United States, 353 F.2d 10 (7th Cir. 1965); United States v. Taylor, 321 F.2d 339 (4th Cir. 1963); State v. Summers, 60 Wash. 2d 702, 375 P.2d 143 (1962); Logan v. People, 138 Colo. 304, 332 P.2d 897 (1958); State v. Moretti, 50 N.J. Super. 223, 141 A.2d 810 (Super. Ct. 1958); Springer v. United States, 148 F.2d 411 (9th Cir. 1945); Redewill v. Superior Court, 43 Ariz. 68, 29 P.2d 475 (1934).

Finally, subsection (b) suggests the impropriety of imposing conditions which achieve such a level of generality as to be of no particular value. Admonitions to live by the golden rule have no particular value to the probationer by way of guidance. At the same time, vague and general conditions result in abdication of the judicial sentencing responsibility to the probation officer. *See* section 3.1(b), *supra*.

Section 3.2(c)

This subsection prescribes typical subjects with which probation conditions might appropriately deal. *Compare* MODEL PENAL CODE § 301.1(2) (P.O.D. 1962). As with the development of standard conditions discussed in section 3.2(a) *supra*, a checklist such as this one may prove of value in the selection of particular conditions for the particular case.

Special note should be made of the condition which might require residence in a facility established for or available to persons on probation. As the institutional aspect of corrections becomes more community oriented, it may be that traditional concepts of probation will be expanded to include community treatment programs using residential group centers. *See* SENTENCING ALTERNATIVES § 2.4 & comment *a-d* at 75–80; L. EMPEY, ALTERNATIVES TO INCARCERATION (1967); P. KEVE, IMAGINATIVE PROGRAMMING IN PROBATION AND PAROLE (1967); Monger, *Probation Hostels in Great Britain*, 31 FED. PROB., Sept. 1967, at 33; Minneapolis, Minnesota Citizen's Council on Delinquency and Crime, Position Statement on Foster Family Group Homes (1966).

Section 3.2(d)

The provision that conditions requiring the payment of a fine, restitution, reparation, or family support should not go beyond the probationer's ability to pay is based on the position of the Advisory Committee with respect to money fines in general. *See* SENTENCING ALTERNATIVES § 2.7 & comment *a-h* at 118–29, § 6.5 & comment *a-d* at 285–94. *See also* MICHIGAN CRIME AND DELINQUENCY COUNCIL, THE SAGINAW PROBATION DEMONSTRATION PROJECT 42–43 (1963); MODEL PENAL CODE § 7.02(3)(a) (P.O.D. 1962).

Section 3.2(e)

The posting of a bond or other surety as a condition of probation seems to stem from the fact that, in early years when probation was without statutory sanction, the nonappearance of violators left the court open to charges of acting extra-legally. Much as with the development of the bail system, the posting of money bond was seen as additional assurance that the offender would comply with the conditions of his release.

The fact remains, however, that the relationship of the prospective probationer's ability to procure a money bond to the desirability of probation is likely to be very small indeed, and indeed so irrelevant as to lead the Advisory Committee to recommend that bonds never be employed. To the extent that financial sanctions are appropriate to the ends of probation, fines, restitution, family support, and other similar devices can perform the function. To the extent that the need is for assurance that the probationer will not violate his probation, a sophisticated system of supervision, combined with reports and visits, should obviate the need for additional financial inducements.

Section 3.2(f)

There are a number of statutes in this country which still permit the imposition of costs of prosecution or probation as a condition. *See, e.g.,* ILL. ANN. STAT. ch. 38, § 117–2 (Smith-Hurd 1964); MASS. GEN. LAWS ANN. ch. 280, § 6 (1959); MICH. COMP. LAWS § 769.3 (1968); N.J. STAT. ANN. § 2A:168–2 (1953); N.M. STAT. ANN., § 40A–29–18 (1964); PA. STAT. ANN. tit. 19, § 1051 (1964); WASH. REV. CODE § 9.95.210 (1959); WIS. STAT. ANN. § 57.01 (1957). The Advisory Committee agrees with the Attorney General's survey that payment of these costs as a condition of probation is unsound:

> [T]he purpose of probation will be defeated from the very outset if those who would otherwise prove good probation material fail to meet the initial requirement of costs because of their poverty. The existence of such a requirement lends the weight of concrete evidence to the oft-repeated charge that American administra-

tion of criminal justice favors the rich over the poor because many persons who might otherwise succeed on probation are denied the benefits for lack of funds to pay the costs of the criminal action against them. Neither the effect which such a law will produce on the minds of those thus denied their liberty, nor the less immediate outcome of the failure to attempt rehabilitation are salutary for society. . . .

2 ATTORNEY GENERAL'S SURVEY OF RELEASE PROCEDURES: PROBATION 222–23 (1939). *But see* Comment, *Conditions of Probation Imposed on Wisconsin Felons: Cost of Prosecution and Restitution,* 1962 WIS. L. REV. 672. The point is equally sound when costs are imposed on an offender who has the ability to pay. Fines, restitution, reparation, family support, and other such conditions which are within the ability of the probationer to pay can accomplish the purpose to the extent that responsibility can be induced through financial sanctions.

3.3 Modification and termination of conditions

Conditions should be subject to modification or termination by the court. All changes in conditions should be presented to the probationer in the manner prescribed in section 3.1 of this Report. Where the proposed modifications would result in a form of confinement as a condition of continued probation, the probationer should be afforded the procedural rights set forth in Part V of this Report.

4.1 Satisfactory completion of probation term

It should be provided that probation automatically terminates upon the successful completion of the term set by the court at the time of sentencing. It is nevertheless desirable that the fact of termination be recorded in an order of the court, a copy of which should be furnished to the probationer.

4.2 Early termination

The sentencing court should have the authority to terminate probation at any time. Such authority should be exercised prior to the term fixed in the original sentence if it appears that the offender has made a good adjustment and that further supervision or enforced compliance with other conditions is no longer necessary.

Commentary

Consistent with the Advisory Committee position of maximum flexibility in the sentencing court at the time of sentence and during probation, this standard encourages discharge at the earliest possible time keyed to the progress of the probationer. Probationers should know that effort and achievement on their part can result in early discharge. Furthermore, it serves little purpose to keep a probationer on as a misleading caseload statistic when in fact supervision is non-existent and conditions are no longer relevant. The mutual benefit of proper early discharge is clear. See SENTENCING ALTERNATIVES § 6.4 & comment *a* at 283.

A number of states authorize such early termination without statutory guidelines as to when the power should be exercised. See, e.g., DEL. CODE ANN. tit. 11, § 4334 (Supp. 1968); KAN. STAT. ANN. § 62–2243 (1964); KY. REV. STAT. ANN. § 439.270 (1963); N.H. REV. STAT. ANN. § 504:4 (1968); VA. CODE ANN. § 53–273 (1967). See also MODEL PENAL CODE § 301.2(1) (P.O.D. 1962); NCCD, STANDARD PROBATION AND PAROLE ACT § 16 (1964). A significantly larger number permit early termination or discharge from further supervision upon the satisfaction of statutory criteria or the taking of certain procedural steps. See, e.g., ALA. CODE tit. 42, § 24 (1958) (showing that probationer has satisfied conditions of probation); ARIZ. REV. STAT. ANN. § 13–1657(d) (1956) (ends of justice will be served and the reformation of the probationer warrants); CONN. GEN. STAT. ANN. § 54–113 (1958) (hearing and a showing of good cause); FLA. STAT. ANN. § 948.05 (1944) (best interests of justice and the welfare of society); GA. CODE ANN. § 27–2712 (Supp. 1968) (best interests of justice and welfare of society); IDAHO CODE ANN. § 19–2604 (1948) (satisfactory fulfillment of conditions); ME. REV. STAT. ANN. tit. 34, § 1634 (1964) (satisfaction of conditions or no further need for supervision); N.J. STAT. ANN. § 2A:168–4 (1953) (best interests of the public and the probationer will be served); N.C. GEN. STAT. § 15–200 (1965) (showing that probationer has satisfied the conditions of probation); N.D. CENT. CODE § 12–53–17 (1960) (ends of justice will be served and the reformation of the probationer warrants); WASH. REV. CODE ANN. § 9.95.230 (1961) (same); WIS. STAT. ANN. § 57.03(2) (1957) (showing that probationer has satisfied the conditions of probation).

The standard takes no position on whether the statute should contain specified criteria, although this should not be understood as sanctioning provisions which unduly discourage the use of the termination power by encumbering it with too many restrictions. The occasion for the exercise of the power is spelled out in the standard and such a statement in the authorizing statute perhaps would add a unifying influence in its application.

4.3 Criminal record

Every jurisdiction should have a method by which the collateral effects of a criminal record can be avoided or mitigated following the successful completion of a term on probation and during its service.

Commentary

In all but five states and the federal system, the deprivation of specified civil rights such as the right to vote, to hold public office or to serve on a jury, follows upon either the conviction of or imprisonment for certain crimes. In addition, the record of conviction can have serious collateral consequences, such as inviting disciplinary action within the defendant's occupation or profession. *See generally* F. COHEN, THE LEGAL CHALLENGE TO CORRECTIONS: IMPLICATIONS FOR MANPOWER AND TRAINING 64–87 (Joint Comm'n on Correctional Manpower and Training 1969); PRESIDENT'S COMM'N, CORRECTIONS 88–92, 171; Note, *Civil Disabilities of Felons,* 53 VA. L. REV. 403 (1967); Note, *Criminal's Loss of Civil Rights,* 16 U. FLA. L. REV. 328 (1963); Note, *The Effect of the Criminal Conviction on Civil Rights in New England,* 42 BOSTON U.L. REV. 110 (1962).

As has been observed in the report of the President's Crime Commission on Corrections,

> The problem with much of the present law in this area is not inherent in the concept of imposing various disabilities and disqualifications as consequences of a conviction of crime, but rather results from the misuse of that concept. Many deprivations during imprisonment can be justified on the grounds of administrative convenience or on the grounds that they are appropriate to punitive aims of imprisonment—thus rights to hold public office or to serve as a juror or to carry on one's business, may properly be considered incompatible with the purpose and nature of imprisonment. Further, it is clear that certain deprivations may be useful as independent sanctions for criminal behavior. Thus suspending or revoking a driver's license for a conviction involving dangerous driving might be a far more appropriate sanction than a fine or term of imprisonment. It is likely to be a highly effective deterrent. It protects society from the particular kind of danger this person poses, thus providing almost as effective incapacitation as imprisonment without its costs or harmful side effects.
>
> But little of the present law in this area can be so justified. As a general matter it has simply not been rationally designed to

accommodate the varied interests of society and the individual convicted person. There has been little effort to evaluate the whole system of disabilities and disqualifications that has grown up. Little consideration has been given to the need for particular deprivations in particular cases. It is quite common to provide for the blanket loss or suspension of "civil rights" or "civil liberties." And even where rights or privileges are dealt with specifically, it is common to provide that conviction of any felony, or any misdemeanor involving moral turpitude, justifies forfeiture. As a result, convicted persons are generally subjected to numerout disabilities and disqualifications which have little relation to the crime committed, the person committing it or, consequently, the protection of society. They are often harsh out of all proportion to the crime committed. And by cutting the offender off from society, including, perhaps, his chosen occupation, they may impede efforts at rehabilitation.

PRESIDENT'S COMM'N, CORRECTIONS 88–89

For the reasons stated by the Commission, the Advisory Committee believes it to be of the utmost importance that at the very least the statutes authorizing a sentence to probation should address the problem of collateral disabilities, and should provide a method by which their effect can be individualized to the particular case. The status of a probated offender, including the basis on which he can participate in normal community life, should be of prime concern to the sentencing court and should be a factor which, like the other conditions of probation, can be tailored in a manner best calculated to effect the rehabilitation of the defendant. The standard thus recommends that the court be given not only authority to deal with collateral disabilities following the successful completion of probation, but also the authority to affect their imposition during the probation term.

There are many forms in which present statutes on this subject are cast. Some, with the consent of the defendant, defer the formal adjudication of guilt through the period of probation and discharge the defendant following successful service without ever declaring him guilty. For a discussion of the practice in Maryland and several other states in this regard, see SENTENCING ALTERNATIVES § 2.3, comment c at 68–69. Others permit the withdrawal of a guilty plea and a dismissal of the charges following the successful service of all or part of a probation term. See, e.g., CAL. PENAL CODE § 1203.4 (West Supp. 1968); NEV. REV. STAT. § 176.225 (1967); N.D. CENT. CODE § 12–53–18 (1960); TEX. CODE CRIM. PROC. ANN. art. 42.12(7) (1966); UTAH

CODE ANN. § 77–35–17 (1953); WASH. REV. CODE ANN. § 9.95.240 (1961). Still others specifically provide in effect for annulment of the conviction following the fulfillment of the conditions of probation prior to or at its termination. *See, e.g.,* DEL. CODE ANN. tit. 11, § 4332(i) (Supp. 1968); WYO. STAT. ANN. § 7–315 (1959). *See also* Note, *The Effect of Expungement on a Criminal Conviction,* 40 S. CAL. L. REV. 127 (1967); Note, *The Effect of a Pardon on License Revocation and Reinstatement,* 15 HASTINGS L.J. 355 (1964); *Annulment of a Conviction of Crime,* 8 CRIME & DELINQ. 97 (1963).

The Advisory Committee is not as concerned with the form which such statutes take as it is with the principle that flexibility should be built into the system and that effective ways should be devised to mitigate the scarlet letter effect of a conviction once the offender has satisfactorily adjusted.

5.1 Grounds for and alternatives to probation revocation

(a) Violation of a condition is both a necessary and a sufficient ground for the revocation of probation. Revocation followed by imprisonment should not be the disposition, however, unless the court finds on the basis of the original offense and the intervening conduct of the offender that:

(i) confinement is necessary to protect the public from further criminal activity by the offender; or

(ii) the offender is in need of correctional treatment which can most effectively be provided if he is confined; or

(iii) it would unduly depreciate the seriousness of the violation if probation were not revoked.

(b) It would be appropriate for standards to be formulated as a guide to probation departments and courts in processing the violation of conditions. In any event, the following intermediate steps should be considered in every case as possible alternatives to revocation:

(i) a review of the conditions, followed by changes where necessary or desirable;

(ii) a formal or informal conference with the probationer to reemphasize the necessity of compliance with the conditions;

(iii) a formal or informal warning that further violations could result in revocation.

Commentary

As set forth in section 1.3(a) of this Report, probation is the recommended disposition of a criminal case in all but three situations:

where confinement is necessary to protect the public from further criminal conduct by the offender; where the offender is in need of correctional treatment which can most effectively be provided in an institutional setting; or where the seriousness of the offense would be unduly depreciated if a sentence less than imprisonment were employed. Given a probationary disposition, the issue for consideration in this section is the related judgment of when the defendant's subsequent conduct justifies the ultimate sanction of revocation followed by a sentence to imprisonment. *See generally* Lohman, Wahl, Carter & Lewis, *The Intensive Supervision Caseload: A Preliminary Evaluation,* THE SAN FRANCISCO PROJECT 28 (1967); Dicerbo, *When Should Probation Be Revoked?,* 30 FED. PROB., June 1966, at 11; Lohman, Wahl & Carter, *The Minimum Supervision Caseload: A Preliminary Evaluation,* THE SAN FRANCISCO PROJECT 31 (1966); WASHINGTON STATE DEP'T OF INSTITUTIONS, AN ANALYSIS OF SIGNIFICANT FACTORS CONCERNING WASHINGTON STATE ADULT CORRECTIONAL INSTITUTIONS 40 (1966); Reed & King, *Factors in the Decision-Making of North Carolina Probation Officers,* 3 J. RESEARCH CRIME & DELINQ. 120 (1967); S. RUBIN, H. WEIHOFEN, G. EDWARDS & S. ROSENZWEIG, THE LAW OF CRIMINAL CORRECTION 208–09 (1963); NEW YORK STATE DIV. OF PROBATION, DEP'T OF CORRECTION, A STUDY OF FELONY CASES IN WHICH PROBATION WAS TERMINATED BY COMMITMENT (1961).

The question does not so much relate to the authority of the court as it does to when and how that authority should be exercised. Probation is of course by its nature a conditional sentence, and by definition is subject to revocation upon a violation of the established conditions. This point is emphasized by the opening sentence of this standard to the effect that violation of a condition is both a necessary and a sufficient basis for revocation and imprisonment.

But the fact that violation of a condition is a *permissible* basis for revocation does not support the idea that revocation should necessarily or automatically follow the establishment of a violation. The fact of a violation, duly established by a proceeding in conformity with section 5.4, *infra,* poses the need for a correctional judgment not unlike the initial sentencing decision. A properly structured system will have preserved for the trial judge the same options as he had at the original sentencing stage of the case, including the option of continuing the offender on probation. *See* section 1.1(f), *supra.* Which of these options should be invoked should depend, it would seem, on the extent to which the facts justify the judgment that was withheld at the time of initial sentencing. Do the intervening events provide the basis for a determination that confinement is now necessary to protect the public from additional criminal conduct by the defendant? Does the intervening conduct justify the conclusion that the defendant can best be dealt with in an institutional setting, *i.e.*, that the objective of preventing a new offense would best be achieved by changing his environment? Has the defendant evidenced such a disregard for the authority of the system that his continuance on probation will be an invitation to others not to respect the conditional nature of their release?

It is the intention of the second sentence of subsection (a) of this standard to invoke criteria such as these for the decision that must follow the violation of a condition. At the same time, however, this subsection is designed to reject the thesis that revocation should inexorably follow a violation because "the defendant has had his chance" or because of similar generalizations which may not fit the facts. As at the time of initial sentencing, the public interest is best served by as sympathetic and honest a judgment as is within the capacity of the trial judge to make, responsive to criteria such as are here set forth. *Compare* MODEL PENAL CODE § 301.3(2) (P.O.D. 1962). For the same reasons as were advanced in support of section 1.3(a), *supra*, it is the submission here that the public is not served by precipitate and automatic imprisonment following what under the circumstances might be either a technical violation or a violation which, though substantial, does not provide the kinds of affirmative reasons for imprisonment which are set forth in this standard.

There are two further objectives of this section. The first is to emphasize, by the first sentence in subsection (b), that standards for the processing of probation violations, developed on a state-wide or department-wide basis, would be helpful. It is clear that *all* violations, no matter how technical or how excusable, should not automatically invoke a revocation hearing. Sound judgment by the probation officer, and ultimately by the trial judge, should be the predicate for such action. The basis on which such judgments should be exercised, and the relationship between judge and probation officer which they necessarily involve, is a matter which can best be dealt with on a less than nationwide basis.

The second objective of the section is to isolate for consideration some of the alternatives to revocation which should be considered as part of this judgment. The alternatives should of course be as flexible as the needs of each case demand, but three common ones are set forth by way of illustration. Each, in the appropriate case, can better serve the needs of the offender and the public than the automatic convening of a revocation proceeding or automatic revocation once a violation has been shown.

5.2 Arrest of probationers

(a) Formal arrests of probationers for the alleged violation of conditions of their probation should be preceded by the issuance of an arrest warrant based upon probable cause that a violation has occurred. Arrests without a warrant should be permitted only when the violation involves the commission of another crime and when the normal standards for arrests without a warrant have otherwise been met.

(b) Probation officers should not be authorized to arrest probationers.

5.3 Proceedings following commission of another crime

A revocation proceeding based solely upon commission of another crime ordinarily should not be initiated prior to the disposition of that charge. However, upon a showing of probable cause that another crime has been committed by the probationer, the probation court should have discretionary authority to detain the probationer without bail pending a determination of the new criminal charge.

Commentary

This standard recognizes the obvious necessity for the commission of a new crime to come within the purview of the probation court. A new criminal offense is typically the most serious way in which the conditions of probation can be violated.

The issue of how to deal with such cases, however, presents sensitive and difficult problems. The irony of the following exchange, occurring during the argument of Mempa v. Rhay, 389 U.S. 128 (1967) in the Supreme Court, illustrates the point:

> Mr. Justice Fortas asked if it was true that . . . [one of the petitioners] had never actually been tried in connection with the criminal charges that led to revocation of his probation, and thus to his imprisonment. This was true, replied . . . [counsel for the petitioners]. Mr. Justice Fortas then commented that this must make for efficient administration of justice. "Very efficient administration," replied . . . [the attorney].

36 U.S. LAW WEEK 3153–54 (1967).

The relative informality of a probation revocation proceeding, as compared to the trial of an original criminal charge, underlines the danger. Relaxation of rules of admissibility of evidence, the absence of a jury, a lesser burden of proof—factors such as these can lead to an abuse of the proceeding by basing revocation upon a new criminal offense when the offense could not be proved in an ordinary criminal trial. Additional complexity is introduced by the position in which the probationer is put as regards his privilege against self-incrimination: a revocation proceeding before trial of the charge on which it is based well could compromise the assertion of this fundamental constitutional right. *Cf.* Marchetti v. United States, 390 U.S. 39 (1968); Garrity v. New Jersey, 385 U.S. 493 (1967); Spevack v. Klein, 385 U.S. 511 (1967).

These problems can be minimized if the probation revocation proceeding is postponed until after the disposition of the new criminal charge. The record will then be clear and the possibilities of unfairness to the probationer will have been sharply reduced, particularly as they involve the privilege against self-incrimination. This standard accordingly suggests such postponement as an operating policy. *Compare* MODEL PENAL CODE § 301.3, comment at 150–51 (Tent. Draft No. 2, 1954).

Two other issues need to be faced. The first relates to the pressure to initiate revocation proceedings which might be applied by the fact that the defendant will be at large, on bail or by some other means, pending the disposition of the new criminal charge. By revoking probation, the court would have the power to prevent this result. The question is whether it should have such power prior to revocation.

The Standard concludes, in agreement with the MODEL PENAL CODE § 301.3(1)(c) (P.O.D. 1962), that the court should have the discretion to exercise such power, conditioned upon a showing of probable cause that a new offense has been committed by the probationer. As an alternative to immediately proceeding to revocation proceedings, in other words, thereby invoking all of the disadvantages of holding the revocation proceeding prior to trial of the new charge, the recommendation is that the probation court be authorized to cause the confinement of the offender until the new charge has been processed to conclusion.

The second issue which needs to be addressed is the effect of an acquittal on the powers of the court to revoke probation. While the standard does not address the point, it is drafted on the assumption that it would be unseemly for the probation court to conclude, counter to the result of a criminal trial, that an offense has occurred and that it could provide the basis for a revocation. On the other hand, as was observed in the commentary to the Model Penal Code.

It may be the case, of course, that quite apart from the commission of a new offense, the conduct of the probationer that gives rise to the criminal charge involves an incidental violation of the conditions of the probation. In that event, we see no reason why the probation court should be required to defer its action. If it does, it may proceed thereafter even though the defendant is acquitted of the charge of crime.

MODEL PENAL CODE § 301.3, comment at 151 (Tent. Draft No. 2, 1954). The Advisory Committee agrees with these observations. *See generally* R. DAWSON, SENTENCING: THE DECISION AS TO TYPE, LENGTH, AND CONDITIONS OF SENTENCE 151–55 (1969).

5.4   Nature of revocation proceedings

(a) The court should not revoke probation without an open court proceeding attended by the following incidents:

(i) a prior written notice of the alleged violation;
(ii) representation by retained or appointed counsel; and
(iii) where the violation is contested, establishment of the violation by the government by a preponderance of the evidence.

Sentence should be imposed following a revocation according to the same procedures as are applicable to original sentencing proceedings.

(b) The government is entitled to be represented by counsel in a contested revocation proceeding.

(c) As in the case of all other proceedings in open court, a record of the revocation proceeding should be made and preserved in such a manner that it can be transcribed as needed.

(d) An order revoking probation should be appealable after the offender has been resentenced.

Section 5.4(a)

The Advisory Committee has stated its conclusions with respect to the procedure attendant to a revocation of probation in SENTENCING ALTERNATIVES § 5.5. The different language used here does not reflect any change in thinking by the Committee. Rather, it is due to the different contexts in which the issues arise in the two reports, and the consequent need for emphasis on different aspects of the problem.

There are at least two points that arise in every proceeding at which probation is revoked. The first is the factual question of whether a violation has occurred. This might be easy to resolve, as where the probationer has already been convicted of another criminal offense or where he readily admits his violation, or it might pose difficult questions, as where the probation officer and the probationer disagree as to the occurrence of material events. The second issue, assuming the establishment of a violation, is the judgmental question of what sentence should be imposed.

The Advisory Committee believes that the second issue—the question of what sentence should be imposed—should be resolved in exactly the same fashion as the original sentencing decision. As developed in SENTENCING ALTERNATIVES Pts. IV–V, the court should have presentence reports available to it, as well as supplemental reports dealing with such matters as physical, mental, and emotional health. The defendant and his attorney should be permitted to advance submissions, both of fact and of opinion, which are relevant to a proper disposition of the case. Additional evidence which must be adduced should be presented in open court with full rights of confrontation, cross-examination, and representation by counsel. See SENTENCING ALTERNATIVES § 5.4. The same procedures for imposition of sentence, set forth in SENTENCING ALTERNATIVES § 5.6, should likewise be followed. The reasons which support such practices at the time of the initial sentencing decision are equally applicable when an essentially similar judgment is made at a later stage of the case.

With regard to the factual question of whether a violation has occurred, the Advisory Committee has isolated three features of the proceeding which deserve emphasis. The probationer should be notified of the details of the alleged violation sufficiently in advance of the proceeding so as to be able to prepare any response he would care to make. He should be permitted the opportunity to obtain representation by counsel, either by retention or through similar appointment channels (perhaps by use of the same attorney) as were available to him at the time of his adjudication of guilt. And the government should have the burden of establishing the occurrence of the violation by a preponderance of the evidence in those cases where the facts are contested. Each of these procedural safeguards is deemed essential by the Advisory Committee to assure the integrity of the revocation proceeding as a truth-seeking inquiry. For further general discussions of these and related issues, see R. DAWSON, SENTENCING: THE DECISION AS TO TYPE, LENGTH, AND CONDITIONS OF SENTENCE 142–51 (1969); Rubin, *Due Process in Probation and Parole Revocation Proceedings,* 23 LEGAL AID BRIEF CASE 219 (1965); Sklar, *Law and Practice in Probation and Parole Revocation Hearings,* 55 J. CRIM. L. C. & P.S. 175 (1965); Kamisar & Choper, *The Right to Counsel in Minnesota: Some Field Findings and Legal-Policy Observations,* 48 MINN. L. REV. 1, 94–101 (1963); Kadish, *The Advocate and the Expert—Counsel in the Peno-Correctional Process,* 45 MINN. L. REV. 803 (1961).

Additional consideration should be given to the question of counsel, particularly in light of the recent Supreme Court decision in Mempa v. Rhay, 389 U.S. 128 (1967). There, the Court considered for the first time the issue of the right to counsel at probation revocation proceedings, and decided—on relatively narrow grounds—that counsel would be required, given the particular legal structure of the State of Washington and given the particular facts involved.*

If taken as a narrow decision portending the denial of a constitutional right to counsel at revocation proceedings generally, the decision is somewhat reminiscent in its approach to the discredited "totality of the circumstances" inquiry posed by Betts v. Brady, 316 U.S. 455, 462 (1942), and following cases. For reasons finally recognized overtly in Gideon v. Wainwright, 372 U.S. 335 (1963), it is not possible to examine a record after the event and determine with any accuracy whether the defendant was "hurt" by the absence of counsel. Nor is it possible or desirable to characterize one type of revocation proceeding as more complex by its very nature than another, and therefore productive of a right to counsel. *Cf.* Chewning v. Cunningham, 368 U.S. 443 (1962). There is always—at least on the judgmental question involved in every case, if not on whether the violation in fact occurred— the potentiality of prejudice which cannot be weighed or assessed in retrospect.

The Advisory Committee therefore believes that the issue should be confronted from a different perspective. With regard to the issue of whether a violation has occurred, it has been observed as follows:

> The central task of ascertaining whether the prisoner has committed the acts alleged, and measuring the acts proven against the standard to which he was obliged to conform is precisely the business of the criminal trial itself where the right to the assistance of counsel has been recognized as one of the "immutable principles of justice." Indeed, in many contested revocation proceedings, the conduct charged actually constitutes the commission of a criminal act. . . . [I]t would seem patently at war with the central concept of procedural justice to deny to a person with his liberty at stake the opportunity to hear and meet the specific charge against him with the benefit of counsel.

Kadish, *The Advocate and the Expert—Counsel in the Peno-Correctional Process*, 45 MINN. L. REV. 803, 833 (1961); *See, e.g.,* Perry v. Williard, 247 Ore. 145, 427 P.2d 1020 (1967); People v. Hamilton,

[* But see *McConnell v. Rhay, supra* at 724.—Eds.]

26 App. Div. 2d 134, 271 N.Y.S.2d 694 (4th Dept. 1966); Hoffman v. State, 404 P.2d 644 (Alaska 1965); Blea v. Cox, 75 N.M. 265, 403 P.2d 701 (1965); Commonwealth *ex rel.* Remeriez v. Maroney, 415 Pa. 534, 304 A.2d 450 (1964). *Contra,* State v. Edge, 96 Ariz. 302, 394 P.2d 418 (1964); Shum v. Fogliani, 82 Nev. 156, 413 P.2d 495 (1966).

The probation revocation proceeding, in other words, involves exactly the same kind of problem as is involved in the criminal trial itself—the ascertainment of historical events about which there may be some dispute and the consideration of these events against a standard of conduct to which the probationer is expected to adhere. The inability of a lay-probationer to adequately protect himself in such a context would seem just as pronounced as it is at the trial itself.

Moreover, the issue of what the sentence should be, given a violation, does not seem to present a markedly different type of question than was posed at the time of initial sentencing in terms of what the governing procedures should be. If, as the Court in *Mempa* seemed to recognize, there is or ought to be a right to counsel at the initial sentencing stage, why should there not be a corresponding right when exactly the same kind of decision is made as to the same defendant later on in the case? Still at issue would be questions such as whether the defendant should be imprisoned at all, whether the imprisonment should be for 10 years or 20, whether parole eligibility should be immediate or postponed for 5 years, or whether commitment should be to one institution or another. The ability of counsel to be helpful on such issues, suggested in SENTENCING ALTERNATIVES § 5.3, would seem undiminished by virtue of the fact that they arise six months or a year after the trial and following an unsuccessful probation experience. *See generally* R. DAWSON, SENTENCING: THE DECISION AS TO TYPE, LENGTH, CONDITIONS OF SENTENCE 155–68 (1969).

The Advisory Committee therefore recommends that as a matter of policy—regardless of what may be constitutionally required—the probationer should be entitled to the representation of counsel at probation revocation proceedings. For similar reasons, the rudimentary requirements of fair notice and hearing should also be the incidents of such a proceeding.

Section 5.4(b)

Subsection (b) is added to give assurance that the Advisory Committee is not thinking only in terms of counsel for the probationer in revocation proceedings. Where there is a contest over whether a violation occurred, it would not seem appropriate to give the defendant an attorney and at the same time make the court and probation officer assume the role of prosecutor. Similarly, there may be cases where contests will develop over information to be used in framing a sentence in addition to that which forms the basis for the revocation. In both instances, there is a proper role for a government attorney, presumably part of the prosecutorial arm. As in the case of initial sentencing, however, the government counsel has a much more limited role to play on the judgmental issue of what the sentence upon revocation should be. See SENTENCING ALTERNATIVES § 5.3(c) & comment c at 242–43.

Section 5.4(c)

The need for a record of the revocation proceeding would seem as great as in any other open court proceeding. See SENTENCING ALTER-NATIVES § 5.7 & comment a-c at 273–76. A record is of course necessary for review of either the merits or the procedure. An available record can also cut short a subsequent collateral inquiry into the type of proceeding that was held, either by habeas corpus or some other form of proceeding. And of course a record of the revocation proceeding and the basis upon which a new sentence to imprisonment was imposed can be of significant value if forwarded to correction authorities at the place of confinement. See SENTENCING ALTERNATIVES § 5.7(b).

Section 5.4(d)

The Advisory Committee also is of the view that a probation revocation order should be appealable, both on grounds relating to the establishment of the violation and on the issue of whether the imposed sentence was excessive. The latter question has been spoken to by the Advisory Committee in a separate report. See ABA STANDARDS, AP-PELLATE REVIEW OF SENTENCES § 1.1(a)(iii) & comment d at 17–18 (Approved Draft 1968). The former question is closely related. See Id. § 3.2(ii) & comment c at 52–53; SENTENCING ALTERNATIVES § 5.5 (b)(iv). See generally Beasley, Revocation of Probation—Appealable Order, 13 ALA. L. REV. 175 (1960).

6.4 Modification of sentence: sentence not involving confinement or sentence to partial confinement

(a) The sentencing court should be authorized to terminate at any time continued supervision or the power to revoke either a sentence not involving confinement or a sentence involving partial confinement. The court should also be authorized to lessen the conditions on which such sentences were imposed at any time, and similarly to shorten the time during which the power to revoke will exist.

(b) The court should be authorized to revoke a sentence not involving confinement or a sentence to partial confinement upon the violation of specified conditions or to increase the conditions under which such a sentence will be permitted to continue in effect. The sentencing alternatives which should be available upon a revocation should be the same as were available at the time of initial sentencing. Specifically, such alternatives should include the imposition of a fine or the imposition of a sentence to partial or total confinement.

(c) The court should not impose a sentence of total confinement upon revocation unless:

(i) the defendant has been convicted of another crime. The sentence in such a case should respect the limitations on consecutive sentences expressed in section 3.4; or

(ii) the defendant's conduct indicates that it is likely that he will commit another crime if he is not imprisoned; or

(iii) such a sentence is essential to vindicate the authority of the court.

If the revocation of a sentence to partial confinement results in a sentence to total confinement, credit should be given for all time spent in custody during the sentence to partial confinement.

Commentary

a. Terminate sentence

Subsection (a) states that the sentencing court should have the power to terminate a sentence of probation at any time, and similarly to terminate any other sentence not involving total confinement. The specific reference is to sentences imposed under sections 2.3 or 2.4, *supra.*

The provision is derived from the Model Penal Code. See MODEL PENAL CODE § 301.2(1), Appendix B, *infra:* "The Court, on application of a probation officer or of the defendant, or on its own motion, may discharge the defendant at any time." Very few statutes contain explicit authority to discharge prior to completion of the original probation term, although the power is no doubt implicitly assumed by most courts. For an example of a statute which is explicit on the point, see ARIZ. REV. STAT. ANN. § 13–1657 (1956).

The basic reason for such a provision is to permit the discontinuance of control over the defendant at the optimal time. The very purpose of probation is to assist the offender's adjustment to the community. Since some will adjust faster than others, the system should be armed with the power to assert its confidence in those who have progressed rapidly at an earlier time than may have been fixed in the original sentence.

b. Revocation

Practically every probation statute, on the other hand, explicitly anticipates that it may be necessary to increase the conditions of probation or to revoke it entirely. This is as it should be. It is inevitable that some defendants will not justify the confidence expressed in them by a sentence to probation or one of its variants.

As does the Model Penal Code, subsection (b) authorizes in the event of revocation the imposition of any sentence which could originally have been imposed. See MODEL PENAL CODE § 301.3(2), Appendix B, *infra*. The statutes of practically every jurisdiction agree. As noted in sections 2.3(b)(iii) and 2.4(b)(iii), *supra*, actual determination of the sentence which should be imposed in response to revocation should await the fact of revocation. For provisions with respect to the procedure at a revocation hearing, see section 5.5(c), *supra*.

c. Limitation

Subsection (c) suggests standards which should govern the issue of whether total incarceration is the proper response to particular violations of probation conditions. It is derived from the Model Penal Code. See MODEL PENAL CODE § 301.3(2), Appendix B, *infra*.

The underlying point is that incarceration should not be the automatic result of a violation of conditions, and that it is at all events improper without detailed consideration of the importance of the violation and the risk which the defendant would pose were he permitted to continue at large. The standards are flexible enough to permit an appropriate response by the court to the numerous types of situations which will arise, and at the same time they accomplish the basic purpose of suggesting that the propriety of a change in conditions or other intermediate sanctions should be explored first. Total incarceration should be a last resort. As with the case of the initial probation decision, the use of a sentence not involving total confinement in most cases will represent less in cost to the taxpayer and offer more in the hope of rehabilitation.

The last sentence of subsection (c) is a reaffirmation in this context of the result that would follow from section 3.6(a), *supra*, with respect to credit for previous incarceration.

❋　❋　❋　❋　❋

4. Fines and Costs

NEW YORK CRIMINAL PROCEDURE LAW (1971)

§ 420.10 Collection of fines

1. **Alternative methods of payment.** When the court imposes a fine upon an individual, the court may direct as follows:

(a) That the defendant pay the entire amount at the time sentence is pronounced;

(b) That the defendant pay the entire amount of the fine at some later date;

(c) That the defendant pay a specified portion of the fine at designated periodic intervals, and in such case may direct that the fine be remitted to a designated official who shall report to the court on any failure to comply with the order;

(d) Where the defendant is sentenced to a period of probation as well as a fine, that payment of the fine be a condition of the sentence.

2. **Imprisonment for failure to pay.** Where the court imposes a fine, the sentence may provide that if the defendant fails to pay the fine in accordance with the direction of the court, the defendant must be imprisoned until the fine is satisfied. Such provision may be added at the time sentence is pronounced or at any later date while the fine or any part thereof remains unpaid, provided, however, that if the provision is added at a time subsequent to the pronouncement of sentence the defendant must be personally present when it is added. In any case where the defendant fails to pay a fine as directed the court may issue a warrant directing a peace officer to take him into custody and bring him before the court.

3. **Period of imprisonment.** When the court directs that the defendant be imprisoned until the fine be satisfied, the court must specify a maximum period of imprisonment subject to the following limits:

(a) Where the fine was imposed for a felony, the period shall not exceed one year;

(b) Where the fine was imposed for a misdemeanor, the period shall not exceed one-third of the maximum authorized term of imprisonment;

(c) Where the fine was imposed for a violation or a traffic infraction the period shall not exceed fifteen days; and

(d) Where a sentence of imprisonment as well as a fine was imposed the aggregate of the period and the term of the sentence shall not exceed the maximum authorized term of imprisonment.

4. Application for resentence. In any case where the defendant is unable to pay a fine imposed by the court, the defendant may at any time apply to the court for resentence. In such case, if the court is satisfied that the defendant is unable to pay the fine, the court must:

(a) Adjust the terms of payment; or
(b) Lower the amount of the fine; or
(c) Where the sentence consists of probation or imprisonment and a fine revoke the portion of the sentence imposing the fine; or
(d) Revoke the entire sentence imposed and resentence the defendant. Upon such resentence the court may impose any sentence it originally could have imposed, except that the amount of any fine imposed shall not be in excess of the amount the defendant is able to pay.

5. Civil proceeding for collection. Notwithstanding that the defendant was imprisoned for failure to pay a fine or that he has served the period of imprisonment imposed, a fine may be collected in the same manner as a judgment in a civil action. The district attorney may, in his discretion, and must, upon order of the court, institute proceedings to collect such fine.

§ 420.20   Collection of fines imposed upon corporations

Where a corporation is sentenced to pay a fine, the fine must be paid at the time sentence is imposed. If the fine is not so paid, it may be collected in the same manner as a judgment in a civil action and if execution issued upon such judgment be returned unsatisfied an action may be brought in the name of the people to procure a judgment sequestering the property of the corporation, as provided by the general corporation law. It shall be the duty of the district attorney to institute proceedings to collect such fine.

§ 420.30   Remission of fines

1. Applicability. The procedure specified in this section shall govern remission of fines in all cases not covered by subdivision four of section 215.10.

2. Procedure. Any superior court which has imposed a fine for any offense, shall have power in its discretion, on five days notice to the district attorney of the county in which such fine was imposed, to remit such fine, or any portion thereof. In case of a fine imposed by a local criminal court for any offense whatever, a superior court judge of the county in which the fine was imposed upon five days notice to the district attorney of the county in which such fine was imposed, shall have the same power.

*   *   *   *   *

WILLIAMS V. ILLINOIS, 399 U.S. 235 (1970) *

MR. CHIEF JUSTICE BURGER delivered the opinion of the Court.

This appeal from Illinois presents an important question involving a claim of discriminatory treatment based upon financial inability to pay a fine and court costs imposed in a criminal case. The narrow issue raised is whether an indigent may be continued in confinement beyond the maximum term specified by statute because of his failure to satisfy the monetary provisions of the sentence. . . .

On August 16, 1967, appellant was convicted of petty theft and received the maximum sentence provided by state law: one year imprisonment and a $500 fine. Appellant was also taxed $5 in court costs. The judgment directed, as permitted by statute, that if appellant was in default of the payment of the fine and court costs at the expiration of the one-year sentence, he should remain in jail pursuant to § 1–7(k) of the Ill. Crim. Code to "work off" the monetary obligations at the rate of $5 per day. Thus, whereas the maximum term of imprisonment for petty theft was one year, the effect of the sentence imposed here required appellant to be confined for 101 days beyond the maximum period of confinement fixed by the statute since he could not pay the fine and costs of $505.

On November 29, 1967, appellant, while still an inmate in the county jail, petitioned the sentencing judge to vacate that portion of the order requiring that he remain imprisoned upon expiration of his one year sentence because of nonpayment of the fine and court costs. Appellant alleged that he was indigent at all stages of the proceedings, was without funds or property to satisfy the money portion of the sentence and that he would "be able to get a job and earn funds to pay the fine and costs if . . . released from jail upon expiration of his one year sentence." The State did not dispute the factual allegations and the trial court granted the State's motion to dismiss the petition

> ". . . for the reason that [appellant] was not legally entitled at that time to the relief requested . . . because he still has time to serve on his jail sentence and when that sentence has been served

---

* Footnotes and concurring opinion omitted.

financial ability to pay a fine might not be the same as it was of the date [of sentencing]."

Appeal was taken directly to the Supreme Court of Illinois, which appears to have rejected any suggestion by the trial court that the petition was premature and went on to decide appellant's constitutional claim on the merits. It held that "there is no denial of equal protection of the law when an indigent defendant is imprisoned to satisfy payment of the fine." *People* v. *Williams,* 41 Ill. 2d 511, 517, 244 N.E.2d 197, 200 (1969).

In addition to renewing the constitutional argument rejected by the state courts, appellant advances a host of other claims which, in light of our disposition, we find unnecessary to reach or decide. Appellant challenges the constitutionality of § 1–7(k) of the Illinois Criminal Code and argues primarily that the Equal Protection Clause of the Fourteenth Amendment prohibits imprisonment of an indigent beyond the maximum term authorized by the statute governing the substantive offense when that imprisonment flows directly from his present inability to pay a fine and court costs. In response the State asserts its interest in the collection of revenues produced by payment of fines and contends that a "work off" system, as provided by § 1–7(k), is a rational means of implementing that policy. That interest is substantial and legitimate but for present purposes it is not unlike the State's interest in collecting a fine from an indigent person in circumstances where no imprisonment is included in the judgment. The State argues further that the statute is not constitutionally infirm simply because the legislature could have achieved the same result by some other means. With that general proposition we have no quarrel but that generality does not resolve the issue.

As noted earlier, appellant's incarceration beyond the statutory maximum stems from separate albeit related reasons: nonpayment of a fine and nonpayment of court costs. We find that neither of those grounds can constitutionally support the type of imprisonment imposed here, but we treat the fine and costs together because disposition of the claim on fines governs our disposition on costs.

The custom of imprisoning a convicted defendant for nonpayment of fines dates back to medieval England and has long been practiced in this country. At the present time all States and the Federal Government have statutes authorizing incarceration under such circumstances. Most States permit imprisonment beyond the maximum term allowed by law, and in some there is no limit on the length of time one may serve for nonpayment. While neither the antiquity of a practice nor the fact of steadfast legislative and judicial adherence to it through the centuries insulates it from constitutional attack, these factors should be weighed in the balance. Indeed, in prior cases this Court seems to have tacitly approved incarceration to "work off" unpaid fines. See *Hill* v. *Wampler*, 298 U.S. 460 (1936); *Ex parte Jackson*, 96 U.S. 727 (1877).

The need to be open to reassessment of ancient practices other than those explicitly mandated by the Constitution is illustrated by the present case since the greatly increased use of fines as a criminal sanction has made nonpayment a major cause of incarceration in this country. Default imprisonment has traditionally been justified on the grounds that it is a coercive device to ensure obedience to the judgment of the court. Thus, commitment for failure to pay has not been viewed as a part of the punishment or as an increase in the penalty; rather, it has been viewed as a means of enabling the court to enforce collection of money which a convicted defendant was obligated by the sentence to pay. The additional imprisonment, it has been said, may always be avoided by payment of the fine.

We conclude that when the aggregate imprisonment exceeds the maximum period fixed by the statute and results directly from an involuntary nonpayment of a fine or court costs we are confronted with an impermissible discrimination which rests on ability to pay, and accordingly, we reverse.

Griffin v. *Illinois*, 351 U.S. 12 (1956), marked a significant effort to alleviate discrimination against those who are unable to meet the costs of litigation in the administration of criminal justice. In holding the failure to provide an indigent criminal defendant with a trial transcript at public expense in order to prosecute an appeal was a violation of the Equal Protection Clause, this Court declared that "[t]here can be no equal justice where the kind of trial a man gets depends on the amount of money he has." *Id.*, at 79. In the years since the *Griffin* case the Court has had frequent occasion to reaffirm allegiance to the basic command that justice be applied equally to all persons. Subsequent decisions of this Court have pointedly demonstrated that the passage of time has heightened rather than weakened the attempts to mitigate the disparate treatment of indigents in the criminal process. Applying the teaching of the *Griffin* case here, we conclude that an indigent criminal defendant may not be imprisoned in default of payment of a fine beyond the maximum authorized by the statute regulating the substantive offense.

A State has wide latitude in fixing the punishment for state crimes. Thus, appellant does not assert that Illinois could not have appropriately fixed the penalty, in the first instance, at one year and 101 days. Nor has the claim been advanced that the sentence imposed was excessive in light of the circumstances of the commission of this particular offense. However, once the State has defined the outer limits of incarceration necessary to satisfy its penological interests and policies, it may not then subject a certain class of convicted defendants to a period of imprisonment beyond the statutory maximum solely by reason of their indigency.

It is clear, of course, that the sentence was not imposed upon appellant because of his indigency but because he had committed a crime. And the Illinois statutory scheme does not distinguish between defendants on the basis of ability to pay fines. But, as we said in *Griffin* v. *Illinois, supra,* "a law nondiscriminatory on its face may be grossly discriminatory in its operation." *Id.,* at 17, n. 11. Here the Illinois statute as applied to Williams works an invidious discrimination solely because he is unable to pay the fine. On its face the statute extends to all defendants an apparently equal opportunity for limiting confinement to the statutory maximum simply by satisfying a money judgment. In fact, this is an illusory choice for Williams or any indigent who, by definition, is without funds. Since only a convicted person with access to funds can avoid the increased imprisonment the Illinois statute in operative effect exposes only indigents to the risk of imprisonment beyond the statutory maximum. By making the maximum confinement contingent upon one's ability to pay, the State has visited different consequences on two categories of persons since the result is to make incarceration in excess of the statutory maximum applicable only to those without the requisite resources to satisfy the money portion of the judgment.

The mere fact that an indigent in a particular case may be imprisoned for a longer time than is a non-indigent convicted of the same offense does not, of course, give rise to a violation of the Equal Protection Clause. Sentencing judges are vested with wide discretion in the exceedingly difficult task of determining the appropriate punishment in the countless variety of situations which appear. The Constitution permits qualitative differences in meting punishment and there is no requirement that two persons convicted of the same offense receive identical sentences. Thus it was that in *Williams* v. *New York,* 337 U.S. 241, 248 (1949), we said "The belief no longer prevails that every offense in a like legal category calls for an identical punishment without regard to the past life and habits of a particular offender."

Nothing in today's decision curtails the sentencing prerogative of a judge because, as noted previously, the sovereign's purpose in confining an indigent beyond the statutory maximum is to provide a coercive means of collecting or "working out" a fine. After having taken into consideration the wide range of factors underlying the exercise of his sentencing function, nothing we now hold precludes a judge from imposing on an indigent, as on any defendant, the maximum penalty prescribed by law.

It bears emphasis that our holding does not deal with a judgment of confinement for nonpayment of a fine in the familiar pattern of alternative sentence of "$30 or 30 days." We hold only that a State may not constitutionally imprison beyond the maximum duration fixed by statute a defendant who is financially unable to pay a fine. A statute permitting a sentence of both imprisonment and fine cannot be parlayed into a longer term of imprisonment than is fixed by the statute since to do so would be to accomplish indirectly as to an indigent that which cannot be done directly. We have no occasion to reach the question whether a State is precluded in any other circumstances from holding an indigent accountable for a fine by use of penal sanction. We hold only that the Equal Protection Clause of the Fourteenth Amendment requires that the statutory ceiling placed on imprisonment for any substantive offense be the same for all defendants irrespective of their economic status.

The State is not powerless to enforce judgments against those financially unable to pay a fine; indeed, a different result would amount to inverse discrimination since it would enable an indigent to avoid both the fine and imprisonment for nonpayment whereas other defendants must always suffer one or the other conviction.

It is unnecessary for us to canvass the numerous alternatives to which the State by legislative enactment—or judges within the scope of their authority—may resort in order to avoid imprisoning an indigent beyond the statutory maximum for involuntary nonpayment of a fine or court costs. Appellant has suggested several plans, some of which are already utilized in some States, while others resemble those proposed by various studies. The State is free to choose from among the variety of solutions already proposed and, of course, it may devise new ones.

We are not unaware that today's holding may place a further burden on States in administering criminal justice. Perhaps a fairer and more accurate statement would be that new cases expose old infirmities which apathy or absence of challenge have permitted to stand. But the constitutional imperatives of the Equal Protection Clause must have priority over the comfortable convenience of the status quo. "Any supposed administrative inconvenience would be minimal since . . . [the unpaid portion of the judgment] could be reached through the ordinary processes of garnishment in the event of default." *Rinaldi* v. *Yeager,* 384 U.S. 305, 310 (1966).

Nothing we hold today limits the power of the sentencing judge to impose alternative sanctions permitted by Illinois law; the definition of such alternatives, if any, lies with the Illinois courts. We therefore vacate the judgment appealed from and remand to the Supreme Court of Illinois for further proceedings not inconsistent with this opinion.

It is so ordered.

❖   ❖   ❖   ❖   ❖

AMERICAN BAR ASSOCIATION PROJECT ON STANDARDS FOR THE ADMINISTRATION OF CRIMINAL JUSTICE, STANDARDS RELATING TO SENTENCING ALTERNATIVES AND PROCEDURES (Approved Draft 1968)

6.5   Modification of sentence: fines; nonpayment

(a) The sentencing court should have the power at any time to revoke or remit a fine or any unpaid portion, or to modify the terms and conditions of payment. When failure to pay a fine is excusable, such authority should be exercised.

(b) Incarceration should not automatically follow the nonpayment of a fine. Incarceration should be employed only after the court has examined the reasons for nonpayment. It is unsound for the length of a jail sentence imposed for nonpayment to be inflexibly tied, by practice or by statutory formula, to a specified dollar equation. The court should be authorized to impose a jail term or a sentence to partial confinement (section 2.3) for nonpayment, however, within a range fixed by the legislature for the amount involved, but in no event to exceed one year. Service of such a term should discharge the obligation to pay the fine, and payment at any time during its service should result in the release of the offender.

(c) The methods available for collection of a civil judgment for money should also be available for the collection of a fine, and should be employed in cases where the court so specifies.

(d) In the event of nonpayment of a fine by a corporation, the court should be authorized to proceed against specified corporate officers under subsection (b) or against the assets of the corporation under subsection (c).

❖   ❖   ❖   ❖   ❖

D. Review of Sentence

Mueller, *Penology on Appeal: Appellate Review of Legal But Excessive Sentences*, 15 VANDERBILT L. REV. 671, 677–84 (1962)*

IV. AMERICAN LAW ON SENTENCE REVIEW TODAY AND TOMORROW

Despite all penological advances, only fifteen American jurisdictions (and England) have either specific statutes authorizing modification of a legal, but excessive sentence, or precedents establishing such a procedure. The remaining jurisdictions either have not had an opportunity to rule on this question or have specifically negated the power of the appellate court so to act. Since the law of each jurisdiction will be examined in detail in Appendix B, we may here restrict the discussion to the practices of a few representative jurisdictions.

A. States With Express Statutory Authorization

The State of Arizona exemplifies a jurisdiction which has specific statutory authorization of appellate modification of legal but excessive sentences. The statute provides:

> Upon an appeal from the judgment or from the sentence on the ground that it is excessive, the court shall have the power to reduce the extent or duration of the punishment imposed, if, in its opinion, the conviction is proper, but the punishment imposed is greater than under the circumstances of the case ought to be inflicted. In such a case, the supreme court shall impose *any legal* sentence, not more severe than that originally imposed, which in its opinion is proper. Such sentence shall be enforced by the court from which the appeal was taken.

Such a statute permits the widest possible latitude. Perhaps the appellate power to substitute its own sentence is undesirably broad, absent mandatory provisions under which the trial judge must submit an opinion in which he assigns the reasons for the sentence he has imposed. For, if the appellate tribunal must operate by guess or from chance remarks and circumstances, it might be better to remand the case for resentencing upon full consideration of all factors, rather than to reduce the sentence at the highest level.

As for the particular Arizona statute, we have no indication that it has led to incongruous dispositions. As a matter of fact, the Arizona Supreme Court has been extremely conservative in its application.[28]

---

[28] State v. Castano, 89 Ariz. 231, 360 P.2d 479 (1961). The sentence was not excessive merely because it did not give the defendant, a first offender, the mini-

Hawaii, similarly, has a statute which authorizes the state supreme court "in a criminal case, if in its opinion the sentence is illegal or excessive, . . . [to] correct the sentence to correspond with the verdict of finding or reduce the same . . . ."[29] This statute has been correctly interpreted as authorizing modification of legal but excessive sentences by the Hawaii Supreme Court.[30]

The appellate courts of Connecticut and Massachusetts (like the English courts[31]) have the specific statutory power to review, to decrease and even to increase sentences imposed below.[32] In both states the grant of these powers is implemented by a unique procedure for sentence review.

Following the example set by Massachusetts in 1943,[33] the Connecticut legislature established a review division composed of three judges of the superior court in a state-wide court of original jurisdiction.[34] With the exception of minor differences,[35] the procedures followed in the two states are similar. The judges meet on an informal basis with the defendant or his counsel and a representative of the prosecuting authority. The trial judge may be consulted. The existence of this review body in no way affects any other procedural remedies.

This new approach to the problem of sentence review has not gone unnoticed, for at least two additional states have established committees to study the feasibility of adopting a similar procedure.[36]

---

mum sentence; nor could the punishment be regarded as "cruel and unusual," since it was within statutory limits; nor does the fact that others, apparently less worthy than defendant, have received lesser sentences, mean that the defendant is denied due process or equal protection of the laws.

[29] HAWAII REV. LAWS § 212–14 (1955).

[30] Territory v. Masami Idemota, 39 Hawaii 152 (Cir. Ct. 1951); Territory v. Kunimoto, 37 Hawaii 591 (Cir. Ct. 1947).

[31] Criminal Appeals Act, 1907, 7 Edw. 7, c. 23, § 4(3); 10 HALSBURY, LAWS OF ENGLAND 541–42 (3d ed. 1955). A summary of the English practice is found in The Principles of Passing Sentence, as Shown by Cases in the Court of Criminal Appeals, 86 JUST. P. 61, 75, 87 (1922).

[32] CONN. GEN. STAT. ANN. § 51–196 (1958); MASS. GEN. LAWS ANN. c. 278, § 28B (1956); see also Act No. 136 of the Philippine Commission § 39 (1901), which allowed an appellate court to increase a legal but excessive sentence.

[33] MASS. ANN. LAWS c. 278, §§ 28 A-D (1956).

[34] CONN. GEN. STAT. ANN. §§ 51–194 to –197 (1958). For a discussion of the Connecticut procedure see Comment, 69 YALE L.J. 1453 (1960).

[35] PRELIMINARY REPORT OF THE MARYLAND STATE BAR ASSOCIATION SPECIAL COMMITTEE TO STUDY THE REVIEW OF SENTENCES IN CRIMINAL CASES (1962) (mimeo) [hereinafter cited as MARYLAND REPORT].

[36] REPORT OF NEW JERSEY SUPREME COURT'S COMMITTEE ON CRIMINAL PROCEDURE (1961) (mimeo). With reference to the State of Maryland, see MARYLAND REPORT, op. cit. supra note 35.

It should be pointed out, however, that while years ago no serious constitutional questions would have arisen,[37] at least as far as these statutes are concerned, contemporary constitutional doctrine may well result in the unconstitutionality of the appellate power to increase the sentence.[38]

B. States With Implied Statutory Authorization

The New York statute bestows upon its appellate tribunals the power of appellate sentence review in a covert manner:

> Upon hearing the appeal the appellate court may, in cases where an erroneous judgment has been entered upon a lawful verdict, or finding of fact, correct the judgment to conform to the verdict or finding; *in all other cases* they must either reverse or affirm the judgment or order appealed from or reduce the sentence imposed to a sentence not lighter than the minimum penalty provided by law for the offense of which the defendant or defendants have been convicted and in cases of reversal, may, if necessary or proper, order a new trial.[39]

The term "erroneous" used in the first part of the statute appears to authorize review of illegal sentences, while "all other cases" has been interpreted to include legal but excessive sentences, so that the New York appellate courts do have the power of appellate review of excessive sentences.[40] Note should be taken of a New York peculiarity. The reviewing power of the New York Court of Appeals (the highest state

---

[37] For a discussion of the constitutional questions see Ocampo v. United States, 234 U.S. 91 (1914) (holding the Philippine Act constitutional, as applied to a defendant whose punishment had been increased after sentence appeal); Kepner v. United States, 195 U.S. 100 (1904) (holding Philippine Act unconstitutional under the double jeopardy clause of the fifth amendment, but only insofar as the act allows sentence increase upon appeal by the government).

[38] See Green v. United States, 355 U.S. 184 (1957), so far extending only to situations involving different degrees of the crime, not *yet* solving the question where the penalty increase is within the same degree of the crime. Conceivably, however, the double jeopardy prohibition may extend that far.

[39] N.Y. CODE CRIM. PROC. § 543(1). (Emphasis added.)

[40] People v. Potskowski, 298 N.Y. 299, 83 N.E.2d 125 (1948) (court of appeals affirming the right of the appellate division to extend mercy by reducing a legal but excessive sentence); People v. Gold, 7 App. Div. 2d 739, 180 N.Y.S.2d 723 (1958) (appellate division reducing a legal but excessive sentence); (People v. Pannone, 8 App. Div. 2d 608, 184 N.Y.S.2d 677 (1959) (on the basis of the court reports and probation record, appellate division modifying a judgment so as to allow separate sentences to run concurrently, rather than consecutively); People v. Downs, 5 App. Div. 2d 935, 172 N.Y.S.2d 377 (1958).

court) is limited by a constitutional provision.[41] On the basis of this limitation it has been held that, save for capital cases, the court of appeals has no power to review the appropriateness of discretionary sentences.[42] Therefore, the review of legal but excessive sentences in New York is limited to the appellate division of the supreme court, except for capital punishment.

Arkansas also has a generally worded statute, judicially interpreted to authorize appellate review of legal but excessive sentences. The statute reads:

> The Supreme Court may reverse, affirm or modify the judgment or order appealed from, in whole or in part and as to any or all parties, and when the judgment or order has been reversed, or affirmed, the Supreme Court may remand or dismiss the cause and enter such judgment upon the record as it may in its discretion deem just . . . .[43]

The Arkansas courts have unhesitatingly accepted this statute as authorization of appellate review of legal but excessive sentences.[44]

Idaho has a similar statute, which reads as follows: "The court may reverse, affirm, or modify any or all of the proceedings subsequent to, or dependent upon, such judgment or order, and may, if proper, order a new trial." [45] In Idaho, however, the court assumes its right to modify a legal, but excessive sentence without the slightest mention of stattory authority.[46]

The last state to be discussed in this group is Pennsylvania. The statute provides: "The supreme court . . . shall have power . . . , as well in criminal as in civil pleas or proceedings, . . . to reverse, modify, or affirm . . . judgments . . . as the law doth or shall direct . . . ." [47] On the basis of this statute, the court for the first time exercised its discretion in reversing a legal but excessive sentence in *Commonwealth v. Garramone*.[48] The defendant, upon arriving home, found that his son had been beaten by a neighbor. The defendant was so provoked by

[41] See N.Y. CONST. art. VI, § 7, providing that, with the exception of a judgment of death, the jurisdiction of the court of appeals is limited to the review of questions of law.
[42] People v. Minjac Corp., 4 N.Y.2d 320, 151 N.E.2d 180 (1958); People v. Speiser, 277 N.Y. 342, 14 N.E.2d 380 (1938).
[43] ARK. STAT. § 27–2144 (1947).
[44] Hadley v. State, 196 Ark. 307, 117 S.W.2d 352 (1938); Simpson v. State, 56 Ark. 8, 19 S.W. 99, 102 (1892); Gugson v. State, 257 S.W.2d 1021 (1952).
[45] IDAHO CODE ANN. § 19–2821 (1947).
[46] State v. Neil, 13 Idaho 539, 90 Pac. 860, *rehearing denied*, 91 Pac. 318 (1907).
[47] PA. STAT. tit. 17, § 41 (1936).
[48] 307 Pa. 507, 161 Atl. 733 (1932); see also Annot., 89 A.L.R. 295 (1934).

seeing his family in a near state of shock that he took the law into his own hands and shot the agitator. Upon review of the death sentence imposed by the trial court, the supreme court held that an abuse of discretion had occurred. The court said that the trial judge abused his authority by not considering the provoking circumstances of the crime, as well as the favorable background of the defendant. It thereupon reversed and remanded with instructions that the defendant be sentenced to life imprisonment.

This view was followed in the much discussed[49] case of *Commonwealth v. Green*,[50] decided in 1959. There the appellate court found that the trial court had abused its discretion by determining the sentence on the basis of the criminal act alone, not having considered the criminal himself.

> The defendant Green was a boy with an I.Q. of 80, convicted of murder and sentenced to end his life at the age of fifteen. The majority of the Pennsylvania Supreme Court found age and I.Q. to have been the only subjective factors which the trial court considered in the exercise of its statutorily imposed discretion to impose the death penalty. One trial judge, however, had considered that Green was part of a crime wave caused by juvenile delinquents. The court's dissenter believed that other subjective factors were considered by the trial court, *i.e.*, the defendant's troubled history, *e.g.*, the psychological report indicating that "social mores were not taught by his family." Obviously, the dissent wanted to make the point that the trial court exercised proper judicial discretion with many subjective factors before it. The majority found an abuse of discretion in *not* considering enough subjective factors. The third possibility, overlooked by both majority and dissent, would have been to find that the trial court abused its discretion because, on the subjective factors before it, the defendant's punishment should not have been death, since, *e.g.*, he certainly cannot be blamed for not having received any moral education from his parents.[51]

The effect of this decision is to create a presumption in favor of the defendant, so that the death penalty is imposable "*only* when it is the sole penalty justified both by the criminal act and the criminal himself . . . ."[52]

---

[49] Mueller, *Criminal Law and Procedure*, 35 N.Y.U.L. Rev. 111, 139 (1959).
[50] 396 Pa. 137, 151 A.2d 241 (1959).
[51] Mueller, *supra* note 49.
[52] Commonwealth v. Green, *supra* note 50, at 247. (Emphasis added.)

In 1959, the State of Pennsylvania amended its murder statute so as to deprive the trial judge of his discretion in determining whether death or life imprisonment shall be imposed. In cases where a jury trial is had, and a verdict of murder in the first degree is entered, "the court shall proceed to receive such additional evidence not previously received in the trial as may be relevant and admissible upon the question of the *penalty* to be imposed upon the defendant, and shall permit such argument by counsel, and deliver such charge thereon as may be just and proper in the circumstances." [53] In the event that the jury can not reach a decision on the punishment imposed, "the court shall sentence the defendant to life imprisonment upon the verdict theretofore rendered by the jury, and recorded as foresaid." [54] The judge has the sole responsibility for selection of the appropriate punishment only in cases decided without a jury.

The statute marks considerable progress in penological practice. At the same time it must be admitted that it imposes serious burdens on the supreme court. For example, since the death penalty lacks any penological basis, what factors, sociological or whatever else, should be considered in selecting this man to die and that man to live?

Nevertheless, the statute is a logical first step in the implementation of the modern penal policy of imposing a socially useful punishment in each case. It is clear that this cannot be done merely upon the evidence admissible on the question of the defendant's liability for the particular crime charged. A separate hearing, after the issue of guilt has been established, is therefore the most appropriate means for receiving evidence bearing solely on the type and amount of punishment called for in the given case. While we believe that the universal introduction of the split sentence statute applicable to all criminal cases would minimíze the need for appellate review of legal but excessive sentences, sound penological theory nevertheless requires a supervision of the sentencing discretion. Indeed, unsupervised discretion ceases to be discretion and becomes absolute power.

C. Appellate Review of Excessive Sentences by Case Law

As late as 1942 it had been relatively certain in New Jersey that an appellate court may not review a legal sentence merely charged to be excessive, since the quantum of the sentence, within the statutory framework, was subject to judicial discretion.[55] But over the years the

---

[53] PA. STAT. tit. 18, § 4701 (Supp. 1959). (Emphasis added.) This statute follows California practice. See CAL. PEN. CODE § 190.7 (Supp. 1959).

[54] PA. STAT. tit. 18, § 4701 (Supp. 1959).

[55] State v. Newman, 128 N.J.L. 82, 88, 24 A.2d 206 (Sup. Ct. 1942).

courts' language sounded less and less emphatic. By 1957 it was said that, quite apart from statutes, New Jersey appellate tribunals have the power to correct not only illegal but also "improper" sentences;[56] and in 1961 this power was actually exercised, in line with what appears to be a national trend, albeit a slow one, statute or no statute. For example, the appellate courts will now correct the sentence if it was "very much greater than the proper protection of society demands."[57]

D. No Appellate Review of Legal but Excessive Sentences

In the vast majority of American states, penology has not yet entered the supreme court temples. Montana is a demonstrative jurisdiction. The Montana appeals statute, of long standing, grants the supreme court the power to "reverse, affirm, or modify the judgment or order appealed from . . . or modify any or all of the proceedings subsequent to, or dependent upon, such judgment or order . . . ."[58] Yet, despite such statute, the Montana Supreme Court thought itself without authority to modify or remand a judgment, even though the sentence appeared greater than deserved. The court felt disinclined to tamper with what it regarded to be executive prerogative.[59]

E. Federal Law

The Judicature Act of 1879[60] allowed the old circuit courts to review and modify legal but excessive sentences as well as illegal sentences imposed by lower federal courts.[61] In 1881, when the appellate jurisdiction of the circuit courts was transferred to the circuit courts of appeals, no similar power was given to these new courts. The review power was deemed abrogated,[62] and such was the unquestioned law until 1960, when the landmark case of *United States v. Wiley* reached the Seventh Circuit for the second time.[63] The defendant had pleaded not guilty to a charge of knowing possession of an interstate shipment of stolen goods. He was tried before a judge and sentenced to three years of imprisonment, and his request for probation was denied. The

[56] State v. Culver, 23 N.J. 495, 505–06, 129 A.2d 715, 721 (1957).
[57] State v. Johnson, 67 N.J. Super. 414, 170 A.2d 830, 840 (Super. Ct. 1961) (quoting Montalto v. State, 51 Ohio App. 6, 199 N.E. 198, 200 (Ct. App. 1935)).
[58] MONT. REV. CODES ANN. § 94–8210 (1947).
[59] State v. Shaffer, 59 Mont. 403, 197 Pac. 986 (1921).
[60] Ch. 176, § 1, 20 Stat. 354.
[61] United States v. Wynn, 11 Fed. 57 (C.C.E.D. Mo. 1882); Bates v. United States, 10 Fed. 92 (C.C.N.D. Ill. 1881).
[62] Jackson v. United States, 102 Fed. 473 (9th Cir. 1900).
[63] 278 F.2d 500 (7th Cir. 1960). See Comment, 10 DE PAUL L. REV. 104, 105 (1960); Note, 109 U. PA. L. REV. 422 (1961).

case went on appeal to the Court of Appeals for the Seventh Circuit. The appeals judges indicated that they would have granted probation had they been in the district court's place, but found that failure to grant probation did not amount to an abuse of discretion. Nevertheless, they regarded the legal sentence as excessive, basing their view on the facts, revealed by the trial record, that the defendant was a minor without prior conviction, whereas the "ringleader," who had four previous felony convictions, had been sentenced to only two years in the penitentiary. The court added that the defendant's not guilty plea should not prejudice his standing.[64] The three-year sentence was set aside and the case was remanded "for a proper sentence not inconsistent with the views herein expressed." [65]

On remand the district court questioned the legality of the court of appeals' disposition.[66] It reaffirmed its belief in the propriety of the three-year sentence and reimposed it. But, "out of my deep respect for the Court of Appeals, and in obedience to its mandate, I also hereby suspend the execution of the said sentence," [67] the trial judge related.

This, then, is the first rumbling presaging a conceivable penological eruption in the federal appellate courts. Despite recent avowals to the contrary,[68] the Supreme Court of the United States may then have to enter the realm of penology after all. . . .

❈ ❈ ❈ ❈ ❈

AMERICAN BAR ASSOCIATION PROJECT ON STANDARDS FOR THE ADMINISTRATION OF CRIMINAL JUSTICE, STANDARDS RELATING TO APPELLATE REVIEW OF SENTENCES (Approved Draft 1968)

PART I. GENERAL PRINCIPLES

1.1 Principle of review

(a) In principle, judicial review should be available for all sentences imposed in cases where provision is made for review of the conviction. This is specifically meant to include

> (i) review of a sentence imposed after a guilty plea or the equivalent, if the case is one in which review of the conviction would be available had the case gone to trial;

---

[64] On this point see also the first appeals decision, United States v. Wiley, 267 F.2d 453 (7th Cir. 1959).

[65] United States v. Wiley, *supra* note 63.

[66] United States v. Wiley, 184 F. Supp. 679 (N.D. Ill. 1960).

[67] *Id.* at 688.

[68] Gore v. United States, 357 U.S. 386, 393 (1958).

(ii) review of a sentence imposed by a trial judge, a trial jury, or the two in combination; and

(iii) review of a re-sentence in the same class of cases.

(b) Although review of every such sentence ought to be available, it is recognized that it may be desirable, at least for an initial experimental period, to place a reasonable limit on the length and kind of sentence that should be subject to review.

1.2   Purposes of review

The general objectives of sentence review are:

(i) to correct the sentence which is excessive in length, having regard to the nature of the offense, the character of the offender, and the protection of the public interest;

(ii) to facilitate the rehabilitation of the offender by affording him an opportunity to assert grievances he may have regarding his sentence;

(iii) to promote respect for law by correcting abuses of the sentencing power and by increasing the fairness of the sentencing process; and

(iv) to promote the development and application of criteria for sentencing which are both rational and just.

PART II. AVAILABILITY OF REVIEW

2.1   Reviewing court

In general, each court which is empowered to review the conviction should also be empowered to review the disposition following conviction. It may be advisable to depart from this principle in some contexts, as, for example, where intermediate appellate courts are available to review sentences and it is deemed unwise to involve the highest court in such matters. In any event, specialized courts should not be created to review the sentence only.

2.2   Procedure and conditions

(a) In all cases where sentence is imposed after a trial on the question of guilt, review of the sentence should be available on the same basis as review of the conviction.

(b) In all cases where a sentence is imposed after a guilty plea or the equivalent, review of the sentence, as well as review of other matters which can be raised, could appropriately be governed by a procedure patterned after the following:

(i) Notice of appeal should be required of the defendant within [15] days of the imposition of sentence. The court should advise the defendant at the time of sentencing of his right to appeal and of the time limit, and should at the same time afford him the opportunity to comply orally with the notice requirement. It should be the responsibility of the attorney who represented the defendant at the sentencing stage to advise him with respect to the filing of the notice of appeal, and to assure that his rights in this respect are protected. Both the sentencing court and the reviewing court should be authorized to enlarge the time for filing the notice of appeal for good cause;

(ii) The sentence appeal should be of right, except to courts where appeal from a conviction after trial would be by leave of court. In cases where leave is required, it may be preferable to follow normal procedures instead of a special procedure patterned after this subsection;

(iii) Unless the defendant is able to retain his own legal assistance or elects not to be represented, an attorney should be appointed as soon as the notice of appeal is filed. Unless it appears inappropriate in a particular instance, it is desirable that the same attorney who represented the defendant at the trial level be appointed to prosecute the sentence appeal;

(iv) The clerk or other responsible official should be required to secure a transcript of the record within [10] days of the filing of the notice of appeal. He should also be required to provide a copy as soon as it is available to the defendant's attorney, to the defendant if he has no attorney, to the state, and to the reviewing court;

(v) All papers in support of the merits of the appeal should be required to be filed within [15] days from the time the attorney, or the defendant if he has no attorney, receives the record, unless the time is enlarged upon application to the reviewing court;

(vi) Any response which the state desires to make should be required to be filed within [10] days of the filing of the defendant's papers, unless the time is enlarged upon application to the reviewing court. The state should promptly notify the court if it has decided not to file a response;

(vii) All written submissions may be typed rather than printed;

(viii) In courts of more than three judges, panels of three may be designated to hear the sentence appeal, without a hearing en banc unless the court sua sponte so orders. The appeal should be decided as expeditiously as is consistent with a fair hearing of the defendant's claims. If possible, time should be allocated each week for the hearing of all appeals which are then ready for disposition, and a decision should be rendered as promptly as the case permits. It may be appropriate in some cases, as where the appeal is patently without merit, to decide the case summarily without a hearing;

(ix) The defendant should commence service of a prison term upon imposition of the sentence, unless bail or the equivalent is granted by the sentencing court or the reviewing court upon special application, or unless either the sentencing court or the reviewing court specifies upon application that the defendant should be detained in a local facility until the sentence appeal has been concluded.

If such a procedure is developed for guilty plea cases, it may also be appropriate to use it in all cases where matters relating to the sentence are the only questions which can be appealed.

2.3 Record on appeal; statement explaining sentence

(a) The following items should be available for inclusion in the record on appeal:

(i) a verbatim record of the entire sentencing proceeding, including a record of any statements in aggravation or mitigation made by the defendant, the defense attorney and the prosecuting attorney, together with any testimony received of witnesses on matters relevant to the sentence, any instructions or comments by the court to the jury in cases where the jury participated in the sentencing decision, and any statements by the court explaining the sentence;

(ii) a verbatim record of such parts of the trial on the issue of guilt, or the proceedings leading to the acceptance of a plea, as are relevant to the sentencing decision;

(iii) copies of the presentence report, the report of a diagnostic facility, or any other reports or documents available to the sentencing court as an aid in passing sentence. The part of the record containing such reports or documents should be subject to examination by the parties only to the extent that such examination was permitted prior to the imposition of sentence.

(b) The record normally should be prepared in each case in the same manner as would any other record to be presented to the court involved.

(c) The sentencing judge should be required in every case to state his reasons for selecting the particular sentence imposed. Normally, this should be done for the record in the presence of the defendant at the time of sentence. In cases in which the sentencing judge deems it in the interest of the defendant not to state fully the reasons for the sentence in the presence of the defendant, he should prepare such a statement for transmission to the reviewing court as a part of the record.

3.1 Duties of reviewing court

(a) It should be the obligation of the reviewing court to make its own examination of the record designed to effect the objectives of sentence review as stated in section 1.2.

(b) In those cases in which it would substantially contribute to the achievement of the objectives of sentence review as stated in section 1.2, the reviewing court should set forth the basis for its disposition in a written opinion. Normally, this should be done in every case in which the sentence is modified or set aside by the reviewing court.

3.2 Powers of reviewing court: scope of review

The authority of the reviewing court with respect to the sentence should specifically extend to review of:

(i) the excessiveness of the sentence, having regard to the nature of the offense, the character of the offender, and the protection of the public interest; and

(ii) the manner in which the sentence was imposed, including the sufficiency and accuracy of the information on which it was based.

3.3 Powers of reviewing court: available dispositions

Every reviewing court should be specifically empowered to:

(i) affirm the sentence under review;

(ii) with the exception stated in section 3.4, substitute for the sentence under review any other disposition that was open to the sentencing court; or

(iii) remand the case for any further proceedings that could have been conducted prior to the imposition of the sentence under review and, with the exception stated in section 3.4, for re-sentencing on the basis of such further proceedings.

CHAPTER 13

Post-Trial Motions

and Appeal

A. Post-Trial Motions

FEDERAL RULES OF CRIMINAL PROCEDURE

Rule 33

NEW TRIAL

The court on motion of a defendant may grant a new trial to him if required in the interest of justice. If trial was by the court without a jury the court on motion of a defendant for a new trial may vacate the judgment if entered, take additional testimony and direct the entry of a new judgment. A motion for a new trial based on the ground of newly discovered evidence may be made only before or within two years after final judgment, but if an appeal is pending the court may grant the motion only on remand of the case. A motion for a new trial based on any other grounds shall be made within 7 days after verdict or finding of guilty or within such further time as the court may fix during the 7-day period.

Rule 34

ARREST OF JUDGMENT

The court on motion of a defendant shall arrest judgment if the indictment or information does not charge an offense or if the court was without jurisdiction of the offense charged. The motion in arrest of judgment shall be made within 7 days after verdict or finding of guilty, or after plea of guilty or *nolo contendere,* or within such further time as the court may fix during the 7-day period.

❋   ❋   ❋   ❋   ❋

UNITED STATES V. SISSON, 399 U.S. 267 (1970)*

MR. JUSTICE HARLAN delivered the opinion of the Court.

The Government seeks to appeal to this Court a decision by a District Court in Massachusetts holding that appellee Sisson could not be criminally convicted for refusing induction into the Armed Forces. The District Court's opinion was bottomed on what that court understood to be Sisson's rights of conscience as a nonreligious objector to the Vietnam War, but not wars in general, under the Free Exercise and Establishment Clauses of the First Amendment and the Due Process Clause of the Fifth Amendment to the Constitution of the United States. The District Court's primary conclusion, reached after a full trial, was that the Constitution prohibited "the application of the 1967 Draft Act to Sisson to require him to render combat service in Vietnam" because as a "sincerely conscientious man," Simmon's interest in not killing in the Vietnam conflict outweighed "the country's present need for him to be so employed," 297 F. Supp. 902, 910 (1969).

The District Court characterized its own decision as an arrest of judgment, and the Government seeks review here pursuant to the "arresting judgment" provision of the Criminal Appeals Act, 18 U.S.C. § 3731, an Act that narrowly limits the Government's right to appeal in criminal cases to certain types of decisions. On October 13, 1969, this Court entered an order postponing further consideration of the question of jurisdiction to the hearing of the case on the merits, 396 U.S. 812 (1969). For reasons which we elaborate in what follows, we conclude that the decision below, depending as it does on facts developed at Sisson's trial, is not an arrest of judgment but instead is a directed acquittal. As such, it is not a decision that the Government can appeal. Consequently, this appeal must be dismissed for lack of jurisdiction without our considering the merits of this case. We, of course, intimate no view concerning the correctness of the legal theory by which the District Court evaluated the facts developed at the trial. . . .

The Government bases its claim that this Court has jurisdiction to review the District Court's decision exclusively on the "arresting judgment" provision of the Criminal Appeals Act. 18 U.S.C. § 3731. The relevant statutory language provides:

> "An appeal may be taken by and on behalf of the United States from the district courts direct to the Supreme Court of the United States in all criminal cases in the following instances:

*   *   *   *   *

---

* Footnotes and concurring and dissenting opinions omitted.

"From a decision arresting a judgment of conviction for insufficiency of the indictment or information, where such decision is based upon the invalidity or construction of the statute upon which the indictment or information is founded."

Thus, three requirements must be met for this Court to have jurisdiction under this provision. First, the decision of the District Court must be one "arresting a judgment of conviction." Second, the arrest of judgment must be for the "insufficiency of the indictment or information." And third, the decision must be "based upon the invalidity or construction of the statute upon which the indictment or information is founded."

Because the District Court's decision rests on facts not alleged in the indictment but instead inferred by the court from the evidence adduced at trial, we conclude that neither the first nor second requirement is met. . . .

The same reason underlying our conclusion that this was not a decision arresting judgment—*i.e.*, that the disposition is bottomed on factual conclusions not found in the indictment but instead made on the basis of evidence adduced at the trial—convinces us that the decision was in fact an acquittal rendered by the trial court after the jury's verdict of guilty.

For purposes of analysis it is helpful to compare this case to one in which a jury was instructed as follows:

"If you find defendant Sisson to be sincere, and if you find that he was as genuinely and profoundly governed by conscience as a martyr obedient to an orthodox religion, you must acquit him because the government's interest in having him serve in Vietnam is outweighed by his interest in obeying the dictates of his conscience. On the other hand, if you do not so find, you must convict if you find that petitioner did willfully refuse induction."

If a jury had been so instructed, there can be no doubt that its verdict of acquittal could not be appealed under § 3731 *no matter how erroneous the constitutional theory underlying the instructions.* As Senator Knox said of the bill that was to become the Criminal Appeals Act:

"Mark this: It is not proposed to give the Government any appeal under any circumstances when the defendant is acquitted *for any error whatever committed by the court.* . . . The Government takes the risks of all the mistakes of its prosecuting officers *and of the trial judge in the trial,* and it is only proposed to give it an appeal upon questions of law raised by the defendant to defeat the trial and if it defeats the trial. The defendant gets the benefit of all errors in the trial which are in his favor, and can challenge all errors in the trial which are against him." 41 Cong. Rec. 2752 (1907).

Quite apart from the statute, it is, of course, well settled that an acquittal can "not be reviewed, on error or otherwise, without putting [the defendant] twice in jeopardy, and thereby violating the Constitution . . . . [I]n this country a verdict of acquittal, although not followed by any judgment, is a bar to a subsequent prosecution for the same offense," *United States* v. *Ball*, 163 U.S. 662, 671 (1896).

There are three differences between the hypothetical just suggested and the case at hand. First, in this case it was the judge—not the jury —who made the factual determinations. This difference alone does not support a legal distinction, however, for judges, like juries, can acquit defendants, see Fed. Rule Crim. Proc. 29. Second, the judge in this case made his decision *after* the jury had brought in a verdict of guilty. Rule 29(c) and (d) of the Federal Rules of Criminal Procedure expressly allows, however, a federal judge to acquit a criminal defendant after the jury "returns a verdict of guilty." And third, in this case the District Court labeled his post-verdict opinion an arrest of judgment, not an acquittal. This characterization alone, however, neither confers jurisdiction on this Court, see n. 6, *supra,* nor makes the opinion any less dependent upon evidence adduced at the trial. In short, we see no distinction between what the court below did, and a post-verdict directed acquittal. . . .

Clarity is to be desired in any statute, but in matters of jurisdiction it is especially important. Otherwise the courts and the parties must expend great energy, not on the merits of dispute settlement, but on simply deciding whether a court has the power to hear a case. When judged in these terms, the Criminal Appeals Act is a failure. Born of compromise, and reflecting no coherent allocation of appellate responsibility, the Criminal Appeals Act proved a most unruly child that has not improved with age. The statute's roots are grounded in pleading distinctions that existed at common law but that in most instances, fail to coincide with the procedural categories of the Federal Rules of Criminal Procedure. Not only does the statute create uncertainty by its requirement that one analyze the nature of the decision of the District Court in order to determine whether it falls within the class of common-law distinctions for which an appeal is authorized, but it has also engendered confusion over the court to which an appealable decision should be brought.

The Solicitor General, at oral argument in this case, forthrightly stated that "there are few problems which occur so frequently or present such extreme technical difficulty in the Solicitor General's office [as] in the proper construction of the Criminal Appeals Act." We share his dissatisfaction with this statute. Nevertheless, until such time as Congress decides to amend the statute, this Court must abide by the limitations imposed by this awkward and ancient Act.

We conclude that the appeal in this case must be dismissed for lack of jurisdiction.

It is so ordered.

☼　☼　☼　☼　☼

NEW YORK CRIMINAL PROCEDURE LAW (1971)

§ 440.10   Motion to vacate judgment

1. At any time after the entry of a judgment, the court in which it was entered may, upon motion of the defendant, vacate such judgment upon the ground that:

(a) The court did not have jurisdiction of the action or of the person of the defendant; or

(b) The judgment was procured by duress, misrepresentation or fraud on the part of the court or a prosecutor or a person acting for or in behalf of a court or a prosecutor; or

(c) Material evidence adduced at a trial resulting in the judgment was false and was, prior to the entry of the judgment, known by the prosecutor or by the court to be false; or

(d) Material evidence adduced by the people at a trial resulting in the judgment was procured in violation of the defendant's rights under the constitution of this state or of the United States; or

(e) During the proceedings resulting in the judgment, the defendant, by reason of mental disease or defect, was incapable of understanding or participating in such proceedings; or

(f) Improper and prejudicial conduct not appearing in the record occurred during a trial resulting in the judgment which conduct, if it had appeared in the record, would have required a reversal of the judgment upon an appeal therefrom; or

(g) New evidence has been discovered since the entry of a judgment based upon a verdict of guilty after trial, which could not have been produced by the defendant at the trial even with due diligence on his part and which is of such character as to create a probability that had such evidence been received at the trial the verdict would have been more favorable to the defendant; provided that a motion based upon such ground must be made with due diligence after the discovery of such alleged new evidence; or

(h) The judgment was obtained in violation of a right of the defendant under the constitution of this state or of the United States.

2. Notwithstanding the provisions of subdivision one, the court must deny a motion to vacate a judgment when:

(a) The ground or issue raised upon the motion was previously determined on the merits upon an appeal from the judgment, unless since the time of such appellate determination there has been a retroactively effective change in the law controlling such issue; or

(b) The judgment is, at the time of the motion, appealable or pending on appeal, and sufficient facts appear on the record with respect to the ground or issue raised upon the motion to permit adequate review thereof upon such an appeal; or

(c) Although sufficient facts appear on the record of the proceedings underlying the judgment to have permitted, upon appeal from such judgment, adequate review of the ground or issue raised upon the motion, no such appellate review or determination occurred owing to the defendant's unjustifiable failure to take or perfect an appeal during the prescribed period or to his unjustifiable failure to raise such ground or issue upon an appeal actually perfected by him; or

(d) The ground or issue raised relates solely to the validity of the sentence and not to the validity of the conviction.

3. Notwithstanding the provisions of subdivision one, the court may deny a motion to vacate a judgment when:

(a) Although facts in support of the ground or issue raised upon the motion could with due diligence by the defendant have readily been made to appear on the record in a manner providing adequate basis for review of such ground or issue upon an appeal from the judgment, the defendant unjustifiably failed to adduce such matter prior to sentence and the ground or issue in question was not subsequently determined upon appeal. This paragraph does not apply to a motion based upon deprivation of the right to counsel at the trial or upon failure of the trial court to advise the defendant of such right; or

(b) The ground or issue raised upon the motion was previously determined on the merits upon a prior motion or proceeding in a court of this state, other than an appeal from the judgment, or upon a motion or proceeding in a federal court; unless since the time of such determination there has been a retroactively effective change in the law controlling such issue; or

(c) Upon a previous motion made pursuant to this section, the defendant was in a position adequately to raise the ground or issue underlying the present motion but did not do so.

Although the court may deny the motion under any of the circumstances specified in this subdivision, in the interest of justice and for good cause shown it may in its discretion grant the motion if it is otherwise meritorious and vacate the judgment.

4. If the court grants the motion, it must, except as provided in subdivision five, vacate the judgment, and must dismiss the accusatory instrument, or order a new trial, or take such other action as is appropriate in the circumstances.

5. Upon granting the motion upon the ground, as prescribed in paragraph (g) of subdivision one, that newly discovered evidence creates a probability that had such evidence been received at the trial the verdict would have been more favorable to the defendant in that the conviction would have been for a lesser offense than the one contained in the verdict, the court may either:

(a) Vacate the judgment and order a new trial; or

(b) With the consent of the people, modify the judgment by reducing it to one of conviction for such lesser offense. In such case, the court must re-sentence the defendant accordingly.

6. Upon a new trial resulting from an order vacating a judgment pursuant to this section, the indictment is deemed to contain all the counts and to charge all the offenses which it contained and charged at the time the previous trial was commenced, regardless of whether any count was dismissed by the court in the course of such trial, except (a) those upon or of which the defendant was acquitted or deemed to have been acquitted, and (b) those dismissed by the order vacating the judgment, and (c) those previously dismissed by an appellate court upon an appeal from the judgment, or by any court upon a previous post-judgment motion.

7. Upon an order which vacates a judgment based upon a plea of guilty to an accusatory instrument or a part thereof, but which does not dismiss the entire accusatory instrument, the criminal action is, in

the absence of an express direction to the contrary, restored to its pre-pleading status and the accusatory instrument is deemed to contain all the counts and to charge all the offenses which it contained and charged at the time of the entry of the plea, except those subsequently dismissed under circumstances specified in paragraphs (b) and (c) of subdivision six. Where the plea of guilty was entered and accepted, pursuant to subdivision three of section 220.30, upon the condition that it constituted a complete disposition not only of the accusatory instrument underlying the judgment vacated but also of one or more other accusatory instruments against the defendant then pending in the same court, the order of vacation completely restores such other accusatory instruments; and such is the case even though such order dismisses the main accusatory instrument underlying the judgment.

§ 440.20 Motion to set aside sentence; by defendant

1. At any time after the entry of a judgment, the court in which the judgment was entered may, upon motion of the defendant, set aside the sentence upon the ground that it was unauthorized, illegally imposed or otherwise invalid as a matter of law.

2. Notwithstanding the provisions of subdivision one, the court must deny such a motion when the ground or issue raised thereupon was previously determined on the merits upon an appeal from the judgment or sentence, unless since the time of such appellate determination there has been a retroactively effective change in the law controlling such issue.

3. Notwithstanding the provisions of subdivision one, the court may deny such a motion when the ground or issue raised thereupon was previously determined on the merits upon a prior motion or proceeding in a court of this state, other than an appeal from the judgment, or upon a prior motion or proceeding in a federal court, unless since the time of such determination there has been a retroactively effective change in the law controlling such issue. Despite such determination, however, the court in the interest of justice and for good cause shown, may in its discretion grant the motion if it is otherwise meritorious.

§ 440.30 Motion to vacate judgment and to set aside sentence; procedure

1. A motion to vacate a judgment pursuant to section 440.10 and a motion to set aside a sentence pursuant to section 440.20 must be made in writing and upon reasonable notice to the people. If the motion is expressly or impliedly based upon the existence or occurrence

of facts, the motion papers must contain sworn allegations thereof, whether by the defendant or by another person or persons. Such sworn allegations may be based upon personal knowledge of the affiant or upon information and belief, provided that in the latter event the affiant must state the sources of such information and the grounds of such belief. The defendant may further submit documentary evidence or information supporting or tending to support the allegations of the moving papers. The people may file with the court, and in such case must serve a copy thereof upon the defendant or his counsel, if any, an answer denying or admitting any or all of the allegations of the moving papers, and may further submit documentary evidence or information refuting or tending to refute such allegations. After all papers of both parties have been filed, and after all documentary evidence or information, if any, has been submitted, the court must consider the same for the purpose of ascertaining whether the motion is determinable without a hearing to resolve questions of fact.

2. If it appears by conceded or uncontradicted allegations of the moving papers or of the answer, or by conclusive documentary evidence or information, that there are circumstances which require denial thereof pursuant to subdivision two of section 440.10 or subdivision two of section 440.20, the court must summarily deny the motion. If it appears that there are circumstances authorizing, though not requiring, denial thereof pursuant to subdivision three of section 440.10 or subdivision three of section 440.20, the court may in its discretion either (a) summarily deny the motion, or (b) proceed to consider the merits thereof.

3. Upon considering the merits of the motion, the court must grant it and vacate the judgment or set aside the sentence, as the case may be, if:

(a) The moving papers allege a ground constituting legal basis for the motion; and

(b) Such ground, if expressly or impliedly based upon the existence or occurrence of facts, is supported by sworn allegations thereof; and

(c) The sworn allegations of fact essential to support the motion are either conceded by the people to be true or are conclusively substantiated by documentary evidence or information.

4. Upon considering the merits of the motion, the court may deny it if:

(a) The moving papers do not allege any ground constituting legal basis for the motion; or

(b) The motion is expressly or impliedly based upon the existence or occurrence of facts and the moving papers do not contain sworn allegations substantiating or tending to substantiate all the essential facts, as required by subdivision one; or

(c) An allegation of fact essential to support the motion is conclusively refuted by documentary evidence or information.

5. If the court does not determine the motion pursuant to subdivisions two, three or four, it must conduct a hearing and make findings of fact essential to the determination thereof. The defendant has a right to be present at such hearing but may waive such right in writing. If he does not so waive it and if he is confined in a prison or other institution of this state, the court must cause him to be produced at such hearing.

6. At such a hearing, the defendant has the burden of proving by a preponderance of the evidence every fact essential to support the motion.

7. Regardless of whether a hearing was conducted, the court upon determining the motion must set forth on the record its findings of fact and the reasons for its determination.

§ 440.40   Motion to set aside sentence; by people

1. At any time not more than one year after the entry of a judgment, the court in which it was entered may, upon motion of the people, set aside the sentence upon the ground that it was invalid as a matter of law.

2. Notwithstanding the provisions of subdivision one, the court must summarily deny the motion when the ground or issue raised thereupon was previously determined on the merits upon an appeal from the judgment or sentence, unless since the time of such appellate determination there has been a retroactively effective change in the law controlling such issue.

3. Notwithstanding the provisions of subdivison one, the court may summarily deny such a motion when the ground or issue raised thereupon was previously determined on the merits upon a prior motion or proceeding in a court of this state, other than an appeal from the judgment or sentence. Despite such circumstance, however, the court, in the interests of justice and for good cause shown, may in its discretion grant the motion if it is otherwise meritorious.

4. The motion must be made upon reasonable notice to the defendant and to the attorney if any who appeared for him in the last proceeding which occurred in connection with the judgment or sen-

tence, and the defendant must be given adequate opportunity to appear in opposition to the motion. The defendant has a right to be present at such proceeding but may waive such right in writing. If he does not so waive it and if he is confined in a prison or other institution of this state, the court must cause him to be produced at the proceeding upon the motion.

5. An order setting aside a sentence pursuant to this section does not affect the validity or status of the underlying conviction, and after entering such an order the court must resentence the defendant in accordance with the law.

6. Upon a resentence imposed pursuant to subdivision five, the terms of which are more severe than those of the original sentence, the defendant's time for taking an appeal from the judgment is automatically extended in the manner prescribed in subdivision four of section 450.30.

* * * * *

LOUISIANA STATUTES ANNOTATED (WEST 1967)
CODE OF CRIMINAL PROCEDURE

Art. 841 When bill of exceptions must be reserved

An irregularity or error in the proceedings cannot be availed of after verdict unless it is objected to at the time of its occurrence and a bill of exceptions is reserved to the adverse ruling of the court on such objection. Failure to reserve a bill of exceptions at the time of an adverse ruling of the court operates as a waiver of the objection and as an acquiescence in the irregularity or ruling.

This requirement shall not apply to:

(1) A ground for arrest of judgment under Article 859, or the court's ruling on a motion in arrest of judgment; or

(2) The court's ruling on a motion for a new trial based on the ground of bills of exceptions reserved during the trial.

Art. 844 Formal bills of exceptions; signing; contents

A. The appellate court shall consider only formal bills of exceptions which have been signed by the trial judge in conformity with Article 845. In a case where the death sentence has been imposed, the appellate court, to promote the ends of justice, may consider bills that have not been timely signed by the trial judge.

B. A formal bill of exceptions shall contain only the evidence necessary to form a basis for the bill, and must show the circumstances and the evidence upon which the ruling was based. When the same evidence has been made part of another bill of exceptions, the evidence may be incorporated by reference to the other bill. Evidence as to guilt or innocence can only be taken down and transcribed as provided by law.

Art. 845   Submission and signing of formal bills of exceptions

The bills of exceptions reserved during the trial shall be submitted to the court and signed by it at any time prior to the granting of an order of appeal; except that if the bills of exceptions are not submitted and signed prior to the order of appeal the court shall fix a later date for the submission and signing of bills of exceptions, which extended date must be not later than the return day for the appeal. The court must sign the formal bills of exceptions, but may attach per curiam comments stating its reasons for the rulings. If the court refuses to sign a formal bill of exceptions, its refusal may be reviewed on a writ of mandamus.

Art. 851   Grounds for new trial

The motion for a new trial is based on the supposition that injustice has been done the defendant, and, unless such is shown to have been the case the motion shall be denied, no matter upon what allegation it is grounded.

The court, on motion of the defendant, shall grant a new trial whenever:

(1) The verdict is contrary to the law and the evidence;

(2) A bill of exceptions reserved during the proceedings shows prejudicial error;

(3) New and material evidence that, notwithstanding the exercise of reasonable diligence by the defendant, was not discovered before or during the trial, is available, and if the evidence had been introduced at the trial it would probably have changed the verdict or judgment of guilty;

(4) The defendant has discovered, since the verdict or judgment of guilty, a prejudicial error or defect in the proceedings that, notwithstanding the exercise of reasonable diligence by the defendant, was not discovered before the verdict or judgment; or

(5) The court is of the opinion that the ends of justice would be served by the granting of a new trial, although the defendant may not be entitled to a new trial as a matter of strict legal right.

Art. 854   Newly discovered evidence; necessary allegations

A motion for a new trial based on ground (3) of Article 851 shall contain allegations of fact, sworn to by the defendant or his counsel, showing:

(1) That notwithstanding the exercise of reasonable diligence by the defendant, the new evidence was not discovered before or during the trial;

(2) The names of the witnesses who will testify and a concise statement of the newly discovered evidence;

(3) The facts which the witnesses or evidence will establish; and

(4) That the witnesses or evidence are not beyond the process of the court, or are otherwise available.

The newly discovered whereabouts or residence of a witness do not constitute newly discovered evidence.

Art. 856   Motion to urge all available grounds; exceptions

A motion for a new trial shall urge all grounds known and available to the defendant at the time of the filing of the motion. However, the court may permit the defendant to supplement his original motion by urging an additional ground, or may permit the defendant to file an additional motion for a new trial, prior to the court's ruling on the motion.

Art. 857   Effect of granting new trial

The effect of granting a new trial is to set aside the verdict or judgment and to permit retrial of the case with as little prejudice to either party as if it had never been tried.

Art. 858   Review of ruling on motion for new trial

Neither the appellate nor supervisory jurisdiction of the supreme court may be invoked to review the granting or the refusal to grant a new trial, except for error of law.

Art. 859   Grounds for arrest of judgment

The court shall arrest the judgment only on one or more of the following grounds:

(1) The indictment is substantially defective, in that an essential averment is omitted;

(2) The offense charged is not punishable under a valid statute;

(3) The court is without jurisdiction of the case;

(4) The tribunal that tried the case did not conform with the requirements of Section 41 of Article VII of the Louisiana Constitution;

(5)   The verdict is not responsive to the indictment, or is otherwise so defective that it will not form the basis of a valid judgment;

(6)   Double jeopardy, if not previously urged; or

(7)   The prosecution was not timely instituted, if not previously urged.

Improper venue may not be urged by a motion in arrest of judgment.

Art. 862   Effect of sustaining motions in arrest of judgment

If the judgment is arrested because of a defect in the indictment, the indictment shall be dismissed and the defendant shall be discharged as to that indictment. However, a new indictment may be filed within the time limitation stated in Article 576.

If the judgment is arrested because the court is without jurisdiction of the case, the defendant shall be discharged, but may be tried by a court of proper jurisdiction.

If the judgment is arrested because the wrong type of tribunal tried the case, or because the verdict is not responsive to the indictment or is otherwise fatally defective, the defendant shall be remanded to custody or bail to await a new trial.

If the judgment is arrested on any other ground, the defendant shall be discharged.

*   *   *   *   *

MICHIGAN COMPILED LAWS ANNOTATED (WEST 1968)

770.1   New trial; reasons for granting

The court in which the trial of any indictment shall be had may grant a new trial to the defendant, for any cause for which by law a new trial may be granted, or when it shall appear to the court that justice has not been done, and on such terms or conditions as the court shall direct.

[Although § 770.2 requires the motion to be made within 30 days, the Michigan judicial interpretation is that a trial court has discretion to accept it at any time. *Millard v. Skillman*, 341 Mich. 461, 67 N.W.2d 708 (1955). This has meant that § 770.1 motions are frequently used as a means of obtaining post-conviction relief, a matter dealt with in Chapter 14. *Cf.* also the provisions of N.Y. Cr. Pro. L. §§ 440.10, 440.20 (1971), *supra* at 812–816. —Eds.]

*   *   *   *   *

B. Appellate Practice

H. LEVY, HOW TO HANDLE AN APPEAL (PLI 1969)
Chapter 11, *Practical Suggestions for Practice in the United States
Courts of Appeals—After July 1, 1968*

On December 4, 1967, the Supreme Court of the United States
promulgated a completely new set of rules of practice governing
appeals to the Federal Courts of Appeals: the Federal Rules of Appellate Procedure, to become effective July 1, 1968, unless rejected or
amended by Congress. These new Rules are reprinted in full as Appendix C to this book *infra*.

For the first time, a uniform practice for civil and criminal appeals,
as well as a uniform practice for all the circuits, is now prescribed.
The new Rules, however, do permit the individual Courts of Appeals
to make local court rules that are not inconsistent with the Federal
Rules of Appellate Procedure (Rule 47, Fed. R. App. P.). This authority may result in minor variations in practice from circuit to circuit.
And, unfortunately, apparently because of statutory problems, different procedures are used in taking different types of appeals.

The genesis of the new Rules has taken several years. In March of
1964, the Committee on Rules of Practice and Procedure of the Judicial
Conference to the United States had proposed "Uniform Rules of Federal Appellate Procedure"; in December 1966, the Committee had
submitted three alternative drafts of proposed Uniform Rule 30, governing reproduction of necessary parts of the record. These proposed
"Uniform Rules of Federal Appellate Procedure," with numerous
amendments, have now emerged as the Federal Rules of Appellate
Procedure.

The material which follows in this chapter gives a step-by-step
breakdown of the complicated procedures to be used by attorneys
handling appeals to the varying United States Courts of Appeals
under the new Federal Rules of Appellate Procedure, which we assume at this writing will be enacted *in haec verba*.

The requirements and methodology of taking the appeal differ,
depending generally upon the type of appeal being prosecuted. These
varying requirements are presented in chart form under 11.1. *infra*,
for easier reference and checking, with citations to the new Rules.

Once the appeal is taken or granted, the timetable is generally as
follows:

a) within ten days thereafter, appellant must order all or parts of the stenographic transcript and serve a statement of issues, and appellee has ten days after service to order other parts;

b) within forty days thereafter, the record is to be filed;

c) in the absence of agreement as to contents of the appendix, appellant makes his designation of what shall be reproduced in the appendix within ten days after the filing of the record, and appellee, within the next ten days, may require appellant to reproduce additional parts thereof;

d) the reproduced appendix and brief of appellant are to be filed by appellant either

  i) within forty days after filing the record, or

  ii) if he uses the "deferred appendix" method, he serves and files his brief within the said forty days, but he need not file the reproduced appendix until twenty-one days after service of appellee's brief;

e) the appellee has thirty days after service of appellant's brief to serve and file his brief.

These provisions, with exceptions and qualifications, are discussed in more detail *infra*. At this point, it seems appropriate to note that the Rules serve the practitioner's convenience by precluding the necessity of consulting myriad statutory requirements (except in cases of review of agency orders). But the major revolutions wrought by the Rules are (1) the use of the compulsory joint appendix (with a heavily restricted option to use the original record and copies thereof), and (2) the option given to appellant to use the deferred appendix method, *i.e.*, to delay the reproduced appendix until after all briefs are served. The use of the new appendix method is discussed at 11.7. *infra*.

11.1 How and When to Take an Appeal

The chart appearing on the next four pages shows the different methodologies to be used in different situations, and the varying time requirements. Usually, it is the existence of many regulatory statutes which necessitates the different requirements, depending upon the type of appeal.

PROCEDURAL REQUIREMENTS FOR TAKING APPEALS

CRIMINAL CASES

1. Time to take appeal:
   (a) Normally

   By defendant, 10 da. after entry; if appeal by U.S., 30 day. R.4(b).

   (b) Extensions of time to take appeal:

   (1) By lower court

   Not more than 30 da. add'l, upon showing of excusable neglect. R.4(b).

   (2) By Court of Appeals

   None. R.26(b).

   (3) By motion for other relief in lower court

   Motion for new trial on newly discovered evidence extends time if made at least 10 da. prior to entry of judgment; other timely motions for new trial or in arrest of judgment. R.4(a).

   (c) Time for cross-appeal.

   None

2. Appeal taken by filing:

   Notice of appeal. R.3(a).

3. Is proof of service necessary?

   No. R.3(d).

4. With which clerk is appealing document to be filed?

   District Court. R.3(a).

5. Number of copies of document to be filed (required or as courtesy to clerk)?

   Courtesy: 2 plus number sufficient for all att'ys of record in case. R.3(d).

6. Must cost bond be filed (assuming party not exempt and no supersedeas bond including such security has been filed) with appealing document?

   No. R.7.

11.2 Appellee's Duty and Opportunity in Connection With the Taking of the Permissive Appeal

Appellee has no duty whatsoever in connection with the taking an appeal as of right, only with its perfecting by designation of parts of the stenographic transcript to be ordered and of parts of the record to be reproduced, together with filing of his brief—and, where an agency is the appellee, the filing of the record itself.

But if appellant has sought a permissive interlocutory appeal under 28 U.S.C. § 1292(b), or an appeal by allowance in bankruptcy proceedings, an adverse party has seven days after the petition is served upon him to file an answer in opposition. Rules 5(b), 6(b).

11.3   Appellant's Duty to Order Stenographic Minutes
Within Ten Days After Notice of Appeal Filed,
and to Serve and File Statement of Issues

In all appeals except those seeking review of agency proceedings, appellant has ten days after the filing of the notice of appeal to order portions of the minutes transcribed and to serve and file a certain statement. . . .

This requirement is not applicable to appeals seeking review of an agency proceeding (Rules 20, 10), as the responsibility is that of the agency to file a complete record.

When do the ten days begin to run if a permissive appeal has been sought? The Rules are silent on this. Although Rules 5(d) and 6(d) provide that the time for transmitting the record and docketing the appeal shall run from the date of the entry of the order granting permission to appeal, they make no provision as to when the time begins to run to order the transcript and serve and file the required statement. However, there is no reason for requiring the transcript to be ordered and notice given prior to the time the appeal is allowed. It may accordingly be assumed that appellant has no such duty until and unless his appeal be allowed, and that the ten days begins to run only then.

11.4   Appellee's Duty to File and Serve Designation of
Additional Parts of Record Within Ten Days After
Service of Appellant's Statement

This duty appertains to all but reviews of agency proceedings. . . .

11.5   Appellant's Duty: Transmission of the Record and
Docketing of the Appeal Within Forty Days After Filing
of Notice of Appeal or Granting of Leave to Appeal:
Extensions and Mechanics

Except in cases seeking review of agency orders (where it is the agency's responsibility to file the entire record), appellant has forty days after the filing of the notice of appeal (or after the granting of permission to appeal if the appeal be not of right) within which to have the record transmitted to the Court of Appeals and to pay the docketing fee. Rules 5, 6, 11, 12. . . .

11.6   Appellant's Failure to Timely Transmit Record or
Pay Docket Fee

11.61 Appellee's Remedy

In the Court of Appeals, appellee may move to dismiss the appeal for appellant's failure to cause timely transmission of the record or to pay the docket fee. The requirements of such motion are clearly set forth in Rules 12(c) and 27.

11.62 Appellant's Duty on Motion: Caveat

Appellant has fourteen days after service to respond to the motion. But he must be careful: unless exempt from payment of the docket fee, his failure to pay it will result in his not being permitted to respond. Rule 12(c). Advice: if the docket fee has not been paid prior to receipt of appellee's motion papers, pay it at once.

11.7   The Reproduced Record—Duties of the Parties

11.71 Possible Use of Original Record and Reproduction of All or Part Thereof

Rule 30(f) provides that a Court of Appeals may by rule applicable to all cases, or to classes of cases, or by order in specific cases, dispense with the requirement of an appendix and permit appeals to be heard on the original record, with such copies of the record, or relevant parts thereof, as the Court may require. This is modelled after the Ninth Circuit's Rule 10, which permits appeals to be heard on the original record and two copies of that record, as a way of reducing costs. Request for the use of this optional procedure in the Ninth Circuit is made in over 95 per cent of the cases. See Advisory Committee's Explanatory Note to Draft C of Rule 30 of the (proposed) Uniform Rules of Federal Appellate Procedure (1966).

Though such a method of proceeding is available in Supreme Court practice by order, we suggest . . . . that the Supreme Court will probably allow this method only where there is a clear cut question of law, as to which factual background and possible issues of fact are lacking. Nevertheless, some of the Courts of Appeals may be willing to experiment, and doubtless the result of their experimentation might change the approach of the Supreme Court of the United States in years to come. Accordingly, even if the rules of your Court of Appeals do not provide for use of the original record plus copies thereof, if such use would incur substantial savings, consider whether you should request permission to so proceed. Bear in mind, however, that pleas for use of the original record method—never intended to be the norm—will sometimes fall on deaf judicial ears, and that it is entirely possible that some Courts of Appeals may by rule severely restrict the availability of this method to *in forma pauperis* cases and exceptional circumstances. Consider also that the method may be uneconomical if the court requires too many copies.

A motion (typewritten, with an original and three copies of the motion filed—see Rule 27) may be made by either party for proceeding by use of the original record plus copies of all or part thereof. If it be denied, use of the deferred appendix and/or deferred brief method may still give ample time to prepare the appendix and brief; if ample time might not be available, ask for extra time for filing the brief and appendix should your motion to proceed on the original record be denied. The request may be coupled with your motion to proceed on the original record.

11.72 If the Original Record is Not Used:
Deferred vs. Non-Deferred Appendix Method

Time requirements for cross-designations of what is to be included in the appendix, and for serving and filing the appendix, differ depending upon whether the "deferred appendix" be used or not. The "deferred appendix" method merely means that the preparation of the appendix may be deferred until after the briefs have been filed, and the service and filing of the appendix may be delayed until twenty-one days after service of appellee's brief. Rule 30(c).

It is the appellant's responsibility to file the appendix, and it is he who chooses whether to proceed by deferred appendix method or not. Or the deferred appendix method may be used if the Court of Appeals so provides for classes of cases or by order in specific cases. *Ibid.*

Rule 30(b) encourages the parties to agree as to the contents of the appendix. If there is such agreement, then the procedures below for designation and cross-designation are inapplicable. Such agreement, however, should be promptly made and reduced to writing. . . .

We turn first to the requirements of the non-deferred appendix method.

11.721 The Non-Deferred Appendix: Time and Cost
Requirements for Non-Deferred Appendix Method

a. *Ten-day requirement* after date of filing record, for appellant to serve on appellee (i) a designation of the parts of the record which he intends to include in the appendix and (ii) a statement of the issues which he intends to present for review. Rule 30(b).

b. *Ten-day requirement,* after date of receiving appellant's designation, for appellee to serve upon appellant a designation of additional parts to be included in the appendix. Rule 30(b).

c. *Forty-day requirement* after date of filing record, for appellant to serve one copy of the reproduced appendix on counsel for each party separately represented and to file ten copies of the appendix. (The Court of Appeals may by rule or order direct the filing or service of a lesser number.) Rule 30(a).

d. *Cost requirement.* Unless otherwise agreed, the costs of producing the appendix shall initially be paid by the appellant, unless he advises the appellee that he considers that parts of the record designated by appellee for inclusion are unnecessary for the determination of issues presented. (There seems to be no precise time requirement for giving such notification.) If such notification be given, the appellee must advance the cost of including such parts. Though the rule is silent as to what happens if he does not so advance the cost, save for the possible use of the disciplinary power of the Court of Appeals under Rule 46(c), it is suggested that in such event the appellant may safely refrain from reproducing such parts. Costs of the appendix are to be taxed as costs, but the court may tax a party for unnecessarily including matter in the appendix. Rule 30(b).

11.722 The Deferred Appendix

a. *Ten-day requirement,* after date of filing record, for appellant to serve and file notice of his election to defer preparation of the appendix. Rule 30(c). (Obviously if a court rule mandates the use of the deferred appendix method, the notice need not be sent.)

b. *Designations deferred until serving of brief.* Designations of the parts of the record to be included in the appendix are to be made by each party when his brief is served (as to time requirements for serving brief, see 11.812. *infra.*) No statement of the issues is necessary. Rule 30(c).

c. *Twenty-one day requirement.* Appellant serves and files the reproduced appendix within twenty-one days after service of appellee's brief. Rule 30(c). See 11.721. (c) *re* number of copies.

11.73 Contents and Arrangement of Appendix

Rule 30(a,d) has precisely the same requirements for contents and arrangement of appendix as required by the Rules of the Supreme Court of the United States, on which see *infra* 12.6123. . . .

If the deferred appendix method is used, the appendix should indicate the original paging of each part of the record by placing in brackets the number of each page at the place in the appendix where that page begins. Alternatively, however, a party may use the "deferred brief" method (see 11.812. *infra*), and refer directly to the pages of the appendix itself. Rule 30(c). The latter method is preferable. . . .

Exhibits may be contained in a separate volume or volumes, suitably indexed. For this purpose, transcripts of a proceeding before an administrative agency, board, commission or officer used in an action in the District Court are treated as exhibits. Four copies of such volume(s) are to be filed with the appendix, and one copy served on counsel for each party separately represented. In most instances it will be preferable to put exhibits in a separate volume so as to make them more handily available to the court. The emphasis upon exhibits by the Rules should warn the appellate attorney that it might well be fatal to fail to furnish relevant exhibits—which, though frequently overlooked by attorneys, may be more important to the court than hundreds of pages of testimony.

11.74 Reproduction of the Appendix

The appendix no longer need be printed; it may be produced either by standard typographic printing or by any duplicating or copying process which produces a clear black image on white paper, except by carbon copies (unless permitted by the court). Rule 32(a). However, the other restrictions on reproduction make arduous the use of other than standard printing methods. These are the restrictions on processes other than printing: (a) the pages must not exceed 8½ by 11 inches; (b) the type matter must not exceed 6½ by 9½ inches; (c) there must be double-spacing between each line of text; (d) they must be bound in volumes. (In patent cases, the pages may be of such size as is necessary to utilize copies of patent documents.) Copies of the reporter's transcript and other papers reproduced in such a manner may be inserted in the appendix.

11.8   The Brief

11.81   Time Requirements

11.811   Non-Deferred Appendix

a. Appellant's brief—Must be served and filed within forty days after record filed.

b. Appellee's brief—Must be served and filed within thirty days after service of appellant's brief.

c. Appellant's reply brief—Must be served and filed within fourteen days after service of appellee's brief, but at least three days before argument except for good cause shown. Rule 31(a).

11.812 Time Requirements—Deferred Appendix—Deferred Brief

Typewritten or page proof briefs may be served and filed within the times set forth in 11.811, *supra*. The final reproduced briefs must then be served within fourteen days after the appendix is filed. Rule 30 (c). . . . The new Rules contain the same procedures as the Supreme Court Rules (except that a fourteen-day requirement is substituted for the ten-day Supreme Court requirement), . . .

11.82 Number Requirements

Twenty-five copies of each brief are to be filed, unless by order a lesser number be directed, and two copies served on counsel for each party separately represented. Rule 31(b).

11.83 Failure to Timely File Briefs

The consequences of failure to file the brief within the time provided, or as extended pursuant to the court's power under Rule 26, may be severe: An appellee may move for dismissal of the appeal—though it is up to the court to decide whether this results in dismissal or merely in additional time to appellant to serve and file his brief. If an appellee fails to file his brief, he will not be heard at oral argument except by permission of the court. Rule 31(c).

11.84 Reproduction of Briefs

The same requirements of reproduction applicable to appendices (11.74 *supra*) are applicable to the briefs. However, Rule 32 lays down quite specific requirements as to the colors of the covers of briefs, applicable when the briefs are produced by a commercial printing or duplicating firm, or if produced otherwise and the covers described are available. The covers of the briefs are required to be the following:

Appellant's: blue
Appellee's: red
Intervenor or Amicus Curiae: green
Any reply brief: grey.

These requirements are to enable a judge to readily know, at any point, whose brief he is reading. In appellate practice, in general, it is most helpful to used different colored covers on the briefs (and records or appendices) of the different parties, unless prohibited.

11.85 Formal Requirements of Briefs

The front covers of the briefs (and of the appendices, if separately printed) must conform with certain formal requirements. Rule 32(a) . . . .

11.86 Length of Briefs

The length of the briefs is limited by Rule 28(g), unless permission of the court be given otherwise, as follows: (a) principal briefs, not more than fifty pages of standard typographic printing or seventy pages of printing by any other process of duplicating or copying (exclusive of pages containing table of contents, table of citations, and any addendum containing statutes, rules, regulations, etc.); (b) reply briefs, not more than twenty-five pages of standard typographic printing or thirty-five pages of printing by any other process of duplicating or copying. It will be at once seen that, if you need the extra pages, statutes, rules and regulations should be printed in an addendum to the brief. Even if you do not need the extra pages, it is far more convenient to a judge to have these items in an addendum.

11.9   Oral Argument

11.91   Prehearing Conference

Federal Rule of Appellate Procedure 33 permits the court to direct the attorneys for the parties to appear before the court or a judge thereof for a prehearing conference to consider the simplification of the issues and such other matters as may aid in the disposition of the proceeding by the court. An order may be made reciting the action taken at the conference and the agreements made by the parties as to any of the matters considered, limiting the issues to those not disposed of by admissions or agreements of counsel. This order, when entered, controls the subsequent course of the proceeding, unless modified to prevent manifest injustice.

To what extent the Courts of Appeals may hold such prehearing conferences, either for all or classes of cases or in specific cases, remains to be seen. Certainly, it would not be worthwhile normally for the entire court to hold a prehearing conference, except in the most complicated cases, or else the prehearing conference would be the equivalent of an oral argument, albeit on a more informal basis. Thus, it is suggested that the Rule will probably be implemented by prehearing conferences held by one appellate judge.

Of course, all that has been said throughout this book as to the key importance of stating the issues correctly would be of considerable importance in any prehearing conference directed towards a so-called "simplification" of the issues. The appellate attorney should be careful to insure that the so-called simplification of the issues does not diminish the effect of the issues as he would state them, since oral argument is yet to follow.

Prehearing conferences will probably be most useful in agency review proceeding and in multi-party appeals. For it is suggested that despite the language of Rule 33, its real purpose is not so much simplification of the issues as setting up time schedules, avoiding duplication, and ironing out procedural difficulties. The prehearing conference might also be used for purposes such as insuring complete appendices or shortening lengthy ones, and for the resolution of preliminary problems whose resolution might aid in the disposition of the case (*e.g.*, possible mootness, intervening legislation, etc.). There may well be situations where counsel will find it appropriate to request a prehearing conference instead of proceeding more formally by motion.

11.92 Time of Oral Argument

You will be notified by the Clerk as to when and where oral argument will be heard; a request for postponement must be made by motion filed reasonably in advance of the date fixed for hearing. Rule 34(a).

If you have never argued a case in your Court of Appeals before, get there a day or so before your argument. . . .

11.93 Time for Oral Argument

Unless otherwise provided by a Court of Appeals rule for all cases or for classes of cases, each side is allowed thirty minutes for argument. Additional time may be requested by letter to the Clerk in advance of the date of the hearing, and is to be liberally granted if cause therefor is shown. (It is suggested that despite the language of the Rule, a strong showing of necessity will be a condition precedent to the granting of additional time.) A party is not obligated to use all of the time allowed, and the court may terminate the argument whenever in its judgment further argument is unnecessary. Rule 34(b).

Oral argument is unnecessary under the Federal Rules of Appellate Procedure if the parties agree that the case may be submitted for decision on the briefs, although the rule may nevertheless direct that the case may be argued. Rule 34(f). Failure of counsel on all sides to appear has the same effect of having the case submitted for decision on the briefs. Rule 34(e). . . .

If one party unilaterally decides not to appear, the consequences are different depending upon whether the non-appearing party is appellant or appellee: If appellant fails to appear it is discretionary with the court whether it will hear argument of appellee if his counsel be present; but if the appellee fails to appear and the appellant be present, the court will hear appellant's argument. Rule 34(e). In any event, if an attorney decides not to appear for oral argument, it is suggested that, as a matter of courtesy, the clerk be so advised in advance, so as to permit the Court of Appeals to better schedule its calendar. Courtesy would also seem to require advising opposing counsel of the same. . . .

11.94 Divided Oral Argument

Unlike the rules of the Supreme Court of the United States . . . , the new rules make no comment either favoring or approving divided oral argument. While the Courts of Appeals are quite used to divided oral arguments, the same considerations as to whether to divide oral argument or not, set forth in 12.633, *infra,* are applicable.

11.95 Physical Exhibits Used at Oral Argument

Where physical exhibits other than documents are to be used at the argument, counsel must arrange to have them placed in the courtroom before the court convenes on the day of the argument. After the argument, counsel must remove them unless the court otherwise directs. Rule 30(g). It should be carefully noted that if exhibits are not reclaimed by counsel within a reasonable time after notice is given by the clerk, they are to be destroyed or otherwise disposed of as the clerk may think best. As your physical exhibits may be quite important, you should be extremely careful to remove them after notice from the clerk as speedily as possible. . . .

11.11 Petition for Rehearing

The detailed and simple requirements for such a petition are set forth in Rule 40. They need not be repeated here.

11.12 General Provisions

11.121 Suspension of Rules

Rule 2 is a catch-all provision, permitting the Court of Appeals, for good cause shown, or in the interest of **expediting** decision, to suspend the requirements or provisions of any **of the** rules, in a particular case, on application of a party or on its own motion. However, the Court of Appeals may not enlarge the time for filing a notice of appeal, a petition for allowance, or a petition for permission to appeal. Nor may it extend the time to seek review of the order of an administrative agency, board, commission or officer, except as specifically authorized by law. Rule 26(b). The only provisions in the Rules themselves permitting extension of time to appeal or seek review are indicated *supra* in the chart at 11.1.

11.122 Filing

All filing is with the Clerk of the Court of Appeals, and it may be accomplished by mail addressed to the Clerk. Filing is not timely unless the papers are received by the Clerk within the allowable time, except (1) that briefs and appendices are deemed filed on the day of mailing if the most expeditious form of delivery by mail, excepting special delivery, is utilized (Rule 25[a]); and (2) if a notice of appeal from a decision of the Tax Court (not other courts) is received after expiration of the last day allowed for filing, the postmark date is deemed the date of delivery, subject to the provisions of § 7502 of the Internal Revenue Code of 1954, as amended, and the regulations promulgated pursuant thereto. (Current regulations are found in 26 C.F.R. § 301.7502–1.) Rule 13(b).

11.123 Proof of Service

Proof of service is either by an acknowledgment of service by the person served, or in the form of a statement of the date and manner of service and of the names of the persons served. It is also recommended that the status of such person served be set forth. It need not be sworn to, but may be certified by the person who made service, whether or not that person be a member of the Bar of the Court. Proof of service may appear on or be affixed to the papers filed. Rule 25(d).

One saving grace: The Clerk may permit papers to be filed without acknowledgment or proof of service, but shall require such to be filed promptly thereafter. *Ibid.* Thus, in case of emergency, proof of service need not be filed with the papers filed; however, it should be filed immediately thereafter. . . .

11.132 Extraordinary Writs

See Rule 21 of the Federal Rules of Appellate Procedure. . . .

11.133 Habeas Corpus Proceedings

See Rules 22 and 23, Federal Rules of Appellate Procedure. . . .

11.134   Proceedings in Forma Pauperis

See Rule 24 of the Federal Rules of Appellate Procedure and Form 4 appended thereto. . . .

11.135   Stays and Release Pending Appeal in Criminal Cases

A death sentence is stayed if an appeal is taken; imprisonment is stayed if an appeal is taken and the defendant is admitted to bail; and the payment of a fine, or of a fine plus costs, if an appeal is taken, may be stayed by the District Court or by the Court of Appeals upon such terms as the court deems proper, including the deposit of all or part of the fine with the District Court, or by giving bond for the payment thereof, or submitting to an examination of assets. Rule 38(a), Federal Rules of Criminal Procedure; Rule 8(c), Federal Rules of Appellate Procedure.

The new Federal Rules of Appellate Procedure govern other release situations. Different procedures obtain depending upon whether release is refused prior to or after conviction. They are set forth in Rule 9.

If an order has been made refusing or imposing conditions or release prior to a judgment of conviction, the District Court must state in writing the reasons for the action taken. The appeal therefrom is to be heard without the necessity of briefs (though of course same may be filed), after reasonable notice to the appellee, upon such papers, affidavits or portions of the record as the parties shall present. It is urged that enough portions of the record be presented so that the appellate court may see that there is a substantial question of law to be reviewed.

If release after judgment of conviction be denied by the District Court, or if it imposes conditions of release, the District Court must state in writing its reasons. However, no relief in the Court of Appeals can be sought until the appeal from the judgment of conviction be taken, so that it is advisable to file the notice of appeal immediately. Once the appeal from the judgment for conviction is taken, a motion is made to the Court of Appeals or to a judge thereof for release; or for modification of the conditions of release. This motion is determined upon such papers, affidavits and portions of the record as the parties shall present and after reasonable notice to the appellee.

The essential difference between the two procedures is this: In the case of denial of bail prior to verdict, there is an *appeal* from the denial, and the court of appeals may thus be limited to considering the record below (despite the broad language as to what it may consider). However, denial of bail after sentence is reviewable not by appeal but by *motion*, when of course new matter may be alleged in affidavits and considered by the court. There is doubt as to which procedure applies to denial of bail between verdict and sentence; however, since such denial would occur prior to a judgment of conviction, the appeal procedure would seem applicable.

Pending the appeal, either before or after conviction, the Court of Appeals—or a judge thereof—may order the release of the appellant. Thus, one should seek from the entire court or a judge thereof the release of the appellant pending the appeal from the denial or imposing conditions of release by the District Court. The Clerk of the Court of Appeals should be consulted as to whether application should be made for such intermediate relief to the Court of Appeals or a judge thereof, by order to show cause or other method.

* * * * *

EDITORS' NOTE

Equal Protection Aspects

The troublesome question of appointment of counsel on appeal and the role of counsel in presenting an appeal is dealt with under the topic of right to counsel [see *infra* at 863]. There are, however, other problems, chiefly ones of equal protection, that the Supreme Court has dealt with recently.

In *Long v. District Court of Iowa* [385 U.S. 192 (1966)], the trial court after a hearing at which the relator was unrepresented by counsel, denied a writ of habeas corpus. Relator then moved for appointment of counsel and a free transcript in order to prosecute an appeal of the habeas ruling; the trial court denied the motion on the ground that habeas corpus proceedings are civil in nature. The Supreme Court reversed and remanded. Having accepted certiorari only on the transcript matter, it made no statements about the question of assigned counsel. But it did rule that the state must provide the relator with a free transcript. Only in that way can the appellate review of his application be as complete as it would be in the case of one with funds.

The ABA Standards

Many of the ABA Standards are quite specific as to the details of procedure that should be followed. A very different approach is taken, however, in the Standards relating to appeal [AMERICAN BAR ASSOCIATION PROJECT ON STANDARDS FOR THE ADMINISTRATION OF CRIMINAL JUSTICE, STANDARDS RELATING TO CRIMINAL APPEALS (Approved Draft 1970)]. These set out quite general guidelines that if adopted should promote a smoothly functioning system.

Necessity of review. The United States Supreme Court has never to date required that a state provide a system of appellate review, whether for civil or criminal cases. Only if a system is in fact provided does the equal protection clause begin to govern the aspects of that appeal that militate against the indigent.

The Standards urge that every criminal conviction should be subject to the possibility of review [§ 1.1(a)]. No kind of a criminal case should become absolutely final and unreviewable on the basis of an action by a single court or judge. To say, however, that review should be available does not necessarily mean that it should be automatic. The Standards take the position that "an appeal is not a necessary and integral part of every conviction," although there is substantial advocacy for such a position. In any event, the equal protection cases have brought about a review of a high percentage of criminal convictions [*see* STANDARDS at 19–21, Commentary to § 1.1].

Structure of courts. The Standards suggest three purposes that an appellate system should promote: (1) protection of defendants against prejudicial legal error, and against convictions unsupported by sufficient evidence, (2) refinement of substantive and procedural doctrine, and (3) fostering uniform criminal procedural standards. However, its drafters oppose the establishment of an appellate court with exclusively criminal jurisdiction, on the grounds that a too narrow judicial specialization may result and that the bar as a whole may ignore its work. If there is a three-tiered judicial system, the Standards affirm that the highest level may take cases on a discretionary basis [§ 1.2].

Scope of defendant's appeal. The Standards assert that every defendant should have the right to appeal a final judgment adverse to him, even though he may have been placed on probation or received a suspended sentence, and even though he may have pleaded guilty or nolo contendere [§ 1.3(a)]. A practical reason for the latter is that it would permit the defendant to object to a pretrial ruling on a motion to suppress without having to go through the form of a trial in order to preserve the point on appeal. In general, interlocutory appeals are not encouraged. However, in three instances the Standards contemplate appeals before final judgment [§ 1.3(b)]. One is in the case of a pretrial ruling, as on a motion to suppress or on an interpretation of the underlying statute, adverse to the defendant, when as far as he is concerned trial would be a formality necessary to preserve the question for appeal. A second is an appeal against an order for a new trial when the defendant maintains that he should have received a final judgment in his favor. A third is against a ruling that the defendant is incompetent to stand trial. Because a period of detention in the guise of hospitalization follows the decision that the defendant is incompetent, direct appeal rather than habeas corpus should be available.

Appeal by the prosecution. The degree if any to which the prosecution should be permitted to appeal is a troublesome question. In most jurisdictions the provision against double jeopardy prevents the state from appealing after a judgment of acquittal has been entered against the defendant, no matter how gross the error may have been against the state's position in procedural or evidentiary matters. The United States Supreme Court has recently indicated clearly that the federal concept of double jeopardy is binding on the states under Fourteenth Amendment due process [*Benton v. Maryland,* 395 U.S. 784 (1969)]. However, there is no double jeopardy problem if a pretrial defense motion has been approved, thus preventing or impairing the ability of the prosecution to proceed to trial. Under these circumstances it is purely a matter of legislative judgment whether to permit the state an interlocutory appeal.

The Standards approve the concept of appeal by the prosecution in certain limited circumstances [§ 1.4(a)]. One is when the trial pleading is dismissed on the basis of a substantive challenge to the statute on which the charge is based or a finding that the pleading form used is inadequate to charge a crime. A second is any pretrial order terminating the prosecution, like a finding of double jeopardy, denial of a speedy trial, or the bar of the statute of limitations. A third is a pretrial order that seriously impedes but does not foreclose prosecution, like an order suppressing a confession or other evidence.

If more than one level of appellate court exist, the prosecution should be able to take the case to the highest court if an intermediate appellate court has ruled favorably on a defendant's appeal [§ 1.4(b)].

How to afford practical protection to a defendant during a period of interlocutory appeal can be a troublesome one. The Standards concern themselves only with the matter of custody pending appeal, taking the position that the defendant should not be held in custody pending determination of the state's appeal unless there is "cogent evidence that he will not abide by the judgment of the appellate court" [§ 1.4(c)]. No mention is made of the problem of expenses of the appeal [*but see* Commentary to § 1.4 at p. 40]. An indigent is protected by the equal protection clause, but a person who is not indigent, yet may become so if forced to pay the costs of an appeal, does not fall within the equal protection concept. Failure to take a stand on this point is regrettable.

Notice of appeal. The Standards recommend that a fixed time, like thirty days, should be stated within which an appeal can be instituted, subject to power in the appellate court to accept a delayed appeal if the delay is excusable [§ 2.1(a)]. The drafters also take the position that it is proper for the sentencing court to assume responsibility to advise the defendant he has a right of review that must be exercised within the specified time, and to suggest that he consult his attorney about appeal [§ 2.1(b)].

Trial counsel duties concerning appeal. The position of the Standards is that trial counsel should continue to represent a defendant during the time a decision is reached whether or not to appeal, and during the appeal itself unless a new attorney is substituted or there is reason for counsel to be permitted to withdraw [§ 2.2(a)]. Presumably an attack on the constitutional competency of trial counsel would be an instance in which withdrawal of counsel "in the interests of justice" would be indicated.

The defense attorney because of his knowledge of the case and the procedures to date should be under a duty, the Standards say, to advise the defendant about the meaning of the trial court judgment, the possible grounds for appeal and the likely outcome of an appeal [§ 2.2 (b)]. Like the decision to plead guilty, however, the ultimate decision whether or not to appeal should lie with the client.

If an appeal is successful and a retrial conducted, the defendant may well be convicted ultimately of something less than the offense currently charged against him. In such a case, it would make procedural sense to permit him to plead after trial but before judgment to a lesser offense, with part of the *quid pro quo* being a waiver of the right of appeal. The Standards would permit waiver of appeal to be considered a part of plea negotiation or the preliminary discussions concerning sentence [§ 2.2(c)].

Inducement and deterrents affecting appeals. Because of the way the existing system of criminal procedure operates, some defendants are encouraged to appeal when they should not, and other meritorious appeals are prevented. The Standards urge certain changes in other parts of criminal procedure law to avoid this effect [§ 2.3(a)]. As examples of improper inducements to taking an appeal, the Standards cite bail pending appeal or detention other than under penitentiary conditions [§ 2.3(b)]. In effect, automatic bail or local detention should not be a part of the system unless based on some sort of informed judgment about the likely outcome of an appeal. As examples of improper deterrents to appeal, the Standards suggest denial of legal assistance to the indigent, denial of costs to successful appellants and the prospect of a more severe sentence on retrial following a successful appeal [§ 2.3(c)]. The equal protection cases have increasingly taken care of the first problem as a matter of constitutional law, and the Supreme Court has held that before the court can impose a longer sentence after retrial it must give specific reasons to show that it is not because of the convict's attack on the first sentence [*North Carolina v. Pearce*, 395 U.S. 711 (1969)].

Screening appeals. The position of the Supreme Court in *Anders* [*Anders v. California*, 386 U.S. 738 (1967)] has made it impossible as a practical matter to screen appeals for frivolity. Therefore, the Standards recommend the elimination of certain traditional screening devices as being functionally useless or even detrimental, including certificates of probable cause and leave to appeal at the first stage of appellate review [§ 2.4(a)]. The drafters find no effective penalty that can be imposed for frivolous appeals other than assessment of costs, which has no impact on indigent appellants who are the source of a heavy percentage of frivolous appeals [§ 2.4(b)]. The only antidote is as speedy as possible a determination of the appeal on its merits or lack thereof.

Supervision of appeal. Appeals that are allowed to drift may remain on the docket for extended periods of time. Therefore, it is important that there be supervision of each criminal appeal. The Standards suggest that it might be helpful to assign each case to a single judge, helped by an administrative aide, so that any procedural problems may be conveniently resolved; most would be resolved by the administrative aide [§ 3.1(a)]. Questions that could be handled this way include the preparation and filing of the record on appeal, appointment of counsel, stays, and the elimination of causes of delay [§ 3.2(b)].

Counsel on appeal. The position of the Standards is that every defendant should have counsel on appeal, including assigned counsel in the case of the indigent [§ 3.2(a)]. This the Constitution requires. However, the drafters of the Standards urge that assigned counsel should be compensated from public funds, presumably at least according to minimum fee schedules.

The *Anders* decision puts assigned defense counsel in a difficult position, in that he is in effect forced to carry through what he believes to be an appeal devoid of merit. The Standards accept this as the necessary basis for a consideration of what an attorney is supposed to do with a frivolous appeal. He is not to withdraw from the case simply because he believes the appeal lacks merit [§ 3.2(b)]. However, he may try to persuade the client either not to appeal or to forget issues that lack substance. If the client insists on continuing, the attorney should present the appeal as best he can without deceiving or misleading the court; submission on briefs is entirely possible.

As a further limitation on indigent appellants who wish to play games with the courts, "unexplained general requests by appellants for dismissal of their assigned counsel should be viewed with disfavor" [§3.2(c)].

Record on appeal. A primary source of both delay and expense is the preparation of the documents for appellate court consideration. The Standards assert that improved techniques are necessary to minimize the cost of making a record [§ 3.3(a)]. In particular, the drafters urge abandonment of the traditional requirement of a printed brief and record and the acceptance of typewritten material reproduced by xerography or any other process now in the market or available in the future, as long as the copies are legible.

Indigents must have necessary documents for appeal supplied them at public expense, under the equal protection cases. This requirement the Standards restate. However, rather than leaving the decision of what is necessary to decision by the court, they recommend that the appellant's counsel be permitted to indicate what in his best judgment is needed for the appeal, subject to appropriate sanctions if he acts "irresponsibly or extravagantly" in making his requests [§ 3.3(b)].

Expediting appeals. As indicated above, the Standards recommend a continuing supervision of appeals [*see* § 3.1, *supra*]. In addition, they urge the affirmative requirement that the appellate court as a body should develop techniques to expedite appeals, including the simplification of the process of appeals and a shortening of the time periods of each stage [§3.4].

❋   ❋   ❋   ❋   ❋

FEDERAL RULES OF CRIMINAL PROCEDURE

Rule 38

STAY OF EXECUTION, AND RELIEF PENDING REVIEW

(a)   **Stay of Execution.**

(1)   **Death.** A sentence of death shall be stayed if an appeal is taken.

(2)   **Imprisonment.** A sentence of imprisonment shall be stayed if an appeal is taken and the defendant is admitted to bail. If the defendant is not admitted to bail, the court may recommend to the Attorney General that the defendant be retained at, or transferred

to, a place of confinement near the place of trial or the place where his appeal is to be heard, for a period reasonably necessary to permit the defendant to assist in the preparation of his appeal to the court of appeals.

(3) **Fine.** A sentence to pay a fine or a fine and costs, if an appeal is taken, may be stayed by the district court or by the court of appeals upon such terms as the court deems proper. The court may require the defendant pending appeal to deposit the whole or any part of the fine and costs in the registry of the district court, or to give bond for the payment thereof, or to submit to an examination of assets, and it may make any appropriate order to restrain the defendant from dissipating his assets.

(4) **Probation.** An order placing the defendant on probation shall be stayed if an appeal is taken. . . .

Rule 52

HARMLESS ERROR AND PLAIN ERROR

(a) **Harmless Error.** Any error, defect, irregularity or variance which does not affect substantial rights shall be disregarded.

(b) **Plain Error.** Plain errors or defects affecting substantial rights may be noticed although they were not brought to the attention of the court.

* * * * *

Note, *Harmless Constitutional Error: A Reappraisal,*
83 HARV. L. REV. 814 (1970)*

It is impossible to make all trials totally free of error. Accordingly, all fifty states and the federal government have adopted a doctrine of "harmless-error," either by constitution,[1] statute,[2] or judicial rule[3] or decision, so that only those errors which "affect the substantial rights of the parties"[4] are grounds for reversal. However, the Supreme Court has determined, in *Chapman v. California,*[5] that a different, often stricter harmless-error rule must apply when the error involves the

---

* Copyright 1970 by The Harvard Law Review Association. Some footnotes have been eliminated.

[1] *E.g.,* CAL. CONST. art. 6, § 13.

[2] *E.g.,* TENN. CODE ANN. § 27–117 (1956).

[3] *E.g.,* ALASKA R. CRIM. P. 47(a) (Supp. 1968).

[4] 28 U.S.C. § 2111 (1964).

[5] 386 U.S. 18 (1967).

denial of a federal constitutional right. Both the need for a federal standard, and the choice of a harmless-error rule rather than a rule of automatic reversal, have been well discussed elsewhere, and lie beyond the scope of this Note. This Note will analyze the kind of harmless-error rule which should be adopted by the federal courts in light of the decision in *Chapman*.

I. *Chapman v. California*

In the nineteenth century, because of the influence of the British "Exchequer Rule," any error, no matter how trivial, called for an automatic reversal of the conviction. Often, "criminal trials became a game for sowing reversible error in the record, only to have repeated the same matching of wits when a new trial had been thus obtained." Eventually, every American jurisdiction rejected this rule, and replaced it with what has been called an "overwhelming" or "untainted" evidence test for harmless errors.

Under such a harmless-error rule the appellate court asks whether the defendant would have been convicted if the error at his trial had not been made. If the error did not change the result at trial, there has been no miscarriage of justice, and the appellate court, if confident of its conclusions, may affirm. This rule appears to be a logical and obvious test to determine when an error is harmless. In *Chapman v. California*, however, the Supreme Court held that a federal harmless-error rule must apply to some errors of constitutional magnitude while others are reversible automatically. The ambiguity of that opinion and dissatisfaction with the "untainted evidence" test prevailing in state courts have together led many to the conclusion that some new test must be applied to constitutional errors.

The *Chapman* opinion is ambiguous but in fact does not compel rejection of an "untainted" or overwhelming" evidence rule with respect to errors which are not automatically reversible. The *Chapman* defendants were tried and covincted of robbery, kidnaping, and murder. At the trial, the prosecutor repeatedly referred to the defendants' failure to testify, and the judge advised the jury that it might take this failure into consideration. Shortly after the conviction, the Supreme Court in *Griffin v. California* [12] held that such conduct violated a person's fifth amendment privilege against self-incrimination. Nevertheless, the California Supreme Court affirmed the convictions, finding the error harmless under the state's constitutional standard.

The Supreme Court reversed, holding that a federal rule must

[12] 380 U.S. 609 (1963).

apply when a federal constitutional right has been violated. The Court stated that "before a federal constitutional error can be held harmless, the court must be able to declare a belief that it was harmless beyond a reasonable doubt," and thus specified the rigor with which the new federal test must be applied. However, the Court gave very little indication of what this new federal rule was to be.

The Court noted that some errors would call for automatic reversal, but specifically rejected such a rule for the case before it.[17] The Court gave little guidance on the matter of determining when an error automatically requires reversal and when it does not. It merely named three constitutional rights to which a rule of automatic reversal would apply,[18] leaving open the question whether the list was exhaustive.

Moreover, the Court was ambiguous as to what harmless-error rule should apply in cases like *Chapman,* when automatic reversal is not required. The California Supreme Court, in upholding Chapman's conviction, interpreted the California harmless-error provision to be an "overwhelming" or "untainted" evidence test. By reversing the California court, the Supreme Court seemingly repudiated the "overwhelming-evidence" approach. Many judges and commentators therefore have assumed that whatever standard the Court adopted did not involve considering whether the defense had been overwhelmed at his trial by the weight of the untainted evidence.

Yet the Court also stated that the advantage of state harmless-error rules was that they avoid reversals for "errors or defects that have little, if any, likelihood of having changed the result of the trial," and that therefore "unimportant and insignificant" constitutional errors do not merit automatic reversal. Additionally, the Court characterized the facts of the *Chapman* case in the following manner:

> And though the case . . . presented a reasonably strong "circumstantial web of evidence" against the petitioners . . . . it was also a case in which, *absent the constitutionally forbidden comments, honest fair-minded jurors might very well have brought in not-guilty verdicts.* Under these circumstances, it is completely impossible for us to say that the State has demonstrated, beyond a reasonable doubt, that the prosecutor's comments and the trial judge's instruction did not contribute to petitioners' convictions. (emphasis added)

---

[17] 386 U.S. at 23.

[18] *Id.* at 23 n.8, citing Payne v. Arkansas, 356 U.S. 560 (1958) (coerced confessions); Gideon v. Wainwright, 372 U.S. 335 (1963) (right to counsel); Tumey v. Ohio, 273 U.S. 510 (1927) (impartial judge).

Naturally, in weighing the evidence against Chapman "absent the constitutionally forbidden comments," the Court was applying a standard overwhelming-evidence test. In finding that a reasonable jury might very well have acquitted on the basis of this evidence, the Court seems to have done what many later assumed it had forbidden. Thus, *Chapman* only established that some errors require automatic reversal and that the federal harmless-error test applied to the remainder requires reversal if the error is not shown harmless beyond a reasonable doubt. *Chapman* did not settle what the content of the federal test is to be.

II. HARMLESS ERRORS

Although *Chapman* does not compel rejection of the untainted-evidence test, and although the test is logically suited to protect the interests of the defendant, the fear has been expressed that there are other important interests it does not address. One of these interests is the need to deter misconduct by the prosecution. In the context of a criminal trial, however, the only way official misconduct can be encouraged is when the prosecutor is given incentives to seek future errors. An untainted-evidence test denies such incentives by reversing all errors which may have changed the result at trial. Of course, an appellate court may err in determining whether the verdict was altered or not. An unscrupulous prosecutor might take advantage of this possibility by introducing tainted evidence when he feels he already has a very strong case. But such a prosecutor would be gambling his strong case on the chance that an appellate court will err in his favor, and the gamble will profit him only if he has an unusual jury which might acquit despite the untainted evidence he has amassed. Since the appellate court will reverse if in doubt about the effect of the error, and since the chances of the jury's being affected are small, it is a bad gamble to take with a good case. Accordingly, the interest of deterring official misconduct is one the untainted-evidence rule addresses and protects.

A second interest the untainted-evidence test has been accused of slighting is the interest of preserving the repute in which constitutional rights are held, particularly among the judiciary. Scrupulous adherence to constitutional procedures as well as substantial fairness in applying them may foster a belief in the importance of these procedures and thereby affect the discretionary decisionmaking of actors in the drama of the criminal trial. Unfortunately, there is no way to be sure that by reversing more convictions than an untainted-evidence rule would require, appellate courts will truly encourage scrupulous attention to constitutional values on the part of the lower judiciary. While some segments of the judiciary may be influenced favorably, other segments may be offended by the seeming technicality of reversing an error which neither harmed the defendant nor encouraged official misconduct. Since there is no way of telling which effect is more likely, this second interest is unassessable, and provides no basis for framing a rule of harmless error more strict than the untainted-evidence rule.

These considerations suggest that for an error to have harmed any of the relevant and assessable interests at stake, it must have meant the difference between acquittal and conviction at trial. Thus they do not derogate but rather support an untainted-evidence rule. Obviously, the influence of an error on the jury cannot be determined with precision. However, in some cases the erroneously admitted evidence will have played a trivial role in the prosecutor's case. In other cases, the erroneously admitted evidence will be merely cumulative, establishing a fact attested by many other convincing pieces of evidence. Such errors are harmless and the convictions may be affirmed. Much of the time, however, the appellate court will be unable to state with confidence that an error had either trivial or cumulative effect. The usual presumption in favor of the defendant and the fact that it was the state which committed the error suggest that the court should reverse unless it can make such a judgment beyond a reasonable doubt.

The overwhelming-evidence test is one of two possible interpretations of *Chapman's* prescription that an error must "contribute to petitioner's conviction" to be reversible. Some have advocated the alternate interpretation: an error "contributed" to a conviction if it played any part in the jury's determination. In practice, however, such a standard would be tantamount to a rule of automatic reversal. Presumably evidence is admitted only if it is relevant to the defendant's guilt or innocence. Thus under the alternative standard there is no piece of evidence that one can state with confidence did not "contribute" to the conviction. Moreover, this test is not logically related to the protection of the defendant's legitimate interests, which are unaffected by errors which were extremely unlikely to have changed the result at trial.

One objection to the overwhelming-evidence test is that it allows the appellate court to usurp the function of the jury, to decide for itself if the defendant should be convicted on a given quantum of evidence. However, this argument misperceives the role the court is assuming. It is not deciding if the defendant should be convicted on the weight of the untainted evidence. It is not deciding whether a yet unsummoned jury would convict at retrial. The court is merely finding that the tainted evidence was highly unlikely to have been a determining factor in the decision of the actual jury which has already heard the case. Moreover, allowing the court to make such a finding is an inherent feature of any harmless-error rule which gauges harm done the defendant in the eyes of the jury. Such a rule necessarily allows judges to estimate the effect of certain evidence on the minds of the jurors.

The overwhelming-evidence test is not only logically compelling but seems to have been approved by the Supreme Court in *Harrington v. California*,[28] its most recent decision interpreting the *Chapman* rule. Glen Martin Harrington was denied his rights under the confrontation clause of the sixth amendment, as interpreted in *Bruton v. United States*,[29] when the inculpatory confessions of his codefendants were introduced into evidence against him. The California Court of Appeals affirmed the conviction, finding that "it is not reasonably probable that a result more favorable to defendant would have been reached had the [*Bruton*] rules been followed." The California Supreme Court declined review, but the United States Supreme Court granted certiorari "to consider whether the violation of *Bruton* on these special facts was harmless error under *Chapman*."

Mr. Justice Douglas, speaking for the majority, stressed that the Court was in no way departing from or diluting *Chapman*, but was rather reaffirming it. The Court then proceeded to uphold Harrington's conviction, finding that the illegally introduced evidence had been "cumulative," and that the state's case against Harrington had been "so overwhelming." Such language in the Court's three page opinion strongly suggests that *Chapman*, either by interpretation or by emendation, now embraces an overwhelming-evidence test for determining when an error is harmless.

III.   AUTOMATIC REVERSALS

The test proposed for determining when a constitutional error is harmless also helps to clarify the second issue raised by *Chapman*: when an error calls for automatic reversal. The overwhelming-evidence test asks whether the error at trial altered the verdict of the jury that heard the case. As noted earlier, this question can be answered when tainted evidence may be segregated and determined to be merely trivial or cumulative. The effect of some errors, however, cannot be so segregated since they affect the entire trial process, and in such cases no answer to the critical question can be given.

[28] 395 U.S. 250 (1969).
[29] 391 U.S. 123 (1968).

Such errors are those which bias the machinery for bringing evidence before the jury and into the record. A defect in this machinery necessarily raises doubts whether all relevant evidence is in the record and whether all evidence in the record is what it purports to be. For example, if the defendant was denied effective counsel or was incompetent to stand trial, there is no way of knowing what additional evidence could have been mustered to support his case or what successful attack could have been made on the evidence of the prosecution. If the prosecutor has manufactured or suppressed one piece of evidence, doubt arises whether other evidence has been unscrupulously handled. If a judge was biased against the defendant, it is uncertain how many of his discretionary decisions were infected with that bias. In all these cases there is no feasible way of segregating the tainted portion of the record and determining its effect on the jury beyond a reasonable doubt. Since there is no way of deciding that the error was harmless, the conviction must be reversed automatically.

There is another error for which the question posed by the overwhelming-evidence test cannot be answered. One cannot ask whether the jury that heard the case would have reached the same decision if there was an error in that jury's composition. The evidence tainted by such an error cannot be segregated; the error affects all the evidence at the trial. An appellate court could, of course, ask whether a properly constituted jury would have convicted on the evidence found in the record. Here, unlike the other cases mentioned, the record had not been affected by the error, but only by the manner in which the evidence was perceived. A court taking such an approach, however, would no longer be deciding if the error altered the verdict of the actual jury that heard the case. It would be evaluating the effect of the evidence as a whole on a hypothetical jury that was never assembled. Its decision would be precisely analogous to as the decision of a trial judge if he were allowed to direct a verdict of guilty at a criminal trial, and would be based on similar grounds. As noted earlier, such an inquiry would intrude into the province of the jury.

Accordingly, errors which concern the basic "trial machinery"—the mechanism for assembling evidence and the mechanism by which it is assessed—should call for automatic reversal. Automatic reversal is compelled by the question the overwhelming-evidence rule poses; by its very nature the rule can only assess the harmlessness of errors which bear on particular evidence.

One merit of this approach is that it provides a framework that would add logical coherence to decisions interpreting Supreme Court rulings. At the present time, if the Supreme Court has ruled that a certain error requires automatic reversal, the courts will reverse whenever that error occurs. But if an error occurs which is merely a corollary of that error, a harmless-error test has been almost invariably applied. In *Jackson v. Wainwright,* for example, a harmless-error rule was applied to a situation in which the district attorney knowingly concealed the testimony of an eyewitness to the crime, testimony which, if believed, would undoubtedly have resulted in the defendant's acquittal. The Fifth Circuit found the error not to be harmless "in the circumstances of the case." Presumably, the court did not automatically reverse because the situation did not fall into one of the neat "automatic reversal" pigeonholes previously recognized by the Supreme Court. If the district attorney had knowingly used perjured testimony, there would have been grounds for an automatic reversal. But suppression of exculpatory testimony was not enough. Such tenuous distinctions are recurring, and the "trial machinery" automatic reversal test would eliminate them.

In addition, the trial machinery formula would provide a logical basis for rationalizing most of the errors now recognized as requiring an automatic reversal. Automatic reversals would continue to be mandatory if the jury was not impartial,[39] if the jury was picked on a discriminatory basis,[40] or if the jury was selected from a community saturated with prejudicial pretrial publicity.[41] Similarly, automatic reversals for defects in the mechanism for bringing evidence before the jury would in the main conform to the existing law. New trials would continue to be automatically granted if the defendant were denied counsel at trial,[42] or at a critical stage of the criminal proceeding,[43] if the defendant were incompetent to stand trial,[44] or if the defendant were denied compulsory process for obtaining witnesses in his behalf.[45] The presence of a biased judge [46] or of a prosecutor who knowingly used perjured testimony [47] would also call for reversals without a showing of prejudice.

Finally, the test would be beneficial because it would significantly reduce the power of lower court judges to surrender to the pressure generated to save a conviction. In order for a judge to uphold a conviction in which an error allegedly occurred involving the "trial machinery," he would specifically have to find that no such error was

---

[39] *See* Parker v. Gladden, 385 U.S. 363 (1966).
[40] *See* Whitus v. Georgia, 385 U.S. 545 (1967)
[41] *See* Sheppard v. Maxwell, 384 U.S. 333 (1966).
[42] *See* Gideon v. Wainwright, 372 U.S. 335 (1963).
[43] *See* White v. Maryland, 373 U.S. 59 (1963).
[44] *See* Pate v. Robinson, 383 U.S. 375 (1966).
[45] *See* Washington v. Texas, 388 U.S. 14 (1967).
[46] *See* Tumey v. Ohio, 273 U.S. 510 (1927).
[47] *See* Miller v. Pate, 386 U.S. 1 (1967).

committed. Such a decision is far easier to review than one based on balancing amounts of prejudice. Moreover, in certain cases it will be virtually impossible for a finding of no error to be made in good faith.

* * * * *

PROCEDURES FOR APPLYING TO THE SUPREME COURT OF THE UNITED STATES FOR A WRIT OF CERTIORARI TO REVIEW AN ORDER OR JUDGMENT OF THE NEW YORK STATE COURTS *

1. Review of the decision of a state court affirming a judgment of conviction or affirming the denial of coram nobis relief may be sought by a Petition for a Writ of Certiorari. Such petition may be filed *only* after appellate review has been timely sought from the State Appellate courts.

2. If your case has been affirmed by the New York Court of Appeals, you may seek certiorari to review the judgment of that Court by filing your petition within 90 days from the date of the Court of Appeals decision.

3. If timely application for leave to appeal to the Court of Appeals was or is denied, you may petition for a writ of certiorari to review the Appellate Division judgment; however, the 90 day time limit for filing such a petition begins to run from the date of the denial of a timely application for leave to appeal to the Court of Appeals.

If you are unable to file your petition within 90 days from the decision of the New York Court of Appeals or the denial of leave to appeal, you may apply to Mr. Justice Harlan for an extension of time to file the Petition. The application for an extension of time *must* be received by the Clerk of the Supreme Court within 90 days from the date of the decision of the Court of Appeals or the denial of leave. Annexed is a copy of Mr. Justice Harlan's memorandum of September 28, 1961, which sets forth the procedure for making such application.

4. Generally the Petition should be divided into six sections:

    A. Opinion Below
    B. Jurisdiction
    C. Questions Presented
    D. Statement
    E. Reasons for Granting the Writ
    F. Conclusion

* New York Legal Aid Society. Form of Advice for Indigent Prisoners.

A. Opinion Below

This section should contain a statement as to whether any opinion was written by any Court in your case. The text of the opinions should appear as an appendix to the Petition, after the Conclusion.

B. Jurisdiction

This section should include a brief statement showing the date of the decision by the Court of Appeals or order denying leave to appeal and state whether any application has been made to extend the time for filing of the Petition for a writ of certiorari.

C. Questions Presented

This section shall include a concise statement of the issues you wish the Court to consider.

D. Statement

This section should contain a statement of the facts of your case as reflected by the Record. Particular attention and emphasis should be given to those facts which relate to the issues you wish the Supreme Court to consider. You should also state when and how the issues or questions you present were first raised. For example, if you claim that there was an illegal search and seizure in your case, you should state whether a motion to suppress evidence was made prior to trial; whether objection to the evidence was taken at trial; and whether the question was raised on appeal. If possible you should refer to the pages in the record which reflect these matters.

E. Reasons for Granting the Writ

This section should contain your arguments as to why you believe the decision in your case to be wrong and why you believe the Supreme Court should review your case.

F. Conclusion

This should merely be a brief statement to the effect that you request the Writ of Certiorari to be granted.

5. In the event any opinions were rendered by the State Courts in your case, copies of the opinion should be annexed to the Petition as an appendix. You should also annex to your Petition, as an appendix copies of the order denying leave to appeal and the Appellate Division order or a copy of the order [Remittitur] of the Court of Appeals if

the case was heard by that Court. Copies may be obtained by writing to the Court issuing the order.

6. If your appeal was heard upon the original record, you should state in your Petition that you are unable to obtain copies of the record because of your indigency.

7. Copies of *all* papers sent to the Supreme Court should be served upon the office of the State Attorney who opposed your appeal in the State Courts and with the papers you send to the Supreme Court you should include an affidavit showing when and upon which District Attorney you served (mailed) a copy of your papers.

8. If you are unable to pay the costs of printing or filing the Petition ($100) you must also send with your Petition an application for leave to proceed *in forma pauperis* which should include your affidavit setting forth your inability to pay the cost of printing and filing. A copy should be served upon the District Attorney.

9. You need only file with the Court one copy of your Petition for Certiorari and your application for leave to proceed *in forma pauparis* and you need serve only one copy of each upon the District Attorney. It is preferable that your papers be typed but if you are unable to have the papers typed they will be accepted *if legible.*

10. Any papers sent to the Supreme Court should be addressed:

Office of the Clerk
Supreme Court of the United States
Washington, D.C. 20543

After your case is given a calendar number by the Clerk, any correspondence concerning the case should refer to that number.

11. No formal action will be taken on the *forma pauperis* application until the Court acts upon the certiorari petition. There is often a period of several months between the filing and the Court's action.

MEMORANDUM
of
Mr. Justice Harlan
Associate Justice Supreme Court of the United States

APPLICATIONS BY INDIGENT LITIGANTS IN THE SECOND CIRCUIT FOR EXTENSIONS OF TIME WITHIN WHICH TO PETITION FOR CERTIORARI

Increasingly I find that applications for extensions of time within which to file petitions for certiorari, coming to me from unrepresented indigent litigants in the Second Circuit, are so un-illuminating as to make intelligent action thereon well nigh impossible.

I recognize that the same degree of compliance with the formalities of the Rules of this Court relating to extensions of time may not be expected from those not represented by counsel as from those who have counsel. However, it is not too much to insist that applications made by unrepresented litigants should contain at least the minimal facts necessary for a determination as to the timeliness of their applications, the probable jurisdiction of this Court over the matter sought to be reviewed, and the reasons justifying an extension of time. Extensions of time are not grantable as a matter of course.

Henceforth, I shall not ordinarily entertain any such applications in criminal or civil cases originating in the Second Circuit which fail to contain the following information:

1. A designation of the court whose judgment or order is sought to be reviewed; and the title of the case.

2. The date on which such judgment or order was made, or on which an application or rehearing with respect thereto was denied.

3. The nature of the matter adjudicated by such judgment or order, together with a copy of, or the citation to, any opinion of the court below, if readily available to the applicant.

4. A general statement of the grounds on which certiorari will be sought.

5. The reasons why the applicant was unable to file a petition for certiorari within the original time allowed by law, and the reasons for the additional time requested.

The Clerk of this Court is requested to arrange for appropriate publication of this memorandum within the Second Circuit, including its transmission to the Clerk of the Court of Appeals for the Second Circuit; to the Clerk of the Court of Appeals of the State of New York; to the Clerk of the Appellate Division of the Supreme Court of Errors of the State of Connecticut; to the Clerk of the Supreme Court of the State of Vermont; to the Director or Warden of the principal federal and state penal institutions situated in the Second Circuit, requesting such authorities to take suitable steps to bring this memorandum to the attention of inmates affected; and to the Editor of the New York Law Journal for publication therein.

Washington, D.C., September 28, 1961.

* * * * *

H. LEVY, HOW TO HANDLE AN APPEAL
1203–08, 1210–14 (P.L.I. 1968)*

12.2 Invoking Jurisdiction: Appeal vs. Certiorari

Though the Supreme Court may clearly have jurisdiction, it may choose not to exercise it. An appellate case in the Court is always a two-stage affair:

(1)   Review must first be sought, by either appeal or certiorari;

(2)   If review is granted (by noting probable jurisdiction of an appeal, or by granting certiorari), then there is full briefing and oral argument on the merits, except for the cases wherein the Court summarily affirms or reverses concurrent with the grant of review.[203]

12.21 Federal Cases

Direct appeals to the Supreme Court from United States district court decisions, and from three-judge federal court determinations, have already been discussed. In general, cases arising in the Court of Claims and the Court of Customs and Patent Appeals are reviewable by certiorari,[205] unless otherwise reviewable by appeal. Cases from a federal court of appeals are always reviewable by certiorari,[206] and by appeal only in rare cases.[207] Such appellate jurisdiction has been rarely invoked, especially in cases involving state statutes, since a federal statute provides that an appeal by a party relying on a state statute held unconstitutional by a federal court of appeals precludes review by certiorari and is limited to the federal questions presented.[208] However, the Supreme Court has ruled that a later amendment to another statute [209] requires such an appeal to be treated as a petition for certiorari.[210]

12.22 State Cases

The Supreme Court's jurisdiction over state cases may be summarized thus: If no question was raised below of the validity of a

---

* Some footnotes omitted.
[203] Still a comparatively rare phenomenon but apparently increasing.
[205] 28 U.S.C. §§ 1255(1), 1256.
[206] 28 U.S.C. § 1254(1).
[207] 28 U.S.C. §§ 1252, 1254(2).
[208] 28 U.S.C. § 1254(2).
[209] 28 U.S.C. § 2103, as amended Sept. 19, 1962.
[210] El Paso v. Simmons, 379 U.S. 497, 502–03 (1965).

statute or treaty, but your client merely claimed that he had been denied a federal constitutional right, you can go up only on certiorari. If the question was raised below of the constitutionality of a federal or state statute, you can go up on certiorari, with the option of going up on appeal if the state statute was held constitutional or the federal statute held unconstitutional.[211]

12.221 State Case Decided on State Grounds

The Supreme Court will not review a state court decision, even if it otherwise satisfies jurisdictional requirements, if the state court decision rests on an adequate and independent state ground, though it will not be bound by the state court's view of this question. Thus, the Court recently granted review[212] of a California Supreme Court decision holding a state statute unconstitutional but dismissed[213] after it became apparent that the California court had held the statute to be violative of the state constitution. Obviously the Supreme Court's decision on the validity of the state statute as against the federal constitution would have been a futile gesture.

12.222 State Court Certificates

If the highest state court has expressly passed upon a federal question, there can be no question as to whether it was properly raised.[214]

---

[211] 28 U.S.C. § 1257, which reads as follows:

"1257. State courts; appeal; certiorari.

"Final judgments or decrees rendered by the highest court of a State in which a decision could be had, may be reviewed by the Supreme Court as follows:

"(1) By appeal, where is drawn in question the validity of a treaty or statute of the United States and the decision is against its validity.

"(2) By appeal, where is drawn in question the validity of a statute of any State on the ground of its being repugnant to the Constitution, treaties or laws of the United States, and the decision is in favor of its validity.

"(3) By writ of certiorari, where the validity of a treaty or statute of the United States is drawn in question or where the validity of a State statute is drawn in question on the ground of its being repugnant to the Constitution, treaties or laws of the United States, or where any title, right, privilege or immunity is specially set up or claimed under the Constitution, treaties or statutes of, or commission held or authority exercised under, the United States. June 25, 1948, c. 646, 62 Stat. 929."

For a fuller discussion, see Stern & Gressman, *op. cit. supra* note 196, at 62–104.

[212] Department of Mental Hygiene v. Kirchner, 379 U.S. 811 (1964).

[213] Department of Mental Hygiene v. Kirchner, 380 U.S. 194 (1965). For a fuller discussion of this problem, see Stern & Gressman, *op. cit. supra* note 196, at 105–116.

[214] Raley v. Ohio, 360 U.S. 423 (1959).

Where there is no such express passing, the attorney's substitute is to secure a certificate from the highest state court—not from a judge thereof—showing clearly which federal questions were considered and necessarily decided in the judgment to be reviewed.[215] In New York, and perhaps in other states, this is done in the form of an amendment to the remittitur. This device, however, may be losing its effectiveness, especially in the cases where the state appellate court record does not bear out the contention. If the record before the Supreme Court does not show the raising of the federal issues, it may be helpful to file with the Supreme Court Clerk such other materials as do, *e.g.*, state court briefs.

12.3 Advantages of Appeal Over Certiorari

Should you go up on appeal in preference to certiorari when you have an option? Appeals historically lie as of right, while the granting of certiorari is discretionary.[216] However, the distinction now is somewhat academic, at least when seeking review of state court cases. For certiorari will be granted "only where there are special and important reasons therefor" (Rule 19),[217] while appeal papers must include "a presentation of the grounds upon which it is contended that the federal questions are substantial[218] which . . . shall include the reasons why the questions presented are so substantial as to require plenary consideration, with briefs on the merits and oral argument, for their resolution" (Rule 15(1)(e)). Since one reason for granting certiorari in a state case is that the state court has decided "a federal question of *substance* not theretofore determined by this court, or has decided it in a way probably not in accord with applicable decisions of this court," (Rule 19(1)(a)),[219] the requirement of substantiality of the federal question would seem to be about the same whether one proceeds by appeal or certiorari.

---

[215] Herb v. Pitcairn, 324 U.S. 117 (1945).

[216] Many years ago, the Supreme Court actually issued a writ of certiorari, *i.e.,* a writ ordering the lower court to certify the record to the Supreme Court. As the Rules now require the certification of the record before the Court will grant certiorari (Rules 21(1), 22(1)), the Court does not actually issue a writ when it grants certiorari.

[217] This and following Rules, appearing in parentheses, are Rules of the U.S. Supreme Court. Printed copies of the Supreme Court Rules are available free on request from the Office of the Clerk of the Supreme Court, Washington, D.C. 20543. They are reprinted in the "Rules" volume of 28 U.S.C.A., but the pamphlet edition is so much easier to work with that it should be part of any appellate lawyer's library.

[218] Zucht v. King, 260 U.S. 174, 176–177 (1922).

[219] Emphasis added.

There is one situation, however, in which an appeal may present advantages over the certiorari method. If a stay of execution is needed, it may be more easily obtained if you proceed by appeal—a survival of the theory that an appeal is a matter of right. Thus, in *Williams v. New York*,[220] a stay had been denied pending the filing of a petition of certiorari, but a stay was granted when the defense attorneys announced that they had decided to take the appeals route to the high Court.

Nearly half of the appeals are heard orally, while certiorari is granted in less than fifteen per cent of the cases in which it is sought.[221] However, one cannot assume that review would be therefore more easily available if the certiorari filer had proceeded by the appellate method. For appeals that are heard usually involve questions of constitutionality of statutes, necessarily of wider scope and applicability than the certiorari case involving only a claimed violation of an individual's rights.

12.31 Appeal in Doubtful Cases

If you clearly have no right to appeal but only to petition for certiorari, do not under any circumstances proceed by appeal. This would be an abuse of Court process. But if you are unsure which method of review to take, you are generally better off proceeding with an appeal.[222] Going up on appeal when you should have petitioned for certiorari is not by itself ground for dismissal; the papers are treated as a petition for certiorari.

If you are taking an appeal in a borderline case, include in your jurisdictional statement all material and type of argument which you would present in a certiorari petition. In general, the jurisdictional statement contains all data necessary to a certiorari petition. The only material differences are that the petition must contain record citations showing that the federal question was timely and properly raised (Rule 23(1)(f)), whereas the jurisdictional statement must similarly

---

[220] 337 U.S. 241 (1949).

[221] Stern & Gressman, *op. cit. supra* note 196, at 279.

[222] That reasonable men may differ in judgment as to whether to seek appeal or certiorari is shown by People v. Fried, 378 U.S. 578 (1964). A jurisdictional statement (taking the appellate route in a case where such judgment was difficult), was filed because it was thought the taking of an appeal would ease the securing of a stay. The stay of execution was granted, but the appeal was dismissed. Three Justices dissented, one of them ruling that probable jurisdiction should have been noted (*i.e.*, that the Court should have accepted the appeal for review), the two others ruling that the appeal should have been treated as an application for certiorari and certiorari granted.

show that the rulings of the court below brought the case within the Court's jurisdiction (Rule 15(1)(d)), and the statement of the case in a certiorari petition must show, if review of a federal court judgment is sought, the basis for federal jurisdiction in the court of first instance (Rule 23(1)(g)). The criteria for granting an appeal are somewhat different than for granting certiorari. Nonetheless, set forth the ways in which you can meet the certiorari criteria. They may be helpful even in a case where only an appeal lies, for meeting certiorari criteria will help to demonstrate the substantiality of the federal question.[223]

12.51 Procedure on Certiorari on Behalf of Petitioner

No notice of appeal is filed, nor need you give any notice in advance of your intention to petition for certiorari. Instead, you file a petition for certiorari when you docket your case. Rule 23 of the

---

[223] The criteria *re* appeals are found in Rule 15(1)(e),(f), reading as follows:

"(e) If the appeal is from a state court, there shall be included a presentation of the grounds upon which it is contended that the federal questions are substantial [Zucht v. King, 260 U.S. 174, 176–177], which shall show that the nature of the case and of the rulings of the court was such as to bring the case within the jurisdictional provisions relied on and the cases cited to sustain the jurisdiction (subparagraph (b) (iv) hereof), and shall include the reasons why the questions presented are so substantial as to require plenary consideration, with briefs on the merits and oral argument, for their resolution.

"(f) If the appeal is from a federal court, there shall similarly be included a statement of the reasons why the questions presented are so substantial as to require plenary consideration, with briefs on the merits and oral argument, for their resolution."

The criteria *re* certiorari are found in Rule 19, reading as follows:

"19. Considerations governing review on certiorari.

"1. A review on writ of certiorari is not a matter of right, but of sound judicial discretion, and will be granted only where there are special and important reasons therefor. The following, while neither controlling nor fully measuring the court's discretion, indicate the character of reasons which will be considered:

"(a) Where a state court has decided a federal question of substance not theretofore determined by this court, or has decided it in a way probably not in accord with applicable decisions of this court.

"(b) Where a court of appeals has rendered a decision in conflict with the decision of another court of appeals on the same matter; or has decided an important state or territorial question in a way in conflict with applicable state or territorial law; or has decided an important question of federal law which has not been, but should be, settled by this court; or has decided a federal question in a way in conflict with applicable decisions of this court; or has so far departed from the accepted and usual course of judicial proceedings, or so far sanctioned such a departure by a lower court, as to call for an exercise of this court's power of supervision.

"2. The same general considerations outlined above will control in respect of petitions for writs of certiorari to review judgments of the Court of Claims, of the Court of Customs and Patent Appeals, or of any other court whose determinations are by law reviewable on writ of certiorari."

Supreme Court Rules sets out in detail the formal contents of the petition and the order in which they must appear. The petition . . . . shows the formal contents required. Your printer will know the technical requirements of the printing.

The petition is not in the same style as a brief. It is not to show the Court why the decision below is in error. You are to show the Court why it should review the case. Thus, argument as to mere error is superfluous.

As the Court's Rule 19 puts it, certiorari "will be granted only where there are special and important reasons therefor." The Rule goes on to list examples of reasons which will be "considered," implying that these are not per se determinative. In general, these reasons are novel federal questions, conflicts in the federal courts of appeals, decisions in conflict with applicable decisions of the Supreme Court, etc.

But whatever you can develop, the stress is always to show why the Court should review the case. The granting of review is in its discretion. The Court generally will not review a case unless it seems sufficiently important, however much injustice may have been done below. Therefore, simply to claim that an injustice has been done will do your client little good. You have to demonstrate to the Court why review should be granted in terms of public importance.

Think up as many arguments as you can to show why the questions presented will fit within the categories of Rule 19. The most persuasive points are conflicts between federal circuits or state courts on issues of general public importance. However, do not cite cases for propositions they do not represent, for the original writ of certiorari may be dismissed, after the expense and trouble of briefing the case on the merits, because review had been improvidently granted.

If your case does not fit within the usual guidelines for granting of review, think of whatever reasons you possibly can as to why review should be granted, quite apart from the normal considerations. In essence, the question to ask yourself is: why should the highest court of the land bother with my case? And it is the answer to this question which you should develop in your petition.

If you rely upon past conflicting Supreme Court decisions, do not quote long passages from very recent opinions. The Justices know the contents of their recent opinions, and lengthy quotes from such cases will try their patience. Recent relevant cases may be, and should be, cited; but lengthy analysis, other than to compare them with the case at bar, is out of order.

Where appropriate, a Brandeis-type petition can be most effective. The Court will be impatient with trivial cases, however unjust the result may seem to be. But by demonstrating important social, economic or political consequences of the decision below, and thus the necessity of having the rule of law settled by the Court, you can best persuade it to exercise its historic function to act as the ultimate arbitor of fundamental questions.

Your application for review should be as brief as possible, for the Court is quite competent to decide which cases it wishes to hear, with minimal assistance of counsel.[229] This attitude was stated by the late Mr. Justice Frankfurter:

> It does not require heavy research to charge the understanding of this Court adequately on the gravity of the issue on which review is sought and to prove to this Court the appropriateness of granting a petition for a writ of certiorari.[230]

In another case, where there had been full judicial exploration of the issues, he indicated that counsel should not take more than a day or two to prepare the petition, particularly if he had handled the case below.[231]

Although his attitude may not be shared wholeheartedly by the present members of the Court, it is symptomatic. Occasionally, a petition may be composed in a couple of days by one thoroughly familiar with the case, but a short petition often requires more time than a long one. But bear in mind Mr. Justice Frankfurter's words, and keep your petition brief. Indeed, says the Court, "The failure of a petitioner to present with accuracy, brevity, and clearness whatever is essential to a ready and adequate understanding of the points requiring consideration will be a sufficient reason for denying his petition" (Rule 23 [4]).

There may be a conflict between brevity, your desire to develop the importance of the issues and the need to show that those issues are present. Nevertheless, use minimal facts, only those which clearly demonstrate the presence of the issues in the case.

12.511 The Questions Presented for Review

If review is granted, you will be limited to questions raised in the petition. So, both in selecting and in wording your questions, be sure to raise all the issues you want and only those issues, and to state them adequately. Here, too, brevity is in order. But even more important is accuracy. For example, if you claim a violation of constitutional right, be specific. Are you attacking the constitutionality of a statute on its face, as applied, or in its operation and effect? Or are you claiming

---

[229] For example, amicus curiae briefs on application for review are discouraged by the Court. Rule 42(1).

[230] Brody v. United States, 77 Sup. Ct. 910 (1957).

[231] Carter v. United States, 75 Sup. Ct. 911 (1955).

that your client was deprived of a constitutional right? If so, which right, and under which provision of the Constitution? And remember that the questions must be "expressed in the terms and circumstances of the case but without unnecessary detail" (Rule 23 [1] [c]).

The scope of the question may be particularly important. For example, in an obscenity case, if all you raise is the constitutionality of the particular statute on its face, you may lose though a new construction of the statute might result in a ruling that the materials involved were not obscene. To get the benefit of such a new ruling you must contend that the statute as construed and applied below is unconstitutional.

The correct formulation of your "Questions Presented" is particularly important. If review is granted, though you may rephrase your questions, you may not raise additional questions or change the substance of the questions presented from that in the certiorari petition. (The Court itself may still notice a plain error. Rule 40 [2].) There is some elasticity in the Court's rule that "the statement of a question presented will be deemed to include every subsidiary question fairly comprised therein" (Rule 23 [1] [c]). But be sure—subject to considerations as to choosing which questions to present—to be careful and thorough in your formulation of the questions.

Nowhere is it more important than in the Supreme Court to write so as to appeal to the individual philosophies of the members of the appellate bench, though this is more important in the brief on the merits and in oral argument than in a certiorari petition.

* * * * *

C. Constitutional Dimensions of the Appellate Process: Right of an Indigent to Appeal

In Re Gault, 387 U.S. 1, 58 (1967)

This Court has not held that a State is required by the Federal Constitution "to provide appellate courts or a right to appellate review at all." In view of the fact that we must reverse the Supreme Court of Arizona's affirmance of the dismissal of the writ of habeas corpus for other reasons, we need not rule on this question in the present case or upon the failure to provide a transcript or recording of the hearings—or, indeed, the failure of the Juvenile Judge to state the grounds for his conclusion. . . .

* * * * *

ANDERS v. CALIFORNIA, 386 U.S. 738 (1967)*

MR. JUSTICE CLARK delivered the opinion of the Court.

We are here concerned with the extent of the duty of a court-appointed appellate counsel to prosecute a first appeal from a criminal conviction, after that attorney has conscientiously determined that there is no merit to the indigent's appeal.

After he was convicted of the felony of possession of marijuana, petitioner sought to appeal and moved that the California District Court of Appeal appoint counsel for him. Such motion was granted; however, after a study of the record and consultation with petitioner, the appointed counsel concluded that there was no merit to the appeal. He so advised the court by letter and, at the same time, informed the court that petitioner wished to file a brief in his own behalf. At this juncture, petitioner requested the appointment of another attorney. This request was denied and petitioner proceeded to file his own brief *pro se*. The State responded and petitioner filed a reply brief. On January 9, 1959, the District Court of Appeal unanimously affirmed the conviction, *People* v. *Anders*, 167 Cal. App. 2d 65, 333 P.2d 854.

On January 21, 1965, petitioner filed an application for a writ of habeas corpus in the District Court of Appeal in which he sought to have his case reopened. In that application he raised the issue of deprivation of the right of counsel in his original appeal because of the court's refusal to appoint counsel at the appellate stage of the proceedings.[1] The court denied the application on the same day, in a brief unreported memorandum opinion. The court stated that it "ha[d] again reviewed the record and [had] determined the appeal [to be] without merit." The court also stated that "the procedure prescribed by In re Nash, 61 A. C. 538, was followed in this case . . . ."[2] On June 25, 1965, petitioner submitted a petition for a writ of habeas

---

* Dissenting opinion omitted.

[1] Previously, on January 24, 1964, petitioner, while on parole, had been arrested and convicted of the felony of burglary which was affirmed on appeal. We granted certiorari, *ante*, p. 264, vacated the judgment below and remanded for further consideration in light of Chapman v. California, *ante*, p. 18.

[2] *In re Nash*, 61 Cal. 2d 491, 393 P. 2d 405 (1964), held that the requirements of *Douglas* v. *California*, 372 U.S. 353 (1963), are met in the event appointed counsel thoroughly studies the record, consults with the defendant and trial counsel and conscientiously concludes, and so advises the appellate court, that there are no meritorious grounds of appeal; and provided that the appellate court is satisfied from its own review of the record, in light of any points personally raised by the defendant, that appointed counsel's conclusion is correct. The appeal then proceeds without the appointment of other counsel and decision is reached without argument.

corpus to the Supreme Court of California, and the petition was denied without opinion by that court on July 14, 1965. Among other trial errors, petitioner claimed that both the judge and the prosecutor had commented on his failure to testify contrary to the holding of this Court in *Griffin* v. *California,* 380 U.S. 609 (1965). We have concluded that California's action does not comport with fair procedure and lacks that equality that is required by the Fourteenth Amendment.

I.

For a decade or more, a continuing line of cases has reached this Court concerning discrimination against the indigent defendant on his first appeal. Beginning with *Griffin* v. *Illinois,* 351 U.S. 12 (1956) where it was held that equal justice was not afforded an indigent appellant where the nature of the review "depends on the amount of money he has," at 19, and continuing through *Douglas* v. *California,* 372 U.S. 353 (1963), this Court has consistently held invalid those procedures "where the rich man, who appeals as of right, enjoys the benefit of counsel's examination into the record, research of the law, and marshalling of arguments on his behalf, while the indigent, already burdened by a preliminary determination that his case is without merit, is forced to shift for himself." At 358. Indeed, in the federal courts, the advice of counsel has long been required whenever a defendant challenges a certification that an appeal is not taken in good faith, *Johnson* v. *United States,* 352 U.S. 565 (1957), and such representation must be in the role of an advocate, *Ellis* v. *United States,* 356 U.S. 674, 675 (1958), rather than as *amicus curiae.* In *Ellis, supra,* we concluded:

> "If counsel is convinced, after conscientious investigation, that the appeal is frivolous, of course, he may ask to withdraw on that account. If the court is satisfied that counsel has diligently investigated the possible grounds of appeal, and agrees with counsel's evaluation of the case, then leave to withdraw may be allowed and leave to appeal may be denied." At 675.

In *Gideon* v. *Wainwright,* 372 U.S. 335 (1963), the Sixth Amendment's requirement that "the accused shall enjoy the right . . . to have the Assistance of Counsel for his defence" was made obligatory on the States by the Fourteenth Amendment, the Court holding that "in our adversary system of criminal justice, any person haled into court, who is too poor to hire a lawyer, cannot be assured a fair trial unless counsel is provided for him." At 344. We continue to adhere to these principles.

II.

In petitioner's case, his appointed counsel wrote the District Court of Appeal, stating:

"I will not file a brief on appeal as I am of the opinion that there is no merit to the appeal. I have visited and communicated with Mr. Anders and have explained my views and opinions to him . . . . [H]e wishes to file a brief in this matter on his own behalf."

The District Court of Appeal, after having examined the record, affirmed the conviction. We believe that counsel's bare conclusion, as evidenced by his letter, was not enough. It smacks of the treatment that Eskridge received, which this Court condemned, that permitted a trial judge to withhold a transcript if he found that a defendant "has been accorded a fair and impartial trial, and in the Court's opinion no grave or prejudicial errors occurred therein." *Eskridge* v. *Washington State Board*, 357 U.S. 214, 215 (1958). Such a procedure, this Court said, "cannot be an adequate substitute for the right to full appellate review available to all defendants" who may not be able to afford such an expense. At 216. And in still another case in which "a state officer outside the judicial system" was given the power to deprive an indigent of his appeal by refusing to order a transcript merely because he thought the "appeal would be unsuccessful," we reversed, finding that such a procedure did not meet constitutional standards. *Lane* v. *Brown*, 372 U.S. 477 (1963). Here the court-appointed counsel had the transcript but refused to proceed with the appeal because he found no merit in it. He filed a no-merit letter with the District Court of Appeal whereupon the court examined the record itself and affirmed the judgment. On a petition for a writ of habeas corpus some six years later it found the appeal had no merit. It failed, however, to say whether it was frivolous or not, but, after consideration, simply found the petition to be "without merit." The Supreme Court, in dismissing this habeas corpus application, gave no reason at all for its decision and so we do not know the basis for its action. We cannot say that there was a finding of frivolity by either of the California courts or that counsel acted in any greater capacity than merely as *amicus curiae* which was condemned in *Ellis, supra*. Hence California's procedure did not furnish petitioner with counsel acting in the role of an advocate nor did it provide that full consideration and resolution of the matter as is obtained when counsel is acting in that capacity. The necessity for counsel so acting is highlighted by the possible disadvantage the petitioner suffered here. In his *pro se* brief, which was filed in 1959, he urged several trial errors but failed to raise the point that both the judge and prosecutor had commented to the jury regarding petitioner's failure to testify. In 1965, this Court in *Griffin* v. *California, supra,* outlawed California's comment rule, as embodied in Art. I, § 13, of the California Constitution.

III.

The constitutional requirement of substantial equality and fair process can only be attained where counsel acts in the role of an active advocate in behalf of his client, as opposed to that of *amicus curiae.* The no-merit letter and the procedure it triggers do not reach that dignity. Counsel should and can with honor and without conflict, be of more assistance to his client and to the court.[3] His role as advocate requires that he support his client's appeal to the best of his ability. Of course, if counsel finds his case to be wholly frivolous, after a conscientious examination of it, he should so advise the court and request permission to withdraw. That request must, however, be accompanied by a brief referring to anything in the record that might arguably support the appeal. A copy of counsel's brief should be furnished the indigent and time allowed him to raise any points that he chooses; the court—not counsel—then proceeds, after a full examination of all the proceedings, to decide whether the case is wholly frivolous. If it so finds it may grant counsel's request to withdraw and dismiss the appeal insofar as federal requirements are concerned, or proceed to a decision on the merits, if state law so requires. On the other hand, if it finds any of the legal points arguable on their merits (and therefore not frivolous) it must, prior to decision, afford the indigent the assistance of counsel to argue the appeal.

This requirement would not force appointed counsel to brief his case against his client but would merely afford the latter that advocacy which a nonindigent defendant is able to obtain. It would also induce the court to pursue all the more vigorously its own review because of the ready references not only to the record, but also to the legal authorities as furnished it by counsel. The no-merit letter, on the other hand, affords neither the client nor the court any aid. The former must shift entirely for himself while the court has only the cold record

---

[3] For comparative purposes see *Tate* v. *United States,* 123 U.S. App. D. C. 261, 359 F. 2d 245, and *Johnson* v. *United States,* 124 U.S. App. D. C. 29, 360 F. 2d 844, which outline the practice followed in the District of Columbia. These guidelines are elaborated in more detail in a "Statement to be Handed by the Clerk to Appointed Counsel" which has been prepared by the Court of Appeals for the District of Columbia Circuit. We indicate no approval of the requirements set out in the statement or in the cases.

which it must review without the help of an advocate. Moreover, such handling would tend to protect counsel from the constantly increasing charge that he was ineffective and had not handled the case with that diligence to which an indigent defendant is entitled. This procedure will assure penniless defendants the same rights and opportunities on appeal—as nearly as is practicable—as are enjoyed by those persons who are in a similar situation but who are able to afford the retention of private counsel.

The judgment is reversed and the case is remanded for further proceedings not inconsistent with this opinion.

It is so ordered.

✿   ✿   ✿   ✿   ✿

CHAPTER 14

Extraordinary Review

A. Habeas Corpus

1. In State Practice

H. WACHTELL, NEW YORK PRACTICE UNDER THE CPLR 356–60
(PLI, 3d ed. 1970)

HABEAS CORPUS

The writ of habeas corpus is a traditional means of inquiring into the legality of a person's detention.[34] If a person is unlawfully imprisoned, it is obvious that the ordinary civil action for false imprisonment will not aid him in obtaining immediate release. Habeas corpus may be used to challenge the detention of persons in official or private custody.

Habeas corpus is a special proceeding.[35] However, due to historical development and constitutional requirement, its procedure varies somewhat from that of the normal special proceeding.[36]

Grounds

The writ of habeas corpus is used where a person is actually imprisoned or otherwise restrained in his liberty at the time the writ is issued.[37] It tests the jurisdiction of the person or authority which presumes to restrain him.[38] Thus, a prisoner detained after the expiration of his sentence is entitled to the writ,[39] as is a person improperly com-

[34] See Third Report 49.
[35] CPLR § 7001.
[36] See Port of New York Authority v. 62 Cortlandt St. Realty Co., 18 N.Y.S.2d 250 (1966), cert. denied sub nom. McInnes v. New York Port Authority, 385 U.S. 1006 (1967); see also Third Report 51, 53.
[37] CPLR § 7002(a); see also N.Y. CONST. art. I, § 4.
[38] See Morhous v. Supreme Court, 293 N.Y. 131 (1944).
[39] People ex rel. Tweed v. Liscomb, 60 N.Y. 559 (1875).

mitted to an insane asylum.[40] Although habeas corpus is not a substitute for appeal in criminal cases, it may nonetheless in certain circumstances be used to challenge a criminal conviction.[41] Habeas corpus may also be, and frequently is, used to test rights to the custody of a child, on the theory that the person in control of the child is detaining him unlawfully.[42]

Procedure

The application for a writ of habeas corpus is made by a written petition verified by the person illegally imprisoned or otherwise restrained in his liberty, or any other person acting on his behalf.[43] The petition is submitted *ex parte*[44] and may be accompanied by affidavits.[45]

The petition is made to: (a) a special term of the Supreme Court held in the judicial district in which the person is detained; (b) the Appellate Division in the department in which he is detained; (c) any justice of the Supreme Court; or (d) a county judge being or residing within the county in which the person is detained, or, if there is no judge within the county capable of issuing the writ or all capable of doing so have refused, to a county judge being or residing within an adjoining county.[46] Where a petition is properly submitted, the court or judge must issue the writ without delay under penalty of a forfeiture of $1,000 to the prisoner.[47] Nonetheless, the writ will not issue if it appears from the petition or accompanying documents that

[40] People *ex rel.* Woodbury v. Hendrick, 215 N.Y. 339 (1915).

[41] See, *e.g.*, People v. Schildhaus, 8 N.Y.2d 33 (1960); *cf.* Morhous v. Supreme Court, 293 N.Y. 131 (1944). See also People *ex rel.* Keitt v. McMann, 18 N.Y.2d 257 (1966); People v. Huntley, 15 N.Y.2d 72, 76 (1965).

[42] Marx v. Holloran, 236 App. Div. 680, 257 N.Y.Supp. 879 (2d Dep't 1932); People *ex rel.* Sisson v. Sisson, 153 Misc. 434, 275 N.Y. Supp. 299 (Sup. Ct. Chenango Co. 1934), *modified*, 246 App. Div. 151, 285 N.Y. Supp. 41, 45 (3d Dep't 1936). See Application of Hebo, 95 N.Y.S.2d 545 (Sup. Ct. N.Y. Co. 1950).

[43] CPLR §§ 7002(a), (c). See also Third Report 57. The petition may also be made by a party in a child abuse proceeding subsequent to an order of the family court.

[44] CPLR § 7002(a).

[45] CPLR § 7002(c). The petitioner must set forth whether any prior application for habeas corpus has been made. See People *ex rel.* Dunn v. McMann, 23 App. Div. 2d 510, 255 N.Y.S.2d 189 (3d Dep't 1965).

[46] CPLR § 7002(b). Note, however, that in a dispute between husband and wife regarding custody of a child, a writ of habeas corpus apparently may only be issued by the Supreme Court, DOM. REL. LAW § 70; People *ex rel.* Burke v. Burke, 47 Misc. 2d 276, 262 N.Y.S.2d 613 (Co. Ct. Allegany Co. 1965); Raffone v. Raffone, 20 Misc. 2d 733, 193 N.Y.S.2d 206 (Dom. Rel. Ct. N.Y. Co. 1959). See also Marx v. Holloran, 236 App. Div. 680, 257 N.Y. Supp. 879 (2d Dep't 1932); People *ex rel.* Sisson v. Sisson, 153 Misc. 434, 275 N.Y. Supp. 299 (Sup. Ct. Chenango Co. 1934).

[47] CPLR §§ 7003(a), (c).

there is no illegal detention or that exclusive jurisdiction with respect to release is vested in the federal judiciary.[48] Furthermore, the petition may be denied where the legality of the detention has been determined by a court of the state in a prior habeas corpus proceeding, the new petition presents no new grounds, and the court is satisfied that the ends of justice will not be served by granting of the new petition.[49]

The writ is issued in the name of the state and, if issued on the application of a private person, must show that it was issued upon his relation.[50] It is directed to the respondent, the person having custody of the person detained.[51] The writ commands the respondent to produce the prisoner before a designated judge "forthwith" or at a specified time and place.[52] However, if the petition does not demand the production of the person detained or if it is clear that there is no factual dispute as to the basis for detention, the court instead of issuing the writ may issue an order requiring the respondent to show cause why the person detained should not be released. The issue of the legality of detention would then be determined without requiring the personal presence of the person detained.[53]

The writ of habeas corpus may be served on any day, including Sunday.[54] Service is made by delivering the writ and a copy of the petition to the respondent. If he cannot with due diligence be found, the writ may be served upon any person having custody of the person detained at the time. If the person detained is in the custody of some person other than the person to whom the writ was directed, it may nonetheless be served on the person having such custody with the same effect as if he had been named as the respondent.[55]

Proceedings on Return

At the time and place specified in the writ (or where the writ commands production of the person detained "forthwith," within twenty-four hours after its service), the person upon whom the writ was served must submit a "return," which is an affidavit fully and explicitly stating the authority and cause of the detention.[56] The respondent must also produce the person detained unless it is proved to the satisfaction of the court that such person is too sick or infirm to be brought

---

[48] CPLR § 7003(a).
[49] CPLR § 7003(b).
[50] CPLR §§ 7004(a), 1301.
[51] CPLR § 7004(b).
[52] CPLR § 7004(d). For restrictions as to place of return, see CPLR § 7004(c); Hogan v. Culkin, 18 N.Y.2d 330 (1966).
[53] CPLR § 7003(a).
[54] CPLR §7005. See Third Report 69.
[55] CPLR § 7005.
[56] CPLR §§ 7008(a), (b).

to the appointed place.[57] If the writ is not complied with, the court before which the writ is returnable, upon proof of its service, must forthwith issue a "warrant of attachment" directing that the respondent be arrested and brought before the court. The respondent may be imprisoned until he complies with the writ.[58] The court may also issue a "precept" directing the person executing the warrant immediately to bring the person detained before the court.[59]

A reply to the return may be made under oath by the petitioner or the person detained stating any facts showing that the person detained is entitled to be discharged.[60] The court must then proceed in a summary manner to hear the evidence and to dispose of the proceeding as justice requires.[61] If, at the hearing, it is determined that the person is illegally detained, a final judgment must be made directing his discharge forthwith.[62] However, where the detention is by virtue of a mandate, the court may not adjudicate the issues in the proceeding until written notice of the time and place of the hearing has been given to certain designated persons specified by statute,[63] e.g., where the mandate was issued in a civil cause, to the person interested in continuing the restraint or his attorney.[64]

✿　✿　✿　✿　✿

2. In Federal Practice

a. Grounds

UNITED STATES CODE, Title 28

§ 2241 Power to grant writ

(a) Writs of habeas corpus may be granted by the Supreme Court, any justice thereof, the district courts and any circuit judge within their respective jurisdictions. The order of a circuit judge shall be entered in the records of the district court of the district wherein the restraint complained of is had.

---

[57] CPLR § 7006(a).
[58] CPLR § 7006(b).
[59] CPLR § 7006(c). Note that where satisfactory proof is presented that a person is wrongfully detained and that he either will be removed from the state or that he will suffer irreparable injury before he can be relieved by habeas corpus, the court will in the first instance, at the time of issuing the writ of habeas corpus, also issue a warrant to an appropriate officer requiring such officer immediately to bring the detained person before the court. CPLR § 7007.
[60] CPLR § 7009(b).
[61] CPLR § 7009(c).
[62] CPLR § 7010(a).
[63] CPLR § 7009(a).
[64] CPLR § 7009(a)(1).

(b) The Supreme Court, any justice thereof, and any circuit judge may decline to entertain an application for a writ of habeas corpus and may transfer the application for hearing and determination to the district court having jurisdiction to entertain it.

(c) The writ of habeas corpus shall not extend to a prisoner unless—

(1) He is in custody under or by color of the authority of the United States or is committed for trial before some court thereof; or

(2) He is in custody for an act done or omitted in pursuance of an Act of Congress, or an order, process, judgment or decree of a court or judge of the United States; or

(3) He is in custody in violation of the Constitution or laws or treaties of the United States; or

(4) He, being a citizen of a foreign state and domiciled therein is in custody for an act done or omitted under any alleged right, title, authority, privilege, protection, or exemption claimed under the commission, order or sanction of any foreign state, or under color thereof, the validity and effect of which depend upon the law of nations; or

(5) It is necessary to bring him into court to testify or for trial.

(d) Where an application for a writ of habeas corpus is made by a person in custody under the judgment and sentence of a State court of a State which contains two or more Federal judicial districts, the application may be filed in the district court for the district wherein such person is in custody or in the district court for the district within which the State court was held which convicted and sentenced him and each of such district courts shall have concurrent jurisdiction to entertain the application. The district court for the district wherein such an application is filed in the exercise of its discretion and in furtherance of justice may transfer the application to the other district court for hearing and determination.

[For a complete analysis of habeas corpus law, see *Developments in the Law: Habeas Corpus*, 83 HARV. L. REV. 1038 (1970). —Eds.]

* * * * *

EDITORS' NOTE

SCOPE OF FEDERAL HABEAS REMEDY

Traditionally, the writ of habeas corpus has been simply a means of obtaining release from custody. Therefore, if the applicant were not in actual custody, or if there were some other alternate lawful basis for retaining him in custody, the writ would not be viewed as available. This was a part of federal practice as well as state [*McNally v. Hill*, 293 U.S. 131 (1934)].

Recently, however, the Supreme Court has gone far to convert federal habeas corpus to a means of post-conviction review for the benefit of present or former state prisoners. In *Carafas v. LaVallee* [391 U.S. 234 (1968)], the New York courts had refused to make available to Carafas certain preliminary transcripts that would have been useful to him on appeal, because he did not have funds to pay for them. While Carafas' federal habeas corpus proceeding was pending, the New York Court of Appeals reversed itself on the matter in light of the United States Supreme Court equal protection cases. However, instead of granting relief to Carafas for what was an evident impairment of constitutional rights, the Second Circuit ruled that Carafas would have to go back to the state courts so that they could grant him relief. The Supreme Court reversed, holding that under those circumstances the federal court should not delay relief, but should grant the writ immediately. The Court did not believe that where there was a clear federal violation mere comity between state and federal courts should serve to delay relief.

In *Walker* [*Walker v. Wainwright*, 390 U.S. 335 (1968)], a state prisoner serving a life sentence sought to attack the propriety of his conviction, but was refused relief because there was another five-year term consecutive to the life sentence that the petitioner would have to begin to serve if the life sentence were not effective. Because the Fifth Circuit felt that *McNally v. Hill* required that immediate release be a possibility before federal habeas corpus could lie, it held that Walker could not attack the life sentence as long as the other sentence remained in effect. The Supreme Court reversed, holding that it was immaterial that another valid sentence might await the petitioner, as long as there was doubt about the constitutional validity of the life sentence he was actually serving.

Peyton v. Rowe [391 U.S. 54 (1968)] presented the converse situation of a prisoner in custody under a sentence he did not attack as invalid wishing to challenge another conviction consecutive to the valid sentence. The district court, again in reliance on *McNally v. Hill*, held that because release could not be ordered until the first valid sentence had been served, the effort to attack the second sentence was premature. The Fourth Circuit reversed the district court on the basis that *Fay v. Noia* [372 U.S. 391 (1963)] and cases following it had so undercut *McNally v. Hill* that it could no longer be considered a bar to relief. The Supreme Court agreed, and overruled *McNally*. The federal habeas corpus statute empowers the court to give whatever relief is appropriate; relief is also to be prompt and expeditious. Delay of the federal writ review until the petitioner actually began to serve his second sentence would mean that witnesses might not be available, thus affecting the propriety of the ruling. Moreover, the procedural delays inherent in habeas review would mean that if the petitioner's attack was well-founded he would spend time in custody on an invalid conviction. Therefore, it was proper to let the petitioner attack the second sentence even though immediate release was not possible under the circumstances.

Also relevant to the question of federal review of state convictions is *Sibron* [*Sibron v. New York*, 392 U.S. 41 (1968)]. Although as one of the stop-and-frisk decisions [*see supra* at 81] it has been considered chiefly of concern in that context, it also contains very useful insights on the nature of the relief available in federal courts. Sibron had already served his misdemeanor sentence by the time the case progressed into the appellate courts. It was argued that this rendered the case moot, so that no decision could be rendered. The Supreme Court disagreed. As long as any disadvantage of whatever kind flowed from the conviction under attack, like voting ineligibility or disability on holding certain offices or receiving certain licenses, then the case was not moot. Therefore, the case could be considered on the merits. Although *Sibron* reached the Supreme Court through a grant of certiorari from the decision of the New York Court of Appeals affirming Sibron's conviction, and not on federal habeas corpus, there seems no reason to deny its applicability to federal habeas corpus proceedings if they follow immediately after exhaustion of state appellate remedies.

One other aspect of *Sibron* also bears on federal review. The state had sought to confess error, thus removing the case from active consideration by the Supreme Court. This it was not permitted to do unless the Court itself concurred. The possibility of determining a federal question is one the Court and not the prosecution should control.

Thus, a state prisoner in actual custody can attack a sentence even though immediate release is not possible. If he is in custody at the beginning of the review proceedings, service of sentence will not render the case moot for purposes of federal habeas corpus as long as any detrimental consequences flow from the conviction under attack. The only aspect not yet formally ruled on would be the availability of federal habeas review if no custody of any kind, but only collateral consequences have flowed from the conviction. Federal habeas, however, has already gone far toward a simple post-conviction remedy for state prisoners similar to that found in some states, and there is little reason not to expect this amplification of the federal remedy to proceed to its logical conclusion, in which a federal district court may review every state conviction on federal constitutional grounds, whether or not the applicant has undergone incarceration at any time.

* * * * *

b. Application

UNITED STATES CODE, Title 28

§ 2242 Application

Application for a writ of habeas corpus shall be in writing signed and verified by the person for whose relief it is intended or by someone acting in his behalf.

It shall allege the facts concerning the applicant's commitment or detention, the name of the person who has custody over him and by virtue of what claim or authority, if known.

It may be amended or supplemented as provided in the rules of procedure applicable to civil actions.

If addressed to the Supreme Court, a justice thereof or a circuit judge it shall state the reasons for not making application to the district court of the district in which the applicant is held.

* * * * *

c. Exhaustion of remedies

UNITED STATES CODE, Title 28

§ 2254 State custody; remedies in Federal courts

(a) The Supreme Court, a Justice thereof, a circuit judge, or a district court shall entertain an application for a writ of habeas corpus in behalf of a person in custody pursuant to the judgment of a State court only on the ground that he is in custody in violation of the Constitution or laws or treaties of the United States.

(b) An application for a writ of habeas corpus in behalf of a person in custody pursuant to the judgment of a State court shall not be granted unless it appears that the applicant has exhausted the remedies available in the courts of the State, or that there is either an absence of available State corrective process or the existence of circumstances rendering such process ineffective to protect the rights of the prisoner.

(c) An applicant shall not be deemed to have exhausted the remedies available in the courts of the State, within the meaning of this section, if he has the right under the law of the State to raise, by any available procedure, the question presented.

* * * * *

FAY v. NOIA, 372 U.S. 391, 435–36, 438–40 (1963)

. . . Noia timely sought and was denied certiorari here from the adverse decision of the New York Court of Appeals on his *coram nobis* application, and therefore the case does not necessarily draw in question the continued vitality of the holding in *Darr* v. *Burford, supra,* that a state prisoner must ordinarily seek certiorari in this Court as a precondition of applying for federal habeas corpus. But what we hold today necessarily overrules *Darr* v. *Burford* to the extent it may be thought to have barred a state prisoner from federal habeas relief if he had failed timely to seek certiorari in this Court from an adverse state decision. Furthermore, our decision today affects all procedural hurdles to the achievement of swift and imperative justice on habeas corpus, and because the hurdle erected by *Darr* v. *Burford* is unjustifiable under the principles we have expressed, even insofar as it may be deemed merely an aspect of the statutory requirement of present exhaustion, that decision in that respect also is hereby overruled. . . .

Although we hold that the jurisdiction of the federal courts on habeas corpus is not affected by procedural defaults incurred by the applicant during the state court proceedings, we recognize a limited discretion in the federal judge to deny relief to an applicant under certain circumstances. Discretion is implicit in the statutory command that the judge, after granting the writ and holding a hearing of appropriate scope, "dispose of the matter as law and justice require," 28 U.S.C. § 2243; and discretion was the flexible concept employed by the federal courts in developing the exhaustion rule. Furthermore, habeas corpus has traditionally been regarded as governed by equitable principles. *United States ex rel. Smith* v. *Baldi,* 344 U.S. 561, 573 (dissenting opinion). Among them is the principle that a suitor's conduct in relation to the matter at hand may disentitle him to the relief he seeks. Narrowly circumscribed, in conformity to the historical role of the writ of habeas corpus as an effective and imperative remedy for detentions contrary to fundamental law, the principle is unexceptionable. We therefore hold that the federal habeas judge may in his discretion deny relief to an applicant who has deliberately bypassed the orderly procedure of the state courts and in so doing has forfeited his state court remedies.

But we wish to make very clear that this grant of discretion is not to be interpreted as a permission to introduce legal fictions into federal habeas corpus. The classic definition of waiver enunciated in *Johnson v. Zerbst*, 304 U.S. 458, 464—"an intentional relinquishment or abandonment of a known right or privilege"—furnishes the controlling standard. If a habeas applicant, after consultation with competent counsel or otherwise, understandingly and knowingly forwent the privilege of seeking to vindicate his federal claims in the state courts, whether for strategic, tactical, or any other reasons that can fairly be described as the deliberate by-passing of state procedures, then it is open to the federal court on habeas to deny him all relief if the state courts refused to entertain his federal claims on the merits—though of course only after the federal court has satisfied itself, by holding a hearing or by some other means, of the facts bearing upon the applicant's default. Cf. *Price* v. *Johnston*, 334 U.S. 266, 291. At all events we wish it clearly understood that the standard here put forth depends on the considered choice of the petitioner.[44] Cf. *Carnley* v. *Cochran*, 369 U.S. 506, 513–517; *Moore* v. *Michigan*, 355 U.S. 155, 162–165. A choice made by counsel not participated in by the petitioner does not automatically bar relief. Nor does a state court's finding of waiver bar independent determination of the question by the federal courts on habeas, for waiver affecting federal rights is a federal question. *E.g., Rice* v. *Olson*, 324 U.S. 786.

The application of the standard we have adumbrated to the facts of the instant case is not difficult. Under no reasonable view can the State's version of Noia's reason for not appealing support an inference of deliberate by-passing of the state court system. For Noia to have appealed in 1942 would have been to run a substantial risk of electrocution. His was the grisly choice whether to sit content with life imprisonment or to travel the uncertain avenue of appeal which, if successful, might well have led to a retrial and death sentence. See, *e.g., Palko* v. *Connecticut*, 302 U.S. 319. He declined to play Russian roulette in this fashion. This was a choice by Noia not to appeal, but under the circumstances it cannot realistically be deemed a merely tactical or strategic litigation step, or in any way a deliberate circumvention of state procedures. This is not to say that in every case where a heavier penalty, even the death penalty, is a risk incurred by taking an appeal or otherwise forgoing a procedural right, waiver as we have defined it cannot be found. Each case must stand on its facts. In the

---

[44] To the extent that any decisions of this Court may be read to suggest a standard of discretion in federal habeas corpus proceedings different from what we lay down today, such decisions shall be deemed overruled to the extent of any inconsistency.

instant case, the language of the judge in sentencing Noia, see note 3, *supra*, made the risk that Noia, if reconvicted, would be sentenced to death, palpable and indeed unusually acute.

* * * * *

d. Habeas corpus practice

Way, *Post-Conviction and Federal Habeas Corpus* *

I. [§ 35.1] Introduction

It has been said that the peremptory common-law and statutory writs are the most powerful weapons in the judicial arsenal. One of these writs is habeas corpus, which has had a considerable effect upon the criminal procedure of the state and nation.[1] Habeas corpus and comparable post-conviction remedies have been the subject of much discussion and no little controversy in recent years. But no matter what position a person may take regarding post-conviction remedies, their effectiveness has motivated persons who have a role in the criminal law process to be far more sensitive to due process considerations.

II. [§ 35.2] Sources of Habeas Corpus

Habeas corpus as a judicial remedy in the federal courts finds its source at least in part in the Constitution of the United States [Article 1, Section 9] which provides:

> The privilege of the writ of habeas corpus shall not be suspended, unless when in cases of rebellion or invasion the public safety may require it.

Substantially, the same provision is to be found in the constitutions of sixteen states. However, the suspension clause in the Constitution re-

---

* This is a revision of an article written and presented for the National District Attorneys Association Pacific Northwest Prosecutors Seminar made possible by a grant from the Department of Justice under the Law Enforcement Assistance Act. Reprint permission granted. Reprinted in PROSECUTOR'S SOURCEBOOK 629–36 (B. GEORGE & I. COHEN, Eds., P.L.I. 1969).

[1] The potency of the writ of habeas corpus, in state and federal judicial systems, has been amply demonstrated in the cases of Gideon v. Wainwright, 372 U.S. 335 (1963) (right to counsel at trial); *In re* Gault, 387 U.S. 1 (1967) (right to counsel, *inter alia*, in certain juvenile court proceedings); Eskridge v. Washington State Board of Prison Terms and Paroles, 372 U.S. 214 (1962) (right to free transcript on appeal); Pate v. Robinson, 383 U.S. 375 (1965) (*sua sponte* hearing on competency to stand trial); Stovall v. Denno, 388 U.S. 293 (1967) (non-retroactive application of Gilbert v. California rule on right to counsel in line-up identification proceedings), and Mempa v. Rhay, 389 U.S. 128 (1967) (right to counsel at probation revocation hearings), to name but a few cases involving the writ of habeas corpus.

lating to habeas corpus does not prohibit legislative bodies from conditioning the availability of the writ.[2]

III. [§ 35.3] Conditions on the Writ

The imposition of conditions upon the availability of the writ is a common feature in both the federal statutory procedures and the procedures of many states. Federal habeas corpus procedure requires with some exceptions that a federal prisoner must first petition the court of conviction for what is known as Section 2255 relief. The federal court in the district in which the prisoner is confined may also entertain an application for the writ.

Conditions are imposed upon the availability of habeas corpus to state prisoners as well. A state prisoner must exhaust the remedies available in the courts of the state before the writ of habeas corpus may be granted in the federal courts, unless there is an absence of available state corrective process "or the existence of circumstances rendering such process ineffective to protect the rights of the prisoner."[3]

State remedies are deemed not to be exhausted as long as the applicant for federal habeas corpus "has the right under the law of the State to raise, by any available procedure, the question presented."[4]

The various federal courts have held different practices to be either an absence of corrective process or an ineffective process. Among these have been: failure to provide waiver of filing fees for indigent prisoners;[5] deeming it a waiver of the right to file a second application when the first fails to state all the applicant's contentions as to the validity of his conviction;[6] deeming the enhanced sentence of a multiple offender, whose earlier offenses were committed outside the State of New York, as not being susceptible to challenge;[7] and not making the process available to parolees.[8]

The federal habeas corpus statute has laid down a set of circumstances under which the record of the state habeas corpus proceeding

[2] St. Clair v. Hiatt, 83 F. Supp. 585 (5th Cir. 1949), *cert. denied,* 339 U.S. 967 (1949).

[3] 28 U.S.C.A. § 2254(b) (Supp. 1968).

[4] 28 U.S.C.A. § 2254(c) (Supp. 1968). *Cf.* Fay v. Noia, 372 U.S. 391 (1962), which held that a decision not to appeal did not constitute a failure to exhaust state remedies that would bar federal habeas corpus relief.

[5] United States *ex rel.* Rhyce v. Cummings, 233 F.2d 190 (2d Cir.), *cert. denied,* 352 U.S. 854 (1956).

[6] McNeil v. North Carolina, 368 F.2d 313 (4th Cir. 1966).

[7] United States *ex rel.* LaNear v. LaValle, 306 F.2d 417 (2d Cir. 1962).

[8] United States *ex rel.* Michelotti v. Price, 230 F.Supp. 505 (W.D. Pa. 1964).

shall not be deemed to be correct.[9] These include: 1) when the merits of the factual dispute have not been resolved at the state hearing; 2) when the state fact-finding procedure was inadequate to afford a full and fair hearing; 3) when the material facts were not fully developed at the state hearing; 4) when the state court lacked either personal or subject matter jurisdiction; 5) when the state court failed to supply an indigent applicant with counsel; 6) when the state hearing was not fully, fairly and adequately conducted; 7) when the applicant was denied due process of law; 8) or, when the federal court determines that the decision of the state court was not supported by the record.

Applications made by prisoners for habeas corpus in federal courts are ordinarily construed with considerable liberality, and if the court can on any reasonable basis find the petitioner alleges an unlawful detention under federal standards, it will entertain the petition. The only statutory requirements concerning applications are that they must be in writing, be verified by the person seeking relief or someone on his behalf, name the person having custody of the applicant, and allege facts as to the illegality of the custody.[10]

IV. [§ 35.4] Indigent's Application

If the petitioner for federal habeas corpus is an indigent and desires to proceed *in forma pauperis,* he must file an affidavit saying that he is unable to pay the costs or fees necessary to institute the proceedings or give security for their payment.[11] If the court grants the petitioner permission to proceed, it must either grant the writ of habeas corpus, order the respondent to show cause why the writ should not be granted, or deny the writ because the petitioner on the basis of the application itself is not entitled to the issuance of the writ.[12] If the court grants the writ of habeas corpus or orders the respondent to show cause why the writ should not be granted, a return must be made and filed with the district court not later than twenty days thereafter.[13]

V. [§ 35.5] Return and Answer—Mechanics

In responding to habeas corpus matters in Washington, the return and answer to the application for a writ of habeas corpus are combined in one pleading. The petitioner is afforded an opportunity under the federal procedure to deny any facts set forth in the return or

[9] 28 U.S.C.A. § 2454(d) (Supp. 1968).
[10] 28 U.S.C.A. § 2242.
[11] 28 U.S.C.A. § 1915.
[12] 28 U.S.C.A. § 2243.
[13] *Ibid.*

allege any other material facts. If the application for the writ of habeas corpus and the return present only issues of law, then the court may decline to require the respondent to produce the petitioner at the hearing on the issues presented.

When application is made for federal habeas corpus, the applicant may at the same time request that an order be entered staying any proceedings in the state courts relating to the habeas corpus proceeding. If a stay of proceedings is not issued or granted by the court, the state may proceed as if no habeas corpus proceeding or appeal were pending.[14] The authority of the federal court to stay the proceeding is ordinarily used only in cases involving the death penalty and extradition proceedings.

The return required to be made by the respondent in accordance with Section 2243 must certify the true cause of the detention of the prisoner. Ordinarily, this is accomplished by reciting in the return the essential details concerning the prisoner's conviction, his sentence and commitment. A certified copy of the judgment and sentence and warrant of commitment should be attached. If the prisoner is held on a charge of having committed a crime, the return should recite the details of the charge. One should also attach copies of the information, indictment or complaint, and the warrant of arrest.

The return in Washington is ordinarily combined with an answer to the prisoner's contention of unlawful detention. The first paragraph is devoted to a statement of the authority of the respondent, i.e., that he is the regularly appointed superintendent of the prison and that it is by law a state correctional institution for the confinement of convicted felons sentenced and committed by the superior courts to serve a term of confinement. The second paragraph of the return contains a recitation of the details relating to the conviction, the sentence and the commitment. Certified copies of the judgment, sentence, and warrant of commitment should be attached. These two paragraphs of the return are all that need be done to satisfy the requirements of Section 2243, but a detailed answer should if at all possible accompany or be combined with the return so that the court can rule on the papers themselves without the necessity of a court appearance.

The allegations contained in the return and answer of the respondent, unless traversed by the prisoner, must be accepted by the court as true, except to the extent that it finds from the evidence they are not true. If the petitioner does not make a responsive pleading to the return and answer of the respondent, the contentions of the petitioner for habeas corpus are rebutted in the return and answer, and there

[14] 28 U.S.C.A. § 2251 (1951).

are no issues of fact in dispute, the court may deny the application for habeas corpus without conducting a hearing.[15]

VI. [§ 35.6] The Answer—Affirmative Defenses

The answer to the application for federal habeas corpus should set forth all available affirmative defenses to the contentions of unlawful detention.

The most common of these are:

(1) Failure of the applicant to exhaust his available state remedies in accordance with the provisions of Section 2254.

(2) Failure of the application for federal habeas corpus to state a federal question under the Constitution, laws or treaties of the United States as required by Section 2241(c)(iii).

(3) Inability under claim made in the application to grant suitable relief.

The doctrine of exhaustion of state remedies requires that the applicant must have unsuccessfully presented his claims of unlawful detention to the highest state court in which the matter may be reviewed.[16] State remedies may be exhausted on the issues presented to the federal court either by appeal from the conviction, or by habeas corpus or a statutory post conviction remedy in the highest state court in which the matter might be reviewed.[17] The effect of the exhaustion of state remedies doctrine is made extremely doubtful, however, by the decision in *Fay v. Noia*.[18] In that case it was held that federal court jurisdiction in habeas corpus cases "is conferred by the allegation of an unconstitutional restraint and is not defeated by anything that may occur in the state court proceedings. State procedural rules plainly must yield to this overriding federal policy."

The affirmative defense of the failure of the applicant to raise a federal question under the Constitution, laws or treaties of the United States is directed to the jurisdiction of the federal court in the cases of state prisoners.[19] Generally, issues raised concerning errors in instructions, the sufficiency of the evidence, the application of state statutory provisions regarding the charge, trial procedure or sentence, do not involve the question of a violation of constitutional rights. An application may state a solid constitutional claim but yet be subject

---

[15] 28 U.S.C.A. § 2248, (1951); Wright v. Dickson, 336 F.2d 878 (9th Cir. 1964).
[16] Stiltner v. Rhay, 258 F. Supp. 487 (S.D. Wash), aff'd, 367 F.2d 148 (9th Cir.), *cert. denied*, 385 U.S. 941 (1965).
[17] 28 U.S.C.A. § 2254 (1951).
[18] *See* note 9 *supra*.
[19] 28 U.S.C.A. § 2241 (1951).

to dismissal if the constitutional error falls within the harmless error rule of *Chapman v. California*.[20] In such cases, the court must find that the claimed constitutional error "was harmless beyond a reasonable doubt."

The affirmative defense of failure to state a claim upon which relief may be granted might also be available if it can be demonstrated that the applicant deliberately and intentionally by-passed state procedural processes. This arises when the defendant, for strategic, tactical or other reasons, knowingly fails to object to the admissibility of evidence or fails to take exception to trial court rulings, constituting a procedural default. In the light of the *Fay* case, however, it is doubtful that this defense can be interposed when the applicant has raised a constitutional question, unless it can be shown that the defendant knowingly waived the possible constitutional defense. . . .

VII. [§35.7] Appeal from the Final Order

An appeal may be taken from the final order in a habeas corpus proceeding only upon obtaining a certificate of probable cause from the federal judge who heard the case, or if the certificate is denied by the trial judge, then obtaining the certificate from a judge of a circuit court of appeals.[25] Once the district court grants the certificate, the circuit court of appeals must permit appellant to proceed *in forma pauperis*, assuming indigency is present.[26] The language of Section 2253 would seem to require that the state, if it is to appeal an adverse decision of the federal district court, must also obtain a certificate of probable cause to perfect its appeal. However, several circuits have held that the state need not obtain such a certificate to appeal an adverse decision of the district court. However, it would of course be advisable to obtain the certificate of probable cause to appeal.

VIII. [§ 35.8] Value of Records and Memoranda

In preventing criminal convictions from being reversed in habeas corpus proceedings, among the most valuable aids to the lawyer defending the application for habeas corpus are records and memoranda concerning the prisoner. Prosecutors and defense lawyers seem to have an aversion for making notes of conferences they have had with each other or with the defendant. Jailers often do not keep logs of communications, either by telephone or mail, or of visitations made to the defendant by his attorney, friends or relatives. Records of this

[20] 386 U.S. 18 (1967).
[25] 28 U.S.C.A. § 2253 (1951).
[26] *See* Nowakowski v. Maroney, 386 U.S. 542 (1967).

sort are invaluable in many cases in which the prisoner, years after his conviction, challenges it on the basis of some alleged happening during his jail custody, which might be easily disproven if records or memoranda had been made at the time.[27]

IX. [§ 35.9] Conclusion

In conclusion, it should be said that of the hundreds of applications for habeas corpus filed each week throughout the United States, very few applicants find their way out of prison as a result of habeas corpus. However, in the face of the constantly advancing change in the criminal law, the prosecutor must keep in mind the post conviction process and its probelms at all stages of the prosecution.

❋ ❋ ❋ ❋ ❋

e. Scope of substantive hearing

UNITED STATES CODE, Title 28

§ 2254 (d)-(f)

(d) In any proceeding instituted in a Federal court by an application for a writ of habeas corpus by a person in custody pursuant to the judgment of a State court, a determination after a hearing on the merits of a factual issue, made by a State court of competent jurisdiction in a proceeding to which the applicant for the writ and the State or an officer or agent thereof were parties, evidenced by a written finding, written opinion, or other reliable and adequate written indicia, shall be presumed to be correct, unless the applicant shall establish or it shall otherwise appear, or the respondent shall admit—

(1) that the merits of the factual dispute were not resolved in the State court hearing;
(2) that the factfinding procedure employed by the State court was not adequate to afford a full and fair hearing;
(3) that the material facts were not adequately developed at the State court hearing;
(4) that the State court lacked jurisdiction of the subject matter or over the person of the applicant in the State court proceeding;

[27] The value of such records and memoranda become especially important in light of the requirements set by 28 U.S.C.A. § 2254(d) as to when a federal court must hold a factual hearing on a habeas corpus application. See also Townsend v. Sain, 372 U.S. 293 (1963).

(5) that the applicant was an indigent and the State court, in deprivation of his constitutional right, failed to appoint counsel to represent him in the State court proceeding;

(6) that the applicant did not receive a full, fair, and adequate hearing in the State court proceeding; or

(7) that the applicant was otherwise denied due process of law in the State court proceeding;

(8) or unless that part of the record of the State court proceeding in which the determination of such factual issue was made, pertinent to a determination of the sufficiency of the evidence to support such factual determination, is produced as provided for hereinafter, and the Federal court on a consideration of such part of the record as a whole concludes that such factual determination is not fairly supported by the record:

And in an evidentiary hearing in the proceeding in the Federal court, when due proof of such factual determination has been made, unless the existence of one or more of the circumstances respectively set forth in paragraphs numbered (1) to (7), inclusive, is shown by the applicant, otherwise appears, or is admitted by the respondent, or unless the court concludes pursuant to the provisions of paragraph numbered (8) that the record of the State court proceeding, considered as a whole, does not fairly support such factual determination, the burden shall rest upon the applicant to establish by convincing evidence that the factual determination by the State court was erroneous.

(e) If the applicant challenges the sufficiency of the evidence adduced in such State court proceeding to support the State court's determination of a factual issue made therein, the applicant, if able, shall produce that part of the record pertinent to a determination of the sufficiency of the evidence to support such determination. If the applicant, because of indigency or other reason is unable to produce such part of the record, then the State shall produce such part of the record and the Federal court shall direct the State to do so by order directed to an appropriate State official. If the State cannot provide such pertinent part of the record, then the court shall determine under the existing facts and circumstances what weight shall be given to the State court's factual determination.

(f) A copy of the official records of the State court, duly certified by the clerk of such court to be a true and correct copy of a finding, judicial opinion, or other reliable written indicia showing such a factual determination by the State court shall be admissible in the Federal court proceeding.

[Subsection (d) incorporates the requirements of *Townsend v. Sain*, 372 U.S. 293 (1963). —Eds.]

* * * * *

B. Special Post-Conviction Proceedings

1. State

EDITORS' NOTE

The Supreme Court has considerably altered the nature of federal habeas corpus review of state convictions [*see supra* at 872]. Similar trends are evident in many of the states. The promulgation of ABA Standards in the area [AMERICAN BAR ASSOCIATION PROJECT ON STANDARDS FOR THE ADMINISTRATION OF CRIMINAL JUSTICE, STANDARDS RELATING TO POST-CONVICTION REMEDIES (Approved Draft 1968)] should accelerate this tendency.

General Character of the Remedy

The Standards recommend a single comprehensive remedy to review either the validity of a judgment of conviction or the legality of custody or supervision [§ 1.1]. All factual claims as well as legal should be determined in this one proceeding. The drafters do not intend to replace habeas corpus, as indeed they could not because by constitutional provision the writ cannot be suspended except in times of war or insurrection. Nevertheless, plenary post-conviction review proceedings can be created, and habeas corpus conditioned on a showing of the inefficacy of those proceedings [*cf.* 28 U.S.C. § 2255], without legally impairing the writ [*see United States v. Hayman*, 342 U.S. 205 (1952)].

In line with the purpose of the unitary post-conviction review proceeding, it should not be considered exclusively civil or criminal [§ 1.2]. Procedures should be geared to the objectives of the remedy, and the proceeding should be considered an extension of the original criminal proceeding, as far as possible.

The moving party should be the person seeking relief, moving in his own name; the respondent should be the governmental entity responsible for the original prosecution [§ 1.3(a)]. The legal officer charged primarily with answering the proceeding should be the attorney-general or other officer with state-wide jurisdiction, unless that officer for sufficient reason delegates the responsibility to a local prosecutor [§ 1.2(b)].

The Standards leave it as a matter of choice whether jurisdiction is vested in a single state-wide court or in the original local courts [§ 1.4(a)]. However, they recommend venue in the court from which the challenged conviction and sentence issued, and not the place of confinement, subject to liberal provisions for change of venue based on convenience [§ 1.4(b)]. The original judge should not be either required to hear the matter or rendered ineligible to do so. The judge, however, should be able to recuse himself without a challenge for bias if he believes another judge should preside [§ 1.4(c)].

Scope of Remedy

The grounds for relief should be quite broad, to comprehend attacks against convictions for federal or state constitutional violations, want of jurisdiction, excessive sentence, newly-discovered evidence, change in statute and any other grounds "properly the basis for collateral attack upon a criminal judgment," and against custody on the grounds that sentence has been fully served or unlawful revocation of conditional release has occurred [§ 2.1].

Post-conviction relief should not be available if regular appeal is still available, and rules should be flexible enough to permit delayed appeals where reason to do so exists. The court should also be empowered to convert delayed appeal proceedings into post-conviction review proceedings if the latter are more appropriate to consider the questions raised [§2.2].

The Standards, anticipating *Peyton v. Rowe,* recommend elimination of a custody requirement, thus permitting post-conviction review even though the applicant has not yet begun to serve the challenged sentence, has completely served it, or received no imprisonment in the sentence [§ 2.3].

The Standards also take the position that it is unwise to put any time limitations on post-conviction review [§ 2.4(a)]. However, it should be considered an abuse of process to withhold a claim until re-prosecution is impossible or correction of error not feasible; in this case relief may be withheld [§ 2.4(b)]. The applicant can also be required to show a present need for relief, as when he has been treated as a multiple offender, experiences delayed parole eligibility, or is under a civil disability because of the challenged conviction [§ 2.4(c)]. The latter anticipated *Sibron.*

The Application

The Standards urge that the system take into account that most petitions will be submitted by laymen in prison [§ 3.1(a)]. Therefore, provision should be made for writing materials, the right to purchase and retain legal materials, access to legal materials in the prison library, and free and uninhibited access to courts and private counsel [§ 3.1(b)]. They also recommend that the state make some form of provision for legal consultation within the prison, and for a prison library and distribution of pamphlets to prisoners explaining in lay language the scope of available post-conviction relief [§ 3.1(c)]. An alternative would be a regular legal aid or public defender branch in the prison, completely separate from the custodial structure [§ 3.1(d)].

To further the same aims, a standard application form should be developed that a layman can cope with [§ 3.2]. Applications should be verified subject to penalties for knowing falsehood, and prisoners should have easy access to notaries [§ 3.3].

The Standards take the position that it is unreasonable to require prisoners to attach supporting affidavits by third parties before an application can be considered. Nor should the applicant be required to indicate how he is to prove his factual allegations; proof should be a matter for later stages of the proceeding [§ 3.4]. Filing fees should also not be required, since proceedings to determine a waiver of fees are more expensive than any fees actually recovered; if fees are required, waiver should be routine [§ 3.5].

Processing Applications

The disposition of an application should be made by judicial officers and not by administrators [§ 4.1(a)]. Disposition should be made as quickly as possible on the merits and not on procedural grounds [§ 4.1(b)].

Because most applications are submitted by laymen, preliminary screening on procedural grounds is unwarranted; an answer should be sought for clarification of factual and legal issues. If there are preliminary review proceedings, dismissal should be limited to "unmistakably frivolous allegations" [§ 4.2].

To promote clarification of the legal issues, a responsive pleading should be required within a specified period of time not to exceed thirty days. Relevant portions of the record should be included [§ 4.3(a)]. The application should have calendar priority if the applicant is imprisoned or subject to the death penalty [§ 4.3(b)]. There should also be power in the court to stay execution of the sentence of death and to permit release of applicants pending final determination [§ 4.3(c)].

After application and response, the court should then determine whether to order additional proceedings, appoint counsel, or conclude the matter. If the decision is to terminate, the court should indicate in advance its reasons and give the applicant the opportunity to reply [§ 4.3(d)]. Disposition without appointment of counsel and hearing is improper if the application requires resolution of a "non-frivolous question of law." Disposition in this way is always improper if there is a material fact issue in the case [§ 4.3(e)].

If more than the initial processing is in order, counsel should be provided for the indigent, with adequate compensation from public funds. The appointed attorney should act through all stages of the proceeding, including review by the United States Supreme Court [§ 4.4].

If there is no factual controversy or the case is submitted on an agreed statement of facts, the application can be determined on the merits without evidentiary hearing and without transporting the applicant from prison to the courtroom [§ 4.5(a)]. There should be discovery proceedings to expedite the determination of facts, including in-prison depositions of applicants to develop the bases for the claims, the production of relevant documents including records of trial proceedings, depositions of witnesses and interrogatories. Representation by counsel is of course necessary to the successful invocation of discovery. The applicant has the protection of the privilege against self-incrimination against creating evidence that might bear on guilt if a retrial is ultimately ordered. If the applicant is indigent, the cost of discovery should be borne by the state [§ 4.5(b)].

If there are material issues of fact, a plenary evidentiary hearing should be held, at which the applicant and his attorney are present. Usual rules of evidence should be applied, except that a transcript of earlier proceedings should be available for use, subject to the possibility of impeachment by either party, and depositions can be used if the witness is unavailable and the right of cross-examination was earlier satisfied. If the judge is in a position of having to testify to events in earlier proceedings, he should not preside over the hearing; the judge should not take into account anything within his personal knowledge unless judicial notice may properly be invoked. Burden of proof is determined according to the underlying substantive law, and is ordinarily by a preponderance of evidence. The court should make specific findings of fact, keeping separate the recital of facts from a legal characterization of them [§ 4.6].

At the conclusion of the hearing, the court should make an appropriate dispositive order. If the judgment favors the state, the application should be dismissed, with an indication of whether this is after a plenary hearing or summarily. If the disposition favors the applicant, the order should indicate clearly which claims were found meritorious. Relief will turn on the nature of the meritorious claims. Release from custody may be ordered unless new trial proceedings are begun within a specified period of time, or a simple declaration of invalidity of judgment entered. If further appeal is possible, the time for appeal is to be specified. The court should have the power to stay its order pending review. A brief opinion should be prepared indicating the legal standards applied, the findings of fact and the specific conclusions of law reached with reference to them [§ 4.7].

Appellate Review

If the application is considered first by a trial-level court, appeal should be in the same form as ordinary appeals against convictions. Normal time limits should apply unless there are practical reasons arising from confinement and difficulty of communication between client and attorney for extending the usual times. Either party should be entitled to an appeal of right from the determination, without any preliminary formality of seeking leave to appeal. If a death penalty is not stayed in the trial court, the appellate court or a constituent judge should be empowered to review the refusal before execution takes place [§ 5.1].

Counsel should be provided for indigents, so that no appeal proceeds *pro se*. If possible, the same attorney should be used that participated in the original proceedings. The appellate court or a component judge should be able to stay execution of lower court orders if on preliminary application the lower court refuses to act. The action of the trial court should be presumed proper [§ 5.2].

The appellate court should have a broad scope of review on both legal and factual matters. A "reasoned opinion" should be entered showing the basis for the appellate court disposition of the appeal [§ 5.3].

Finality of Judgments

Once an issue has been fully litigated, it should not be relitigated. Therefore, complete records should be retained of proceedings. A case is fully litigated when the highest court to which there is an appeal of right has decided on the issue. Finality is an affirmative defense pleaded and proved by the respondent. Claims should be fully and finally determined even though they were not so determined in the original trial proceedings. If the applicant "deliberately and inexcusably" failed to raise a question on trial or during appeal, this is considered an abuse of process warranting refusal of relief on post-conviction proceedings. However, the respondent must allege that there was an abuse of process and the defendant with the assistance of counsel given the opportunity to reply to the allegation. There should be a reluctance to deny relief on purely procedural grounds; the court should reach the underlying merits despite procedural flaws [§ 6.1].

How far an earlier determination is final should turn on how far the matter was litigated the first time. If dismissal occurred because allegations were insufficient, a later application indicating an adequate claim should be heard. If there was a plenary hearing, all findings of fact and issues of law fully and finally litigated and decided should be final unless a contrary ruling is required "in the interests of justice." If the applicant "deliberately and inexcusably" failed to raise an issue of which he was aware on an earlier post-conviction proceeding or appeal, this should be considered an abuse of process barring relief. Further prosecution should be possible as long as it does not conflict with the basis on which post-conviction relief was granted; new proceedings can commence at the point necessary to cure error, without repeating valid procedures [§ 6.2].

If there is a subsequent prosecution or resumption of prosecution followed by conviction, or a sentence has been set aside, the sentencing court should not be able to impose a more severe penalty than that originally imposed, and credit toward both minimum and maximum sentence should be given for any time served under the earlier conviction or sentence successfully attacked in the post-conviction proceeding [§ 6.3].

* * * * *

UNIFORM POST-CONVICTION PROCEDURE ACT (Second Revision 1966)

Section 1. [Remedy—To Whom Available—Conditions.]

(a) Any person who has been convicted of, or sentenced for, a crime and who claims:

(1) that the conviction or the sentence was in violation of the Constitution of the United States or the Constitution or laws of this state;

(2) that the court was without jurisdiction to impose sentence;

(3) that the sentence exceeds the maximum authorized by law;

(4) that there exists evidence of material facts, not previously presented and heard, that requires vacation of the conviction or sentence in the interest of justice;

(5) that his sentence has expired, his probation, parole, or

conditional release unlawfully revoked, or he is otherwise unlawfully held in custody or other restraint; or

(6) that the conviction or sentence is otherwise subject to collateral attack upon any ground of alleged error heretofore available under any common law, statutory or other writ, motion, petition, proceeding, or remedy;

may institute, without paying a filing fee, a proceeding under this Act to secure relief.

(b) This remedy is not a substitute for nor does it affect any remedy incident to the proceedings in the trial court, or of direct review of the sentence or conviction. Except as otherwise provided in this Act, it comprehends and takes the place of all other common law, statutory, or other remedies heretofore available for challenging the validity of the conviction or sentence. It shall be used exclusively in place of them.

Section 2. [Exercise of Original Jurisdiction in Habeas Corpus.]

[(The Supreme Court, Circuit Court, District Court) in which, by the Constitution of this state, original jurisdiction in habeas corpus is vested, may entertain in accordance with its rules a proceeding under this Act in the exercise of its original jurisdiction. In that event, this Act, to the extent applicable, governs the proceeding.]

Section 3. [Commencement of Proceedings—Verification—Filing— Service.]

A proceeding is commenced by filing an application verified by the applicant with the clerk of the court in which the conviction took place. An application may be filed at any time. Facts within the personal knowledge of the applicant and the authenticity of all documents and exhibits included in or attached to the application must be sworn to affirmatively as true and correct. The [Supreme Court, Court of Appeals] may prescribe the form of the application and verification. The clerk shall docket the application upon its receipt and promptly bring it to the attention of the court and deliver a copy to the [prosecuting attorney, county attorney, state's attorney, attorney general].

Section 4. [Application—Contents.]

The application shall identify the proceedings in which the applicant was convicted, give the date of the entry of the judgment and sentence complained of, specifically set forth the grounds upon which the application is based, and clearly state the relief desired. Facts within the personal knowledge of the applicant shall be set forth separately from other allegations of facts and shall be verified as provided in section 3 of this Act. Affidavits, records, or other evidence supporting its allegations shall be attached to the application or the application shall recite why they are not attached. The application shall identify all previous proceedings, together with the grounds therein asserted, taken by the applicant to secure relief from his conviction or sentence. Argument, citations, and discussion of authorities are unnecessary.

Section 5. [Inability to Pay Costs.]

If the applicant is unable to pay court costs and expenses of representation, including stenographic, printing, and legal services, these costs and expenses shall be made available to the applicant in the preparation of the application, in the trial court, and on review.

Section 6. [Pleadings and Judgment on Pleadings.]

(a) Within [30] days after the docketing of the application, or within any further time the court may fix, the state shall respond by answer or by motion which may be supported by affidavits. At any time prior to entry of judgment the court shall take account of substance regardless of defects of form. The court may make appropriate orders for amendment of the application or any pleading or motion, for pleading over, for filing further pleadings or motions, or for extending the time of the filing of any pleading. In considering the application the could shall take account of substance, regardless of defects of form. If the application is not accompanied by the record of the proceedings challenged therein, the respondent shall file with its answer the record or portions thereof that are material to the questions raised in the application.

(b) When a court is satisfied, on the basis of the application, the answer or motion, and the record, that the applicant is not entitled to post-conviction relief and no purpose would be served by any further proceedings, it may indicate to the parties its intention to dismiss the application and its reasons for so doing. The applicant shall be given an opportunity to reply to the proposed dismissal. In light of the reply, or on default thereof, the court may order the application dismissed or grant leave to file an amended application or direct that the proceedings otherwise continue. Disposition on the pleadings and record is not proper if there exists a material issue of fact.

(c) The court may grant a motion by either party for summary disposition of the application when it appears from the pleadings, depositions, answers to interrogatories, and admissions and agreements of fact, together with any affidavits submitted, that there is no genuine issue of material fact and the moving party is entitled to judgment as a matter of law.

Section 7. [Hearing—Evidence—Order.]

The application shall be heard in, and before any judge of, the court in which the conviction took place. A record of the proceedings shall be made and preserved. All rules and statutes applicable in civil proceedings including pre-trial and discovery procedures are available to the parties. The court may receive proof by affidavits, depositions, oral testimony, or other evidence and may order the applicant brought before it for the hearing. If the court finds in favor of the applicant, it shall enter an appropriate order with respect to the conviction or sentence in the former proceedings, and any supplementary orders as to rearraignment, retrial, custody, bail, discharge, correction of sentence, or other matters that may be necessary and proper. The court shall make specific findings of fact, and state expressly its conclusions of law, relating to each issue presented. This order is a final judgment.

Section 8. [Waiver of or Failure to Assert Claims.]

All grounds for relief available to an applicant under this Act must be raised in his original, supplemental or amended application. Any ground finally adjudicated or not so raised, or knowingly, voluntarily and intelligently waived in the proceeding that resulted in the conviction or sentence or in any other proceeding the applicant has taken to secure relief may not be the basis for a subsequent application, unless the court finds a ground for relief asserted which for sufficient reason was not asserted or was inadequately raised in the original, supplemental, or amended application.

Section 9. [Review.]

A final judgment entered under this Act may be reviewed by the [Supreme Court, Court of Appeals] of this state on [appeal, writ of error] brought either by the applicant within —————— or the state within —————— from the entry of the judgment.

Section 10. [Uniformity of Interpretation.]

This Act shall be so interpreted and construed as to effectuate its general purpose to make uniform the law of those states which enact it.

Section 11. [Short Title.]

This Act may be cited as the Uniform Post-Conviction Procedure Act.

Section 12. [Severability.]

If any provision of this Act or the application thereof to any person or circumstance is held invalid, the invalidity does not affect other provisions or applications of the Act which can be given effect without the invalid provision or application, and to this end the provisions of this Act are severable.

Section 13. [Repeal.]

The following Act is repealed: "(An Act (etc.)————————————"

or

The following Acts and parts of Acts are repealed:

(1) "An Act (etc.) ————————————————"
(2) "Section ———— of 'An Act (etc.)' ————————————"

Section 14. [Time of Taking Effect.]

This Act shall take effect ————————————————————

* * * * *

According to Appendix C of American Bar Association Project on Standards for the Administration of Criminal Justice, Standards Relating to Post-Conviction Remedies 112 (Approved Draft 1968), special post-conviction proceedings of some sort are to be found in the following statutes and rules:

Alaska R. Crim. P. 35 (Supp. 1963).
Ariz. Rev. Stat. Ann. §§ 13–2001 to 13–2027 (1956).
Ark. R. Crim. P. 1 (1965).
Colo. R. Crim. P. 35 (1962).
Del. R. Crim. P. 35 (1953).
Fla. R. Crim. P. 1 (1963).
Ill. Ann. Stat. c. 38, §§ 122–1 to 122–7 (1964).
Kan. Stat. Ann. § 60–1507 (1964).
Ky. R. Crim. P. 11.42 (1964).
Me. R. Crim. P. 35 (b), following tit. 14, Me. Rev. Stat. Annot. (Supp. 1966).
Md. Ann. Code art. 27, § 645 (Supp. 1965) and R. Crim. P. Bk 40–48 (1963).

Mo. Sup. Ct. R. 27.26 (1953).

Neb. Rev. Stat. §§ 29–3001 to 29–3004 (Cum. Supp. 1965).

N.J. Ct. R. 3:10A (Supp. 1965).

N.Y. proposed act, §§ 880–87 and §§ 517–28, Leg. Doc. (1959) 65[L].

N.C. Gen. Stat. §§ 15–217 to 15–222 (1965).

Ohio Rev. Code §§ 2953.21 to 2953.24 (Supp. 1966).

Ore. Rev. Stat. §§ 138.510 to 138.680 (1963).

Pa. Laws 1965, No. 554.

Vt. Stat. Ann. tit. 13, §§ 7131–7137 (Law Pamphlet 1966).

Wyo. Stat. Ann. tit. 7, §§ 7–408.1 to 7–408.8 (1963).

28 U.S.C. § 2255 (1964).

Second Revised Uniform Post-Conviction Procedure Act §§ 1–14.

See the summary of American Bar Association Project on Standards for the Administration of Criminal Justice, Standards Relating to Post-Conviction Remedies (Approved Draft 1968), *supra* at 886–91.

❊   ❊   ❊   ❊   ❊

2. Federal

UNITED STATES CODE, Title 28

§ 2255   Federal custody; remedies on motion attacking sentence

A prisoner in custody under sentence of a court established by Act of Congress claiming the right to be released upon the ground that the sentence was imposed in violation of the Constitution or laws of the United States, or that the court was without jurisdiction to impose such sentence, or that the sentence was in excess of the maximum authorized by law, or is otherwise subject to collateral attack, may move the court which imposed the sentence to vacate, set aside or correct the sentence.

A motion for such relief may be made at any time.

Unless the motion and the files and records of the case conclusively show that the prisoner is entitled to no relief, the court shall cause notice thereof to be served upon the United States attorney, grant a prompt hearing thereon, determine the issues and make findings of fact and conclusions of law with respect thereto. If the court finds that the judgment was rendered without jurisdiction, or that the sentence imposed was not authorized by law or otherwise open to collateral attack, or that there has been such a denial or infringement of the constitutional rights of the prisoner as to render the judgment vulnerable to collateral attack, the court shall vacate and set the judgment aside and shall discharge the prisoner or resentence him or grant a new trial or correct the sentence as may appear appropriate.

A court may entertain and determine such motion without requiring the production of the prisoner at the hearing.

The sentencing court shall not be required to entertain a second or successive motion for similar relief on behalf of the same prisoner.

An appeal may be taken to the court of appeals from the order entered on the motion as from a final judgment on application for a writ of habeas corpus.

An application for a writ of habeas corpus in behalf of a prisoner who is authorized to apply for relief by motion pursuant to this section, shall not be entertained if it appears that the applicant has failed to apply for relief, by motion, to the court which sentenced him, or that such court has denied him relief, unless it also appears that the remedy by motion is inadequate or ineffective to test the legality of his detention.

❋ ❋ ❋ ❋ ❋

C. Constitutional Aspects

GARDNER v. CALIFORNIA, 393 U.S. 367 (1969) *

MR. JUSTICE DOUGLAS delivered the opinion of the Court.

Petitioner is a California state prisoner who filed *pro se* various papers with the State Superior Court alleging state action that interfered with his access to the courts for determination of his claims. The Superior Court, which granted a hearing and designated the Public Defender's office to represent petitioner at that hearing, treated the papers as requests for habeas corpus relief. After hearing, it made findings and held that the State had not impaired petitioner's rights of access to the courts.

Under California law, while the State has an appeal from an order discharging a defendant in a habeas corpus proceeding, the defendant has no appeal where his petition is denied. See *Loustalot* v. *Superior Court*, 30 Cal. 2d 905, 913, 186 P.2d 673. But he may file a petition for habeas corpus either in the intermediate Court of Appeal or in the Supreme Court. As petitioner in the instant case desired to pursue his remedy in the higher courts, he asked for a free transcript of the evidentiary hearing before the Superior Court. His motion was denied

* Footnotes and concurring and dissenting opinions omitted.

and he sought review of that denial by certiorari to the District Court of Appeal. It was denied, as was a timely petition for a hearing in the Supreme Court. We granted the petition for a writ of certiorari, 391 U.S. 902, to consider whether the rulings below squared with our decisions in *Griffin* v. *Illinois,* 351 U.S. 12, and *Long* v. *District Court,* 385 U.S. 192.

We reverse the judgment below. If this involved an appeal from the Superior Court's denial of habeas corpus, the rule of the *Griffin* case would prevent California from not allowing petitioner, an indigent, access to the record which makes any appellate review meaningful, while according full review to all who have the money to pay their own way. This, however, is not an appeal but the drafting of a new original petition for habeas corpus to the higher court. That new petition must reflect what has transpired in the Superior Court. The statute provides:

> "Every application for a writ of habeas corpus must be verified, and shall state whether any prior application or applications have been made for a writ in regard to the same detention or restraint complained of in the application and if any such prior application or applications have been made, the later application must contain a brief statement of all proceedings had therein, or in any of them, to and including the final order or orders made therein, or in any of them, on appeal or otherwise."

It is argued that since petitioner attended the hearing in the Superior Court, he can draw on his memory in preparing his application to the appellate court. And that court, if troubled, can always obtain the transcript in the lower court. But we deal with an adversary system where the initiative rests with the moving party. Without a transcript the petitioner, as he prepared his application to the appellate court, would have only his own lay memory of what transpired before the Superior Court. For an effective presentation of his case he would need the findings of the Superior Court and the evidence that had been weighed and rejected in order to present his case in the most favorable light. Certainly a lawyer, accustomed to precise points of law and nuances in testimony, would be lost without such a transcript, save perhaps for the unusual and exceptional case. The lawyer, having lost below, would be conscious of the skepticism that prevails above when a second hearing is sought and would as sorely need the transcript in petitioning for a hearing before the appellate court as he would if the merits of an appeal were at stake. A layman *a fortiori* needs the transcript even more.

It is said that the appellate court may send for the transcript and deduce from it whether there is merit in this new application for another hearing. That philosophy would make the appellate tribunal *parens patriae* of the indigent habeas corpus litigant. If that would suffice for appellate hearings in habeas corpus, why not in review of cases on appeal? Since our system is an adversary one, a petitioner carries the burden of convincing the appellate court that the hearing before the lower court was either inadequate or that the legal conclusions from the facts deduced were erroneous. A transcript is therefore the obvious starting point for those who try to make out a case for a second hearing. The State can hardly contend that a transcript is irrelevant to the second hearing, where it specifically provides one, upon request, to the appellate court and the State attorney. So long as this system of repeated hearings exists and so long as transcripts are available for preparation of appellate hearings in habeas corpus cases, they may not be furnished those who can afford them and denied those who are paupers.

There is no suggestion that in the present case there is any adequate substitute for a full stenographic transcript. We conclude that in the context of California's habeas corpus procedure denial of a transcript to an indigent marks the same invidious discrimination which we held impermissible in the *Griffin* and *Long* cases where a State granted appeals in criminal cases but in practical effect denied effective appellate review to indigents.

Reversed.

CHAPTER 15

Juvenile Proceedings

IN RE GAULT, 387 U.S. 1 (1967) *

. . . Appellants allege that the Arizona Juvenile Code is unconstitutional or alternatively that the proceedings before the Juvenile Court were constitutionally defective because of failure to provide adequate notice of the hearings. No notice was given to Gerald's parents when he was taken into custody on Monday, June 8. On that night, when Mrs. Gault went to the Detention Home, she was orally informed that there would be a hearing the next afternoon and was told the reason why Gerald was in custody. The only written notice Gerald's parents received at any time was a note on plain paper from Officer Flagg delivered on Thursday or Friday, June 11 or 12, to the effect that the judge had set Monday, June 15, "for further hearings on Gerald's delinquency."

A "petition" was filed with the court on June 9 by Officer Flagg, reciting only that he was informed and believed that "said minor is a delinquent minor and that it is necessary that some order be made by the Honorable Court for said minor's welfare." The applicable Arizona statute provides for a petition to be filed in Juvenile Court, alleging in general terms that the child is "neglected, dependent or delinquent." The statute explicitly states that such a general allegation is sufficient, "without alleging the facts." There is no requirement that the petition be served and it was not served upon, given, or shown to Gerald or his parents.

The Supreme Court of Arizona rejected appellants' claim that due process was denied because of inadequate notice. It stated that "Mrs. Gault knew the exact nature of the charge against Gerald from the day he was taken to the detention home." The court also pointed out that the Gaults appeared at the two hearings "without objection." The court held that because "the policy of the juvenile law is to hide youthful

* Footnotes and concurring and dissenting opinions eliminated.

errors from the full gaze of the public and bury them in the graveyard of the forgotten past," advance notice of the specific charges or basis for taking the juvenile into custody and for the hearing is not necessary. It held that the appropriate rule is that "the infant and his parents or guardian will receive a petition only reciting a conclusion of delinquency. But no later than the initial hearing by the judge, they must be advised of the facts involved in the case. If the charges are denied, they must be given a reasonable period of time to prepare."

We cannot agree with the court's conclusion that adequate notice was given in this case. Notice, to comply with due process requirements, must be given sufficiently in advance of scheduled court proceedings so that reasonable opportunity to prepare will be afforded, and it must "set forth the alleged misconduct with particularity." It is obvious, as we have discussed above, that no purpose of shielding the child from the public stigma of knowledge of his having been taken into custody and scheduled for hearing is served by the procedure approved by the court below. The "initial hearing" in the present case was a hearing on the merits. Notice at that time is not timely; and even if there were a conceivable purpose served by the deferral proposed by the court below, it would have to yield to the requirements that the child and his parents or guardian be notified, in writing, of the specific charge or factual allegations to be considered at the hearing, and that such written notice be given at the earliest practicable time, and in any event sufficiently in advance of the hearing to permit preparation. Due process of law requires notice of the sort we have described—that is, notice which would be deemed constitutionally adequate in a civil or criminal proceeding. It does not allow a hearing to be held in which a youth's freedom and his parents' right to his custody are at stake without giving them timely notice, in advance of the hearing, of the specific issues that they must meet. Nor, in the circumstances of this case, can it reasonably be said that the requirement of notice was waived. . . .

Appellants charge that the Juvenile Court proceedings were fatally defective because the court did not advise Gerald or his parents of their right to counsel, and proceeded with the hearing, the adjudication of delinquency and the order of commitment in the absence of counsel for the child and his parents or an express waiver of the right thereto. The Supreme Court of Arizona pointed out that "[t]here is disagreement [among the various jurisdictions] as to whether the court must advise the infant that he has a right to counsel." It noted its own decision in Arizona State Dept. of Public Welfare v. Barlow, 80 Ariz. 249, 296 P.2d 298 (1956), to the effect "that *the parents* of an infant in a juvenile proceeding cannot be denied representation by counsel of their choosing." (Emphasis added.) It referred to a provision of the Juvenile Code which it characterized as requiring "that the probation officer shall look after the interests of neglected, delinquent and dependent children," including representing their interests in court. The court argued that "The parent and the probation officer may be relied upon to protect the infant's interests." Accordingly it rejected the proposition that "due process requires that an infant have a right to counsel." It said that juvenile courts have the discretion, but not the duty, to allow such representation; it referred specifically to the situation in which the Juvenile Court discerns conflict between the child and his parents as an instance in which this discretion might be exercised. We do not agree. Probation officers, in the Arizona scheme, are also arresting officers. They initiate proceedings and file petitions which they verify, as here, alleging the delinquency of the child; and they testify, as here, against the child. And here the probation officer was also superintendent of the Detention Home. The probation officer cannot act as counsel for the child. His role in the adjudicatory hearing, by statute and in fact, is as arresting officer and witness against the child. Nor can the judge represent the child. There is no material difference in this respect between adult and juvenile proceedings of the sort here involved. In adult proceedings, this contention has been foreclosed by decisions of this Court. A proceeding where the issue is whether the child will be found to be "delinquent" and subjected to the loss of his liberty for years is comparable in seriousness to a felony prosecution. The juvenile needs the assistance of counsel to cope with problems of law, to make skilled inquiry into the facts, to insist upon regularity of the proceedings, and to ascertain whether he has a defense and to prepare and submit it. The child "requires the guiding hand of counsel at every step in the proceedings against him." Just as in Kent v. United States, supra, 383 U.S., at 561–562, 86 S.Ct., at 1057–1058, we indicated our agreement with the United States Court of Appeals for the District of Columbia Circuit that the assistance of counsel is essential for purposes of waiver proceedings, so we hold now that it is equally essential for the determination of delinquency, carrying with it the awesome prospect of incarceration in a state institution until the juvenile reaches the age of 21.

During the last decade, court decisions, experts, and legislatures have demonstrated increasing recognition of this view. In at least one-third of the States, statutes now provide for the right of representation by retained counsel in juvenile delinquency proceedings, notice of the right, or assignment of counsel, or a combination of these. In other States, court rules have similar provisions.

The President's Crime Commission has recently recommended that in order to assure "procedural justice for the child," it is necessary that "Counsel * * * be appointed as a matter of course wherever coercive action is a possibility, without requiring any affirmative choice by child or parent." As stated by the authoritative "Standards for Juvenile and Family Courts," published by the Children's Bureau of the United States Department of Health, Education, and Welfare:

> "As a component part of a fair hearing required by due process guaranteed under the 14th Amendment, notice of the right to counsel should be required at all hearings and counsel provided upon request when the family is financially unable to employ counsel." Standards, at p. 57.

This statement was "reviewed" by the National Council of Juvenile Court Judges at its 1965 Convention and they "found no fault" with it. The New York Family Court Act contains the following statement:

> "This act declares that minors have a right to the assistance of counsel of their own choosing or of law guardians in neglect proceedings under article three and in proceedings to determine juvenile delinquency and whether a person is in need of supervision under article seven. This declaration is based on a finding that counsel is often indispensable to a practical realization of due process of law and may be helpful in making reasoned determinations of fact and proper orders of disposition."

The Act provides that "At the commencement of any hearing" under the delinquency article of the statute, the juvenile and his parent shall be advised of the juvenile's "right to be represented by counsel chosen by him or his parent * * * or by a law guardian assigned by the court * * *." The California Act (1961) also requires appointment of counsel.

We conclude that the Due Process Clause of the Fourteenth Amendment requires that in respect of proceedings to determine delinquency which may result in commitment to an institution in which the juvenile's freedom is curtailed, the child and his parent must be notified of the child's right to be represented by counsel retained by them, or if they are unable to afford counsel, that counsel will be appointed to represent the child.

At the habeas corpus proceeding, Mrs. Gault testified that she knew that she could have appeared with counsel at the juvenile hearing. This knowledge is not a waiver of the right to counsel which she and her juvenile son had, as we have defined it. They had a right expressly to be advised that they might retain counsel and to be confronted with the need for specific consideration of whether they did or did not choose to waive the right. If they were unable to afford to employ counsel, they were entitled in view of the seriousness of the charge and the potential commitment, to appointed counsel, unless they chose waiver. Mrs. Gault's knowledge that she could employ counsel is not an "intentional relinquishment or abandonment" of a fully known right. . . .

Appellants urge that the writ of habeas corpus should have been granted because of the denial of the rights of confrontation and cross-examination in the Juvenile Court hearings, and because the privilege against self-incrimination was not observed. The Juvenile Court Judge testified at the habeas corpus hearing that he had proceeded on the basis of Gerald's admissions at the two hearings. Appellants attack this on the ground that the admissions were obtained in disregard of the privilege against self-incrimination. If the confession is disregarded, appellants argue that the delinquency conclusion, since it was fundamentally based on a finding that Gerald had made lewd remarks during the phone call to Mrs. Cook, is fatally defective for failure to accord the rights of confrontation and cross-examination which the Due Process Clause of the Fourteenth Amendment of the Federal Constitution guarantees in state proceedings generally.

Our first question, then, is whether Gerald's admission was improperly obtained and relied on as the basis of decision, in conflict with the Federal Constitution. For this purpose, it is necessary briefly to recall the relevant facts.

Mrs. Cook, the complainant, and the recipient of the alleged telephone call, was not called as a witness. Gerald's mother asked the Juvenile Court Judge why Mrs. Cook was not present and the judge replied that "she didn't have to be present." So far as appears, Mrs. Cook was spoken to only once, by Officer Flagg, and this was by telephone. The judge did not speak with her on any occasion. Gerald had been questioned by the probation officer after having been taken into custody. The exact circumstances of this questioning do not appear but any admissions Gerald may have made at this time do not appear in the record. Gerald was also questioned by the Juvenile Court Judge at each of the two hearings. The judge testified in the habeas corpus proceeding that Gerald admitted making "some of the lewd statements * * * [but not] any of the more serious lewd statements." There was conflict and uncertainty among the witnesses at the habeas corpus proceeding—the Juvenile Court Judge, Mr. and Mrs. Gault, and the probation officer—as to what Gerald did or did not admit.

We shall assume that Gerald made admissions of the sort described by the Juvenile Court Judge, as quoted above. Neither Gerald nor his parents was advised that he did not have to testify or make a statement, or that an incriminating statement might result in his commitment as a "delinquent."

The Arizona Supreme Court rejected appellant's contention that Gerald had a right to be advised that he need not incriminate himself. It said: "We think the necessary flexibility for individualized treatment will be enhanced by a rule which does not require the judge to advise the infant of a privilege against self-incrimination."

In reviewing this conclusion of Arizona's Supreme Court, we emphasize again that we are here concerned only with proceedings to determine whether a minor is a "delinquent" and which may result in commitment to a state institution. Specifically, the question is whether, in such a proceeding, an admission by the juvenile may be used against him in the absence of clear and unequivocal evidence that the admission was made with knowledge that he was not obliged to speak and would not be penalized for remaining silent. In light of Miranda v. State of Arizona, 384 U.S. 436, 86 S.Ct. 1602, 16 L.Ed.2d 694 (1966), we must also consider whether, if the privilege against self-incrimination is available, it can effectively be waived unless counsel is present or the right to counsel has been waived. . . .

The privilege against self-incrimination is, of course, related to the question of the safeguards necessary to assure that admissions or confessions are reasonably trustworthy, that they are not the mere fruits of fear or coercion, but are reliable expressions of the truth. The roots of the privilege are, however, far deeper. They tap the basic stream of religious and political principle because the privilege reflects the limits of the individual's attornment to the state and—in a philosophical sense—insists upon the equality of the individual and the State. In other words, the privilege has a broader and deeper thrust than the rule which prevents the use of confessions which are the product of coercion because coercion is thought to carry with it the danger of unreliability. One of its purposes is to prevent the State, whether by force or by psychological domination, from overcoming the mind and will of the person under investigation and depriving him of the freedom to decide whether to assist the State in securing his conviction.

It would indeed be surprising if the privilege against self-incrimination were available to hardened criminals but not to children. The language of the Fifth Amendment, applicable to the States by operation of the Fourteenth Amendment, is unequivocal and without exception. And the scope of the privilege is comprehensive. As Mr. Justice White, concurring, stated in Murphy v. Waterfront Commission, 378 U.S. 52, at 94, 84 S.Ct. 1594, at 1611, 12 L.Ed.2d 678 (1964):

> "The privilege can be claimed in *any proceeding*, be it criminal or civil, administrative or judicial, investigatory or adjudicatory. * * * it protects *any disclosures* which the witness may reasonably apprehend *could be used in a criminal prosecution or which could lead to other evidence that might be so used.*" (Emphasis supplied.)

With respect to juveniles, both common observation and expert opinion emphasize that the "distrust of confessions made in certain situations" to which Dean Wigmore referred in the passage quoted above, is imperative in the case of children from an early age through adolescence. In New York, for example, the recently enacted Family Court Act provides that the juvenile and his parents must be advised at the start of the hearing of his right to remain silent. The New York statute also provides that the police must attempt to communicate with the juvenile's parents before questioning him, and that a confession may not be obtained from a child prior to notifying his parents or relatives and releasing the child either to them or to the Family Court. In In Matters of W. and S., referred to above, the New York Court of Appeals held that the privilege of self-incrimination applied in juvenile delinquency cases and requires the exclusion of involuntary confessions, and that People v. Lewis, 260 N.Y. 171, 183 N.E. 353, 86 A.L.R. 1001 (1932), holding the contrary, had been specifically overruled by statute.

The authoritative "Standards for Juvenile and Family Courts" concludes that, "Whether or not transfer to the criminal court is a possibility, certain procedures should always be followed. Before being interviewed [by the police] the child and his parents should be informed of his right to have legal counsel present and to refuse to answer questions or be fingerprinted if he should so decide."

Against the application to juveniles of the right to silence, it is argued that juvenile proceedings are "civil" and not "criminal," and therefore the privilege should not apply. It is true that the statement of the privilege in the Fifth Amendment, which is applicable to the States by reason of the Fourteenth Amendment, is that no person "shall be compelled in any *criminal case* to be a witness against himself." However, it is also clear that the availability of the privilege does not turn upon the type of proceeding in which its protection is invoked, but upon the nature of the statement or admission and the exposure which it invites. The privilege may, for example, be claimed in a civil or administrative proceeding, if the statement is or may be inculpatory.

It would be entirely unrealistic to carve out of the Fifth Amendment all statements by juveniles on the ground that these cannot lead to "criminal" involvement. In the first place, juvenile proceedings to determine "delinquency," which may lead to commitment to a state institution, must be regarded as "criminal" for purposes of the privilege against self-incrimination. To hold otherwise would be to disregard substance because of the feeble enticement of the "civil" label-of-convenience which has been attached to juvenile proceedings. Indeed, in over half of the States, there is not even assurance that the juvenile will be kept in separate institutions, apart from adult "criminals." In those States juveniles may be placed in or transferred to adult penal institutions after having been found "delinquent" by a juvenile court. For this purpose, at least, commitment is a deprivation of liberty. It is incarceration against one's will, whether it is called "criminal" or "civil." And our Constitution guarantees that no person shall be "compelled" to be a witness against himself when he is threatened with deprivation of his liberty—a command which this Court has broadly applied and generously implemented in accordance with the teaching of the history of the privilege and its great office in mankind's battle for freedom.

In addition, apart from the equivalence for this purpose of exposure to commitment as a juvenile delinquent and exposure to imprisonment as an adult offender, the fact of the matter is that there is little or no assurance in Arizona, as in most if not all of the States, that a juvenile apprehended and interrogated by the police or even by the juvenile court itself will remain outside of the reach of adult courts as a consequence of the offense for which he has been taken into custody. In Arizona, as in other States, provision is made for juvenile courts to relinquish or waive jurisdiction to the ordinary criminal courts. In the present case, when Gerald Gault was interrogated concerning violation of a section of the Arizona Criminal Code, it could not be certain that the Juvenile Court Judge would decide to "suspend" criminal prosecution in court for adults by proceeding to an adjudication in Juvenile Court.

It is also urged, as the Supreme Court of Arizona here asserted, that the juvenile and presumably his parents should not be advised of the juvenile's right to silence because confession is good for the child as the commencement of the assumed therapy of the juvenile court process, and he should be encouraged to assume an attitude of trust and confidence toward the officials of the juvenile process. This proposition has been subjected to widespread challenge on the basis of current reappraisals of the rhetoric and realities of the handling of juvenile offenders.

In fact, evidence is accumulating that confessions by juveniles do not aid in "individualized treatment," as the court below put it, and that compelling the child to answer questions, without warning or advice as to his right to remain silent, does not serve this or any other good purpose. In light of the observations of Wheeler and Cottrell, and others, it seems probable that where children are induced to confess by "paternal" urgings on the part of officials and the confession is then followed by disciplinary action, the child's reaction is likely to be hostile and adverse—the child may well feel that he has been led or tricked into confession and that despite his confession, he is being punished.

Further, authoritative opinion has cast formidable doubt upon the reliability and trustworthiness of "confessions" by children. . . .

We conclude that the constitutional privilege against self-incrimination is applicable in the case of juveniles as it is with respect to adults. We appreciate that special problems may arise with respect to waiver of the privilege by or on behalf of children, and that there may well be some differences in technique—but not in principle—depending upon the age of the child and the presence and competence of parents. The participation of counsel will, of course, assist the police, juvenile courts and appellate tribunals in administering the privilege. If counsel is not present for some permissible reason when an admission is obtained, the greatest care must be taken to assure that the admission was voluntary, in the sense not only that it has not been coerced or suggested, but also that it is not the product of ignorance of rights or of adolescent fantasy, fright or despair.

The "confession" of Gerald Gault was first obtained by Officer Flagg, out of the presence of Gerald's parents, without counsel and without advising him of his right to silence, as far as appears. The judgment of the Juvenile Court was stated by the judge to be based on Gerald's admission in court. Neither "admission" was reduced to writing, and, to say the least, the process by which the "admissions" were obtained and received must be characterized as lacking the certainty and order which are required of proceedings of such formidable consequences. Apart from the "admission," there was nothing upon which a judgment or finding might be based. There was no sworn testimony. Mrs. Cook, the complainant, was not present. The Arizona Supreme Court held that "sworn testimony must be required of all witnesses including police officers, probation officers and others who are part of or officially related to the juvenile court structure." We hold that this is not enough.

No reason is suggested or appears for a different rule in respect of sworn testimony in juvenile courts than in adult tribunals. Absent a valid confession adequate to support the determination of the Juvenile Court, confrontation and sworn testimony by witnesses available for cross-examination were essential for a finding of "delinquency" and an order committing Gerald to a state institution for a maximum of six years.

The recommendations in the Children's Bureau's "Standards for Juvenile and Family Courts" are in general accord with our conclusions. They state that testimony should be under oath and that only competent, material and relevant evidence under rules applicable to civil cases should be admitted in evidence. The New York Family Court Act contains a similar provision.

As we said in Kent v. United States, 383 U.S. 541, 554, 86 S.Ct. 1045, 1053, 16 L.Ed.2d 84 (1966), with respect to waiver proceedings, "there is no place in our system of law for reaching a result of such tremendous consequences without ceremony * * *." We now hold that, absent a valid confession, a determination of delinquency and an order of commitment to a state institution cannot be sustained in the absence of sworn testimony subjected to the opportunity for cross-examination in accordance with our law and constitutional requirements. . . .

Appellants urge that the Arizona statute is unconstiutional under the Due Process Clause because, as construed by its Supreme Court, "there is no right of appeal from a juvenile court order. * * * " The court held that there is no right to a transcript because there is no right to appeal and because the proceedings are confidential and any record must be destroyed after a prescribed period of time. Whether a transcript or other recording is made, it held, is a matter for the discretion of the juvenile court.

This Court has not held that a State is required by the Federal Constitution "to provide appellate courts or a right to appellate review at all." In view of the fact that we must reverse the Supreme Court of Arizona's affirmance of the dismissal of the writ of habeas corpus for other reasons, we need not rule on this question in the present case or upon the failure to provide a transcript or recording of the hearings—or, indeed, the failure of the juvenile court judge to state the grounds for his conclusion. Cf. Kent v. United States, supra, 383 U.S., at 561, 86 S.Ct., at 1057, where we said, in the context of a decision of the juvenile court waiving jurisdiction to the adult court, which by local law, was applicable: "* * * it is incumbent upon the Juvenile Court to accompany its waiver order with a statement of the reasons or considerations therefor." As the present case illustrates, the consequences of failure to provide an appeal, to record the proceedings, or to make findings or state the grounds for the juvenile court's conclusion may be to throw a burden upon the machinery for habeas corpus, to saddle the reviewing process with the burden of attempting to reconstruct a record, and to impose upon the juvenile judge the unseemly duty of testifying under cross-examination as to the events that transpired in the hearings before him.

For the reasons stated, the judgment of the Supreme Court of Arizona is reversed and the cause remanded for further proceedings not inconsistent with this opinion. It is so ordered.

Judgment reversed and cause remanded with directions.

* * * * *

In Re Winship, 397 U.S. 358 (1970) *

Mr. Justice Brennan delivered the opinion of the Court.

Constitutional questions decided by this Court concerning the juvenile process have centered on the adjudicatory stage at "which a determination is made as to whether a juvenile is 'delinquent' as a result of alleged misconduct on his part, with the consequence that he may be committed to a state institution." *In re Gault,* 387 U.S. 1, 13 (1967). *Gault* decided that, although the Fourteenth Amendment does not require that the hearing at this stage conform with all the requirements of a criminal trial or even of the usual administrative proceeding, the Due Process Clause does require application during the adjudicatory hearing of "the essentials of due process and fair treatment." *Id.,* at 30. This case presents the single, narrow question whether proof beyond a reasonable doubt is among the "essentials of due process and fair treatment" required during the adjudicatory stage when a juvenile is charged with an act which would constitute a crime if committed by an adult.

Section 712 of the New York Family Court Act defines a juvenile delinquent as "a person over seven and less than sixteen years of age who does any act which, if done by an adult, would constitute a crime." During a 1967 adjudicatory hearing, conducted pursuant to § 742 of the Act, a judge in New York Family Court found that appellant, a 12-year-old boy, had entered a locker and stolen $112 from a woman's pocketbook. The petition which charged appellant with delinquency alleged that his act, "if done by an adult, would constitute

---

* Footnotes and concurring and dissenting opinions omitted.

the crime or crimes of Larceny." The judge acknowledged that the proof might not establish guilt beyond a reasonable doubt, but rejected appellant's contention that such proof was required by the Fourteenth Amendment. The judge relied instead on § 744(b) of the New York Family Court Act which provides that "[a]ny determination at the conclusion of [an adjudicatory] hearing that a [juvenile] did an act or acts must be based on a preponderance of the evidence." During a subsequent dispositional hearing, appellant was ordered placed in a training school for an initial period of 18 months, subject to annual extensions of his commitment until his 18th birthday, six years in appellant's case. . . .

We turn to the question whether juveniles, like adults, are constitutionally entitled to proof beyond a reasonable doubt when they are charged with violation of a criminal law. The same considerations which demand extreme caution in factfinding to protect the innocent adult apply as well to the innocent child. We do not find convincing the contrary arguments of the New York Court of Appeals. *Gault* rendered untenable much of the reasoning relied upon by that court to sustain the constitutionality of § 744 (b). The Court of Appeals indicated that a delinquency adjudication "is not a 'conviction' (§ 781); that it affects no right or privilege, including the right to hold public office or to obtain a license (§ 782); and a cloak of protective confidentiality is thrown around all the proceedings (§§ 783–784)." 24 N.Y.2d, at 200, 247 N.E.2d, at 255–256. The court said further: "The delinquency status is not made a crime; and the proceedings are not criminal. There is, hence, no deprivation of due process in the statutory provision [challenged by appellant] . . . ." 24 N.Y.2d, at 203, 247 N.E.2d, at 257. In effect the Court of Appeals distinguished the proceedings in question here from a criminal prosecution by use of what *Gault* called the " 'civil' label of convenience which has been attached to juvenile proceedings." 387 U.S., at 50. But *Gault* expressly rejected that distinction as a reason for holding the Due Process Clause inapplicable to a juvenile proceeding. 387 U.S., at 50–51. The Court of Appeals also attempted to justify the preponderance standard on the related ground that juvenile proceedings are designed "not to punish, but to save the child." 24 N.Y.2d, at 197, 247 N.E.2d, at 254. Again, however, *Gault* expressly rejected this justification. 387 U.S., at 27. We made clear in that decision that civil labels and good intentions do not themselves obviate the need for criminal due process safeguards in juvenile courts, for "[a] proceeding where the issue is whether the child will be found to be 'delinquent' and subjected to the loss of his liberty for years is comparable in seriousness to a felony prosecution." *Id.*, at 36.

Nor do we perceive any merit in the argument that to afford juveniles the protection of proof beyond a reasonable doubt would risk destruction of beneficial aspects of the juvenile process. Use of the reasonable-doubt standard during the adjudicatory hearing will not disturb New York's policies that a finding that a child has violated a criminal law does not constitute a criminal conviction, that such a finding does not deprive the child of his civil rights, and that juvenile proceedings are confidential. Nor will there be any effect on the informality, flexibility, or speed of the hearing at which the factfinding takes place. And the opportunity during the post-adjudicatory or dispositional hearing for a wide-ranging review of the child's social history and for his individualized treatment will remain unimpaired. Similarly, there will be no effect on the procedures distinctive to juvenile proceedings which are employed prior to the adjudicatory hearing.

The Court of Appeals observed that "a child's best interest is not necessarily, or even probably, promoted if he wins in the particular inquiry which may bring him to the juvenile court." 24 N.Y.2d, at 199, 247 N.E.2d, at 255. It is true, of course, that the juvenile may be engaging in a general course of conduct inimical to his welfare which calls for judicial intervention. But that intervention cannot take the form of subjecting the child to the stigma of a finding that he violated a criminal law and to the possibility of institutional confinement on proof insufficient to convict him were he an adult.

We conclude, as we concluded regarding the essential due process safeguards applied in *Gault*, that the observance of the standard of proof beyond a reasonable doubt "will not compel the States to abandon or displace any of the substantive benefits of the juvenile process." *Gault, supra,* at 21.

Finally, we reject the Court of Appeals' suggestion that there is, in any event, only a "tenuous difference" between the reasonable-doubt and preponderance standards. The suggestion is singularly unpersuasive. In this very case, the trial judge's ability to distinguish between the two standards enabled him to make a finding of guilt which he conceded he might not have made under the standard of proof beyond a reasonable doubt. Indeed, the trial judge's action evidences the accuracy of the observation of commentators that "the preponderance test is susceptible to the misinterpretation that it calls on the trier of fact merely to perform an abstract weighing of the evidence in order to determine which side has produced the greater quantum, without regard to its effect in convincing his mind of the truth of the proposition asserted." Dorsen & Reznek, *supra,* at 26–27.

In sum, the constitutional safeguard of proof beyond a reasonable doubt is as much required during the adjudicatory stage of a delinquency proceeding as are those constitutional safeguards applied in *Gault*—notice of charges, right to counsel, the rights of confrontation and examination, and the privilege against self-incrimination. We therefore hold, in agreement with Chief Judge Fuld in dissent in the Court of Appeals, "that, where a 12-year-old child is charged with an act of stealing which renders him liable to confinement for as long as six years, then, as a matter of due process . . . the case against him must be proved beyond a reasonable doubt." 24 N.Y.2d, at 207, 247 N.E.2d, at 260.

Reversed.

* * * * *

Isaacs, *The Role of the Lawyer in Representing Minors in the New Family Court,* 12 BUFF. L. REV. 501, 508–18 (1963) *

III

COUNSEL'S ROLE IN JUVENILE DELINQUENCY AND PERSON IN NEED OF SUPERVISION PROCEEDINGS UNDER ARTICLE 7 OF THE ACT

Cases which were denominated as juvenile delinquency proceedings under the former Children's Court Act and Domestic Relations Court Act [32] have now been subdivided into two categories—"juvenile delinquent" and "person in need of supervision." The label "juvenile delinquent" is now applied to a person over seven and under sixteen who does any act which, is done by an adult, would constitute a crime.[33] The new category of "person in need of supervision" encompasses a male less than sixteen years of age and a female less than eighteen years of age who is habitually truant, or incorrigible, ungovernable or habitually disobedient and beyond the lawful control of parent or other lawful authority.[34] Counsel should be aware that there are important distinctions in terms of procedure and judicial power between these two categories of cases.

A. *Proceedings Preliminary to the Filing of Petition*

In the rare instances in which counsel is retained as soon as the parent has been notified that the child has been taken into custody or that the filing of a petition under article 7 of the Family Court Act is

---

* Copyright 1963 by Buffalo Law Review. Reprinted by permission.

[32] N.Y. Children's Ct. Act § 2(2); N.Y. Dom. Rel. Ct. Act § 2(15).

[33] N.Y. Family Ct. Act § 712(a).

[34] N.Y. Family Ct. Act § 712(b).

contemplated, the first concern of counsel may be the propriety of temporary detention of his client pending the filing of a petition. The Family Court Act reflects a strong legislative policy against the use of temporary detention pending the initiation of Family Court proceedings except in very restricted circumstances, and it is a proper function of counsel to insist that this policy be observed.[35]

Although the Act authorizes arrest without a warrant by a police officer where it appears that an act of juvenile delinquency has been committed,[36] there is no statutory authority for taking a child into custody on the ground that he is or appears to be a person in need of supervision. When arrest is authorized, if the arresting officer does not release a child to the custody of his parent or person responsible for his care, he is required to bring the child forthwith to the Family Court, without his first being taken to a police station house, or to a place designated by rules of court for the reception of children.[37] Rules of Court authorize the probation services to release a child in custody if the case appears to be one involving a person in need of supervision proceeding rather than juvenile delinquency, and in the latter cases custody can be continued only if there are special circumstances requiring detention.[38] A child who is not released must promptly be brought before a judge of the court, if practicable, and no child may be held for more than forty-eight hours without a hearing.[39]

If a child in custody is brought before a judge of the Family Court before the filing of a petition, the court is required to hold a hearing to determine whether the court appears to have jurisdiction over the child.[40] On such a hearing counsel is under a duty to oppose continued detention of his client unless a proper showing is made that the court has jurisdiction, that the events occasioning the taking into custody involve juvenile delinquency and that there is a substantial probability that the child will not appear in court on the return date or that there

[35] See N.Y. Joint Legis. Committee on Court Reorganization, Rep. II (The Family Court Act) 10, 11 (1962).

[36] N.Y. Family Ct. Act § 721.

[37] N.Y. Family Ct. Act § 724. Rules of court have delegated the power of designating children's shelters to the respective Appellate Divisions. N.Y.R. Family Ct. 7.1. "Confessions" taken in a police station may not be admissible in evidence. See Matter of Rutane, 234 N.Y.S.2d 777 (Family Ct. 1962). A bill presently awaiting action by the governor would amend section 724(b) so as to authorize a police officer to take a child for questioning to a facility designated for such purpose by the appellate division of each department. [This bill has been signed—Ed.]

[38] N.Y.R. Family Ct. 72; N.Y. Family Ct. Act § 727.

[39] N.Y. Family Ct. Act § 729. Legislation pending would alter the time to take week-end detention into account. [This bill did not pass.—Ed.]

[40] N.Y. Family Ct. Act § 728.

is a serious risk that he may commit a criminal act before the return date.[41]

Both the Family Court Act [42] and the Rules of Court [43] adopted pursuant thereto contemplate the utilization of an intake procedure preliminary to the filing of a petition for the purpose of screening out cases which do not require judicial attention either because the necessary jurisdictional elements are manifestly lacking or because the matter is amenable to adjustment on an informal voluntary basis. In the larger cities and counties of the State this function will be handled by the probation service of the court or a specialized unit thereof, while in less populous areas intake may be handled through public or private welfare or other family or children's agencies. Counsel is rarely retained as early as the intake level. However, in the rare instances when counsel is in the picture at this early stage, he may serve a valuable function by bringing to the attention of the intake officer any facts or circumstances either related to the particular acts in issue or the family or child which might militate in favor of efforts toward voluntary adjustment. Cooperation by counsel in developing a plan for voluntary adjustment may also help to avoid the need for formal proceedings. Statements made during intake procedures cannot be admitted in evidence at any subsequent adjudicatory hearing or, if the proceeding is transferred to a criminal court, at any time prior to a conviction.[44] They may, however, be considered in the dispositional process later discussed.

B. *The Petition*

All proceedings under the Family Court Act are instituted by the filing of a petition. Juvenile delinquency petitions are usually made by peace officers or by an individual who has allegedly suffered injury as a result of the acts complained of. Parents constitute the petitioners in the great preponderance of person in need of supervision cases, and authorized agencies in almost all the rest. These four categories encompass the authorized petitioners in proceedings under article 7 of the Family Court Act.[45]

The required contents of a petition filed under article 7 are particularized in some detail by the Act. In a juvenile delinquency case the

[41] N.Y. Family Ct. Act § 728(b).
[42] N.Y. Family Ct. Act § 734.
[43] N.Y.R. Family Ct. 7.3.
[44] N.Y. Family Ct. Act § 735.
[45] N.Y. Family Ct. Act § 733.

petition must specify the act, which, if done by an adult, would constitute a crime and the time and place of its commission and must allege that the respondent was under sixteen at the time of the alleged act and that he requires supervision, treatment or confinement.[46] The petition in a person in need of supervision case must set forth, in addition to the required age allegations, the specific acts on which the allegations of habitual truancy, incorrigibility, habitual disobedience or ungovernability are based and the time and place of their occurrence, and that the respondent requires supervision or treatment.[47] Although petitions are prepared by court clerks, most of whom are not lawyers, there will rarely be occasion for counsel to interpose objection to them if the official forms adopted by the Judicial Conference are properly used.[48] However, it is clear that it was the intention of the Legislature that the petitioner be given adequate notice of the nature and circumstances of the particular acts alleged, and the sufficiency of a petition which does not meet these requirements and which substitutes vague, generalized or conclusory allegations is properly subject to attack by motion.[49]

In localities having a permanent law guardian staff, counsel may be assigned after a petition has been filed and before the first hearing of the court. In other localities counsel will not usually be assigned until requested at the initial hearing. A brief comment may be appropriate at this juncture with respect to ethical problems of representation that may arise. The problem of potential divided loyalty will never confront the law guardian since by statutory prescription his sole loyalty is to the child he represents. The possibility of adverse interest may arise, however, where private counsel is retained by a parent to represent a child in a juvenile delinquency or person in need of supervision proceeding. In some cases proper defense of the child may require the elicitation of facts reflecting adversely on the parent and which could, in fact, result in the substitution of a petition charging the parent with neglect for that pending before the court at the outset of the proceeding. In such circumstances it would appear to be the ethical duty of counsel either to request that a law guardian be assigned to represent the child or to advise the parent of the potential adverse interest, of his intention to defend the child to the utmost without regard to possible serious consequences to the parent and possibly even to suggest that the parent retain separate counsel.

[46] N.Y. Family Ct. Act § 731.
[47] N.Y. Family Ct. Act § 732.
[48] Family Ct. Forms, No. 7-6, 7-7.
[49] See Schinitsky, *supra* note 4, at 16; Procedure and Evidence in the Juvenile Court, *op. cit. supra* note 31, at 12.

C. *Hearings*

The new Family Court Act attempts to distinguish the basically legal aspects of a proceeding under article 7 from the primarily social aspects by providing that hearings be held in two phases, the first designated as an "adjudicatory hearing" and the second as a "dispositional hearing." [50] The legal aspects are largely embodied in the "adjudicatory hearing," the function of which is to determine whether the respondent did the particular acts on which the allegations of juvenile delinquency or person in need of supervision are based.[51] The social aspects of the proceeding are emphasized in the dispositional hearing which is designed to determine whether, in the case of a person alleged to be in need of supervision, there is need for supervision or treatment, and, in the case of a person alleged to be a juvenile delinquent, whether the respondent requires supervision, treatment or confinement.[52] No final adjudication of delinquency or person in need of supervision can be made until both hearings have been held.

Counsel coming into the Family Court for a hearing for the first time may be surprised, if not dismayed, by the lack of courtroom formality. The judge, not wearing a robe, may be sitting behind an ordinary conference table with probation personnel, the respondent and counsel sitting as if at an informal meeting. The proceedings may be conducted in what appears to be purely a conversational manner with little regard for the courtroom niceties adhered to in other courts. Forensic ability or intimate acquaintance with the technicalities of courtroom procedures seem to have little place in the picture. Unauthorized persons are generally barred from the court.[53] In a properly conducted court, where informality merely means the absence of technical formalities which tend to confuse or coerce the child,[54] counsel will learn that such informality is desirable as a means of conveying to the child that the court is seeking to help rather than punish him, and that it can be achieved without sacrificing dignity or respect for the authority which the court represents. Counsel must be on his guard, however, that the cloak of "informality" is not used as a disguise for abuse or deprivation of important rights.

In this connection, some note should be made of the special problem confronting the law guardian who is permanently assigned to a single

---

[50] The same concept of dual hearings is found in Standards for Specialized Courts Dealing with Children 53 (1954), which is published by the Children's Bureau of the U.S. Department of Health, Education and Welfare.

[51] N.Y. Family Ct. Act § 742.

[52] N.Y. Family Ct. Act § 743.

[53] N.Y. Family Ct. Act § 741(b).

[54] Lou, Juvenile Courts in the United States 129 (1927).

court. He may sit opposite a single judge day after day, and case after case for an extended period of time, and his regular duties will normally bring him into almost daily contact with the probation staff of the court. Under these circumstances the lawyer must exercise constant vigilance and preserve unyielding independence lest his desire to maintain amicable relations with his judicial cohort and with the court and probation personnel reduce him to an ineffective rubber stamp.

1. *The Adjudicatory Hearing*

An adjudicatory hearing must commence not more than three days after the filing of the petition if the respondent is in detention.[55] The issue presented on an adjudicatory hearing in a juvenile delinquency case is generally well defined and limited, namely, whether the respondent committed the particular criminal act or acts alleged. In person in need of supervision cases the issue may tend to be more diffuse since proof of incorrigibility or ungovernability may involve a general pattern of conduct rather than an isolated occurrence and it may be difficult to pinpoint the legal issue to be adjudicated. For example, a substantial portion of these cases involve children who have repeatedly run away from home, who are brought to court on the petition of their parents whose vociferous disclaimers of any desire to have the child restored to the home are met with the child's vehement assertion that he will run away again if forced to return home. It is hard to find a justifiable issue in these cases, the only real question being a social one, namely, what created this situation and what is to be done about it.

Counsel will have to determine prior to hearing whether to advise his client to admit the commission of the acts alleged in the petition or to require that the issues be put to proof. The term "put to proof" is used advisedly since the Family Court Act has no requirement for the entry of anything akin to a plea in a criminal proceeding, and the respondent can, in effect, require that the allegations of the petition be established without either admitting or denying his culpability.[56]

In cases where the child protests his innocence, it is, of course, the responsibility of counsel to require that proper and sufficient proof be adduced.[57] In cases where the operative facts are admitted, however,

[55] N.Y. Family Ct. Act § 747.

[56] N.Y. Family Ct. Act §§ 742, 744.

[57] "If we consider the problems that might confront the lawyer, we see that he could not, with an understanding of the court's philosophy and objectives, experience a conflict between its needs and his client's. It is of course the judge's function to determine on the facts presented whether an adjudication will be made. Thus if the respondent desires to present facts to contravene the petition or the prospective disposition it is no more the function of the lawyer in the juvenile case than in any other to overrule the client in this respect. . . ." Procedure and Evidence in the Juvenile Court, *op. cit. supra* note 31, at 43.

counsel should not automatically decide to waive the necessity of proof without further investigation. As a general rule it would appear desirable for counsel to interview at least the complaining witnesses so that he can verify the true nature and extent of his client's complicity and so as to discourage the growth in the court of a cavalier attitude toward the necessity of supporting allegations in the petition with proper proof.[58] Where such verification appears to confirm the child's admission, the child's interest would rarely be served by insisting on a contested hearing, and, in these circumstances, counsel should usually advise the court of his client's willingness to admit the allegations of the petition at the outset of the hearing, reserving, however, if deemed necessary, the right to adduce matter which may have some bearing on the true quality of or motivations for the youth's conduct. In some instances, however, counsel properly may decide to require proof of the allegations of the petition where he feels that only by a full examination of the complaining and other witnesses can the *de minimis* nature of his client's conduct be fully developed.

The Family Court Act directs that "only evidence that is competent, material and relevant may be admitted in an adjudicatory hearing" in delinquency and person in need of supervision cases.[59] Invocation by counsel of exclusory rules of evidence should be guided by intelligence conditioned with sympathetic understanding of the court's objectives and problems. Since there is no prosecuting attorney, the proceeding is not truly adversary in character, and accordingly greater leeway must be accorded in the elicitation of the affirmative case than might be proper in a criminal trial, in order to avoid placing the judge in the role of the dogged prosecutor. Objections to the form of questions will rarely serve much purpose. The reasons for the rules of evidence rather than all the details of the rules themselves should be counsel's guide. Evidence, such as hearsay statements, which is objectionable because it is inherently untrustworthy or improperly prejudicial should be vigorously resisted, but objections should not be motivated by the desire to display legal acumen or merely to establish a technical basis for possible reversal on appeal.

Neither records of the respondent's prior history in the court nor social evaluation reports prepared by the probation department are properly considered by the court during an adjudicatory hearing, and any effort to inject such information should be opposed.[60] Little difficulty should be encountered by counsel in evaluating the relevancy or

---

[58] The dangers of unquestioning acceptance of a child's admissions are discussed in Schinitsky, *supra* note 4, at 25.

[59] N.Y. Family Ct. Act § 744(a).

[60] N.Y. Family Ct. Act § 746; Procedure and Evidence in the Juvenile Court, *op. cit. supra* note 31, at 57.

materiality of proffered evidence in juvenile delinquency cases in view of the limited issue presented as to whether a particular act was committed by the respondent. Greater difficulty will be encountered in person in need of supervision cases since the petition may rest on a mosaic of conduct, and it may be difficult to assign irrelevancy or immateriality to any information which bears on the respondent's family background or conduct.

Whether the respondent should be advised to invoke his right to remain silent will depend on the particular circumstances of the case. In juvenile delinquency proceedings where the respondent protests his innocence and there has been an insufficient affirmative showing of the acts alleged, counsel is certainly under no duty to advise his client to subject himself to examination. On the other hand, where evidentiary basis for the allegations of the petition has been offered, it is usually wise to permit the respondent to rebut the adverse testimony.

There would appear to be few, if any, person in need of supervision cases where resort to the privilege of remaining silent will serve the best interests of the respondent. In the overwhelming majority of these cases it is only if the respondent is given the opportunity to explain the origins and motivations of his conduct or the attitudes and actions of his parents which precipitated the filing of the petition, that the real issues can be seen in their true perspective and a determination made as to whether the issue is incorrigibility or parental neglect. In this connection it should be noted that the court, on motion of counsel or on its own motion, may at any time in the proceedings substitute a person in need of supervision petition for a delinquency petition or a neglect petition for either a delinquency or person in need of supervision petition.[61]

The term "adjudicatory hearing" is a misnomer since adjudicatory hearings do not conclude with an adjudication or the entry of an order unless the petition is dismissed at this stage.[62] The statute merely contemplates that, as a prerequisite for further proceedings, the court must make a finding at the conclusion of the adjudicatory hearing that the acts on which the petition is predicated have in fact been committed by the respondent. Such determination must be based on a pre-

[61] N.Y. Family Ct. Act § 716.

[62] An essential element of the petition is that "the respondent requires supervision, treatment or confinement" in juvenile delinquency cases and "supervision or treatment" in person in need of supervision cases. N.Y. Family Ct. Act §§ 731, 732. Since by definition these issues are to be determined on the dispositional hearing (N.Y. Family Ct. Act § 743) no final adjudication can be made until the dispositional hearing has been held. A bill now awaiting action by the governor would change the name of "Adjudicatory Hearings" to "Fact-Finding Hearings." [This bill has been signed—Ed.]

ponderance of the evidence and for this purpose, an uncorroborated confession of the respondent made out of court is not sufficient.[63] Counsel contemplating the possibility of an appeal should press for detailed findings so that the exact basis of the determination is made clear on the record.

Counsel may on occasion find himself subjected to pressure from the judge not to press for dismissal in a case where there is insufficient competent evidence to sustain the petition on the ground that the child requires the court's "help." There is no justification for counsel to succumb to such blandishments. If the Legislature had desired to make amenability to the "help" of the court a ground for jurisdiction, it would have so prescribed. The policy of the Legislature as expressed in the statute is that the interposition of judicial authority is authorized only where there has been a proper showing of the commission of the acts or existence of the circumstances defined by the Act. If this is not the correct policy, then correction lies in the hands of the Legislature and not with the court or counsel.[64]

2. Dispositional Hearings

The Act permits the commencement of a dispositional hearing immediately after the adjudicatory hearing has been completed and the required findings made.[65] However, the Act also contemplates that for purposes of determining disposition an inquiry will be made, usually in the form of a probation department investigation, "into the surroundings, conditions and capacities of the respondent," and it authorizes adjournments of the dispositional hearing for this purpose.[66] Unless it is clear that a probation or medical or psychiatric investigation is not required, it is usually wise for counsel to urge that the dispositional hearing be adjourned until the results of such investigation are available. In this connection it should be noted that there are limitations imposed by the state on the number and length of such adjournments, with special restrictions being imposed in cases where the respondent

[63] N.Y. Family Ct. Act § 744.

[64] "The conditions under which the State is empowered to intervene in the upbringing of a child should be specifically and clearly delineated in the statutes. Whenever the State seeks to intervene, it should be required to show that those conditions do in fact exist with respect to a child and that its intervention is necessary to protect the child or the community, or both. The State should not be able to interfere with the rights of the parents with respect to their child and assume jurisdiction over such child on the generalized assumption that the child is in need of the care or protection of the State. . . ." Standards for Specialized Courts Dealing with Children, op. cit. supra note 50, at 7.

[65] N.Y. Family Ct. Act § 746.

[66] N.Y. Family Ct. Act § 749.

is being detained.[67] While counsel may consent to waive the statutory limitations, such consent should be given only where a clear showing of the necessity therefor is made. Where the limitations are violated over counsel's objections, counsel should not hesitate to resort to a writ of habeas corpus to obtain release of the respondent from custody.

In view of the fact that the dispositional hearing is primarily social in function, it is difficult at this early date to describe the lawyer's role therein with any particularity or confidence. However, certain general observations should be made. Since the primary purpose of the Family Court is not to deal with the "what" but rather with the "why" of the anti-social conduct, the dispositional hearing process is probably the most important stage of the proceeding. The potential of the lawyer's role in this stage has sometimes been unduly minimized. For example, it is important to note that the findings made at the conclusion of an adjudicatory hearing do not in and of themselves provide the basis for sustaining the petition. There remains for establishment at the dispositional hearing the necessary allegations in the petition that the respondent requires supervision, treatment or confinement, in the case of a juvenile delinquency proceeding, or supervision or treatment in the case of a person in need of supervision proceeding.[68] Accordingly, if counsel can establish that notwithstanding the commission of the acts alleged in the petition no real purpose would be served by suspending judgment, probationary supervision, placement or commitment, there would be basis for dismissal of the petition and avoidance of whatever stigma or disability might otherwise attach to an adjudication of delinquency or person in need of supervision.

Even in cases in which dismissal of the petition cannot be achieved the lawyer can utilize his training and experience to good purpose. A probation evaluation must be predicated at least in part on a factual investigation of the background of the matter. Probation staffs are usually understaffed and overworked and often cannot make the investigation to the full extent really needed. Counsel with his special abilities for adducing and collating facts can offer his cooperation to the probation service and make available information which otherwise might not be adduced.

The Act authorizes the court, in its discretion, to withhold from or disclose, in whole or in part, probation reports to counsel.[69] In my view counsel should request disclosure of such reports in almost every case,

[67] N.Y. Family Ct. Act § 749.
[68] N.Y. Family Ct. Act §§ 731, 732.
[69] N.Y. Family Ct. Act § 746(b).

and there are few circumstances under which a court should deprive counsel of that privilege. There is, however, a concomitant responsibility on the part of counsel not to use such reports in such way as may be detrimental to the child he represents or the child's family. In evaluating probation reports counsel should understand and respect the particular expertise and talents which the probation officer brings into play. This does not mean, however, that he must forfeit his common sense and acquiesce in whatever evaluation or recommendations are forthcoming. Social workers like all humans are sometimes prone to incompetence, laziness and even bias, and it is the duty of counsel to guard his clients against the consequence of such inadequacies. If counsel feels that the report contains or is based upon inaccurate or incomplete facts, it is the duty of counsel to bring these matters to the attention of the court and to adduce the correct or additional information during the course of the dispositional hearing.

At stake on a dispositional hearing may be the "rights of a child to remain at liberty without interference by the State and the rights of the parents to legal custody of a child." [70] Due process of law, therefore, is equally applicable to this part of the hearing. The statutory requirements as to evidence which may be received on a dispositional hearing differ from those applicable to an adjudicatory hearing only in the omission of the requirement of competency.[71]

Counsel should be aware of the broad range of dispositional powers available to the court,[72] including suspended judgment,[73] probation,[74] placement,[75] and orders of protection [76] in the cases of persons in need of supervision and delinquency cases,[77] and the additional power of commitment in delinquency cases.[78] Generally counsel should attempt to resist dispositions which involve institutionalization unless there is

[70] Standards for Specialized Courts Dealing with Children, *op. cit. supra* note 50, at 57.

[71] N.Y. Family Ct. Act § 745.

[72] N.Y. Family Ct. Act §§ 753, 754.

[73] N.Y. Family Ct. Act § 755.

[74] N.Y. Family Ct. Act § 757.

[75] N.Y. Family Ct. Act § 756.

[76] N.Y. Family Ct. Act § 759.

[77] The court also has power to discharge a person in need of supervision with a warning. N.Y. Family Ct. Act § 754(a). It would appear, however, that in any case where a warning is the only dispositive action deemed required, dismissal of the petition on the ground that no supervision or treatment is required would be warranted.

[78] N.Y. Family Ct. Act § 758. A bill presently awaiting action by the governor would permit the placement of persons in need of supervision in state training schools. No such authority existed in the statute as originally exacted. [This bill has been signed—Ed.]

no practicable alternative,[79] and counsel may perform a valuable service to his client by suggesting and attempting to implement programs of treatment which might avoid resort to institutional placement or commitment. Sometimes the persistent ingenuity of counsel may obtain a concededly preferable form of disposition after the well-meaning but overworked social worker has failed in similar efforts.

At the conclusion of the dispositional hearing, unless the petition is dismissed, the court will make its final adjudication of either delinquency or person in need of supervision, setting forth the grounds therefor and the final order of disposition is thereupon entered.[80]

D. Post-Dispositional Proceedings

The entry of a dispositional order may not terminate the need for counsel's services. Motions for a new hearing or to stay, modify, set aside or vacate any order issued in the course of the proceeding may be made.[81] A petition may be filed for an order terminating the placement or commitment directed in the dispositional order.[82] Counsel may also have to re-enter the picture if the respondent is charged with failure to comply with the terms or conditions of a suspended judgment, or with the terms of placement at home or in an authorized agency, or with the terms of probation.[83] There is also available, of course, the ultimate remedy of appeal. Appeals from the Family Court are taken in the first instance to the Appellate Division of the Supreme Court.[84]

*   *   *   *   *

George, *Juvenile Delinquency Proceedings: The Due Process Model*, 40 Colo. L. Rev. 315, 315–36 (1968)*

I. Background: Structure of Juvenile Proceedings

None of the rights set out for juveniles by *Gault* is new. Instead, it is the context in which they are to be applied that is unique. In the name of benevolence juvenile court proceedings have been almost totally ignored as far as due process is concerned, simply because the "tunnel vision" of lawyers and judges has kept only civil and criminal proceedings and the activities of administrative tribunals in view. With *Gault*

---

[79] Kahn, For Children in Trouble 65 (1957); Interim Rep. XI, Juvenile Delinquency Evaluation Project of the City of New York (1958).

[80] N.Y. Family Ct. Act §§ 751–754.

[81] N.Y. Family Ct. Act §§ 761–763.

[82] N.Y. Family Ct. Act §§ 764–768.

[83] N.Y. Family Ct. Act §§ 776–779.

[84] N.Y. Family Ct. Act art. 10.

* Copyright 1968 by Colorado Law Review. Reprinted by permission.

we are on the threshold of "wide-screen" due process for all "protective" proceedings, whether judicial or administrative in nature. As indicated above, the catalog of *Gault* requirements is brief. But the clear intent of the decision is to convert juvenile delinquency proceedings into adversary proceedings, albeit specialized ones of a "quasi-criminal" character. As the participation of attorneys in delinquency proceedings increases, it will be a relatively short time until the bulk of procedural guarantees established for regular criminal actions are transferred to juvenile delinquency proceedings. True, the extension of due process guarantees will undoubtedly be a selective one, because whatever the changes decreed, juvenile proceedings will never be the exact equivalent of regular criminal proceedings. But there will be substantial overlap in the respective lists of safeguards.

Because the test used to adapt due process standards to delinquency proceedings will be the flexible one of indispensability of the particular guarantee to objective fairness, the process of adaptation cannot be confined simply to the adjudicational stage of a delinquency proceeding, whatever the Court's representations to that effect may have been. *Gault* itself is not so limited; the right to counsel clearly extends to all phases of the delinquency proceeding,[7] as does the privilege against self-incrimination.[8] Nor can the selective extension of due process rights be long confined to delinquency proceedings. Custody, dependency and neglect proceedings will also be affected by many of the *Gault* and post-*Gault* expansions of due process; the decision is already being cited by analogy in civil commitment cases, welfare contests and school disciplinary cases.[9] The question is no longer *whether* due process applies to these proceedings, but rather what variations from traditional due process in criminal procedure are permitted or required.

In presenting the potential scope of due process after *Gault*, one can either break the delinquency down into its several stages and catalog

---

[7] While directly concerned with the adjudicational stage, the Court declared that "the child requires the guiding hand of counsel at every step in the proceedings against him." 387 U.S. at 36, citing Powell v. Alabama, 287 U.S. 45, 69 (1932). In this respect, *Gault* clearly implies a constitutional, as opposed to statutory, basis for the recent decision in Kent v. United States, 383 U.S. 541 (1966), which held that the right to counsel extends to a waiver hearing.

[8] 387 U.S. at 44–45. For a full discussion of the privilege against self-incrimination see pp. 329–30 *infra*.

[9] *E.g.*, Parker v. Heryford, 379 F.2d 556 (10th Cir. 1967) (remanding a habeas corpus proceeding concerning a juvenile's civil commitment for reconsideration in light of *Gault*); Maders v. Board of Educ., 386 F.2d 778 (2nd Cir. 1967), *rev'g* 267 F. Supp. 356 (S.D.N.Y. 1967) (although *Gault* not applicable to early "conference" stage of school disciplinary hearing, court implied student would be entitled to an attorney later in the proceeding). See B. George, *supra* note 6, at 84–95, for a full discussion of the potential impact of *Gault* on welfare proceedings.

the guarantees that are likely to affect each stage,[10] or consider the specific guarantees to see in how many contexts they might apply and with what modifications. I have chosen the second approach because it stresses the process of analogy by which due process extensions come about.

However, it is well to keep in mind that there are normally three stages that are functionally visible in delinquency proceedings.[11] The first is the intake or jurisdictional phase, in which the court decides whether to take further action in the matter. The second is the fact-finding or adjudicational hearing, at which the determination of delinquency or non-delinquency is to be made. The third is the dispositional phase, in which the degree of official interference in the lives of the juvenile and his family is determined.

If the juvenile is of an age at which his case can be waived to an adult criminal court for trial, there may be a statutory fourth stage consisting of a waiver hearing,[12] usually intervening between intake and adjudication.[13] Although the right to counsel and the privilege against self-incrimination apply to waiver hearings,[14] the extent to which other rights are applicable must rest on the function the waiver hearing is to play,[15] a matter on which neither the juvenile codes nor the decisions interpreting them are in agreement. One view is that it is designed to screen the respondent's background to determine whether he is more appropriately to be dealt with by juvenile court-related services, or whether the lack of appropriate services, the availability of special facilities for young adult offenders, the age or background of the particular offender, or whatever, suggests that the respondent should be tried in the regular criminal courts.[16]

Should the foregoing be adopted as the primary function of the waiver hearing, then whether or not a delinquent act has in fact been committed is not of much moment. On the other hand, some judges apparently view the waiver hearing as dispositional in nature, so that the fact of delinquency must first be established before the question

[10] See Dorsen & Rezneck, *In re Gault and the Future of Juvenile Law*, 1 Family L.Q. 1–46 (Dec. 1967). For the contrasting approach, see Ketcham, *Guidelines from Gault: Revolutionary Requirements and Reappraisal*, 53 Va. L. Rev. 1700 (1967).

[11] See generally Children's Bureau, U.S. Dep't of Health, Educ., and Welfare, Standards for Specialized Courts Dealing With Children 40–41, 53–60, 63–82 (1954) [hereinafter cited as "Standards"].

[12] See generally Note, *Separating the Criminal from the Delinquent: Due Process in Certification Procedure*, 40 S. Cal. L. Rev. 158 (1967).

[13] Standards 54.

[14] See authorities cited notes 7 & 8 and accompanying text *supra*.

[15] See text accompanying notes 27 & 57 *infra*.

[16] E.g., Cal. Welf. & Inst'ns Code § 707 (West Supp. 1967).

of waiver can be dealt with.[17] If this is what the legislature intended, economy of judicial time dictates that the waiver hearing follow the fact-finding or adjudicational stage and not precede it. Yet apparently waiver proceedings are always disposed of first. For present purposes, the point is that a decision on the extent of due process coverage of waiver hearings will be meaningful only when the function of waiver has been firmly established. The determination of what the waiver hearing is to accomplish, however, is not itself one of constitutional interpretation but of statutory construction; due process governs how the proceeding is to be conducted and not what its "substantive" aim is.

One other point should be stressed. It must be recognized that these stages may extend over several hearings in a seriously contested delinquency proceeding. It has apparently been the practice to blend together the jurisdictional and adjudicational or the adjudicational and dispositional hearings without a clear-cut delineation of the purposes of the particular court session.[18] In uncomplicated and uncontested proceedings this may continue to be the practice, but in a serious delinquency case no two stages can safely be intermingled. Moreover, each stage may require two or more separate hearings. Once more, the analogy is the ordinary criminal proceeding. For convenience one may speak of the pretrial stage, trial and sentencing. Yet the pretrial stage comprehends such separate procedures as the initial appearance to answer the indictment or information, an adjourned hearing at which the defendant's plea is taken if he was earlier unrepresented by counsel, and various pretrial motion hearings on motions to dismiss or quash the pleading, motions for a bill of particulars, motions to suppress, applications for bail or modification of bail, and motions for a change of venue. Some or all of these functions will manifest themselves in the "jurisdictional" stage of delinquency proceedings. In short, we will have to refine our classifications of procedural activity for delinquency proceedings.

With this as background, let us consider the notice function, the objective limitations on trial proceedings themselves, the fact-finding and adjudicating process, and the problem of review.

II. NOTICE

The Court in *Gault* requires that there be timely notice of the proceeding so that adequate preparation is possible.[19] This problem, how-

---

[17] *See, e.g.*, Appendix to Opinion of the Court, Kent v. United States, 383 U.S. 541, 565–68 (1966). *Cf.* Peyton v. Nord, 437 P.2d 716 (N.M. 1967).
[18] Standards 53.
[19] 387 U.S. at 31–34.

ever, must be analyzed further before its extension to the various stages of a delinquency proceeding can be determined.

Notice of procedural activity. In *Gault*, the Court observed that no notice was given to the juvenile's parents that their son had been taken into custody or that a hearing on the petition of the arresting officer was to be held the following day, although they did in fact appear for the hearing. One dimension, therefore, is that written notification must be given of the time and place of every procedural act, whatever the stage of the proceeding. If a juvenile is taken into custody notice of that fact should be communicated to the parents. This is frequently provided for by statute, but the requirement probably has a constitutional foundation after *Gault*. In short, whatever the hearing or procedure, written notice of its time and place must be given reasonably in advance.

Recipients of notice. The Court declares that "the child *and his parents or guardian*" must be notified in writing of the pending charges.[20] In a footnote it indicates that both civil and criminal proceedings are subject to this due process requirement.[21] However, the civil decisions cited, particularly *Armstrong v. Manzo*,[22] do not in fact provide a direct analogy for delinquency proceedings. The purpose of the civil notice requirement is to ensure that *persons whose legal rights may be directly affected* by a pending judicial action are given notice sufficiently in advance of the proceedings to enable them to enter the litigation. Timeliness is certainly a major factor in this, and to that extent *Armstrong* is direct precedent.

Armstrong was principally concerned, however, with delineating those persons to whom notice must be given. The case involved an adoption proceeding in juvenile court. After a divorce in which the mother was awarded custody of the child of the marriage and the father ordered to pay child support, the mother remarried. Subsequently, the stepfather sought to adopt the child. No notice was given to the natural father. Under the Texas statute the father's consent to an adoption was unnecessary if he had not "contributed substantially" to the support of the child for a two-year period. The juvenile court approved the adoption on the representation of the mother and stepfather that the natural father had not contributed to the child's support for the required period. The Supreme Court held this a violation of due process because the stepfather knew the natural father's where-

[20] *Id.* at 33 (emphasis added).
[21] *Id.* at 33 n.53.
[22] 380 U.S. 545 (1965). Mullane v. Central Hanover Bank & Trust Co., 339 U.S. 306 (1950), holding that when notice is required it must be provided by the best means available, was also cited in support. 387 U.S. at 33 n.53.

abouts and could have given him notice so that he could appear and contest the adoption. The contention that due process was satisfied since the natural father could and did move to vacate the adoption decree after he learned of it was rejected. If the natural father had appeared in the original proceeding, the burden would have been on the mother and stepfather to show the fitness of the stepfather to become an adoptive parent and to establish the grounds for dispensing with the natural father's consent. On the motion to vacate, the burden was on the natural father to show the impropriety of the juvenile court's ruling on both points. As a result, the failure to notify him worked procedurally as well as substantively to his disadvantage and denied him due process.

The difficulty lies in how to adapt this idea to juvenile delinquency proceedings. *Armstrong* seems obviously to cover all custody proceedings since parental rights are directly affected by a change in custody. It is also persuasive precedent for most, if not all, dependency or neglect proceedings since parental activity is directly or indirectly involved in the determination of neglect, and the orders that a juvenile court is empowered to make often operate directly on the parents. But a delinquency proceeding does not functionally involve the parents in their own right; their only personal stake in the outcome is deprivation of their child's custody if he is incarcerated, and this is probably not an "interest" in a traditional legal sense.

On the other hand, the reason for requiring notice to parents or guardian in juvenile cases is to allow them to assist the juvenile respondent in a procedural sense. This suggests a constitutional guardianship ad litem. However, some caution should be exercised in delineating parental right to participate in delinquency proceedings, particularly from defense counsel's point of view. The attorney for the juvenile respondent represents only the respondent, and not the parents. He should not be considered in the same position, for example, as counsel retained by a lay guardian ad litem in a personal injury action. The maximum permissible function of notice to the parents ought to be to enable them to ensure the juvenile's presence when he is not in detention, and to permit them to observe the proceedings.

Content of the notice. It is obvious from the notice portion of the *Gault* opinion that the Court is chiefly concerned about the contents of the notice to be given, and in particular about the pleading on the basis of which the adjudicational hearing is to be held. It is here that the criminal procedure cases are important. Under the sixth amendment the accused in a criminal prosecution has the right "to be informed of the nature and cause of the accusation" against him. This in turn has been incorporated into fourteenth amendment due process binding on the states.[23] The specific objectives of this right were set forth in an early Michigan case [24] as follows:

> *First,* to identify the particular transaction charged as criminal, so that the defendant shall not be liable to be put upon his trial for an offense different from that for which the grand jury have found the bill, or . . . different from that to which the person verifying the information intended to swear; *second,* that the defendant's conviction or acquittal may enure to his subsequent protection, should he be again prosecuted for the same offense . . . ; *third,* to inform the defendant of the particular transaction constituting the offense for which he is to be tried, that he may be able to prepare for his defense; and *fourth,* to enable the court, looking at the record after conviction, to decide whether the facts, as charged, are sufficient to support the conviction and warrant the judgment; . . . .

To what extent do these functions apply to juvenile delinquency proceedings? The first is intended to make sure that the incident that is tried is the same incident that the person initially responsible for the pleading had in mind. This means that specific acts of delinquency must be set forth in the pleadings, and that without supplementary pleadings the proof at the adjudicational hearing must be restricted to these acts. This may create problems under some of the sweeping definitions of delinquency found in the statutes, a matter to be touched on below from another angle.[25]

The second is designed to give effect to the double jeopardy provision. As far as fourteenth amendment due process is concerned, this function lies in the future only since the Court has not recently reconsidered its decision in *Palko v. Connecticut* [26] which holds, in effect, that double jeopardy under the fifth amendment is not applicable to the states under the fourteenth amendment.* However, nothing in *Palko* suggests that a state would ever be permitted arbitrarily to try an adult criminal defendant a second time after his acquittal in a trial free from legal error, and there is no reason to expect that the same

[23] *In re* Oliver, 333 U.S. 257 (1948); Cole v. Arkansas, 333 U.S. 196 (1948).

[24] Merwin v. People, 26 Mich. 297, 299–300 (1873).

[25] See text accompanying notes 28–31 *infra.*

[26] 302 U.S. 319 (1937). Certiorari was vacated as improvidently granted in the case that was expected to provide the vehicle for a re-examination of the matter. Cichos v. Indiana, 385 U.S. 76 (1966).

* [*Palko* was overruled in Benton v. Maryland, 395 U.S. 784 (1969)—Eds.]

act of delinquency will ultimately be available for successive delinquency proceedings.

The third is the function that the Court obviously has in mind in *Gault*—notice which enables defense counsel to prepare. If the delinquency petition is based on a specific act that would be a crime if committed by an adult, then for preparation purposes it is probably safe to use the same pleading form that is used for a regular indictment or information. This might well include the "short-form" indictment or information, provided there is a duty imposed on the state to supply a mandatory bill of particulars at the request of defense counsel. This, however, concerns only the substantive content of the charges; adequate notice for preparation of a delinquency case may also include an indication of the purpose of the particular proceeding. This would be particularly important in notices to juveniles and their parents who are not yet represented by counsel or who have validly waived counsel.

The fourth is intended to protect against a variance between pleading and proof. This, too, will be of increasing functional significance as some of the controls on evidence stemming from the privilege against self-incrimination and the right of confrontation become effective. The juvenile court judge will have the responsibility of setting out in his decision the basis for his conclusion that the act of delinquency has been proven. As in the adult criminal cases, the petition must be specific enough for the judge to decide whether there is a variance between pleading and proof.

Therefore, to qualify as adequate notice the petition in a delinquency case will have to identify in considerable detail the conduct charged as delinquent, and will probably also have to include some indication of the purpose of the particular hearing to which it relates. Notice content may vary from stage to stage. The initial jurisdictional hearing notice may stress only the factors of age, past delinquency record, etc., on which the power to proceed rests; the description of the delinquent activity should reflect the degree to which the court actually considers the presence or absence of delinquency a factor in deciding whether to proceed further. The contents of a waiver hearing notice must be judged in light of the purposes of that hearing; as indicated above, the courts are generally quite vague about what its thrust is.[27] It is imperative that the substance of the alleged delinquency be included in the notice of the adjudicational hearing. Notice of the dispositional hearing may be nothing more than an

[27] See text accompanying notes 12–17 *supra*.

indication of time and place, at least if the analogy to the adult criminal proceeding is followed. Convenience may suggest that the "content" notice be given as early as possible, and that this then be supplemented by successive "procedural" notices indicating time, place and purpose of each hearing. These are the procedural details that *Gault's* requirement of notice leaves to be supplied.

Validity of substantive statutes. Inadequacy of the pleadings by sixth amendment standards is one means (the other being instructions to the jury) by which vagueness and indefiniteness of the underlying criminal statute can be brought to light. If a charge couched in the language of the statute conveys nothing or so little that the functional tests of the sixth amendment pleading requirement cannot be met, or if almost any detail supplied at the election of the prosecutor properly fits within the language of the statute, the legislation is subject to challenge as unconstitutionally vague and indefinite.[28] The lack of any strict pleading requirements in juvenile proceedings before *Gault* precluded attacks against delinquency standards on vagueness grounds. However, the foundation for such an attack is plain once one departs from delinquency based on activity that would be a crime if committed by an adult. The language of vagrancy legislation now under attack [29] is, if anything, less broad than the sweeping phrases in much delinquency legislation; [30] the latter will probably not long survive attack. The result of sustaining a constitutional challenge on this ground, incidentally, will be to narrow the actual effective jurisdiction of the juvenile courts, a recommendation made by the President's Crime Commission,[31] though with legislative rather than judicial reform in mind. Nor, it should be noted, is the potential vagueness attack limited to delinquency proceedings. The statutory bases for custody, neglect and dependency proceedings are often couched in extremely broad language, and may in time be challenged as vigorously as the delinquency definitions themselves.

---

[28] *E.g.,* Winters v. New York, 333 U.S. 507 (1948) (statute outlawing magazines principally made up of news or stories of criminal deeds of bloodshed or lust).

[29] *See, e.g.,* Alegata v. Commonwealth, 231 N.E.2d 201 (Mass. 1967); Parker v. Municipal Judge, 427 P.2d 642 (Nev. 1967); Fenster v. Leary, 20 N.Y.2d 309, 229 N.E.2d 426, 282 N.Y.S.2d 739 (1967).

[30] Cf. language in Mich. Stat. Ann. § 27.3178(598.2) (1962) ("repeatedly disobedient to the reasonable and lawful commands of his parents"; "repeatedly associates with immoral persons, or who is leading an immoral life"; "habitually idles away his or her time"); and in N.Y. Family Ct. Act § 712(b) (1963) ("an habitual truant or who is incorrigible, ungovernable or habitually disobedient and beyond the lawful control of parents or other lawful authority").

[31] U.S. President's Comm'n on Law Enforcement and Administration of Justice, The Challenge of Crime in a Free Society 85 (1967).

Charge by a grand jury? Will a concomitant of the new notice and pleading requirements be a movement toward grand jury indictment in delinquency cases? This is doubtful. The Supreme Court has shown no indication that it proposes to overrule its decision in *Hurtado v. California*,[32] which held that the fourteenth amendment does not include the right to a grand jury indictment. However, the constitutional fairness of the information system rests, at least in part, on the usual prohibition against filing an information in a felony or high misdemeanor case unless a preliminary examination has been held or waived, as well as the common limitation on the contents of the information to what is revealed in the transcript of the examination, or to the complaint if examination was waived. These restrictions are intended to provide the same safeguard against unwarranted *ex parte* action on the part of the prosecuting attorney that the grand jury has traditionally been thought to provide.[33] It may be that in juvenile delinquency proceedings the initial jurisdictional hearing provides comparable protection. If not, some functional equivalent to the preliminary examination had best be devised if an attack alleging fundamental unfairness in the charging procedure is to be forestalled.

III. Due Process Limitations on Hearings

Assuming that the notice requirements of *Gault* have been fulfilled, what are the objective constitutional limitations on delinquency hearing procedures that can be posited as a result of *Gault*?

The *Gault* opinion has nothing to say about the objective trappings of juvenile court procedures, other than to require counsel (not that this is an unimportant right). Indeed, it concerns itself principally with the fact-finding process. Nevertheless, when one examines the procedural guarantees applicable to adult criminal proceedings, it is evident that some, though not all of them, have similar functional roles to play in delinquency proceedings.

Discovery. The Supreme Court has not yet ruled directly that there is a right, based on fourteenth amendment due process, to discovery of prosecution material that may eventually be used as evidence. The content of the amended Federal Rules of Criminal Procedure [34] and certain language in *Giles v. Maryland* [35] may presage this, but the de-

---

[32] 110 U.S. 516 (1884).

[33] *See generally* 27 Am. Jur. *Indictments and Informations* § 14 (1940).

[34] Fed. R. Crim. P. 16.

[35] 386 U.S. 66 (1967). "The State's pursuit is justice, not a victim. If it has in its exclusive possession specific, concrete evidence which is not merely cumulative or embellishing and which may exonerate the defendant or be of material importance to the defense . . . the State is obliged to bring it to the attention of the court and the defense." *Id.* at 100 (Fortas, J., concurring in judgment).

cision lies in the future. However, there are certain disclosure requirements that should be kept in mind.

There is, first, the prosecution's constitutional duty to make available to the defendant any evidence that is mitigating or exculpatory.[36] In other words, although the prosecutor may not yet be under a duty to make available the results of official investigations or private cooperation that support the state's case, he must volunteer material that suggests innocence or reduced responsibility. There is no reason to suppose that this requirement will not be extended to delinquency cases.

A second possibility is that the right to counsel coupled with the equal protection clause may dictate that some kinds of material in the prosecutor's hands must be made available so that defense counsel can prepare adequately.[37] It will probably be through this avenue that a constitutional right of discovery will be ultimately established. Indeed, although the constitutional stature of the opinion is unclear, the Court's recent decision in *Kent v. United States* appears to follow this reasoning in holding that at a waiver hearing respondent's counsel is entitled to access to the "social records" to be considered by the court in making its decision.[38] Since *Gault* guarantees the indigent respondent the right to counsel, the equal protection concept should extend right of discovery to all stages of a delinquency proceeding;[39] it may in time result in a right to state-subsidized preparation in delinquency matters.

Speedy trial. In *Klopfer v. North Carolina*,[40] the Supreme Court has recently incorporated the right to a speedy trial into fourteenth amendment due process. The prosecutor in *Klopfer* had used a special *nolle prosequi* device against a civil rights demonstrator that would have

[36] *E.g.,* Miller v. Pate, 386 U.S. 1 (1967); Napue v. Illinois, 360 U.S. 264 (1959); Mooney v. Holohan, 294 U.S. 103 (1935).

[37] *Cf.* text accompanying cases cited notes 70–75 *infra.* A right of this nature might require that a pistol be handed over for an independent ballistics test, or that an earlier medical report be made available to a psychiatrist who will testify for the defense on the issue of insanity.

[38] 383 U.S. 541, 562 (1966):

> With respect to access by the child's counsel to the social records of the child, we deem it obvious that since these are to be considered by the Juvenile Court in making its decision to waive, they must be made available to the child's counsel.

The opinion by Mr. Justice Fortas rests on statutory grounds. *Id.* at 562. Although *Gault* implies a constitutional basis to the right to counsel aspect of the *Kent* decision, 387 U.S. at 36, the right of discovery was not discussed in *Gault* and is obviously still an open question.

[39] See the related discussion on the right to confrontation pp. 328–29 *infra.*

[40] 386 U.S. 213 (1967).

permitted the case to be revived at any time in the prosecutor's discretion. The procedure, evidently designed to place a curb on future civil rights activity of the defendant, was declared an impairment of the defendant's right to a speedy trial.

It would seem that similar considerations are present in a delinquency proceeding in which the processing of a delinquency complaint is deferred indefinitely on condition that the juvenile "behave himself." The President's Crime Commission recommended increased use of pre-judicial disposition out of court and informal disposition of cases in juvenile court short of adjudication.[41] There should be no objection to either practice as long as the original act of delinquency is not kept hanging over the juvenile's head as a deterrent to further misconduct. Subsequent delinquency can of course be promptly prosecuted but any revival of the original delinquency invites application of the *Klopfer* doctrine.

Compulsory process. In *Washington v. Texas*[42] the Court held that fourteenth amendment due process includes the right to compulsory process, and that this right was denied when a Texas statute was invoked to prevent the defendant from calling an accomplice to the stand to testify to facts that would have been useful to the defense. The applicability of this right to the jurisdictional and adjudicational stages of the delinquency proceeding seems undeniable. It may extend to the dispositional hearing as well, although there is no precise parallel in the sentencing phase of an adult criminal proceeding. Once established in the context of the delinquency proceeding, it may be difficult to prevent the right from slipping over into custody and neglect proceedings as well.

Public proceedings. The right to a public trial is guaranteed by the sixth amendment, and is incorporated in fourteenth amendment due process.[43] Its purpose is to guarantee the purity of trial proceedings, excluding the public only when absolutely necessary to preserve decorum and order, and even here an absolute cloture is rarely permitted.

This right, however, raises serious problems in the context of juvenile proceedings. The juvenile court tradition has been to close juvenile proceedings to the general public and to limit those in attendance to persons related in some way to the juvenile or having some legitimate interest in the work of the court.[44] An offshoot of this

---

[41] President's Comm'n, *supra* note 31, at 81–82, 84.

[42] 388 U.S. 14 (1967).

[43] *In re* Oliver, 333 U.S. 257 (1948).

[44] *E.g.*, Cal. Wel. & Inst'ns Code §§ 675–76 (West 1966); Colo. Rev. Stat. Ann. § 22-1-7(1) (Supp. 1967); N.J. Ct. R. 6:9-1 (Supp. 1967); N.Y. Family Ct. Act § 741(b) (1963).

has been that juvenile court records are ordinarily confidential.[45] The right to completely public proceedings could be annexed to delinquency proceedings only at the expense of a thorough restructuring of the aims of delinquency proceedings. True, the Court in *Gault* evinced distrust of the protective principle,[46] but it did not necessarily say that all policy factors embodied in that principle were beyond consideration. A fair proceeding can probably be ensured through the guarantees expressly provided in *Gault,* and it is probable that the claim to public proceedings will be among the last to be transferred from the adult criminal action.

A related matter is press publicity. In the adult criminal proceeding the concern has been over excessive publicity.[47] In the juvenile field, the usual ban has been on publication of the names of juveniles in the press, presumably enforced by contempt power in case of a breach. This might present a first amendment problem, but it should be noted that members of the press have not been given standing to object to publicity restrictions in regular criminal cases.[48] Unless in some future Term the Court completely repudiates the protective principle and in effect converts delinquency proceedings into a special variety of ordinary criminal trial, it appears unlikely that news media will be permitted to overturn restrictions on press coverage on first amendment grounds.

Jury trial. The Supreme Court recently held the sixth amendment right to a jury trial binding on the states under fourteenth amendment due process in all criminal cases except those involving *"petty offenses."* [49] While the Court found it unnecessary to settle the exact location of the line between petty offenses and serious crimes, it will undoubtedly be presented in the near future with an opportunity to determine the applicability of the holding to delinquency actions. *In re Whittington,* [50] remanded by the Court for reconsideration in light of *Gault,* might yet provide such an opportunity.

[45] See President's Comm'n, *supra* note 31, at 87–88; U.S. President's Comm'n on Law Enforcement and Administration of Justice, Task Force Report: Juvenile Delinquency and Youth Crime 38–40 (1967).

[46] Its attitude is perhaps best summarized in its statement that "juvenile court history has again demonstrated that unbridled discretion, however benevolently motivated, is frequently a poor substitute for principle and procedure." *Id.* at 18.

[47] Sheppard v. Maxwell, 384 U.S. 333 (1966); Estes v. Texas, 381 U.S. 532 (1965).

[48] United Press Associations v. Valente, 308 N.Y. 71, 123 N.E.2d 777 (1954).

[49] Duncan v. Louisiana, 36 U.S.L.W. 4414 (U.S. May 20, 1968).

[50] 13 Ohio App. 2d 11, 233 N.E.2d 333, *cert. granted,* 88 S. Ct. 112 (1967), *vacated and remanded,* 36 U.S.L.W. 4466 (U.S. May 20, 1968). A three-judge federal district court in New York recently held that *Gault* requires the right to a jury trial in actions under the Federal Juvenile Delinquency Act. Nieves v. United States. 36 U.S.L.W. 2580 (S.D.N.Y. Mar. 5, 1968).

While apparently it did not do so in *Duncan,* if the Court should eventually be persuaded to look at potential length of incarceration alone, and stress the "community judgment" aspect of jury trial, then one might expect an extension of the jury trial right to the same delinquency cases with which *Gault* was concerned—those "which may result in commitment to an institution in which the juvenile's freedom is curtailed." [51] However, this would be a triumph of form over function. The principal "moral" judgments in a delinquency proceeding are probably reached at the jurisdictional hearing, the waiver hearing and the dispositional hearing, and it is doubtful that the Court would hold the sixth amendment protections applicable to other than the adjudicational hearing.[52] Moreover, under the typical statute, "delinquency" is not divided into degrees. If the delinquency alleged is homicide, for example, there would be no scope to decide whether it constitutes first-degree murder, second-degree murder or manslaughter; it is delinquency in any event. Nor could the jury content itself with a finding of "guilty" or "proven"; it would probably have to prepare a lengthy report of its findings if its participation were to make any practical difference.

Another factor that should be kept in mind is that one of the major problems in treating delinquency is the "generational gap" between the adults who administer the juvenile justice machinery and the juveniles who are its raw material. Only a juvenile jury could adequately serve the function of piercing the juvenile front on the one hand and of applying contemporary youthful standards to alleged delinquent conduct on the other. To state the matter another way, if the objective is a jury of "peers," no jury drawn from the regular jury venire will be suitable from the respondent's standpoint; if anything, the lay adult judgment is likely to be generally harsher and less understanding than the judgment of adult professionals who have at least some understanding of the juvenile milieu. Since eighteen-year-olds cannot vote, however, it is unlikely that sixteen-year-olds will be made eligible for jury duty by either legislative or constitutional mandate. If lay participation is desired, attention should probably be given to utilizing lay assessors, preferably quite young ones, on the pattern of Japanese and Scandinavian family and juvenile court procedures.[53]

Impartial tribunal. A person who may be adversely affected by a proceeding has a right to trial by a judge who has no interest in the

[51] 387 U.S. at 41.

[52] However, the state by its own constitution or legislation can, of course, provide this additional protection. See Peyton v. Nord, 437 P.2d 716 (N.M. 1968), concerning jury trial of the fact of delinquency when a determination on that point is a condition precedent to a waiver hearing.

[53] *See, e.g.,* Grobe, *Juvenile Delinquency in Sweden,* 53 Ky. L.J. 247–50 (1965).

case, and who has not been prejudiced by earlier events.[54] This applies today to juvenile proceedings in the obvious cases of a court's relationship to the complainant or to the injury resulting from the respondent's acts. However, there is a more refined aspect of this idea that may become visible after *Gault*. The system of adult criminal trials is arranged so that those who pass on preliminary matters rarely make the final adjudication as well. Thus, the magistrate who conducts the preliminary examination in a felony case does not serve as trial judge. Citizens who serve on the grand jury are ineligible to become petit jurors in the same matter. Even certain pre-trial hearings in a court of general jurisdiction may prejudice the judge in a particular case so that he must disqualify himself from conducting the main trial, particularly if jury trial has been waived. Serious question may arise in juvenile delinquency proceedings whether a judge who presides, for example, over a contested jurisdictional or waiver hearing can make an impartial ruling on the evidence before him in the adjudication hearing which must, by itself, prove the act of delinquency charged; he may have heard too much about the juvenile's background and past record of delinquency to be able to weigh the evidence objectively. If this consideration prevails, it may be necessary to rotate juvenile court judges on assignment, so that the judge who makes the jurisdictional or waiver determination does not preside over a contested adjudication hearing.

These, then, are the principal issues that can be expected to arise concerning the external forms of delinquency proceedings. They may have limited application to other classes of juvenile court proceedings as well. However, the same can probably not be said of the principles stemming from *Gault* that govern the fact-finding process, the matter to which we now turn.

IV. Controls of the Fact-Finding Process

The *Gault* decision directly dictates two major constitutional limitations affecting proof processes. Both require the almost complete reformation of trial practice in delinquency proceedings.

Confrontation. The first is the right to confront and cross-examine all witnesses on whom the state relies in establishing delinquency. Since the right of confrontation was already within fourteenth amendment due process,[55] it was no radical extension to require that the witnesses whose evidence is necessary to show the act of alleged delinquency be present in court to be confronted by the respondent and subjected to cross-examination.

[54] *In re* Murchison, 349 U.S. 133 (1955).
[55] Brookhart v. Janis, 384 U.S. 1 (1966); Pointer v. Texas, 380 U.S. 400 (1965).

There appears to be no rational basis on which to restrict this protection to the adjudicational hearing. The court's decisions regarding jurisdiction and waiver are, if anything, more important than its ultimate determination of whether an act of delinquency took place. Therefore, the respondent should have the right to confront and cross-examine the sources of the information marshalled in favor of assumption or waiver of jurisdiction. Though there may be greater latitude in the use of documentary evidence in these stages than at the fact-finding hearing, this should be compensated for by pre-hearing discovery [56] coupled with an option to insist that the source be called.[57]

Whether the same right applies at the dispositional hearing is open to debate. The adult criminal does not have a constitutional right at the present time to confront the sources of the data on which sentence is assessed,[58] though a recent criminal sexual psychopath decision [59] may presage a change or modification of that position. It is probably safe to assume, however, that as changes are made in the adult sentencing process in favor of either discovery or confrontation, corresponding changes will appear in the juvenile dispositional hearing.

By the same token, since custody, neglect and dependency proceedings can have an extremely adverse impact on the juvenile and his family, it will be difficult to deny for long a right on the part of respondents to confront the source of information on which state authorities purport to act in regulating the family's future. This may not be "right to confrontation" in the strict sense, but it seems to be "due process of law."

Privilege against self-incrimination. Secondly, *Gault* extends the privilege against self-incrimination to juvenile respondents. While there is no need to repeat the language in the opinion on the in-court application of the privilege,[60] several aspects of the application of the privilege to juvenile court proceedings should be stressed.

Once again, the analogy is to the defendant's privilege in adult criminal proceedings. The privilege does not merely protect the defendant against those questions he declines to answer. Instead, it prevents him from being called at all at the instance of the state. From the time the petition is filed through the adjudicational stage, the juvenile respondent is clearly within the defendant privilege and cannot be

---

[56] See text and notes 37–39 *supra.*

[57] This latter might be analogized to the limited right to an informer's identity during a criminal trial. Smith v. Illinois, 88 S. Ct. 748 (1968); Roviaro v. United States, 353 U.S. 53 (1957); Commonwealth v. Carter, 427 Pa. 53, 233 A.2d 284 (1967).

[58] Williams v. New York, 337 U.S. 241 (1949).

[59] Specht v. Patterson, 386 U.S. 605 (1967).

[60] *See* 387 U.S. at 47–51, 55.

questioned against his will by the judge, probation officer or prosecutor in attendance. The basis for proceeding further will have to be established by independent evidence and not by the respondent's judicial admissions.

A second aspect of extending this privilege to juvenile proceedings is that although it is possible to waive it, the Court stresses that there can be no waiver of a right of which the juvenile is ignorant. Therefore, for both in-court and out-of-court questioning, the Court seems to require that the respondent be explicitly advised of the privilege and of the consequences of waiver.[61] This requirement obtains whether or not the respondent is represented by counsel at the time, though the presence of and participation by counsel will necessarily affect the determination of whether a purported waiver was valid.[62]

A third consideration is that the witness privilege can be invoked by other juvenile participants or by parents if the information sought will incriminate them. This has always been true in theory, but will probably be increasingly evident in practice. This may mean that the state will either have to develop immunity devices for witnesses whose testimony it wants, or that it will need to defer juvenile court proceedings until the witness has been acquitted, convicted or adjudged delinquent, so that he can no longer be incriminated by the answers sought. The invocation of the witness privilege may be encountered more frequently in custody and neglect cases than in delinquency proceedings, because parental misconduct is commonly the basis for juvenile court intervention, and the sweep of criminal provisions on child neglect, nonsupport and abuse almost guarantees that the information which establishes juvenile court jurisdiction will incriminate the parents as well. It is for this reason that the state may have to choose which avenue it wishes to pursue, neglect proceedings or criminal prosecution, and grant immunity against the latter if it wishes to move promptly along the civil route.

A fourth aspect of the privilege involves improper consideration of the respondent's failure to testify. The problem has arisen in the adult proceeding when the prosecutor has commented to the jury on the defendant's failure to take the stand.[63] As long as the jury is not a part of juvenile court proceedings, of course, the issue will not be encountered. However, one procedural result of *Gault* will probably be the elaboration in the court's judgment of the bases of its actions. If

[61] *Id.* at 44–45.

[62] *Id.* at 55.

[63] Griffin v. California, 380 U.S. 609 (1965). *Cf.* Chapman v. California, 386 U.S. 18 (1967).

the court should be unwise enough to mention that the respondent failed to exculpate himself, present his side of the story, or whatever, it should be reversible error.

Other restrictions on evidence. Extension of the rights of confrontation and self-incrimination means that the standard rules of evidence will be applicable to the adjudicational hearing. For the most part, they will apply to jurisdictional and waiver hearings as well. One application of this will undoubtedly be the corpus delicti rule, so that the juvenile's extra-judicial statements, even if they are "voluntary" under *Gault's* adaptation of the *Miranda* requirements, cannot be used unless the fact of a delinquent act has been established by independent evidence. The reverse of this is that confessions must be corroborated to be usable. Furthermore, the *Gault* right to notice of the content of the charges implies that objections to the materiality and relevance of otherwise valid evidence may be entered.

Plea of guilty. It may be that in some instances neither the juvenile nor his attorney will desire to contest the factual allegations of the pleading. This raises the question of whether an equivalent to the guilty plea in an adult action can be developed in juvenile court practice. This can be best accomplished by a revision of statutes or rules of court. If the same safeguards are provided that have been held to apply to pleas of guilty under fourteenth amendment due process,[64] it will almost certainly be a constitutionally valid procedure, though the Court's concern over the trustworthiness of juvenile confessions[65] may spill over into the context of formal judicial proceedings as well.

Meanwhile, since *Gault* assumes that a waiver of the privilege against self-incrimination is valid if the court has expressly informed the juvenile that the privilege protects him and that its invocation cannot be used to his detriment, it may be that a juvenile acting on advice of counsel can indicate early in the proceedings that he will waive the privilege. Information provided at this stage by the juvenile concerning the act of delinquency may considerably abbreviate the proof process.

Role of the witness. Actual witnesses to the delinquency will testify on the same basis as a witness in a regular criminal proceeding and will recount what they have observed. Close attention, however, will have to be paid to expert witnesses, particularly those attached to or

[64] Machibroda v. United States, 368 U.S. 487 (1962) (guilty plea must be voluntary and not induced by promises and threats); DeMeerleer v. Michigan, 329 U.S. 663 (1947) (defendant must be apprised of the consequences of a plea of guilty).

[65] *See* 387 U.S. at 51–55.

invited to participate by the court. Most if not all of what experts have traditionally offered in the adjudicational hearing bears not on delinquency but on the proper disposition to be made of the respondent should he be found delinquent. This cannot be permitted after *Gault.* The purpose of the adjudicational hearing is to determine whether the respondent committed the delinquent act with which he is charged. Only in those rare instances in which the equivalent of a substantive defense is being asserted [66] is there likely to be any legitimate basis for expert testimony. If the expert attempts to testify about the respondent's general character or background, an objection should be entered, and if the witness persists, the equivalent to a mistrial should be sought.

A counterpart to all this is that in order to protect the respondent's rights of confrontation and impartial adjudication, and to maintain intact the purpose of the adjudicational hearing, the juvenile court judge should under no circumstances see background reports on the respondent until the adjudication has been made on the basis of the evidence presented in court. This is another reason why there may have to be two juvenile court judges in the case, one to preside over preliminary proceedings and the other at the adjudication.

Burden of persuasion. It has seldom been necessary to consider the burden of persuasion or proof in the traditionally informal juvenile proceeding. While in a handful of jurisdictions there is a statutory right to demand a jury, it is in fact almost unheard of to request one. This in turn has meant that there has been no occasion to develop the elaborate instructions of law, including those on burden of persuasion, that characterize civil and criminal trials.

Even if the Supreme Court should decree that the sixth amendment right to jury trial applies to delinquency proceedings, and even though attorneys should participate frequently in those proceedings, it seems unlikely that the actual incidence of jury trials will markedly increase. The disposition upon adjudication is usually the most significant decision from the respondent's point of view, and the jury has nothing to say about this. As long as the jury is not a part of juvenile delinquency proceedings in fact, the burden of persuasion or proof is likely to remain substantially undefined.

However, the significance traditionally attached to burdens of proof by the legal profession may be sufficiently great that revised juvenile codes should state what the ostensible burden is. If a specific delin-

---

[66] *Cf. In re* Winburn, 32 Wis. 2d 152, 145 N.W.2d 178 (1966), permitting the equivalent to a defense of insanity when the charge of delinquency was based on a homicide.

quent act is charged, then the formula of "beyond a reasonable doubt" is the most prudent for the legislature to select, since it will preclude attacks on the statute.* In fact, a "preponderance of the evidence" standard is currently being tested before the Ohio courts in *In re Whittington*.[67] In other phases of juvenile court jurisdiction, such as custody and neglect proceedings, the "clear and convincing proof" standard is perhaps preferable to the "preponderance" standard, again because it forestalls challenge. But whatever the standard, there is room for intervention by an appellate court only if the judge states an improper test of burden on the record.

V. REVIEW AND RECORD

Though the *Gault* opinion mentioned the disadvantages of a failure to provide a regular avenue of appeal or to maintain an adequate record of the proceedings—principally the need to litigate the matter on habeas corpus [68]—it did not require either. The summary treatment accorded these problems is in part explainable by the abundance of other specific denials of constitutional protection which rendered moot the question of the adequacy of Arizona's system of reviewing juvenile court adjudications. In any event, a decision on either issue would have been premature.

A decision on availability of appeal would have been anomalous. As has been indicated above, the *Gault* rights are functionally derivative from constitutional restrictions previously imposed by the Court on state criminal proceedings. It was not the rights themselves but the context that was new. This would not have been true, however, of a right of appeal, because as the Court points out, it has not yet directly held that the Constitution requires each state "to provide appellate courts or a right to appellate review at all." [69] It may be that the Court is gradually moving toward a decision to that effect, but it would have been incongruous to utilize the pioneer decision on the application of due process guarantees to delinquency proceedings as a vehicle to that end.

On the matter of the right to a transcript, on the other hand, decision was essentially unnecessary. If there is no federal constitutional right to an appeal, there is no occasion to examine the detailed attributes

* [See *In re Winship, supra* at 910.—Eds.]

[67] 13 Ohio App. 2d 11, 233 N.E.2d 333, *cert. granted*, 88 S. Ct. 112 (1967), *vacated and remanded*, 36 U.S.L.W. 4466 (U.S. May 20, 1968). The recent case of *In re* Urbasek, 232 N.E.2d 716 (Ill. 1967), held, on the basis of *Gault*, that "delinquency" must be proven beyond a reasonable doubt.

[68] See 387 U.S. at 58.

[69] *Id.* at 58, citing Griffin v. Illinois, 351 U.S. 12, 18 (1956).

that such a right necessarily includes. Determination of the issue was not essential, in addition, because of the equal protection decisions already in existence. For, though a state does not have to provide an appeal from a criminal conviction, if it does decide to do so it cannot set up procedural requirements that work to the disadvantage of the indigent. It is a denial of equal protection to refuse an indigent appellant a transcript at state expense,[70] to permit the judge to screen out frivolous appeals by indigents when no similar screening applies generally,[71] to reject an application for coram nobis because no transcript is supplied,[72] or to refuse a free transcript to a habeas corpus petitioner.[73] If appeal is of right, the state must provide counsel[74] who prosecutes the appeal vigorously.[75] *Gault* itself extends the right to counsel to the indigent, and it would require little imagination to project the equal protection cases into any statutory system of appeals from juvenile delinquency adjudications. But the matter was properly reserved for another day.

It is clear, however, that the system of review for juvenile courts badly needs renovation. In a great many states the juvenile court is, or is a part of, a court not of record. Appeals from these courts are usually in the form of a de novo trial, which is not only expensive and time-consuming, but raises the question whether the court of record in which the retrial is had (which may lack the court-related staff and services of the juvenile court) can then remand the matter to the juvenile court for administration if its decision is inconsistent with the juvenile court's. Even in states that provide for review in a regular appellate court, review is rare because of the expense. Whatever the theoretical availability of appeal in juvenile delinquency proceedings, the President's Crime Commission Task Force concluded that "the juvenile court system has operated without appellate surveillance."[76]

Federal habeas corpus is another dimension of review that should be considered in forecasting the juvenile appellate review system after

[70] Griffin v. Illinois, 351 U.S. 12 (1956).

[71] Draper v. Washington, 372 U.S. 487 (1963).

[72] Lane v. Brown, 372 U.S. 477 (1963).

[73] Long v. District Court, 385 U.S. 192 (1966). Equal protection also extends to a free transcript of the preliminary examination. Roberts v. LaVallee, 88 S. Ct. 194 (1967).

[74] Douglas v. California, 372 U.S. 353 (1963).

[75] Entsminger v. Iowa, 386 U.S. 748 (1967); Anders v. California, 386 U.S. 738 (1967).

[76] U.S. President's Comm'n on Law Enforcement and Administration of Justice, Task Force Report: Juvenile Delinquency and Youth Crime 40 (1967). In illustration, it cited figures for 1959–1960 in New York that only four of 20,000 cases of delinquent or neglected children were appealed and reviewed by an appellate court.

Gault. The federal habeas corpus statute permits examination into the detention of a state prisoner to determine whether he is "in custody in violation of the Constitution . . . of the United States." [77] By virtue of this, the federal courts have become more and more a reviewing agency in state criminal cases; the broader the regulation of state criminal procedure under fourteenth amendment due process and equal protection, the greater the number of state cases that qualify for federal review. This trend has accelerated as a result of two 1963 decisions of the Supreme Court. One, *Fay v. Noia,*[78] held that a federal district court has the discretionary power to entertain an application for the federal writ even though the relator may not in fact have availed himself of state remedies theoretically available to him.[79] The other, *Townsend v. Sain,*[80] requires the federal court to hold a factual hearing on the allegations in the petition unless the record forwarded from the state court adequately covers both the legal and factual issues set forth.

Because *Gault* rests on federal due process grounds, it obviously opens up the possibility of federal habeas corpus proceedings to review delinquency adjudications. No state tribunal by its own efforts can forestall federal habeas review. Most important, and as the Court noted in passing in *Gault,*[81] if no record has been made of the juvenile

[77] 28 U.S.C. § 2241(c)(3) (1965).

[78] 372 U.S. 391 (1963).

[79] The test, borrowed from Johnson v. Zerbst, 304 U.S. 458, 464 (1938), is whether there has been "an intentional relinquishment or abandonment of a known right or privilege." The Court stated:

> If a habeas applicant, after consultation with competent counsel or otherwise, understandingly and knowingly forewent the privilege of seeking to vindicate his federal claims in the state courts, whether for strategic, tactical, or any other reasons that can fairly be described as the deliberate by-passing of state procedures, then it is open to the federal court on habeas to deny him all relief if the state courts refused to entertain his federal claims on the merits— though of course only after the federal court has satisfied itself, by holding a hearing or by some other means, of the facts bearing upon the applicant's default. . . . At all events we wish it clearly understood that the standard here put forth depends on the considered choice of the petitioner. . . . A choice made by counsel not participated in by the petitioner does not automatically bar relief. Nor does a state court's finding of waiver bar independent determination of the question by the federal courts on habeas, for waiver affecting federal rights is a federal question. 372 U.S. at 439.

Since Noia, convicted of first-degree murder and sentenced to life imprisonment on his first trial, would have been subject to the death penalty upon a retrial after a successful appeal, his failure to appeal, on the facts of his case, did not constitute a binding waiver of his state procedural rights.

[80] 372 U.S. 293 (1963).

[81] *See* 387 U.S. at 58.

court proceeding or of any de novo trial in a state court of record, under *Townsend* the federal district court has no choice but to hold a complete factual inquiry into the way the state courts processed the matter. Advisedly, then, a stenographic or mechanical recording will be made of post-*Gault* delinquency proceedings, for it is cheaper to maintain adequate records in the first place than to have all the participants, including the juvenile court judge, appear to testify at some later time in federal court.

There are two practical limitations on the scope of federal review after *Gault*. One is the matter of retroactivity of the *Gault* decision itself. State decisions are already split over whether it has retroactive effect.[82] If the decision ultimately is applied prospectively only, federal habeas review will be limited to those cases adjudicated after May 15, 1967.

The other is that habeas corpus traditionally has required actual physical detention of the relator before the writ will lie.[83] Because most juvenile delinquents are kept in actual detention for only a relatively brief period of time, few will be in a position to seek federal habeas corpus relief before they are released. However, the Supreme Court has agreed to review a recent case dispensing with the custody requirement for habeas if the prisoner is under some sort of control,[84] which may signal a relaxation of the strict custody rule. Alternatively, the Court might make *coram nobis* [85] or some other noncustodial form of review available to cover cases in which the juvenile is not physically detained. At any rate, it seems doubtful that the Court will long keep the federal courts out of the review picture simply because brief incarceration or probation is the general practice in delinquency cases.

In summary, the equal protection and habeas corpus cases dictate

[82] Holding that *Gault* is not retroactive: *In re* Harris, 434 P.2d 615, 64 Cal. Rptr. 319 (Sup. Ct. 1967); Hammer v. State, 238 A.2d 567 (Md. Ct. Spec. App. 1968); State v. Hance, 2 Md. App. 162, 233 A.2d 326 (1967); Cradle v. Peyton, 156 S.E.2d 874 (Va. 1967). Holding that it is: Nieves v. United States, 36 U.S.L.W. 2580 (S.D.N.Y. Mar. 5, 1968); Marsden v. Commonwealth, 227 N.E.2d 1 (Mass. 1967); LaFollette v. Circuit Court, 155 N.W.2d 141 (Wis. 1967). The Washington Supreme Court applied *Gault* without comment to a juvenile court adjudication rendered before *Gault*. *In re* Lesperance, 434 P.2d 602 (Wash. 1967). *See also* Dorsen & Reznick, *supra* note 10, at 28–31.

[83] McNally v. Hill, 293 U.S. 131 (1934).

[84] Peyton v. Rowe, 88 S. Ct. 782 (1968), reviewing Rowe v. Peyton, 383 F.2d 709 (4th Cir. 1967). *See also* Cameron v. Mullen, 387 F.2d 193 (D.C. Cir. 1967); Williams v. Peyton, 372 F.2d 216 (4th Cir. 1967); Martin v. Virginia, 349 F.2d 781 (4th Cir. 1965); Note, *Postconviction Remedies: The Need for Legislative Change,* 55, Georgetown L.J. 851, 860–64 (1967).

[85] *See* United States v. Morgan, 346 U.S. 502 (1954), holding that a federal court can set aside a conviction and sentence by a proceeding in the nature of *coram nobis* even though defendant has served his full term.

a revised juvenile procedural system embodying improved methods of recording proceedings and clear-cut avenues of appeal, preferably to an ordinary appellate court. All stages of the delinquency proceeding should be recorded, although an actual transcript need not be prepared unless appeal or federal habeas review is contemplated.[86] With transcripts available, the de novo trial would become an anachronism and should be eliminated as a mode of review.[87]

[86] On the practical problem of coping with large numbers of prisoner requests for transcripts, see Holmes v. United States, 383 F.2d 925 (D.C. Cir. 1967).

[87] A complementary problem is the secrecy of the records that are maintained. The report of the President's Comm'n, *supra* note 31, at 87–88, pointed up abuses of the confidentiality of juvenile court records, and urged that access to records be controlled by the court and granted only to those who seek them for the same purpose for which they were originally compiled. See also the comment on the problem in the *Gault* opinion. 387 U.S. at 23–25. The juvenile court judge should regulate access to court records, and records of court-related public agencies, by rule of court.

TABLE OF STATUTES

(Numerals in **bold face** refer to text of statute)

949

PAGES

TABLE OF CASES

(Numerals in **bold face** refer to text of case)

INDEX